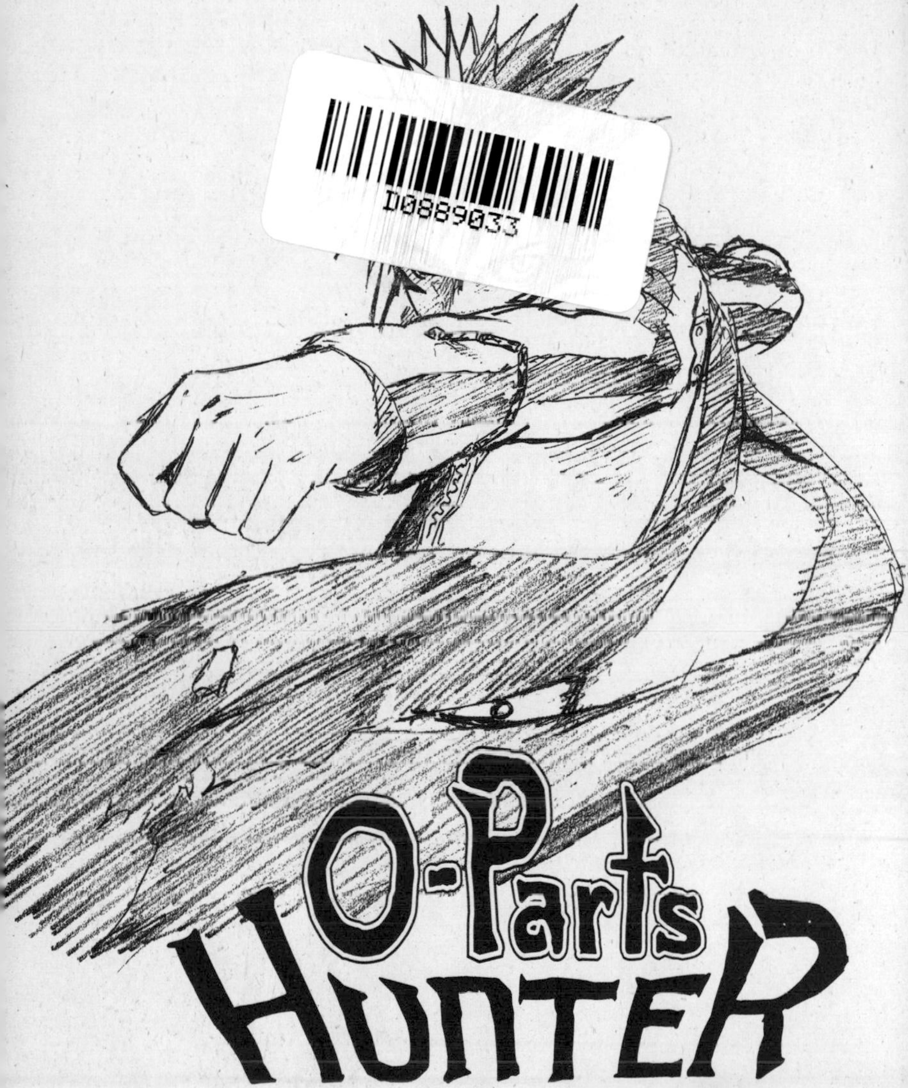

O-Parts HUNTER

SEISHI KISHIMOTO

14

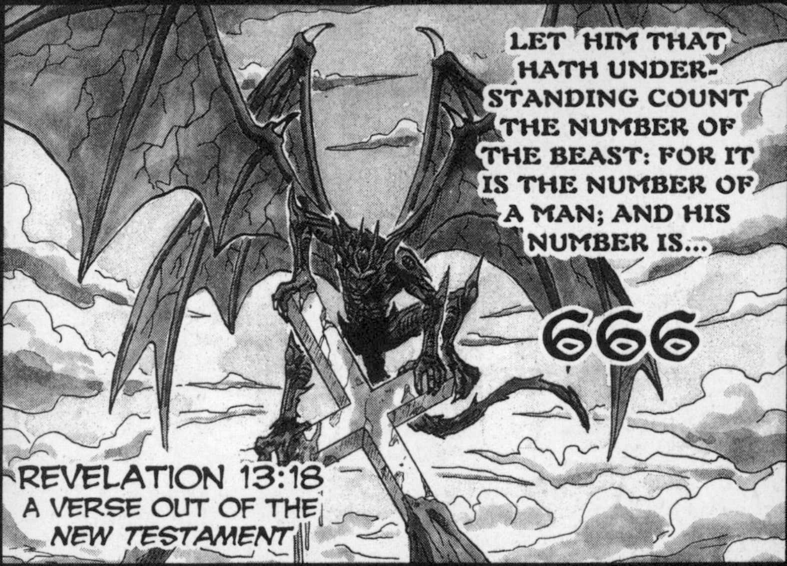
LET HIM THAT HATH UNDER-STANDING COUNT THE NUMBER OF THE BEAST: FOR IT IS THE NUMBER OF A MAN; AND HIS NUMBER IS...
666
REVELATION 13:18 A VERSE OUT OF THE *NEW TESTAMENT*

O-Parts Hunter

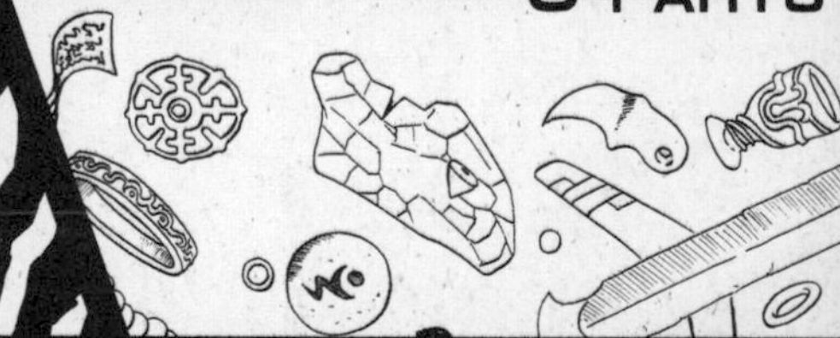
O-PARTS

O-Parts: Amazing artifacts with mystical powers left from an ancient civilization. They have been excavated from various ruins around the world. Depending on their Effects, O-Parts are given a rank from E to SS within a seven-tiered system.

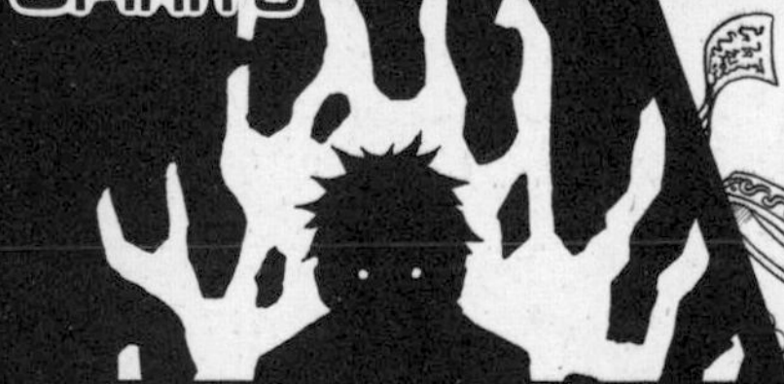
SPIRITS

Spirit: A special energy force which only the O.P.T.s have. The amount of Spirit they have within them determines how strong of an O.P.T. they are.

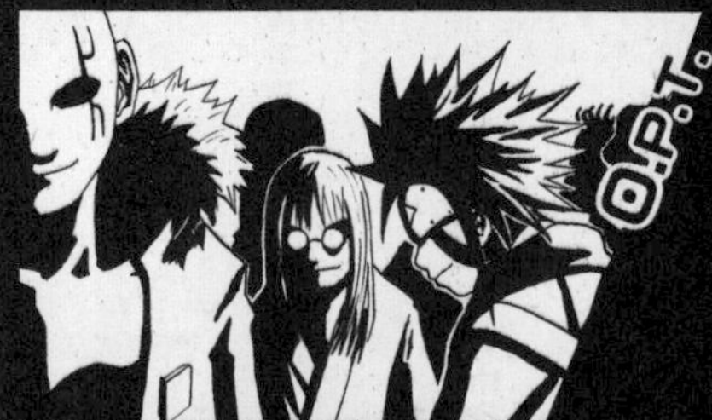
O.P.T.

O.P.T.: One who has the ability to release and use the powers of the O-Parts. The name O.P.T. is an abbreviated form of O-Part Tactician.

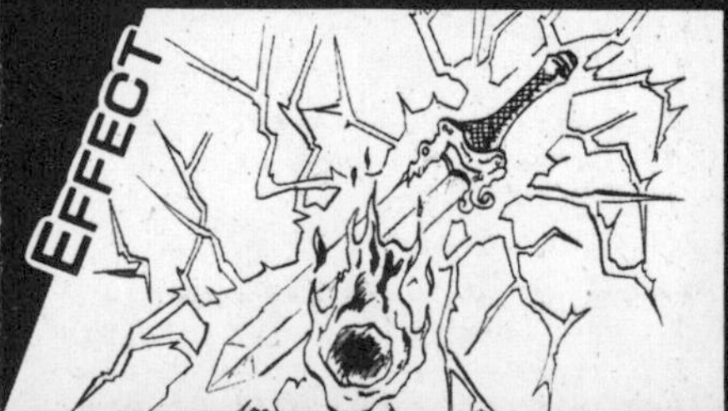
EFFECT

Effect: The special energy (power) the O-Parts possess. It can only be used when an O.P.T. sends his Spirit into an O-Part.

CHARACTERS

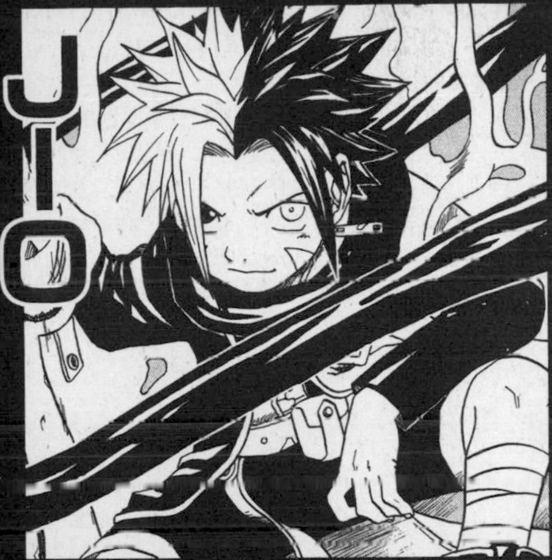
JIO

Jio Freed
A wild O.P.T. boy whose dream is world domination! He has been emotionally damaged by his experiences in the past, but is still gung-ho about his new adventures! O-Part: New Zero-shiki (Rank B)
Effect: Triple (Increasing power by a factor of three)

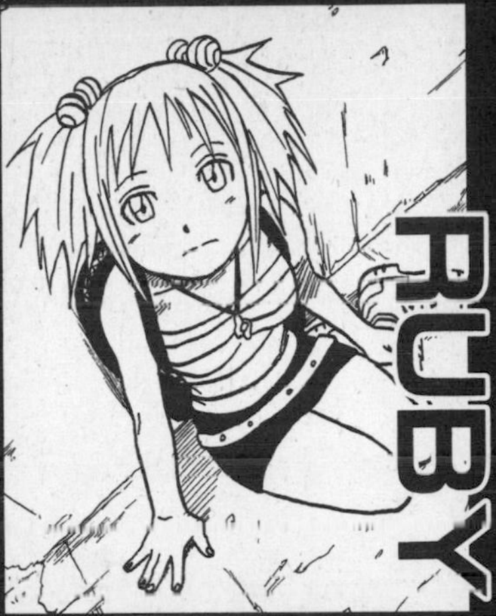
RUBY

Ruby
A treasure hunter who can decipher ancient texts. She meets Jio during her search for a legendary O-Part.

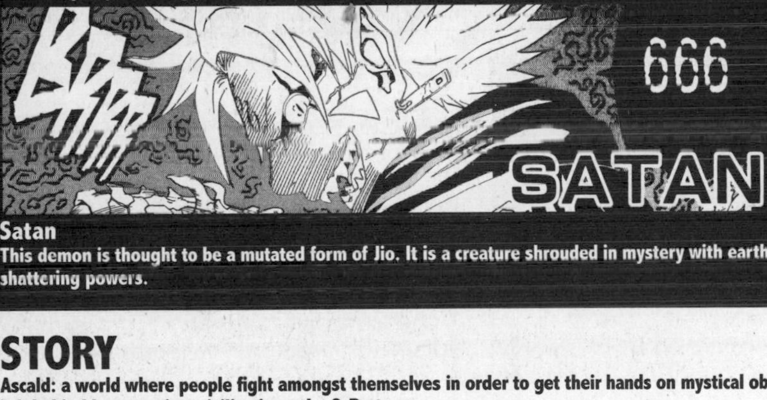
666
SATAN

Satan
This demon is thought to be a mutated form of Jio. It is a creature shrouded in mystery with earth-shattering powers.

STORY

Ascald: a world where people fight amongst themselves in order to get their hands on mystical objects left behind by an ancient civilization...the O-Parts.

In that world, a monster that strikes fear into the hearts of the strongest of men is rumored to exist. Those who have seen the monster all tell of the same thing–that the number of the beast, 666, is engraved on its forehead.

***

Jio, an O.P.T. boy who wants to rule the world, travels the globe with Ball, a novice O.P.T., and Ruby, a girl searching for both her missing father and a legendary O-Part. Coming to Rock Bird in search of the legendary O-Part, Jio and his friends have succeeded in defeating Ikaros, the ruler of the town—but as a result, Satan has taken over Jio's mind. Cross, who is out to get revenge on Satan, turns out to be an Angel of the Kabbalah, and a deadly battle ensues. Ruby intervenes by deciding to make contact with Satan, who has deeply rooted himself in Jio's mind.

O-Parts Hunter

14

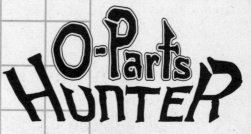

Table of Contents

CHAPTER 53 CONNECTION

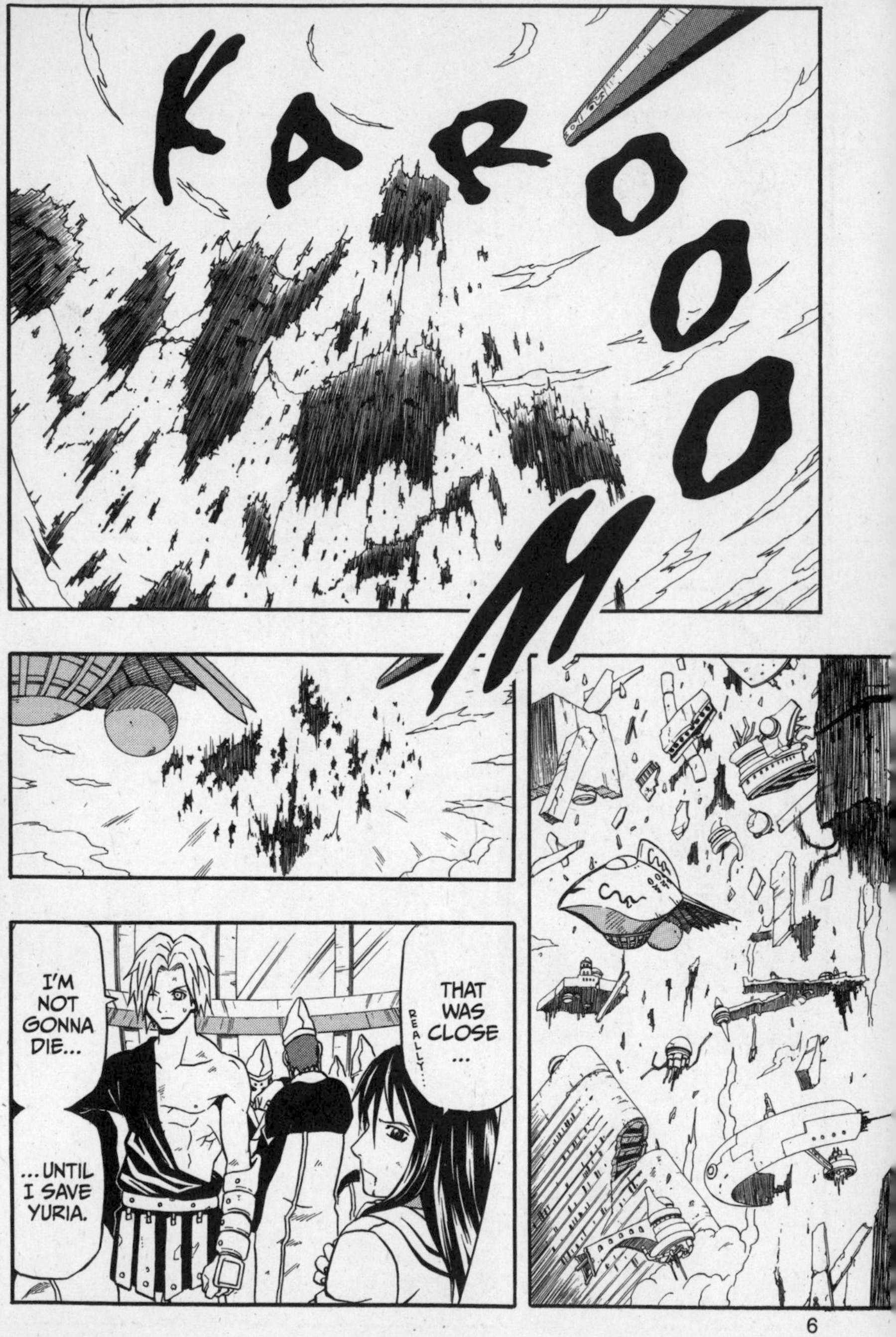
KAROOOOM
THAT WAS CLOSE ...
REALLY...
I'M NOT GONNA DIE...
...UNTIL I SAVE YURIA.

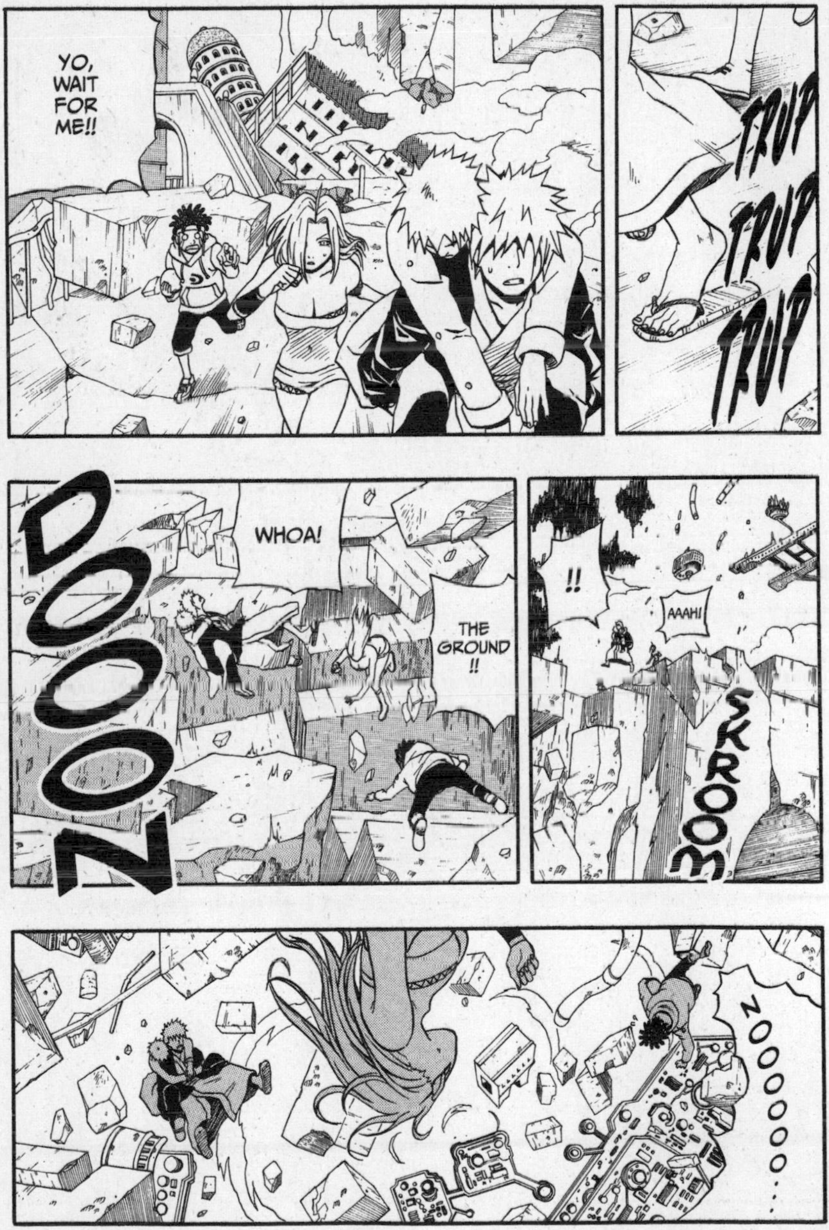
TRUP
TRUP
TRUP
YO, WAIT FOR ME!!
!!
AAAH!
SKROOM
WHOA!
THE GROUND !!
DOOOZ
ZOOOOOO...

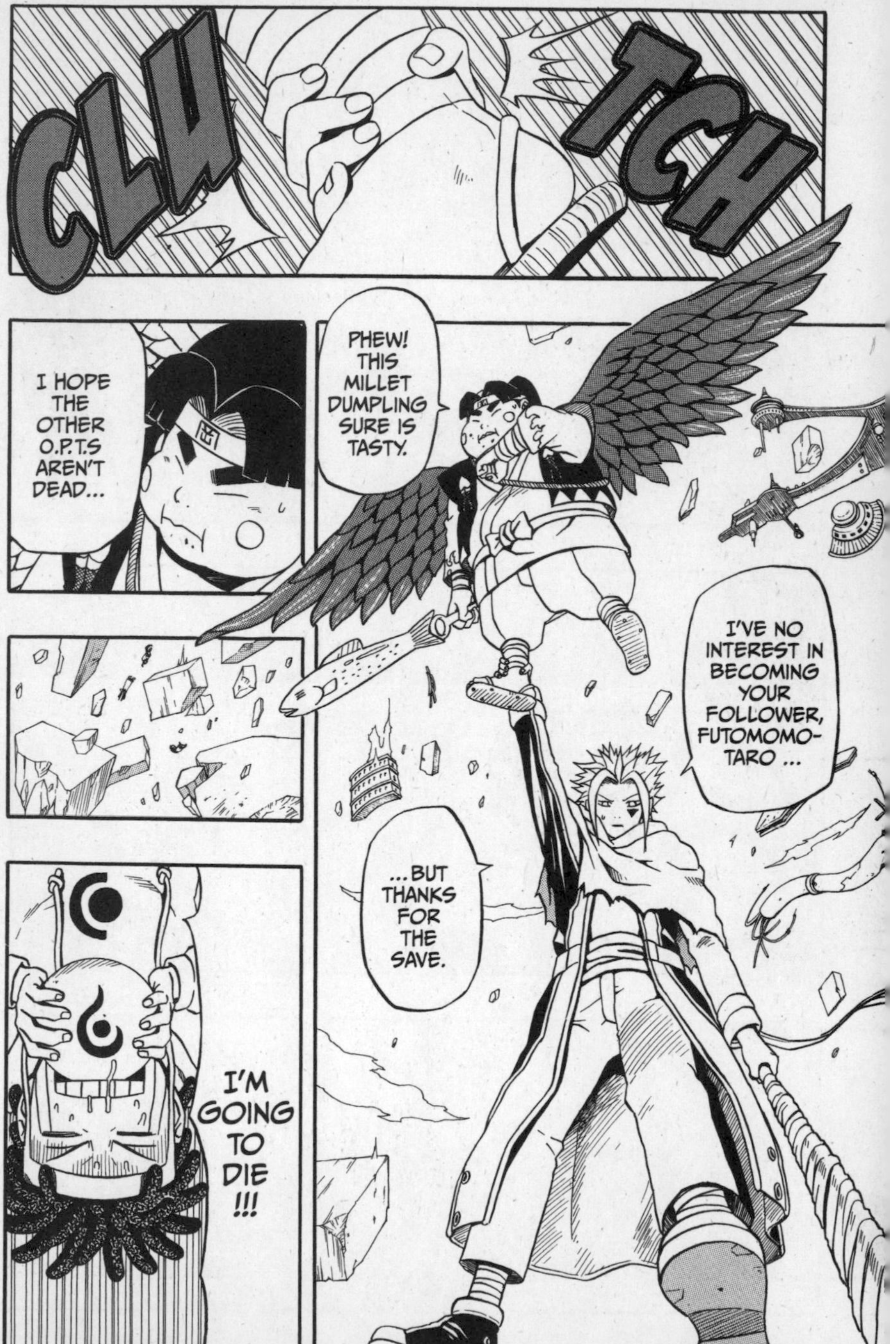
CLUTCH
PHEW! THIS MILLET DUMPLING SURE IS TASTY.
I'VE NO INTEREST IN BECOMING YOUR FOLLOWER, FUTOMOMO-TARO ...
...BUT THANKS FOR THE SAVE.
I HOPE THE OTHER O.P.T.S AREN'T DEAD...
I'M GOING TO DIE!!!

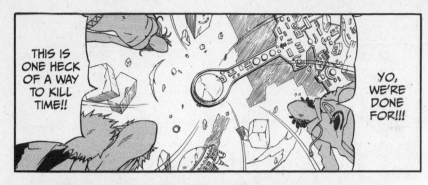

YO, WE'RE DONE FOR!!!
THIS IS ONE HECK OF A WAY TO KILL TIME!!
SHWOOM
!
THWUMP
AGH!
THUD
!

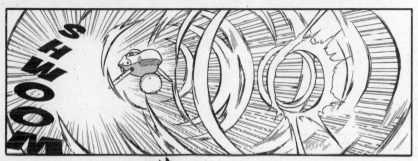

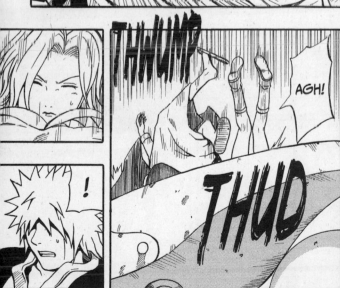

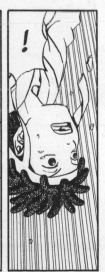

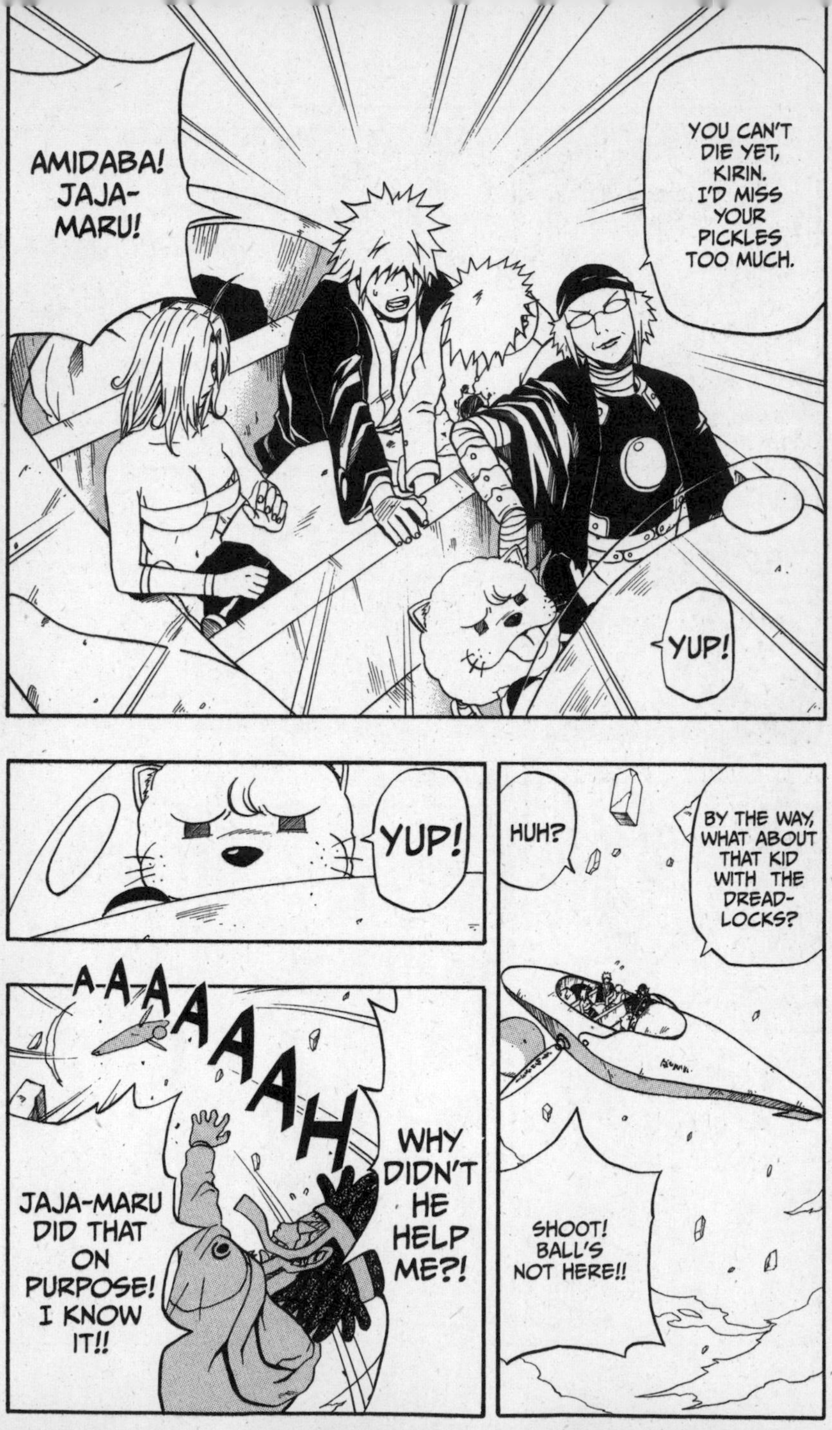
YOU CAN'T DIE YET, KIRIN. I'D MISS YOUR PICKLES TOO MUCH.
AMIDABA! JAJA-MARU!
YUP!
BY THE WAY, WHAT ABOUT THAT KID WITH THE DREAD-LOCKS?
HUH?
SHOOT! BALL'S NOT HERE!!
YUP!
A-A-AAAAAH
WHY DIDN'T HE HELP ME?!
JAJA-MARU DID THAT ON PURPOSE! I KNOW IT!!

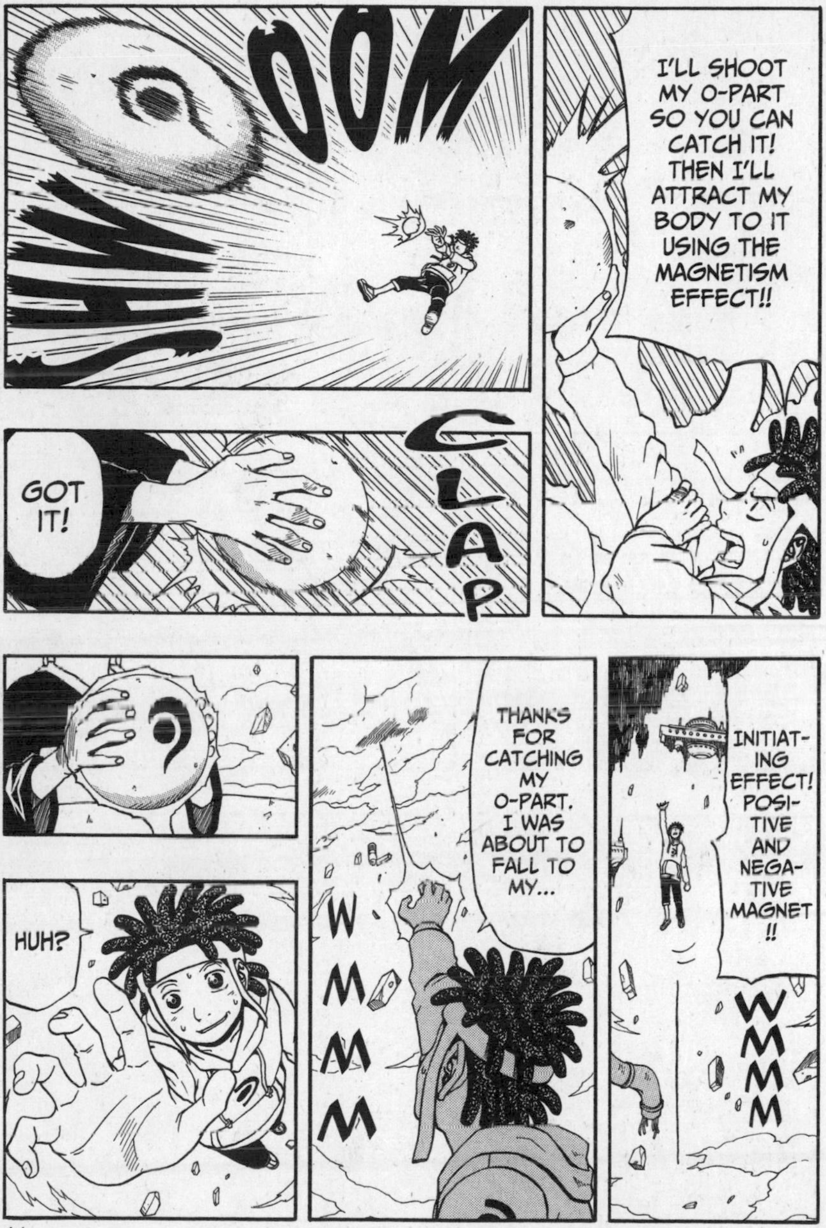
I'LL SHOOT MY O-PART SO YOU CAN CATCH IT! THEN I'LL ATTRACT MY BODY TO IT USING THE MAGNETISM EFFECT!!
SHWOOM
CLAP
GOT IT!
INITIATING EFFECT! POSITIVE AND NEGATIVE MAGNET!!
WMMM
THANKS FOR CATCHING MY O-PART. I WAS ABOUT TO FALL TO MY...
WMMM
HUH?

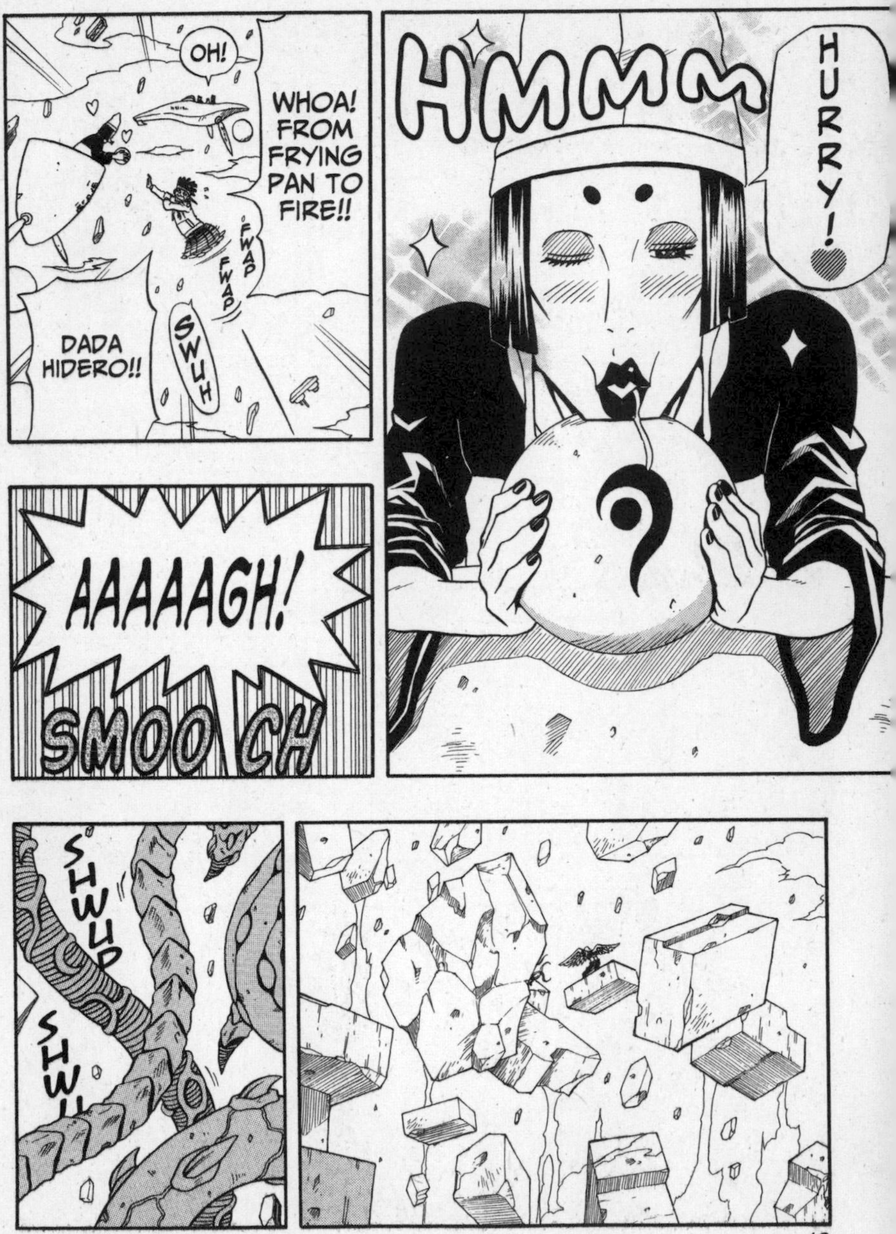
HMMM
HURRY!
OH!
WHOA! FROM FRYING PAN TO FIRE!!
FWAP
FWAP
SWUH
DADA HIDERO!!
AAAAGH!
SMOOCH
SHWUP

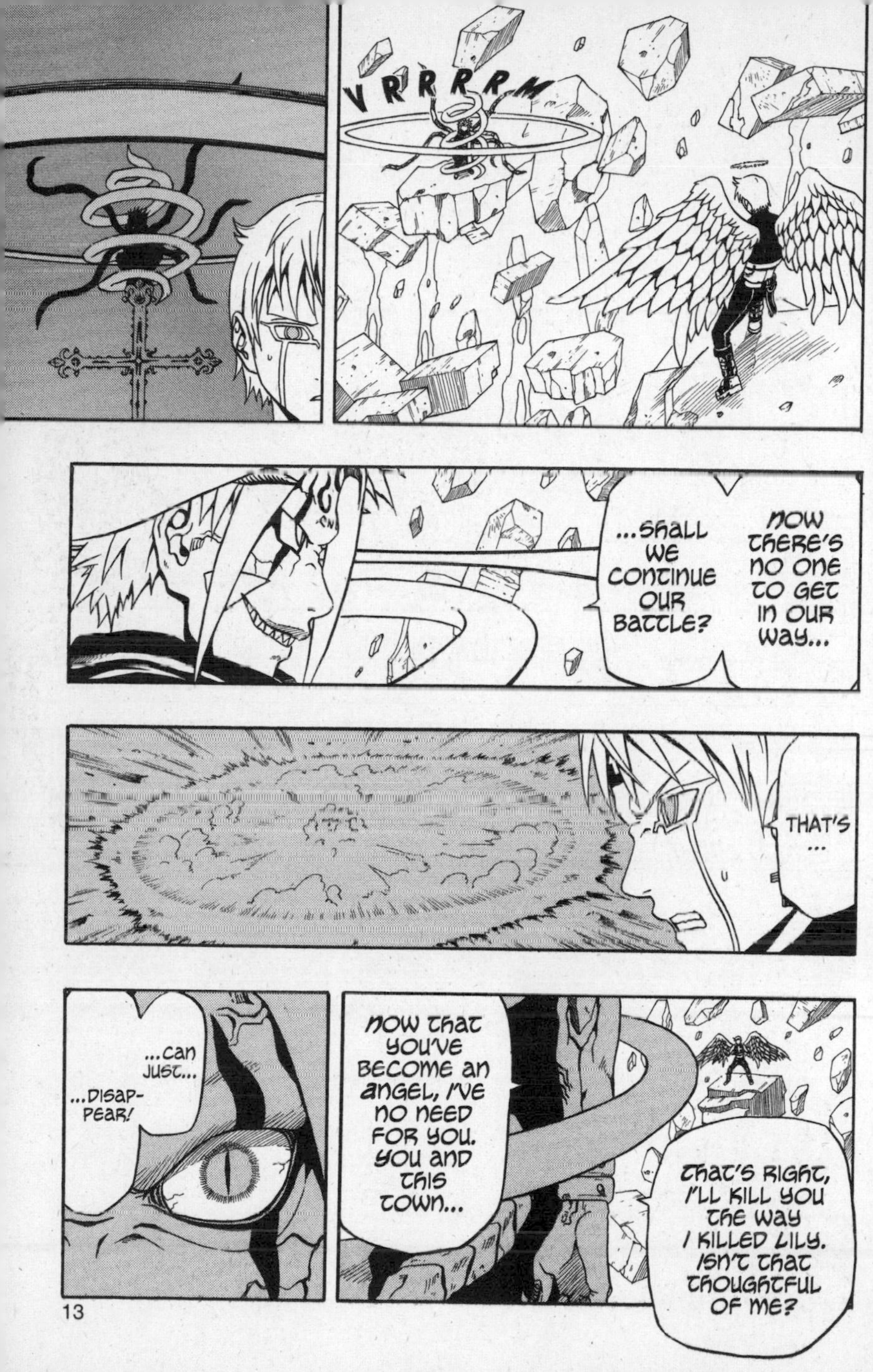
VRRRRM
NOW THERE'S NO ONE TO GET IN OUR WAY...
...SHALL WE CONTINUE OUR BATTLE?
THAT'S ...
THAT'S RIGHT, I'LL KILL YOU THE WAY I KILLED LILY. ISN'T THAT THOUGHTFUL OF ME?
NOW THAT YOU'VE BECOME AN ANGEL, I'VE NO NEED FOR YOU. YOU AND THIS TOWN...
...CAN JUST...
...DISAP-PEAR!

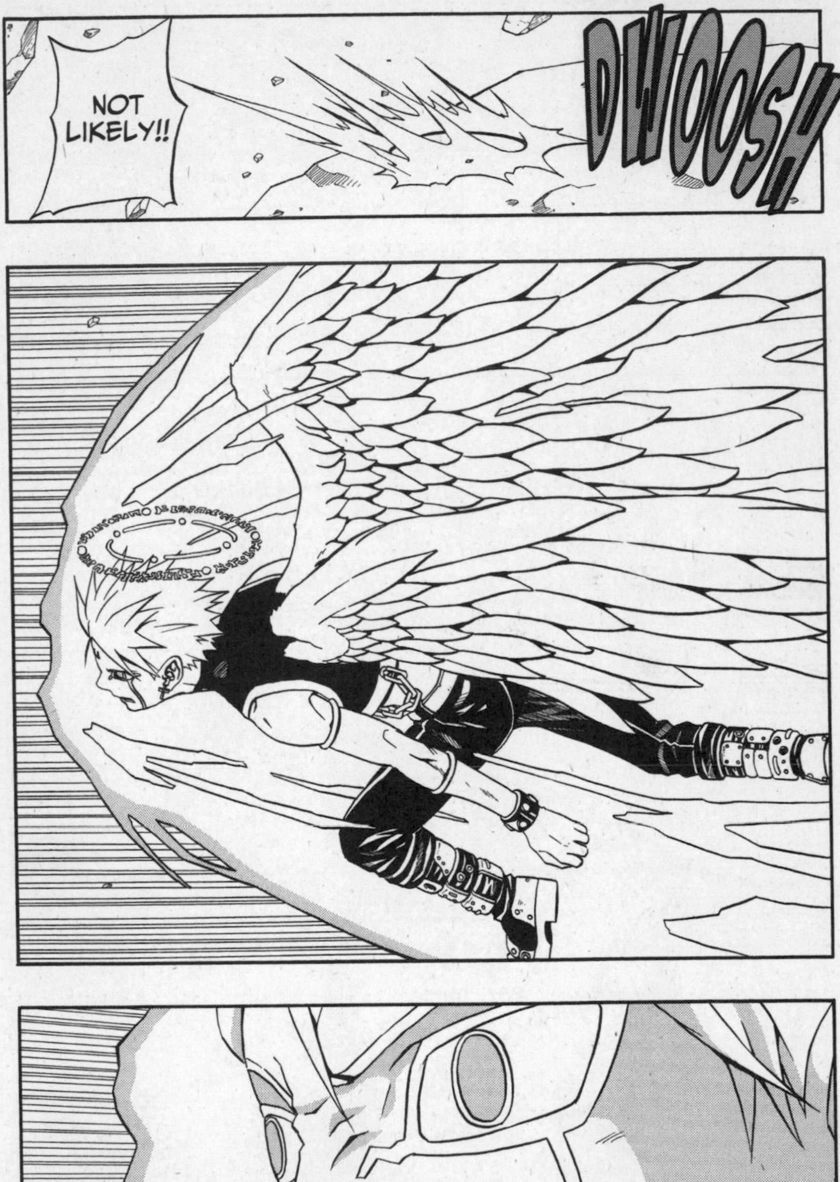
DWOOSH
NOT LIKELY!!

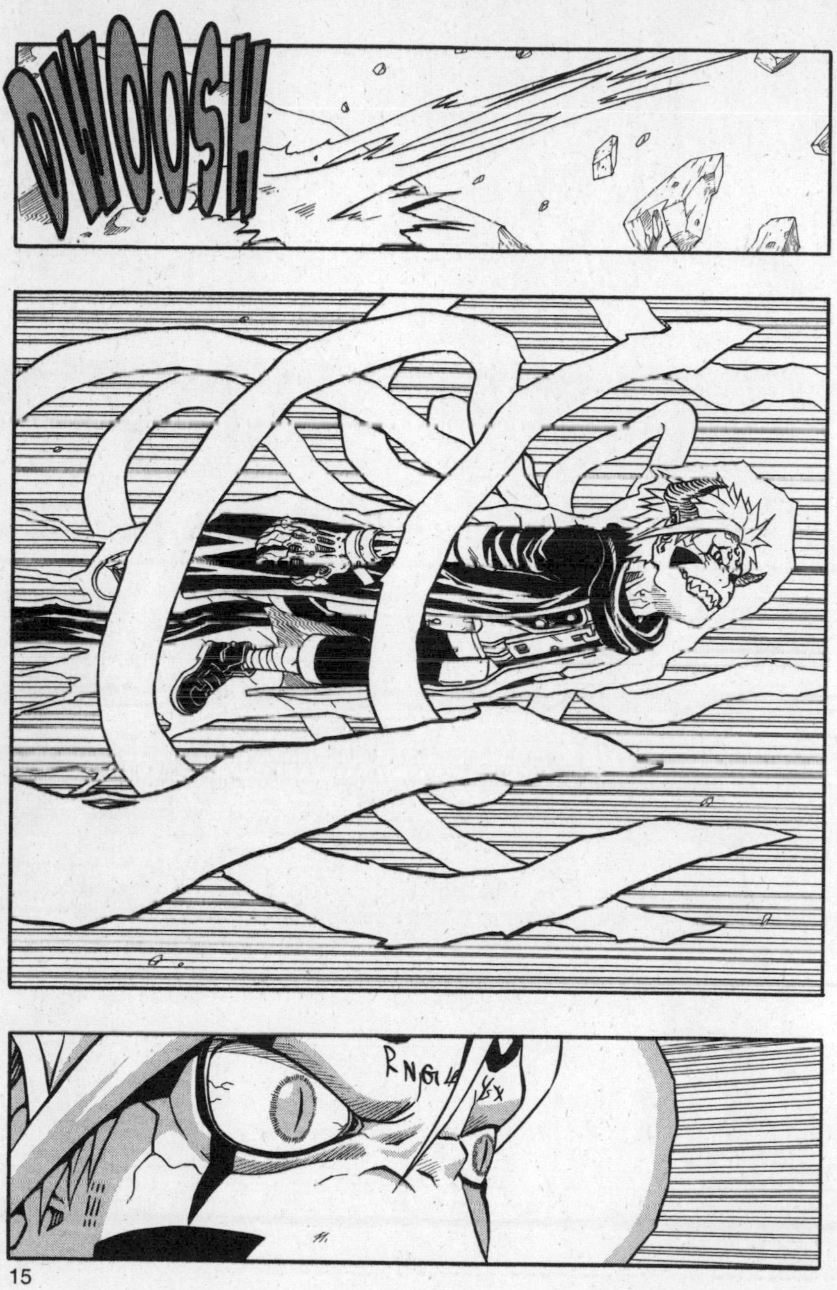
DWOOSH

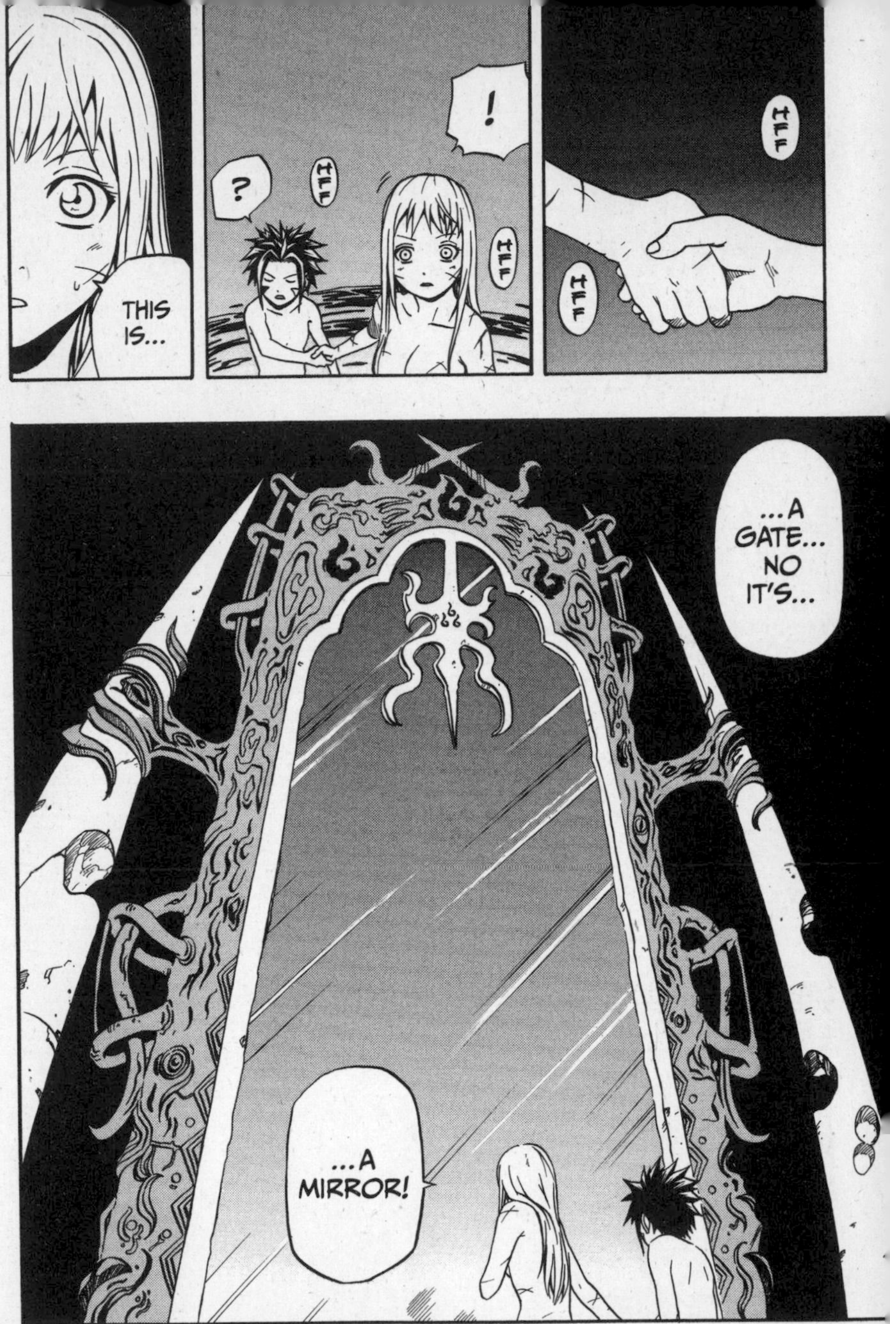
HFF
HFF
!
?
HFF
HFF
THIS IS...
...A GATE... NO IT'S...
...A MIRROR!

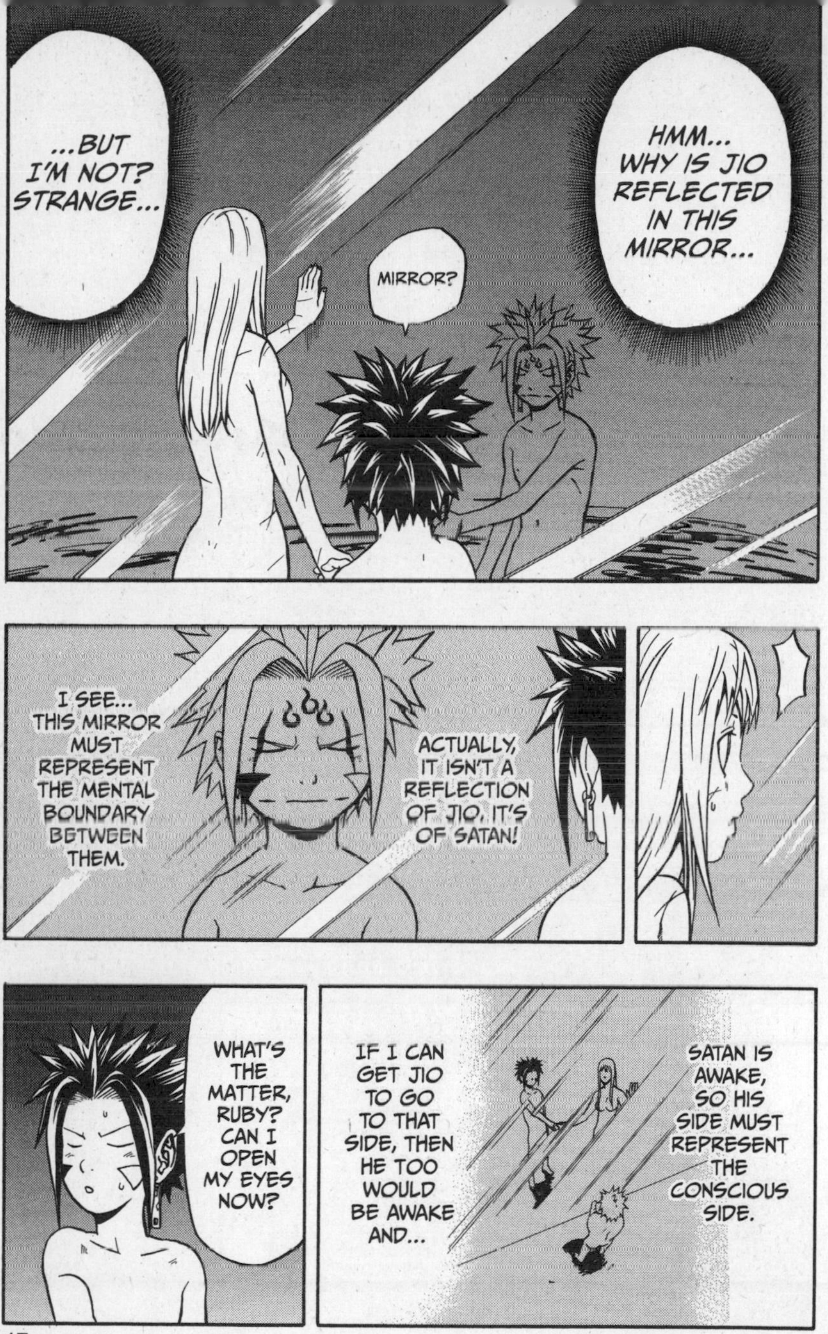
HMM... WHY IS JIO REFLECTED IN THIS MIRROR...
...BUT I'M NOT? STRANGE...
MIRROR?
ACTUALLY, IT ISN'T A REFLECTION OF JIO. IT'S OF SATAN!
I SEE... THIS MIRROR MUST REPRESENT THE MENTAL BOUNDARY BETWEEN THEM.
SATAN IS AWAKE, SO HIS SIDE MUST REPRESENT THE CONSCIOUS SIDE.
IF I CAN GET JIO TO GO TO THAT SIDE, THEN HE TOO WOULD BE AWAKE AND...
WHAT'S THE MATTER, RUBY? CAN I OPEN MY EYES NOW?

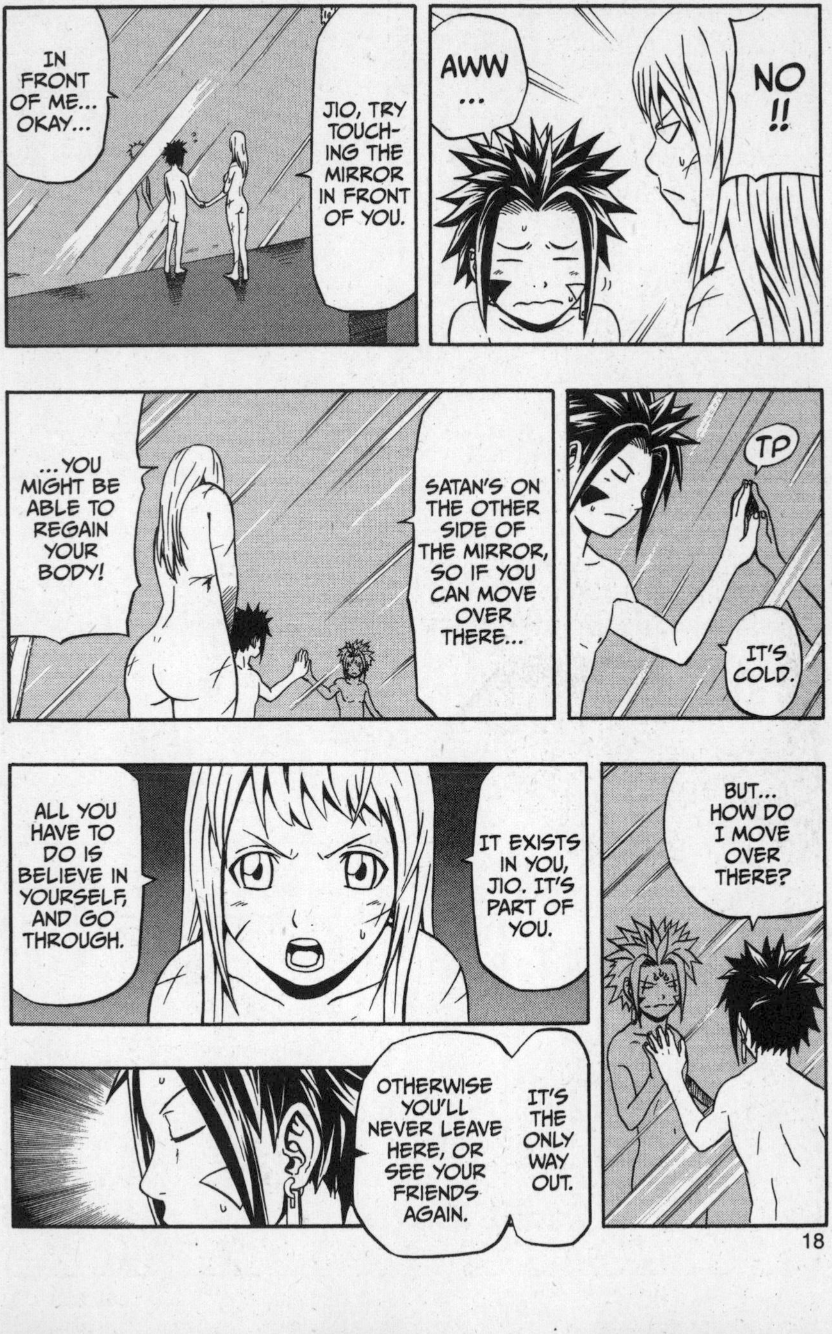
NO!!
AWW...
JIO, TRY TOUCHING THE MIRROR IN FRONT OF YOU.
IN FRONT OF ME... OKAY...
TP
IT'S COLD.
SATAN'S ON THE OTHER SIDE OF THE MIRROR, SO IF YOU CAN MOVE OVER THERE...
...YOU MIGHT BE ABLE TO REGAIN YOUR BODY!
BUT... HOW DO I MOVE OVER THERE?
IT EXISTS IN YOU, JIO. IT'S PART OF YOU.
ALL YOU HAVE TO DO IS BELIEVE IN YOURSELF, AND GO THROUGH.
IT'S THE ONLY WAY OUT.
OTHERWISE YOU'LL NEVER LEAVE HERE, OR SEE YOUR FRIENDS AGAIN.

...NOT ALONE!

SLUP

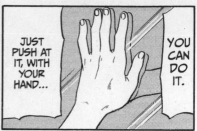

JUST PUSH AT IT, WITH YOUR HAND...

YOU CAN DO IT.

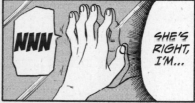

NNN

SHE'S RIGHT, I'M...

YOU'RE DOING IT!

SLUUP

URRRRRGH!

HUH?

RUBY, NOW YOU...

WOW! THE MIRROR SUCKS YOU OVER TO THIS SIDE.

SLUP

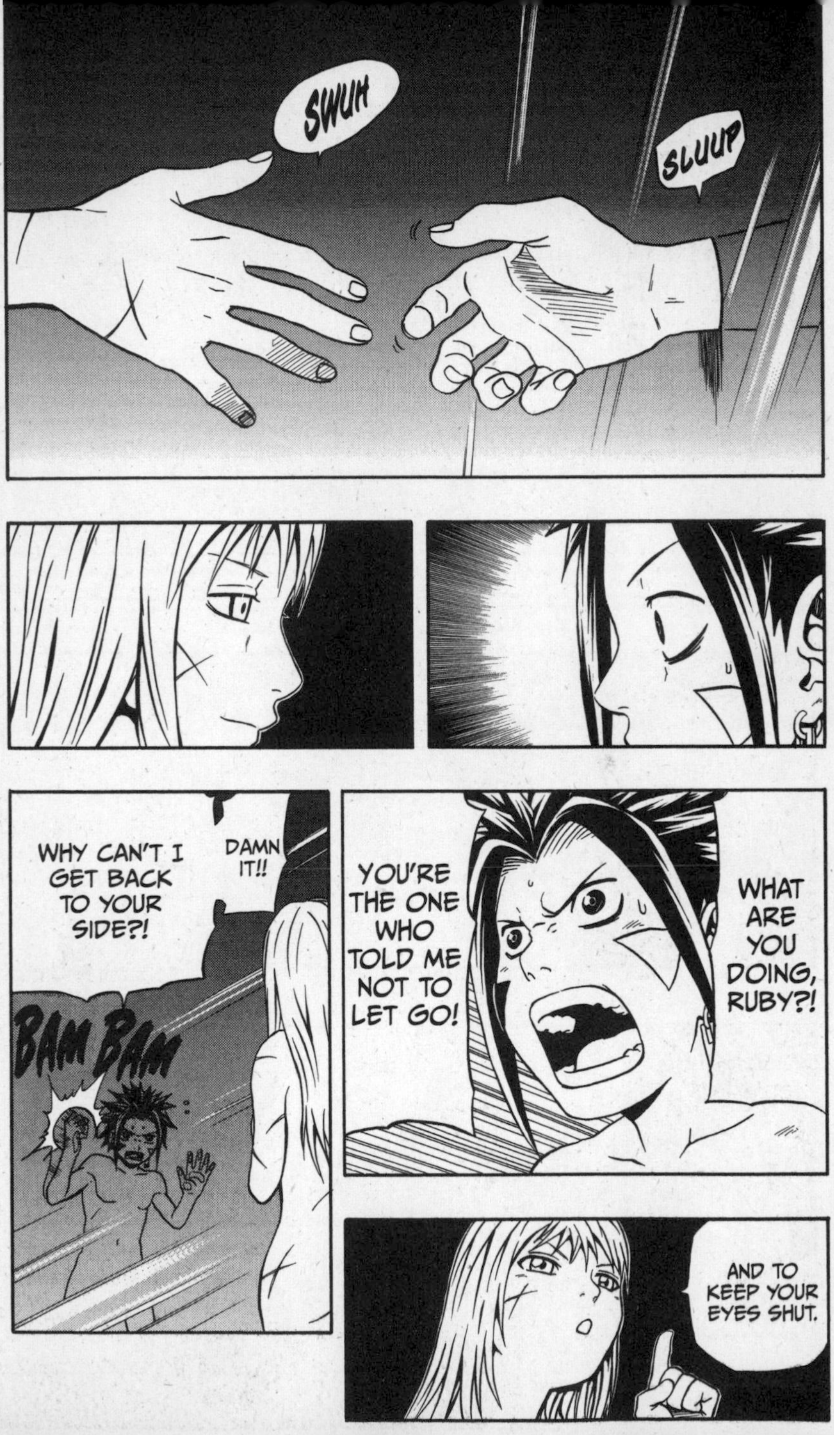
SLUUP
SWUH
WHAT ARE YOU DOING, RUBY?!
YOU'RE THE ONE WHO TOLD ME NOT TO LET GO!
AND TO KEEP YOUR EYES SHUT.
DAMN IT!!
WHY CAN'T I GET BACK TO YOUR SIDE?!
BAM BAM

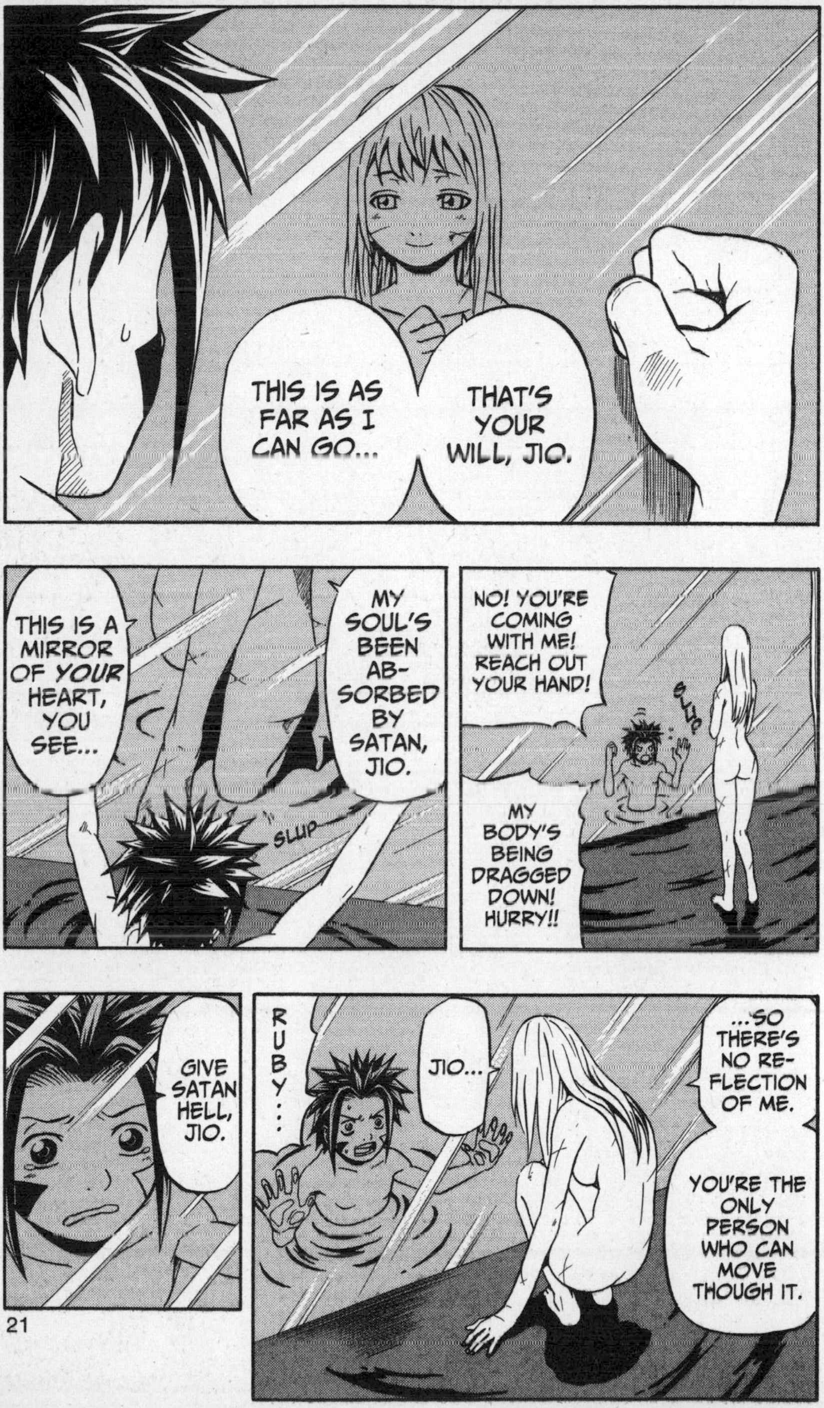
THAT'S YOUR WILL, JIO.
THIS IS AS FAR AS I CAN GO...
NO! YOU'RE COMING WITH ME! REACH OUT YOUR HAND!
SLUP
MY BODY'S BEING DRAGGED DOWN! HURRY!!
MY SOUL'S BEEN AB-SORBED BY SATAN, JIO.
THIS IS A MIRROR OF *YOUR* HEART, YOU SEE...
SLUP
...SO THERE'S NO RE-FLECTION OF ME.
YOU'RE THE ONLY PERSON WHO CAN MOVE THOUGH IT.
JIO...
RUBY...
GIVE SATAN HELL, JIO.

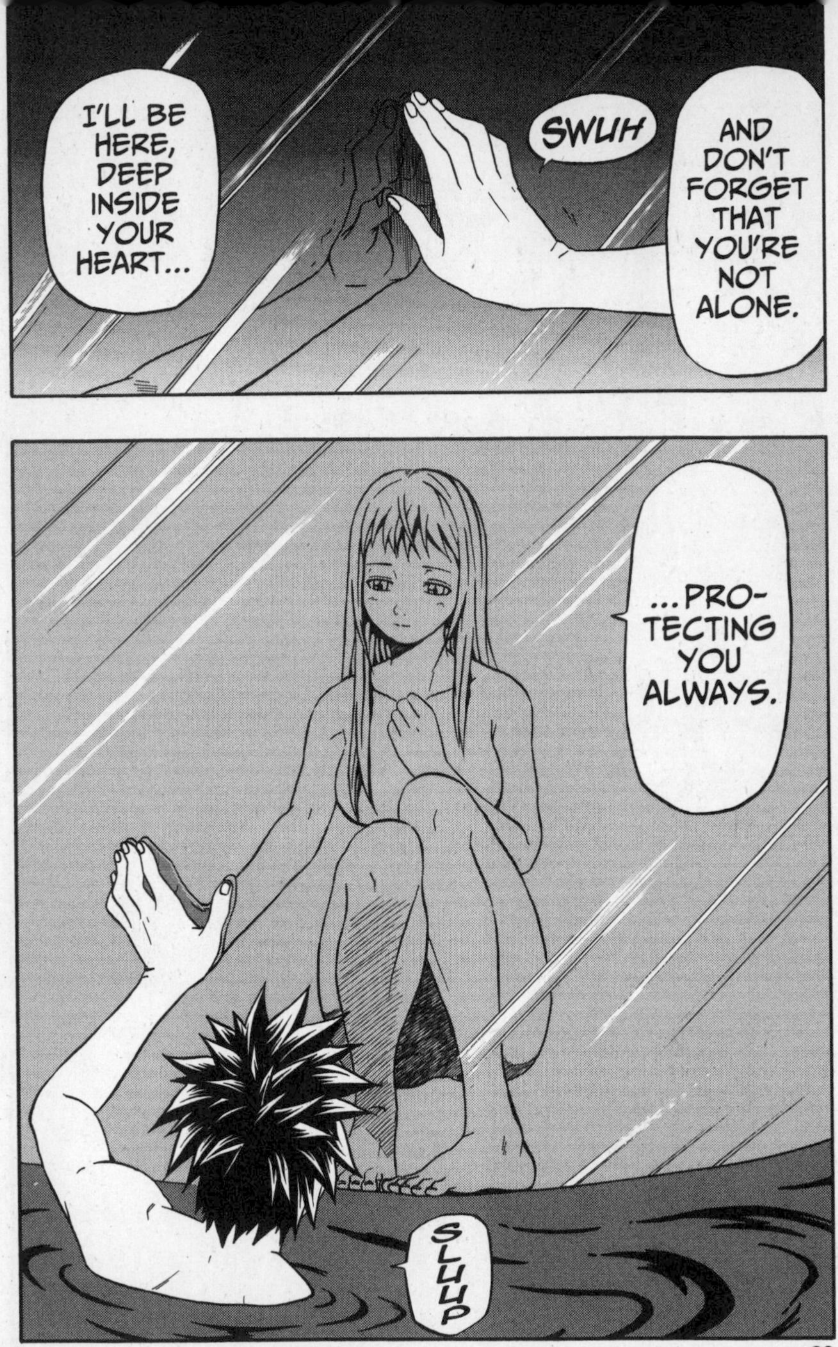
AND DON'T FORGET THAT YOU'RE NOT ALONE.
SWUH
I'LL BE HERE, DEEP INSIDE YOUR HEART...
...PROTECTING YOU ALWAYS.
SLUUP

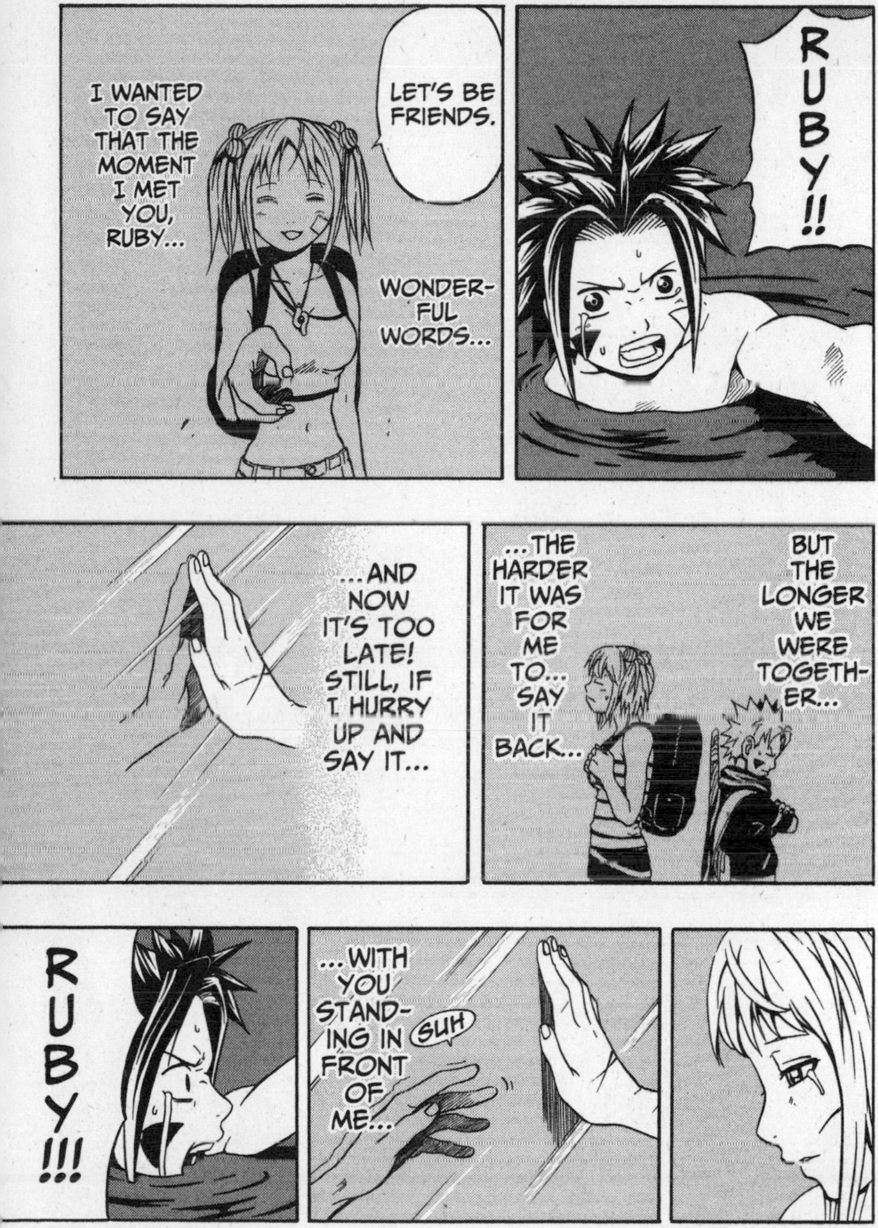
RUBY!!
LET'S BE FRIENDS.
I WANTED TO SAY THAT THE MOMENT I MET YOU, RUBY...
WONDERFUL WORDS...
BUT THE LONGER WE WERE TOGETHER...
...THE HARDER IT WAS FOR ME TO... SAY IT BACK...
...AND NOW IT'S TOO LATE! STILL, IF I HURRY UP AND SAY IT...
...WITH YOU STANDING IN FRONT OF ME...
SUH
RUBY!!!

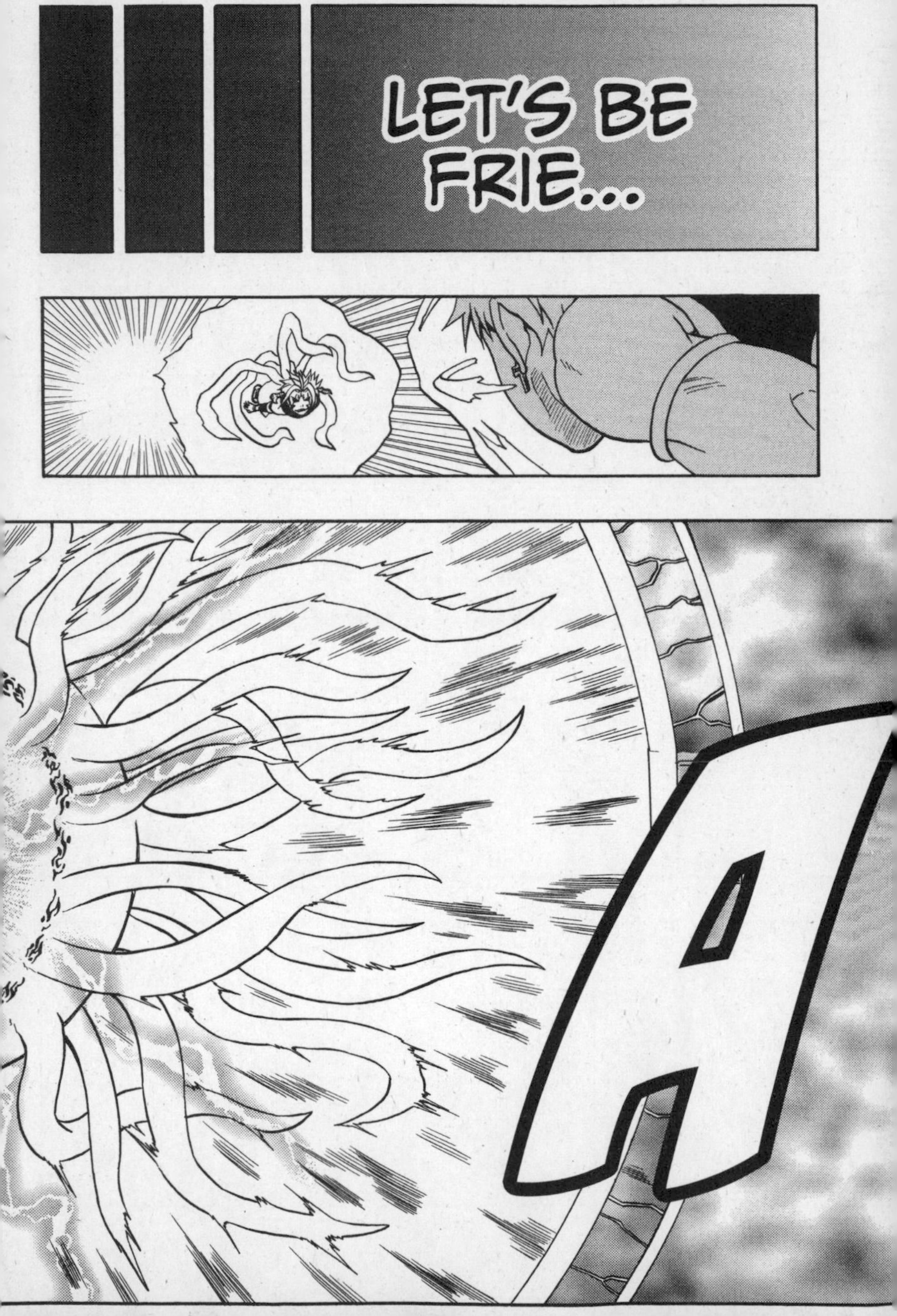
LET'S BE FRIE...
A

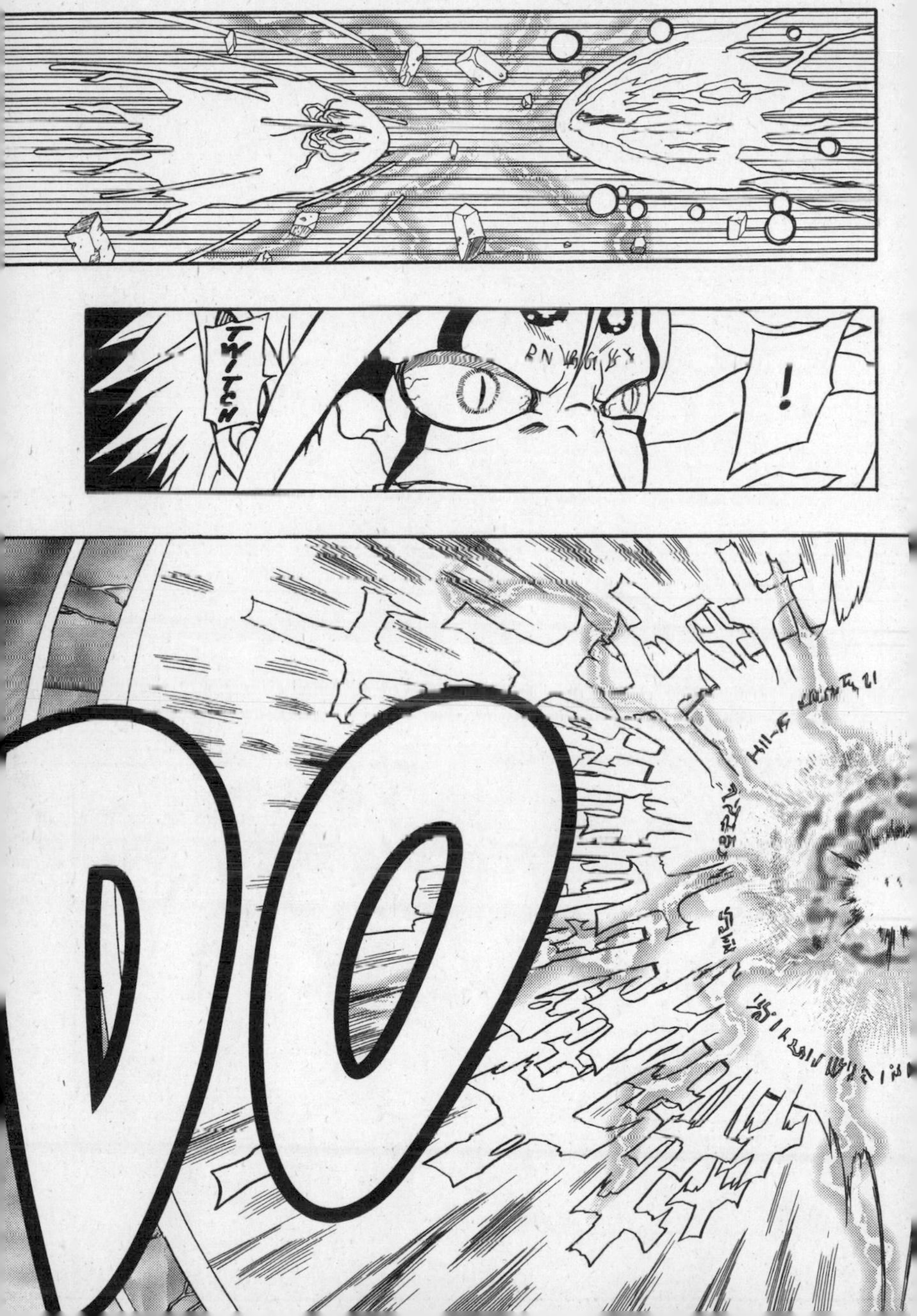
!
TWITCH

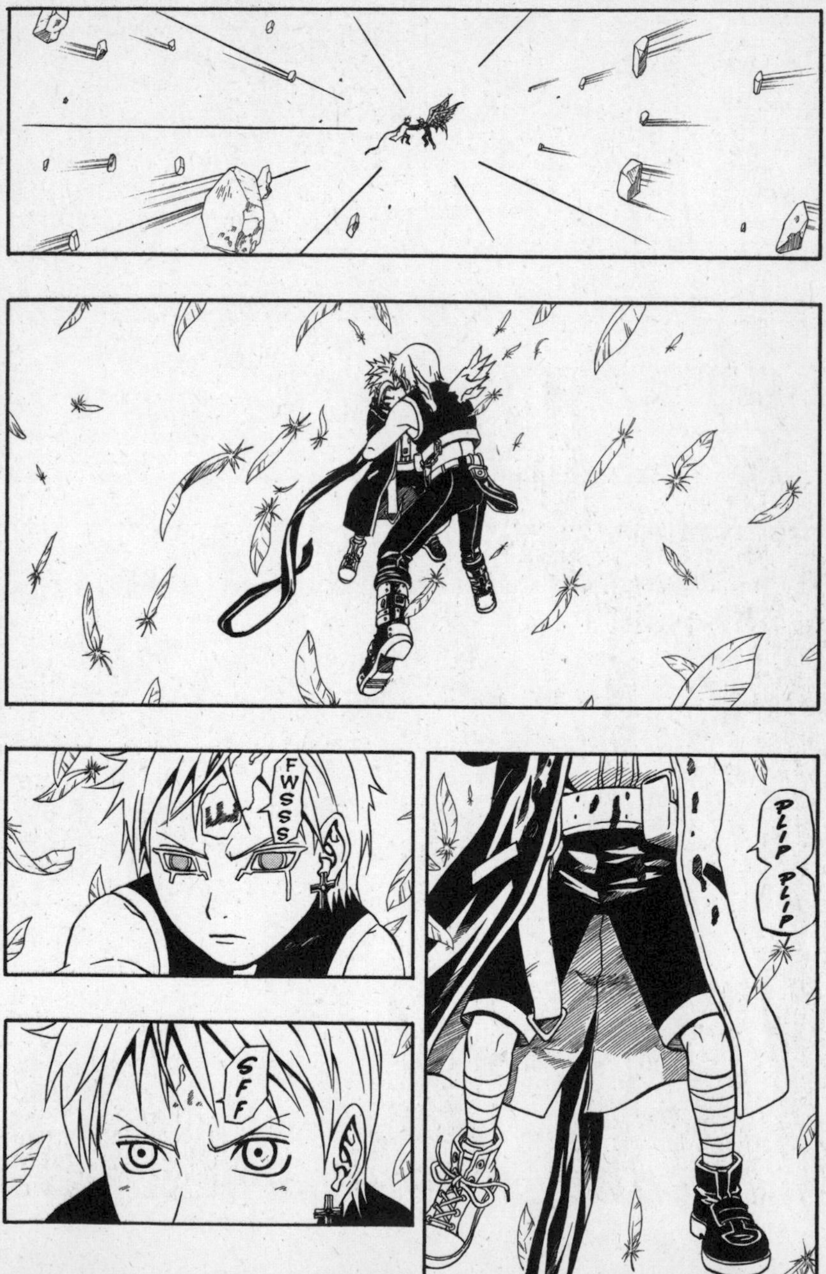
PLIP PLIP
FWSSS
SFF

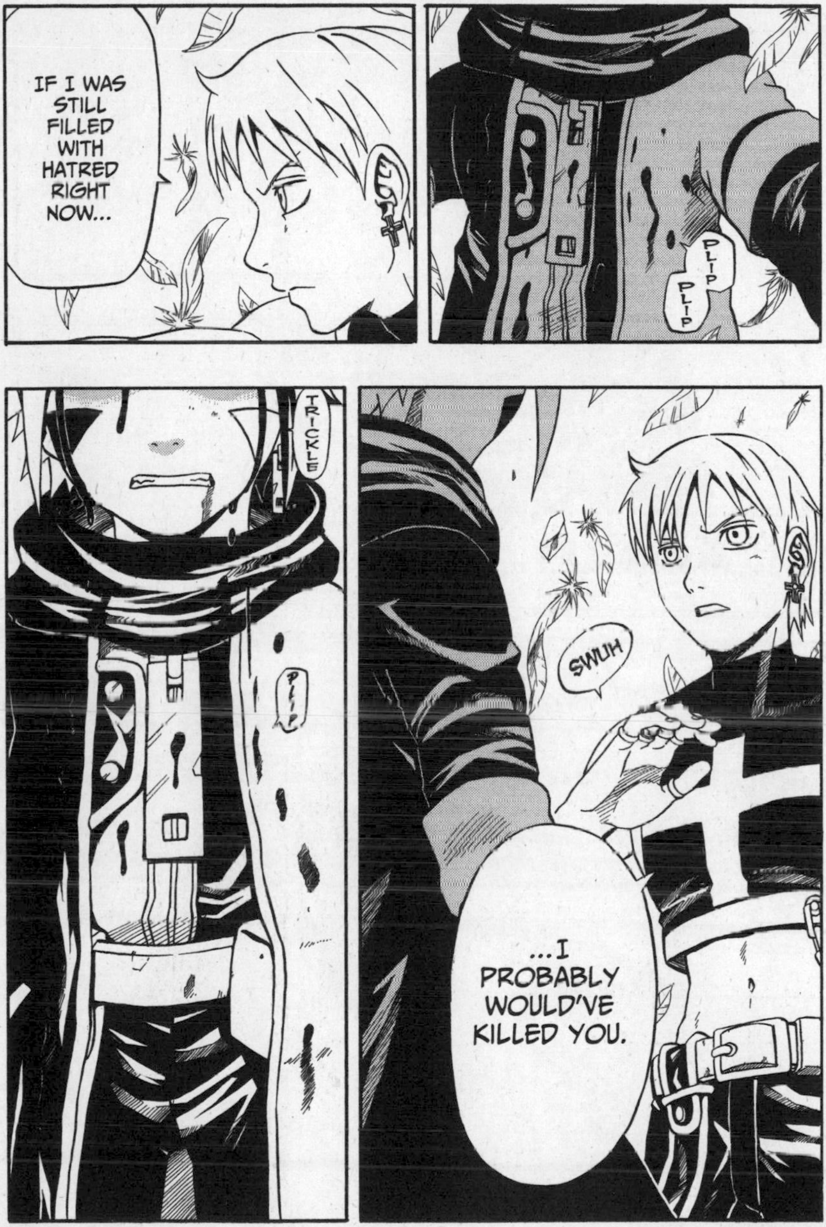
PLIP
PLIP
IF I WAS STILL FILLED WITH HATRED RIGHT NOW...
SWUH
...I PROBABLY WOULD'VE KILLED YOU.
TRICKLE
PLIP

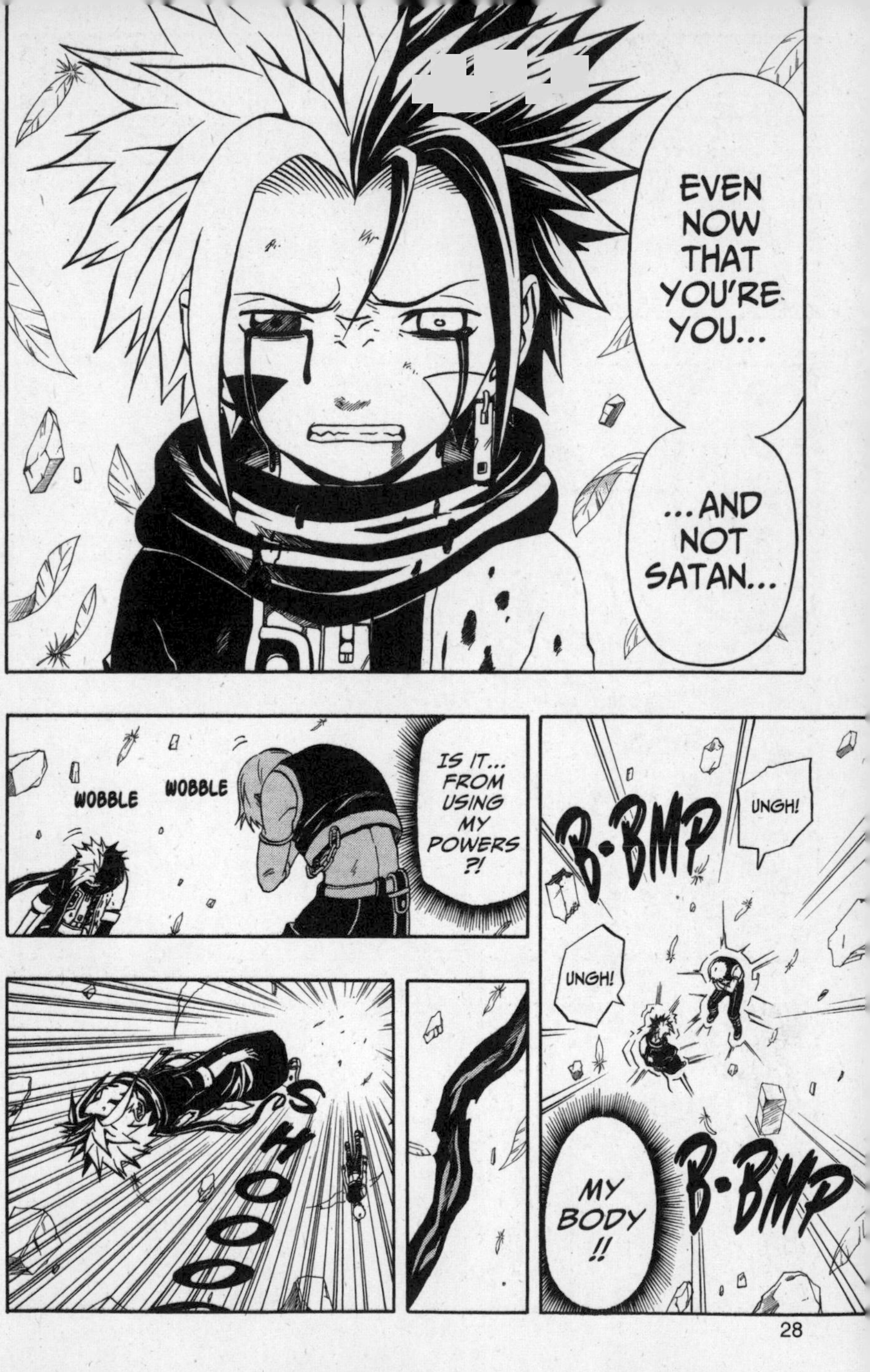
EVEN NOW THAT YOU'RE YOU...
...AND NOT SATAN...
UNGH!
B-BMP
UNGH!
B-BMP
MY BODY!!
IS IT... FROM USING MY POWERS?!
WOBBLE
WOBBLE
SHOOOOO

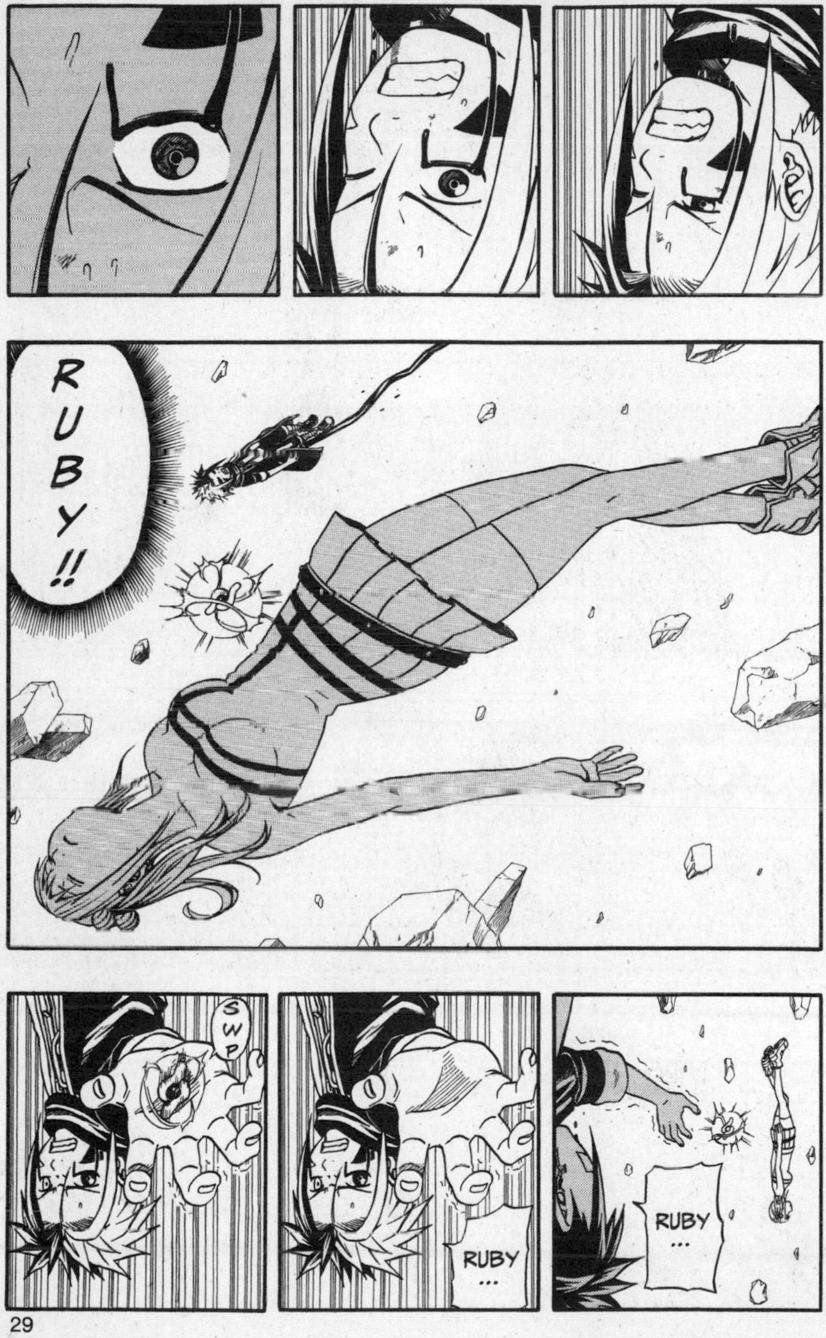
RUBY!!
RUBY ...
RUBY ...
SWP

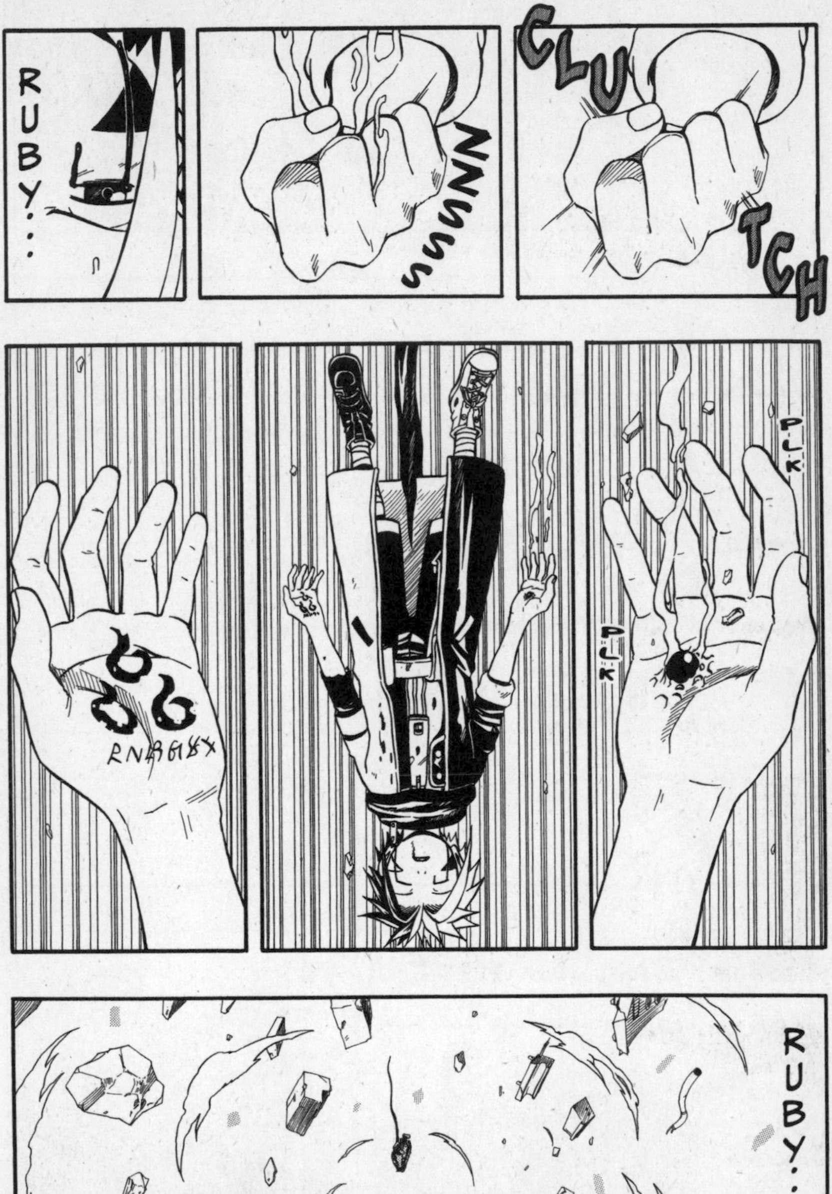
CLUTCH
SSSSSNNN
RUBY...
PLK
PLK
RUBY...

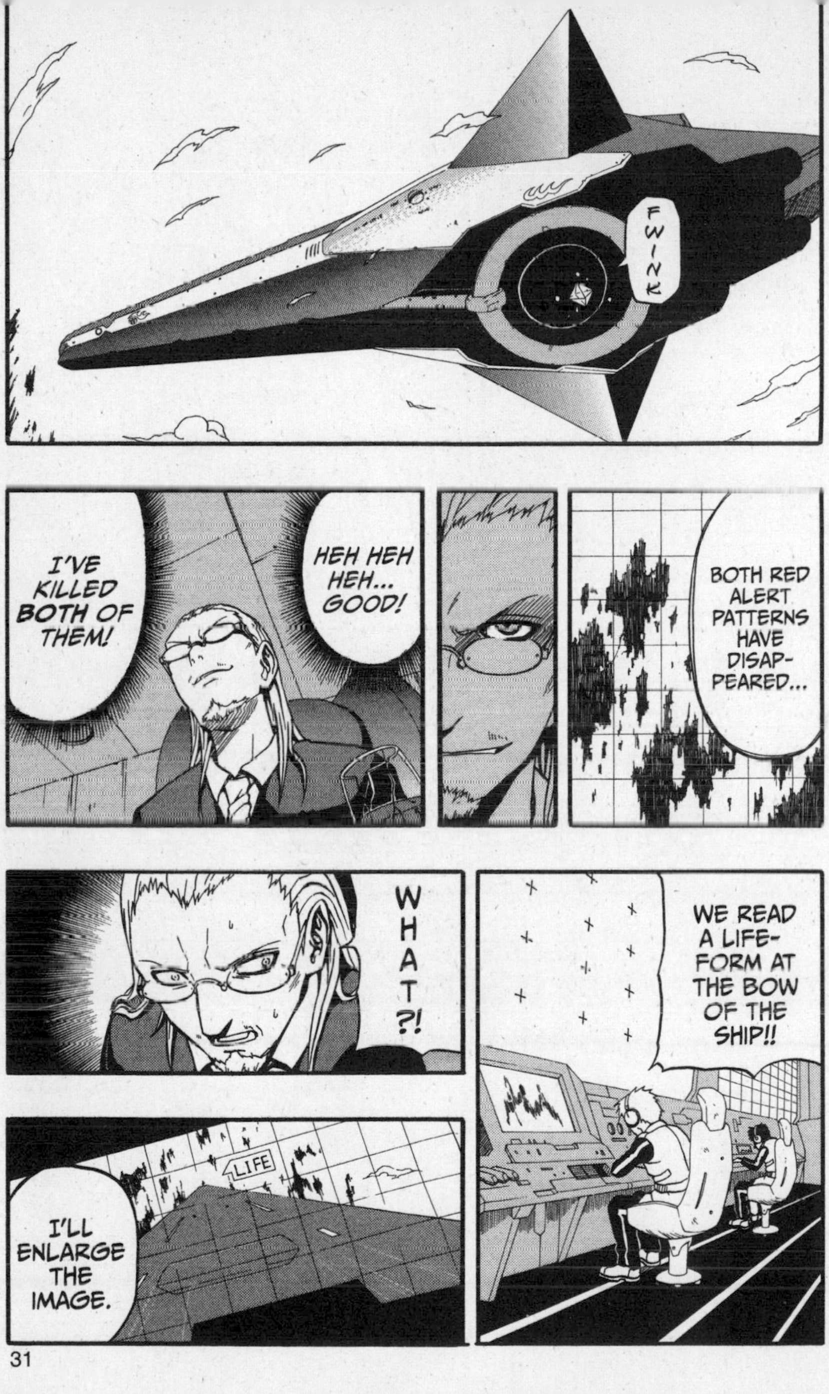
FWINK
BOTH RED ALERT PATTERNS HAVE DISAPPEARED...
HEH HEH HEH... GOOD!
I'VE KILLED BOTH OF THEM!
WE READ A LIFE-FORM AT THE BOW OF THE SHIP!!
WHAT?!
LIFE
I'LL ENLARGE THE IMAGE.

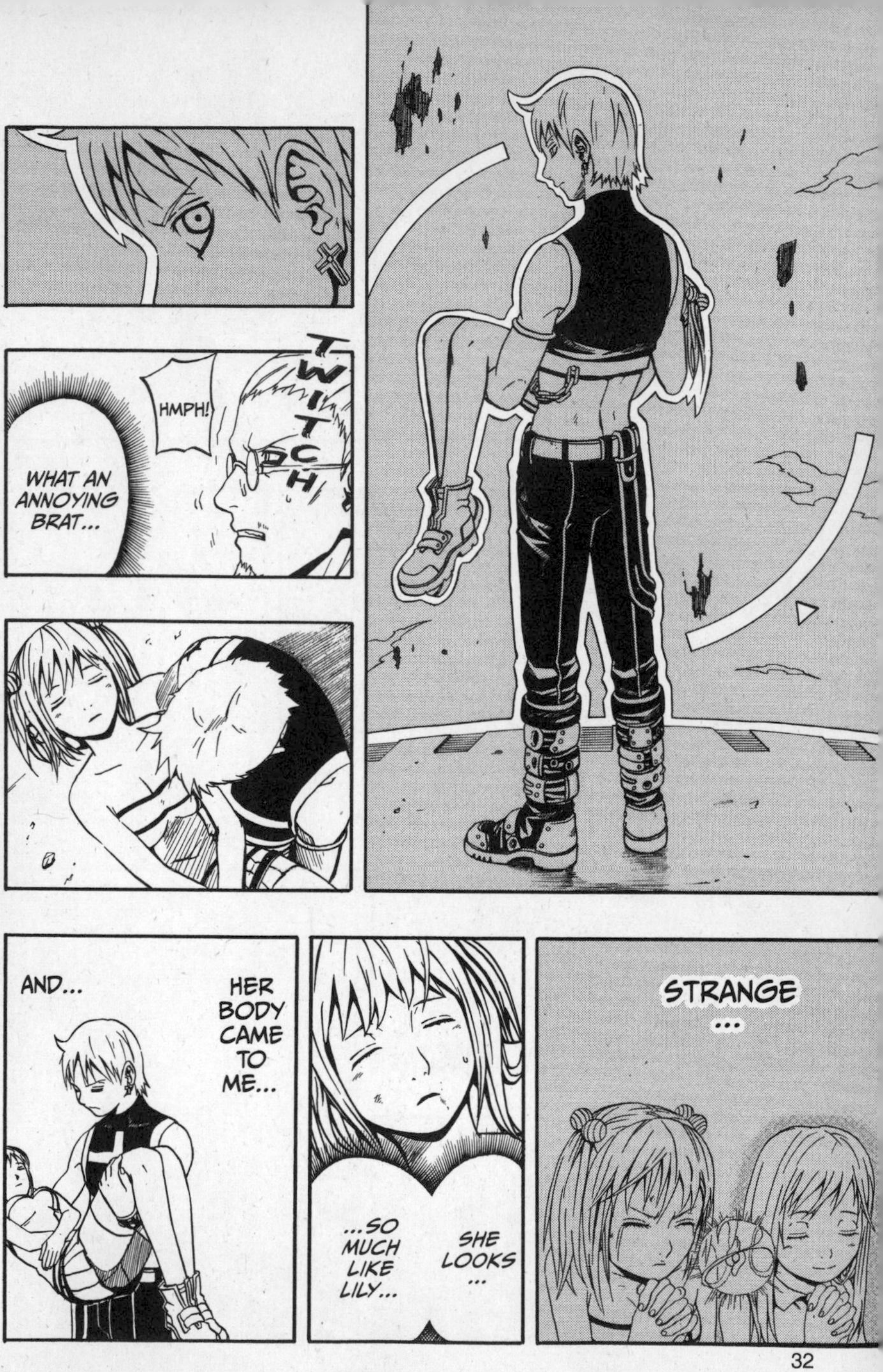
TWITCH
HMPH!
WHAT AN ANNOYING BRAT...
STRANGE ...
SHE LOOKS ...
...SO MUCH LIKE LILY...
HER BODY CAME TO ME...
AND...

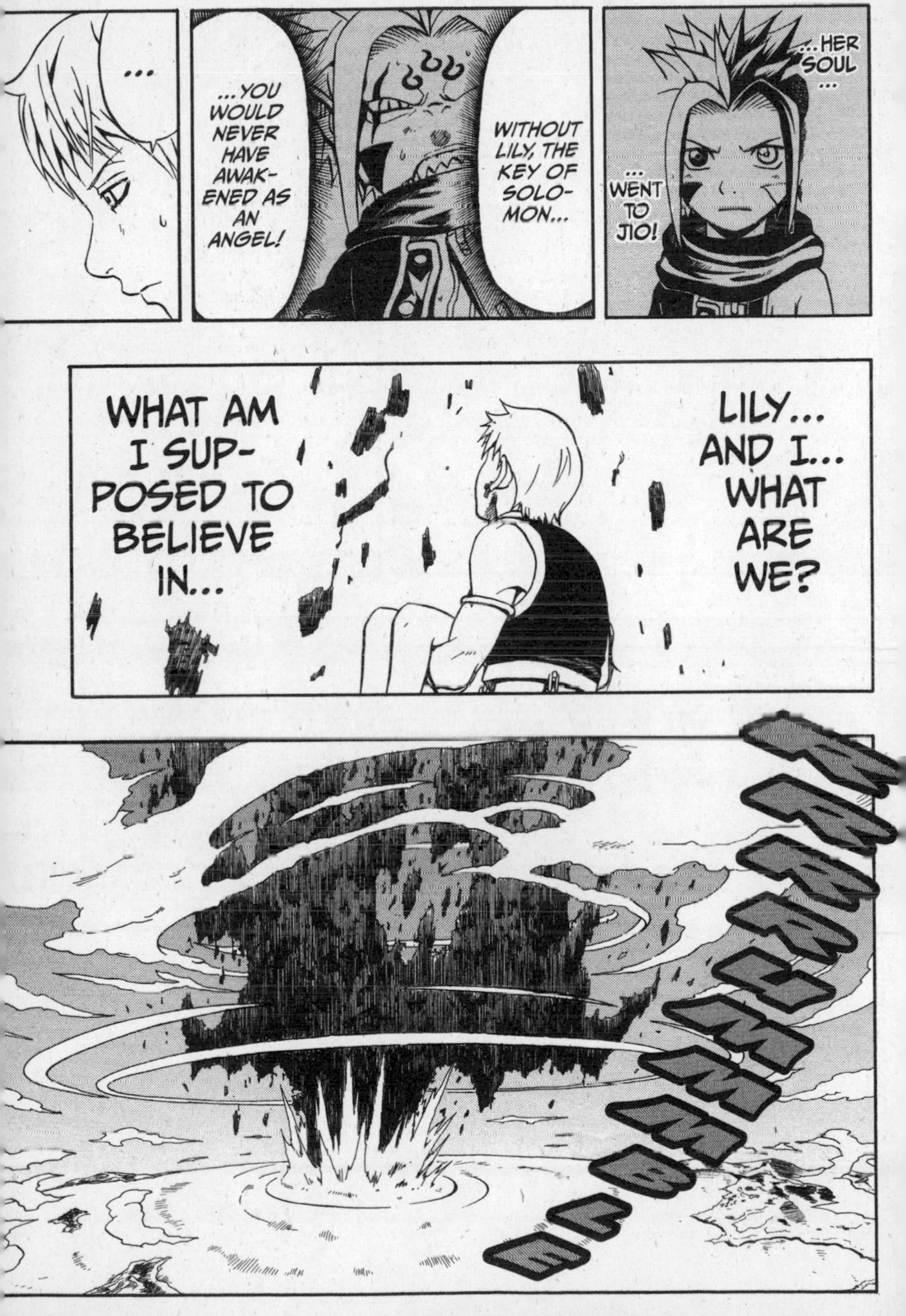
...HER SOUL ...
...WENT TO JIO!
WITHOUT LILY, THE KEY OF SOLO-MON...
...YOU WOULD NEVER HAVE AWAK-ENED AS AN ANGEL!
...
LILY... AND I... WHAT ARE WE?
WHAT AM I SUP-POSED TO BELIEVE IN...

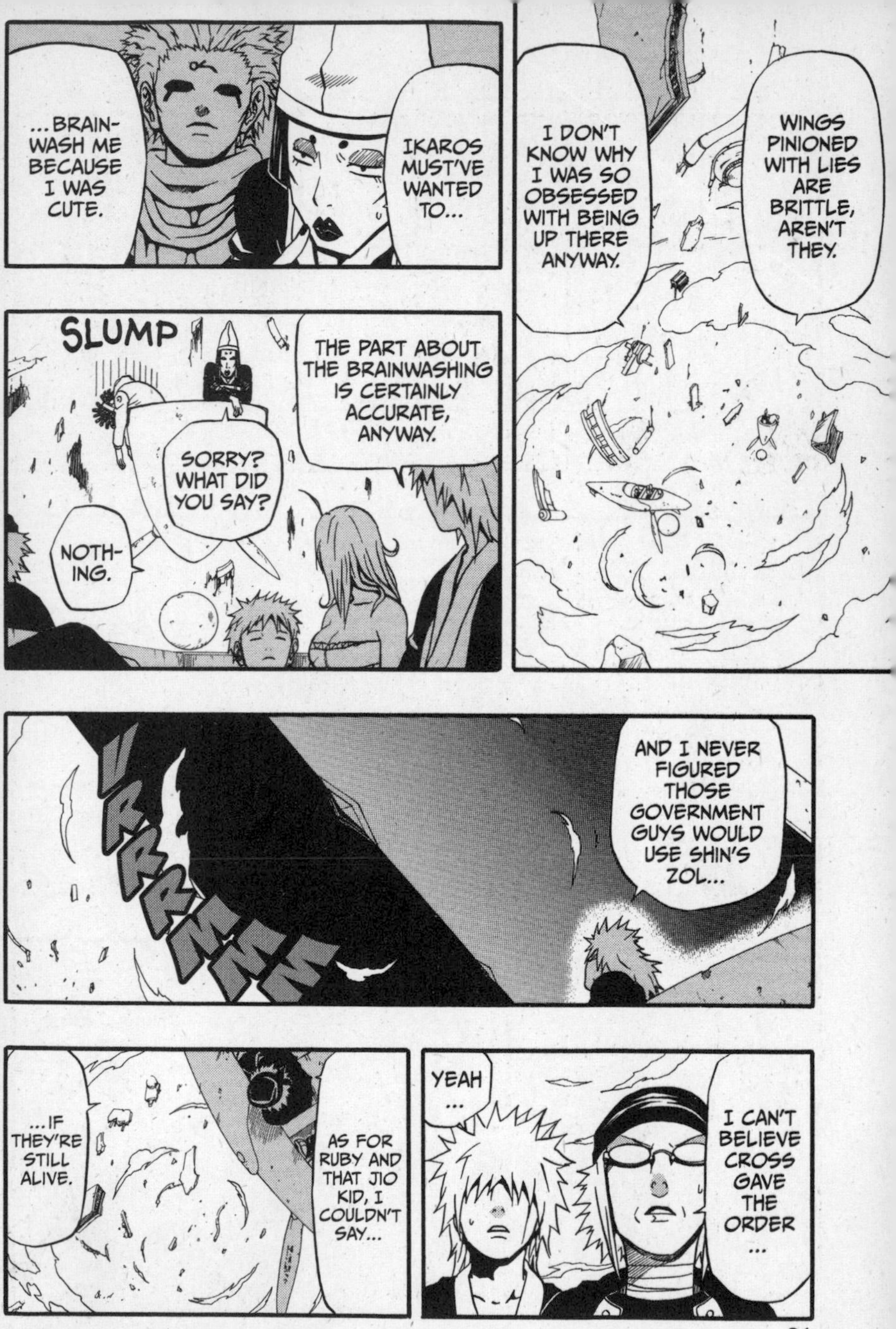
WINGS PINIONED WITH LIES ARE BRITTLE, AREN'T THEY.
I DON'T KNOW WHY I WAS SO OBSESSED WITH BEING UP THERE ANYWAY.
IKAROS MUST'VE WANTED TO...
...BRAIN-WASH ME BECAUSE I WAS CUTE.
THE PART ABOUT THE BRAINWASHING IS CERTAINLY ACCURATE, ANYWAY.
SLUMP
SORRY? WHAT DID YOU SAY?
NOTH-ING.
AND I NEVER FIGURED THOSE GOVERNMENT GUYS WOULD USE SHIN'S ZOL...
VRRMMMN
I CAN'T BELIEVE CROSS GAVE THE ORDER...
YEAH...
AS FOR RUBY AND THAT JIO KID, I COULDN'T SAY...
...IF THEY'RE STILL ALIVE.

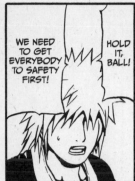

DON'T TALK LIKE THAT! OF COURSE THEY'RE STILL ALIVE!!
WE'RE GONNA GO BACK AN' HELP 'EM!!
HE... HEY...
HOLD IT, BALL!
WE NEED TO GET EVERYBODY TO SAFETY FIRST!
DON'T YOU HAVE FAITH IN JIO AND RUBY?
UH... I DO, BUT...
I'M SURE BOTH JIO AND RUBY ARE FINE.
SEE? MY FEELINGS... MALSE'S AND JIO'S TOO...
...HAVE CHANGED THE RUKO ORE...

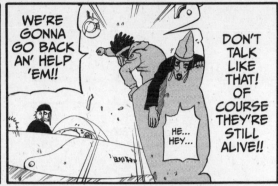

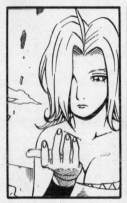

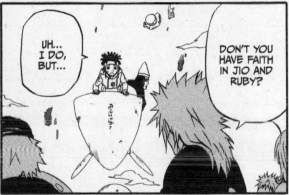

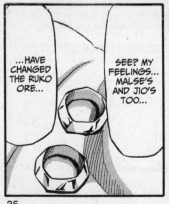

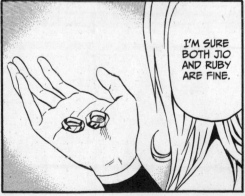

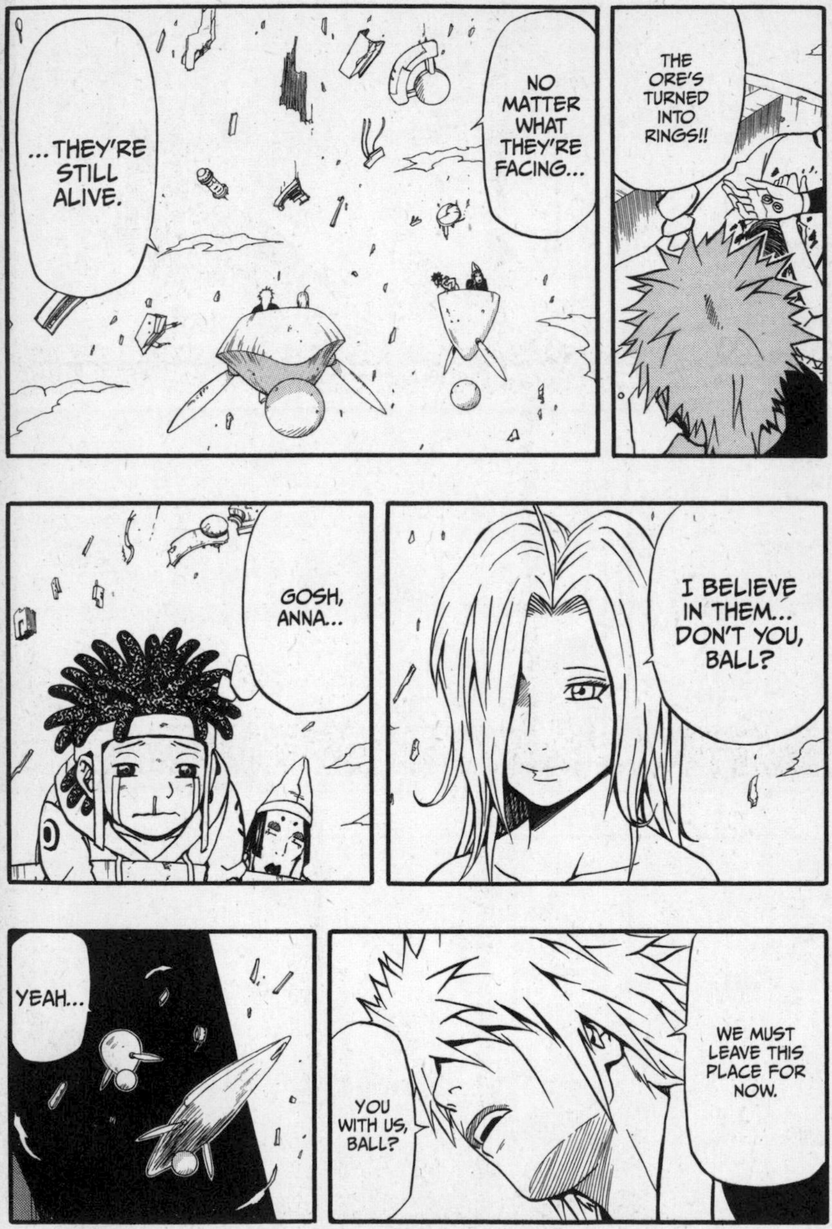
THE ORE'S TURNED INTO RINGS!!
NO MATTER WHAT THEY'RE FACING...
...THEY'RE STILL ALIVE.
I BELIEVE IN THEM... DON'T YOU, BALL?
GOSH, ANNA...
WE MUST LEAVE THIS PLACE FOR NOW.
YOU WITH US, BALL?
YEAH...

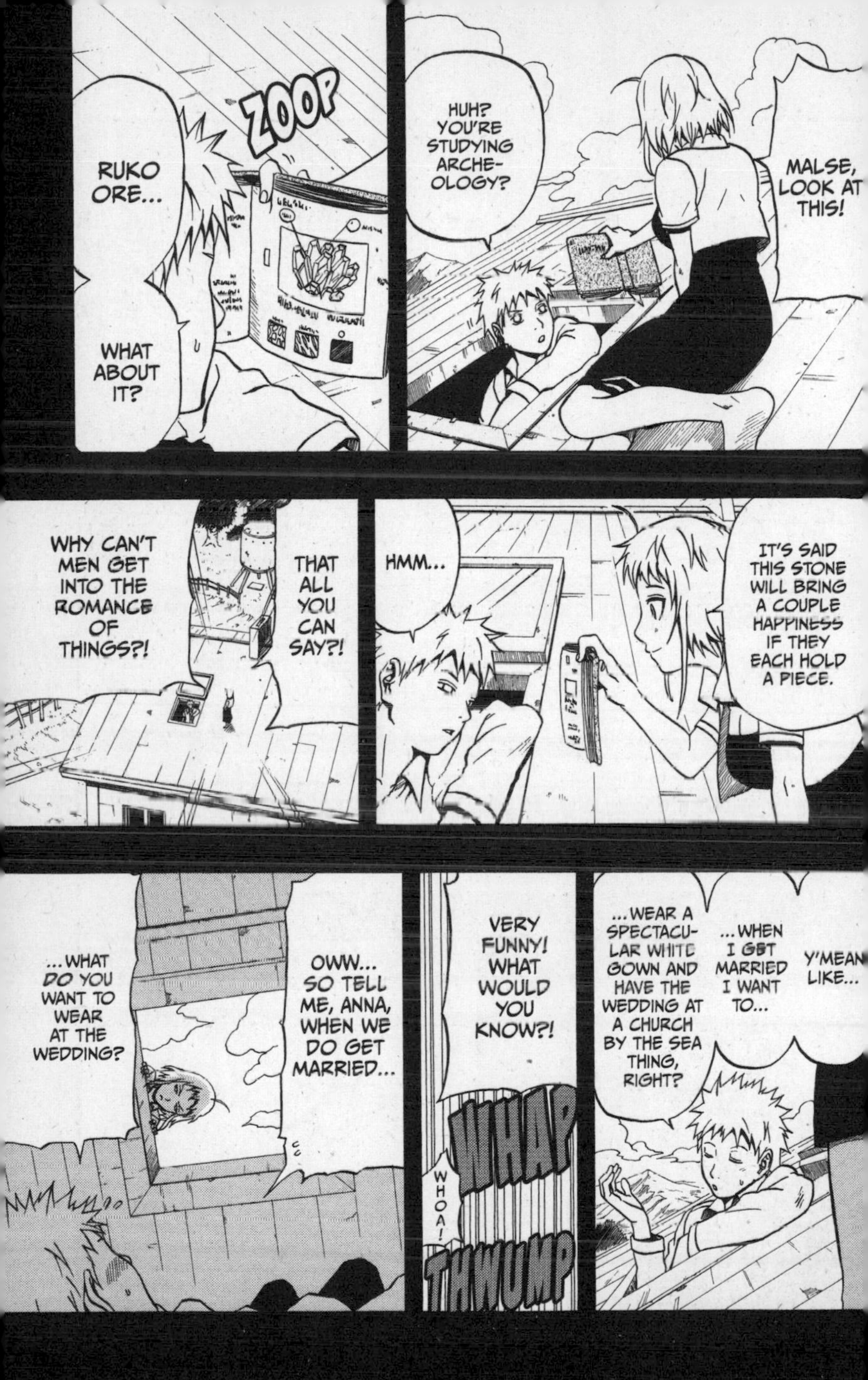
MALSE, LOOK AT THIS!
HUH? YOU'RE STUDYING ARCHE-OLOGY?
ZOOP
RUKO ORE...
WHAT ABOUT IT?
IT'S SAID THIS STONE WILL BRING A COUPLE HAPPINESS IF THEY EACH HOLD A PIECE.
HMM...
THAT ALL YOU CAN SAY?!
WHY CAN'T MEN GET INTO THE ROMANCE OF THINGS?!
Y'MEAN LIKE...
...WHEN I GET MARRIED I WANT TO...
...WEAR A SPECTACULAR WHITE GOWN AND HAVE THE WEDDING AT A CHURCH BY THE SEA THING, RIGHT?
VERY FUNNY! WHAT WOULD YOU KNOW?!
WHAP
WHOA!
THWUMP
OWW... SO TELL ME, ANNA, WHEN WE DO GET MARRIED...
...WHAT *DO* YOU WANT TO WEAR AT THE WEDDING?

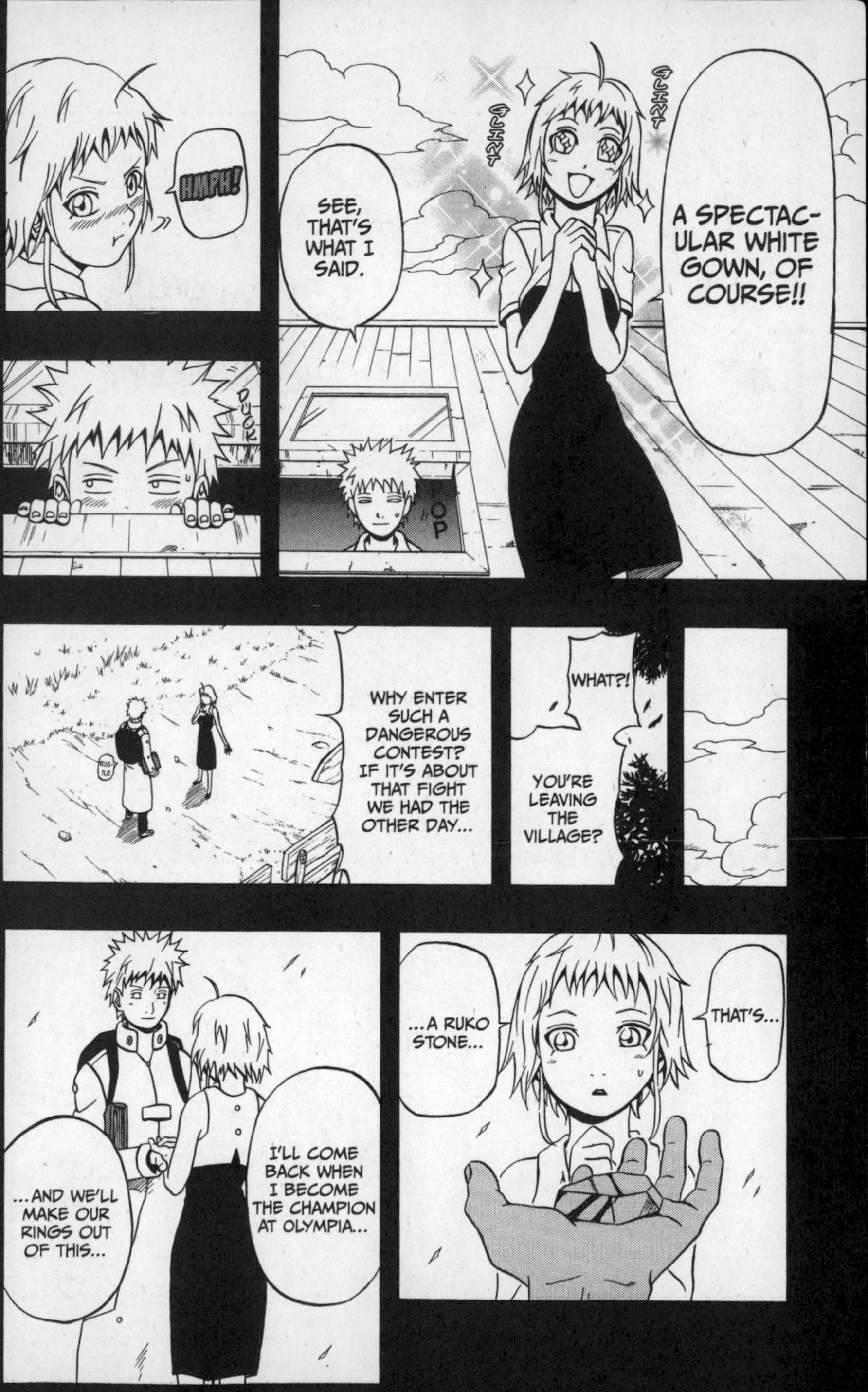
A SPECTACULAR WHITE GOWN, OF COURSE!!
GLINT
GLINT
SEE, THAT'S WHAT I SAID.
POP
HMPH!
DUCK
WHAT?!
YOU'RE LEAVING THE VILLAGE?
WHY ENTER SUCH A DANGEROUS CONTEST? IF IT'S ABOUT THAT FIGHT WE HAD THE OTHER DAY...
RUSTLE
THAT'S...
...A RUKO STONE...
I'LL COME BACK WHEN I BECOME THE CHAMPION AT OLYMPIA...
...AND WE'LL MAKE OUR RINGS OUT OF THIS...

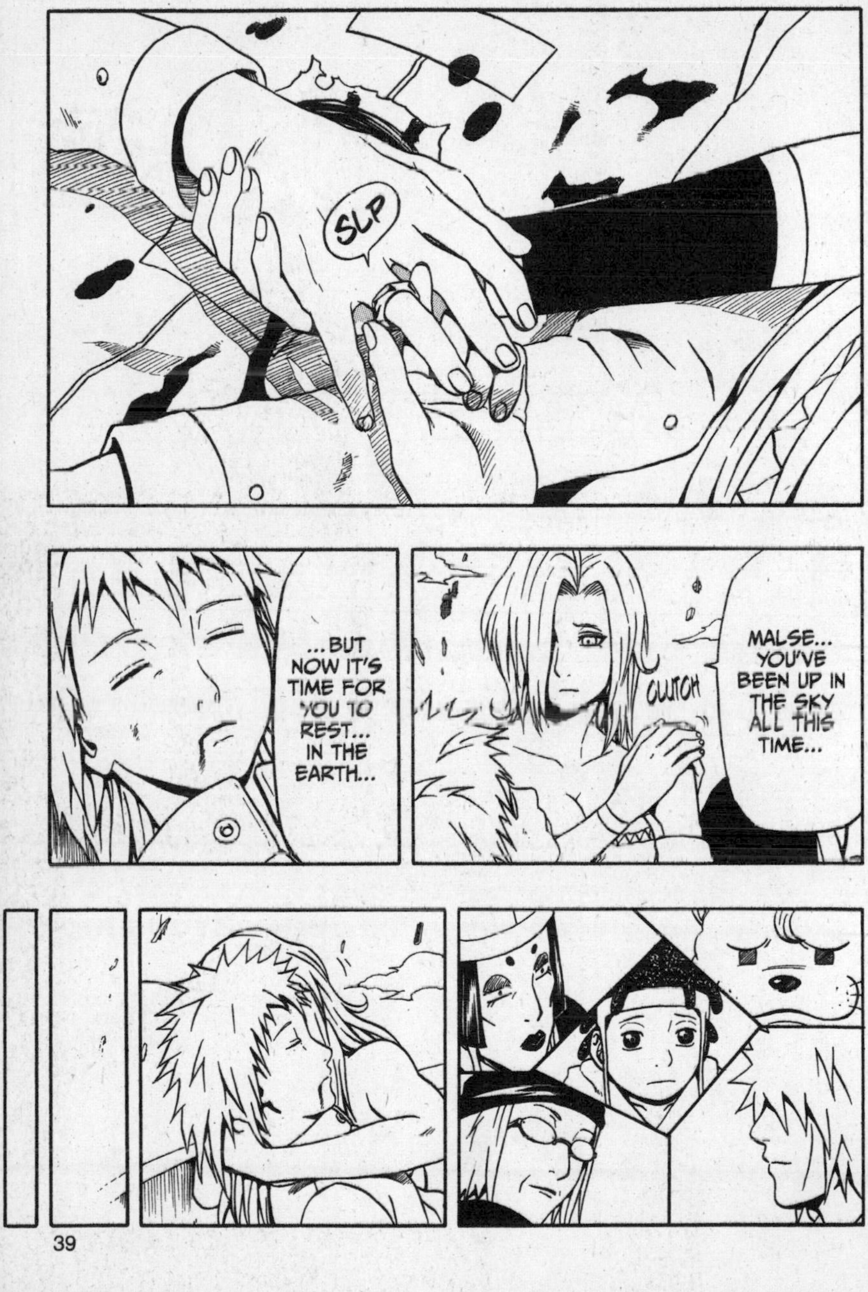
SLP
MALSE... YOU'VE BEEN UP IN THE SKY ALL THIS TIME...
CLUTCH
...BUT NOW IT'S TIME FOR YOU TO REST... IN THE EARTH...

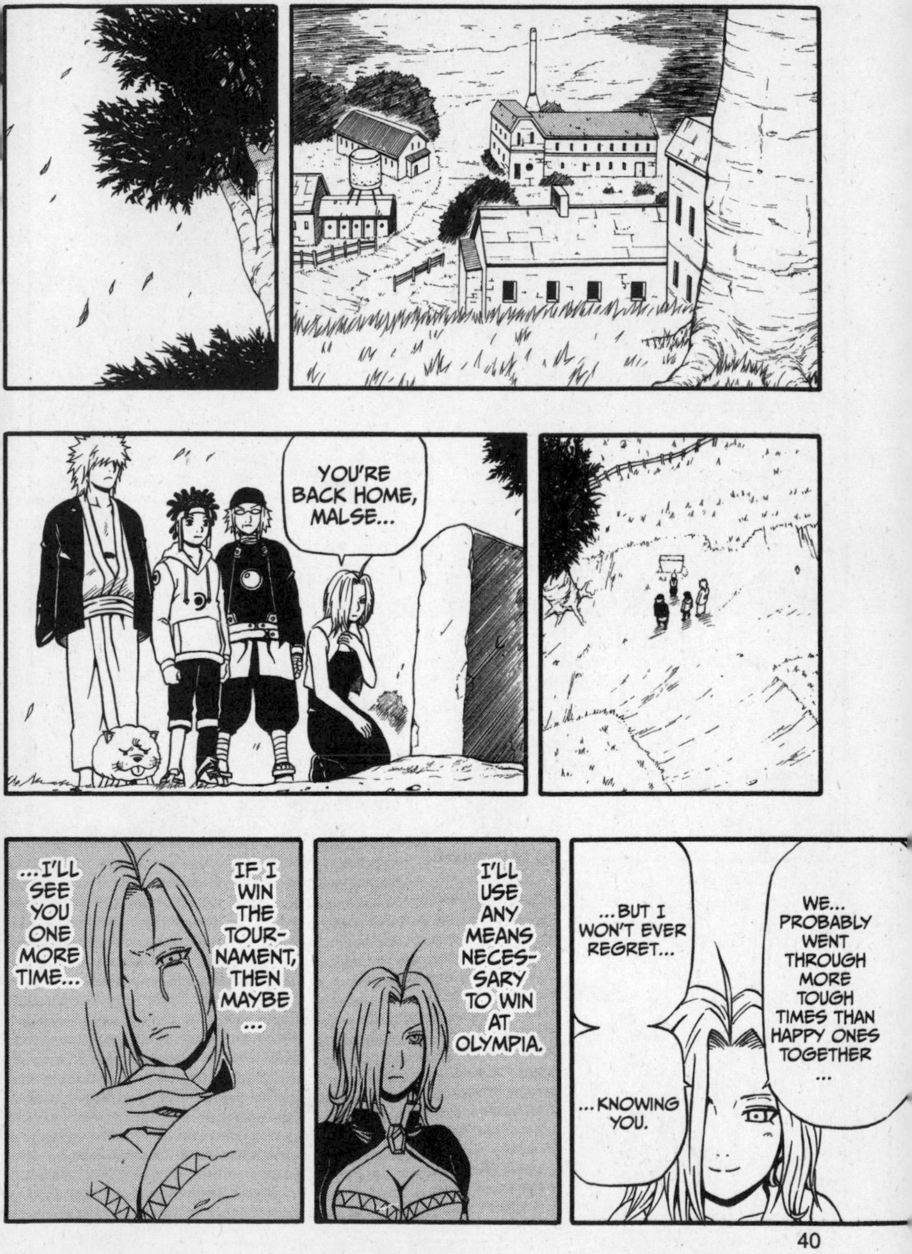
YOU'RE BACK HOME, MALSE...
WE... PROBABLY WENT THROUGH MORE TOUGH TIMES THAN HAPPY ONES TOGETHER ...
...BUT I WON'T EVER REGRET...
...KNOWING YOU.
I'LL USE ANY MEANS NECESSARY TO WIN AT OLYMPIA.
IF I WIN THE TOURNAMENT, THEN MAYBE ...
...I'LL SEE YOU ONE MORE TIME...

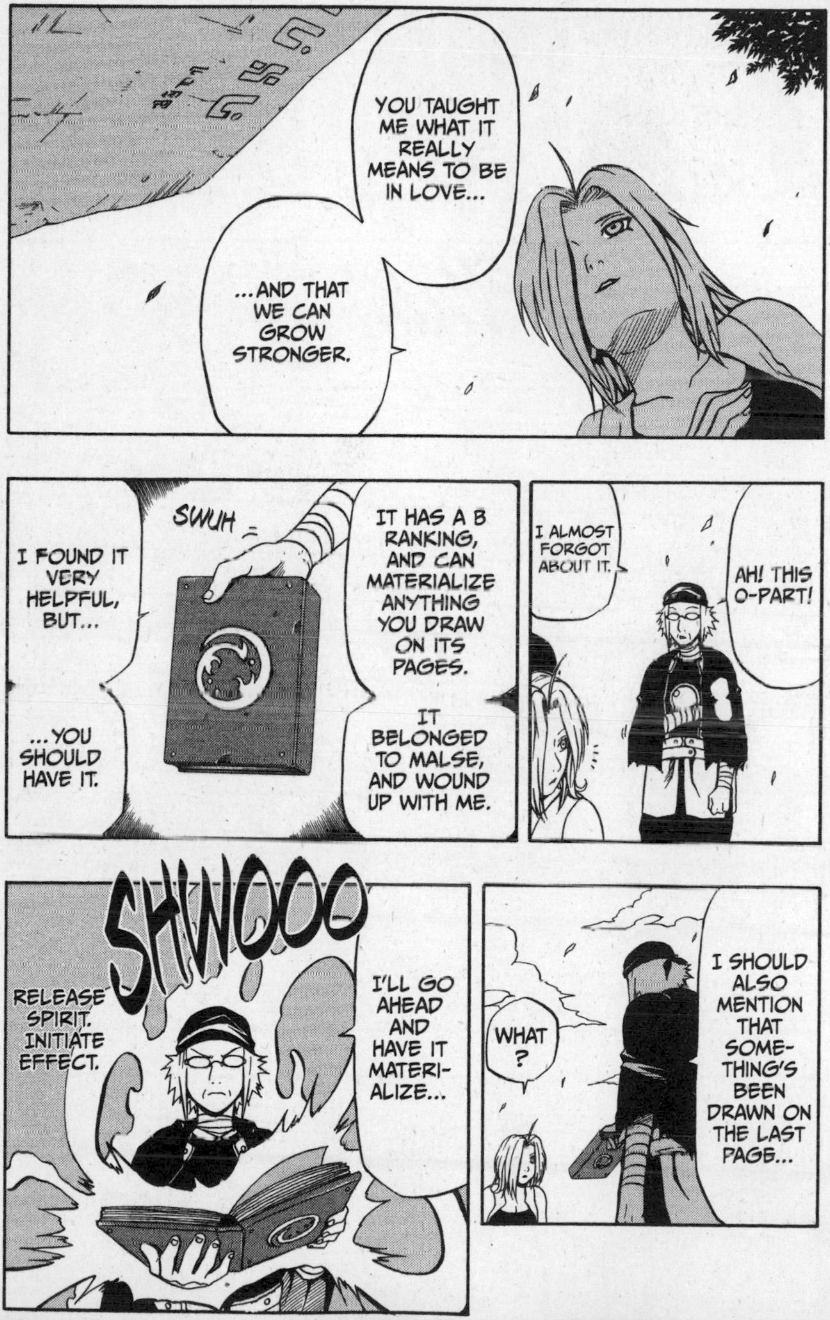
YOU TAUGHT ME WHAT IT REALLY MEANS TO BE IN LOVE...
...AND THAT WE CAN GROW STRONGER.
AH! THIS O-PART!
I ALMOST FORGOT ABOUT IT.
IT HAS A B RANKING, AND CAN MATERIALIZE ANYTHING YOU DRAW ON ITS PAGES.
IT BELONGED TO MALSE, AND WOUND UP WITH ME.
SWUH
I FOUND IT VERY HELPFUL, BUT...
...YOU SHOULD HAVE IT.
I SHOULD ALSO MENTION THAT SOME-THING'S BEEN DRAWN ON THE LAST PAGE...
WHAT?
I'LL GO AHEAD AND HAVE IT MATERI-ALIZE...
SHWOOO
RELEASE SPIRIT. INITIATE EFFECT.

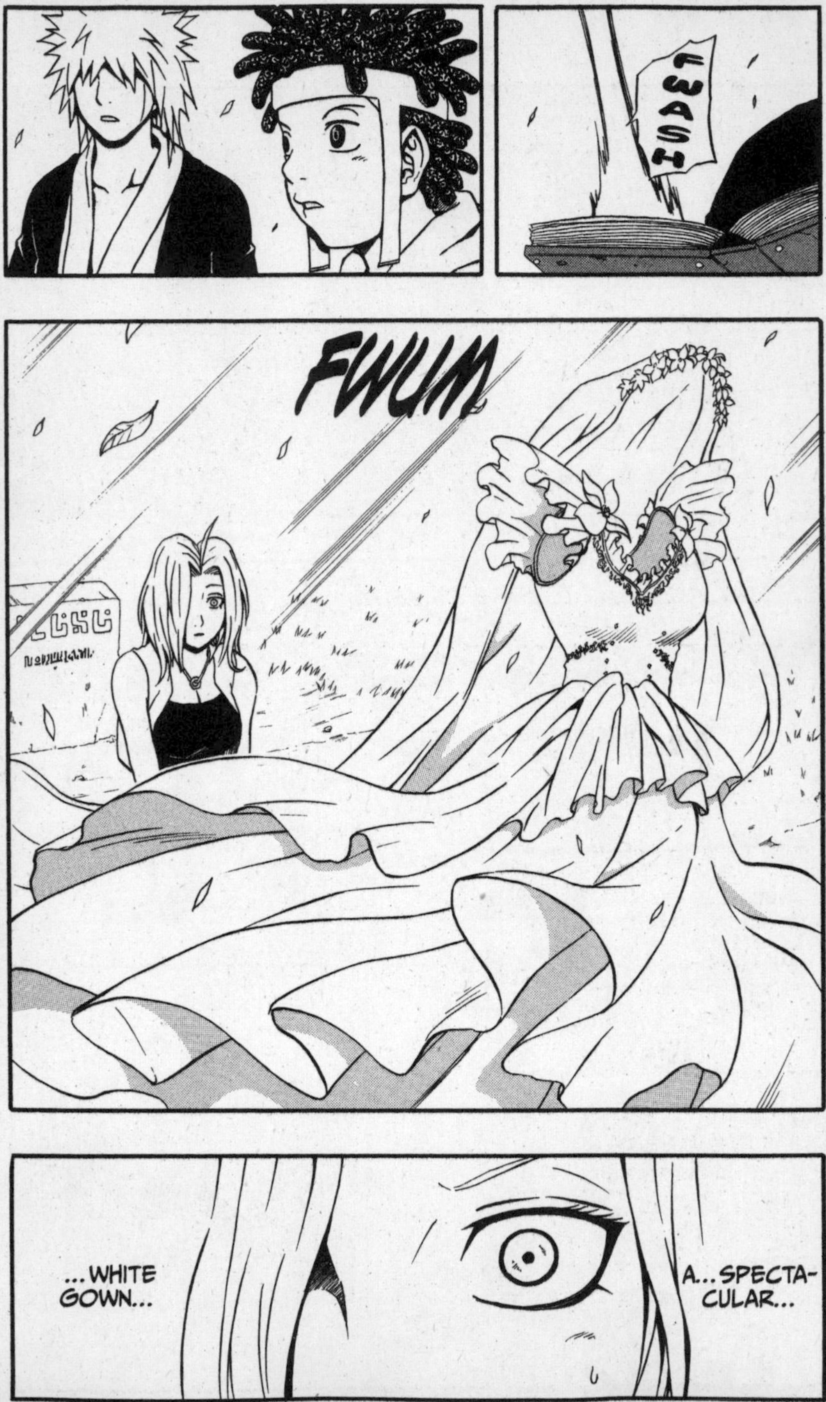
FWASH
FWUM
A... SPECTA-
CULAR...
...WHITE
GOWN...

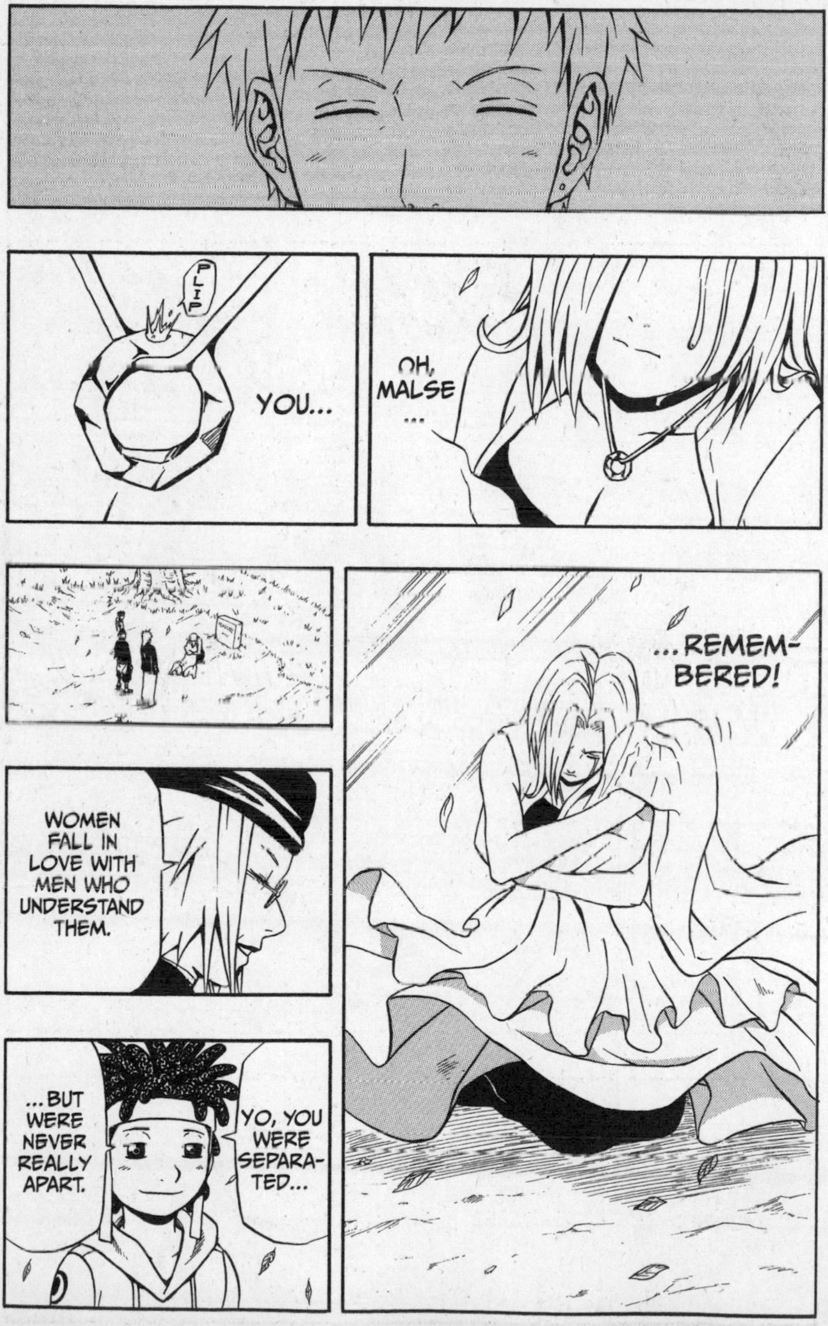
OH, MALSE ...
PLIP
YOU...
...REMEM-BERED!
WOMEN FALL IN LOVE WITH MEN WHO UNDERSTAND THEM.
YO, YOU WERE SEPARA-TED...
...BUT WERE NEVER REALLY APART.

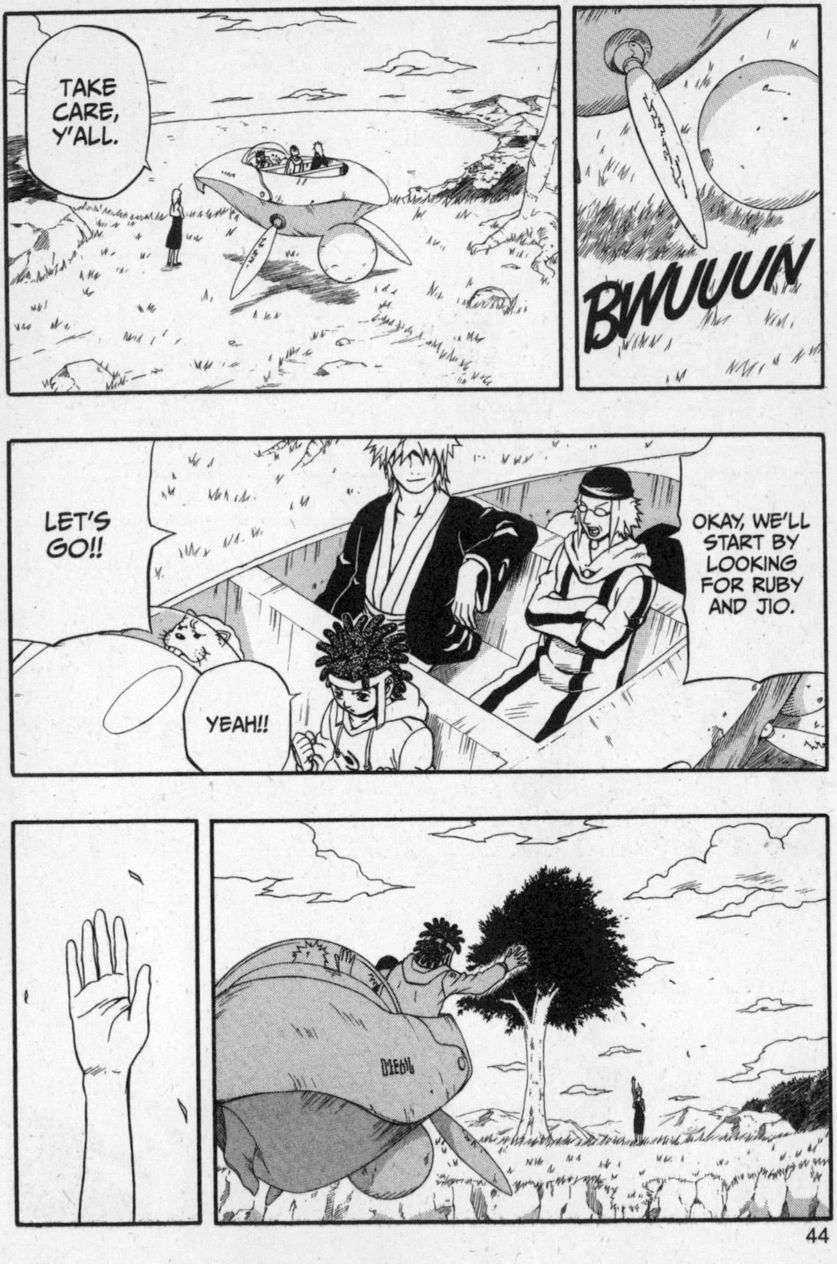
BWUUUN
TAKE CARE, Y'ALL.
OKAY, WE'LL START BY LOOKING FOR RUBY AND JIO.
LET'S GO!!
YEAH!!

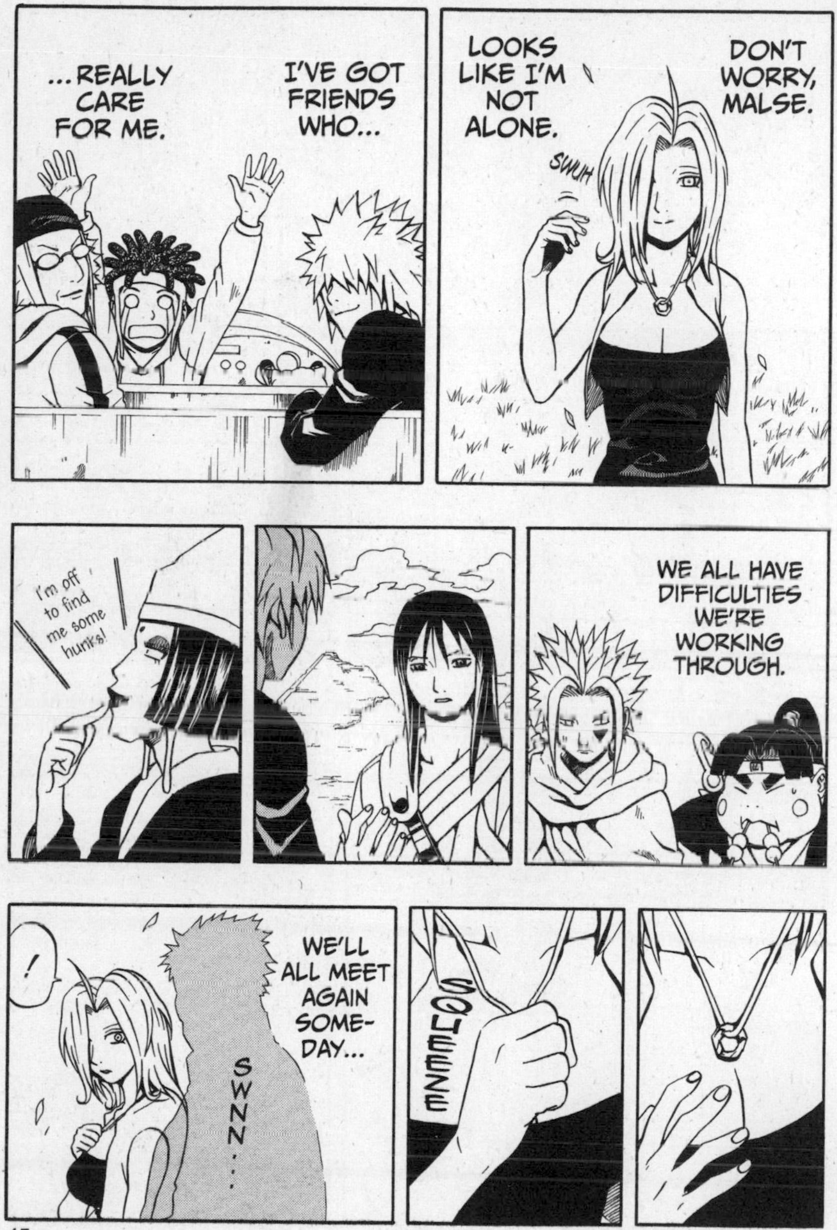
DON'T WORRY, MALSE.
LOOKS LIKE I'M NOT ALONE.
SWUH
I'VE GOT FRIENDS WHO...
...REALLY CARE FOR ME.
WE ALL HAVE DIFFICULTIES WE'RE WORKING THROUGH.
I'm off to find me some hunks!
SQUEEZE
WE'LL ALL MEET AGAIN SOME-DAY...
!
SWNN...

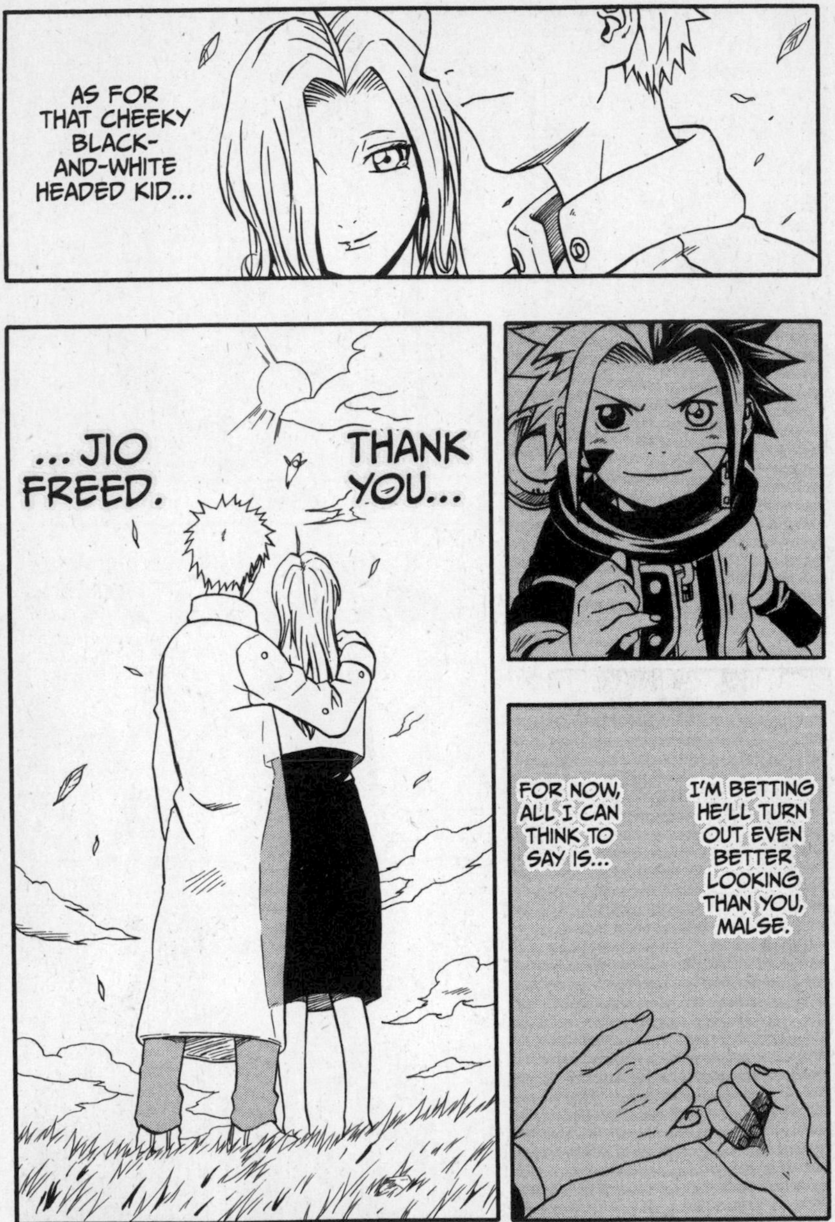
AS FOR THAT CHEEKY BLACK-AND-WHITE HEADED KID...
I'M BETTING HE'LL TURN OUT EVEN BETTER LOOKING THAN YOU, MALSE.
FOR NOW, ALL I CAN THINK TO SAY IS...
THANK YOU...
...JIO FREED.

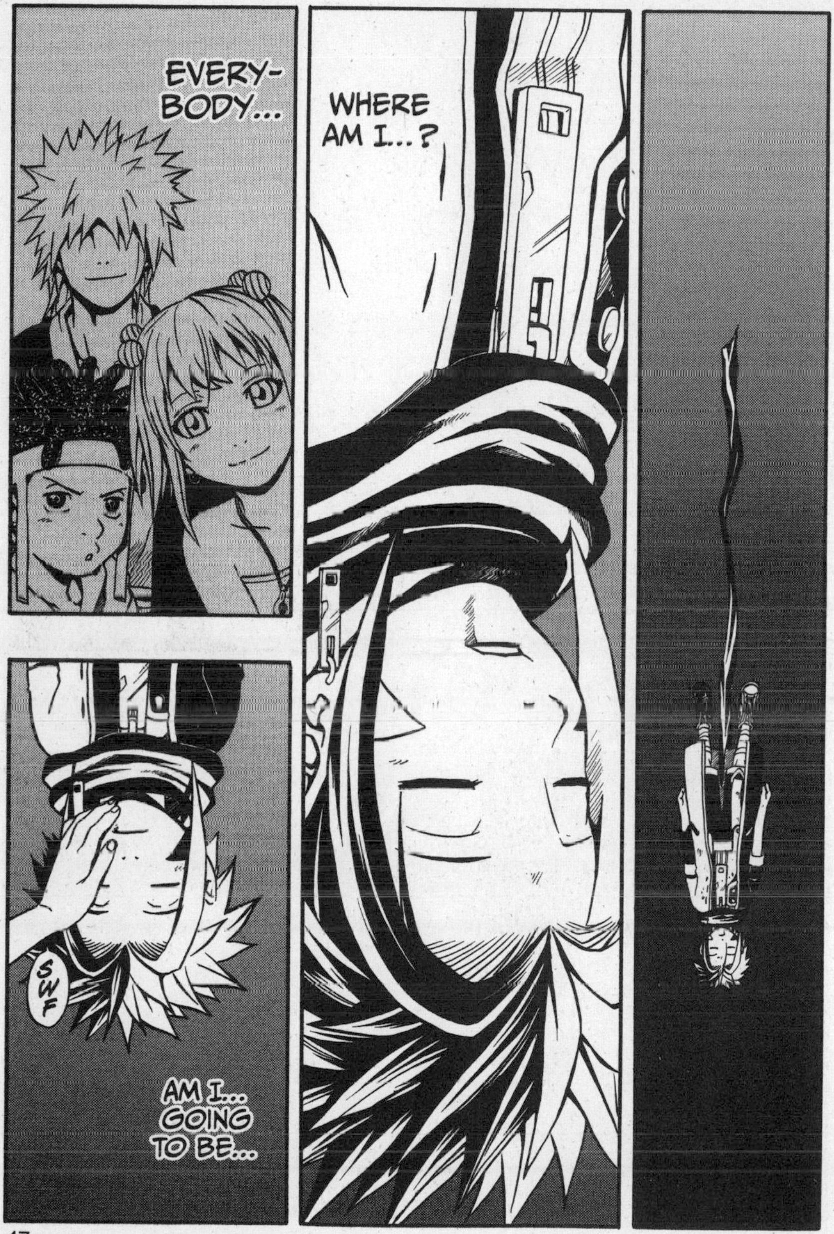
WHERE AM I...?
EVERY-BODY...
SWF
AM I... GOING TO BE...

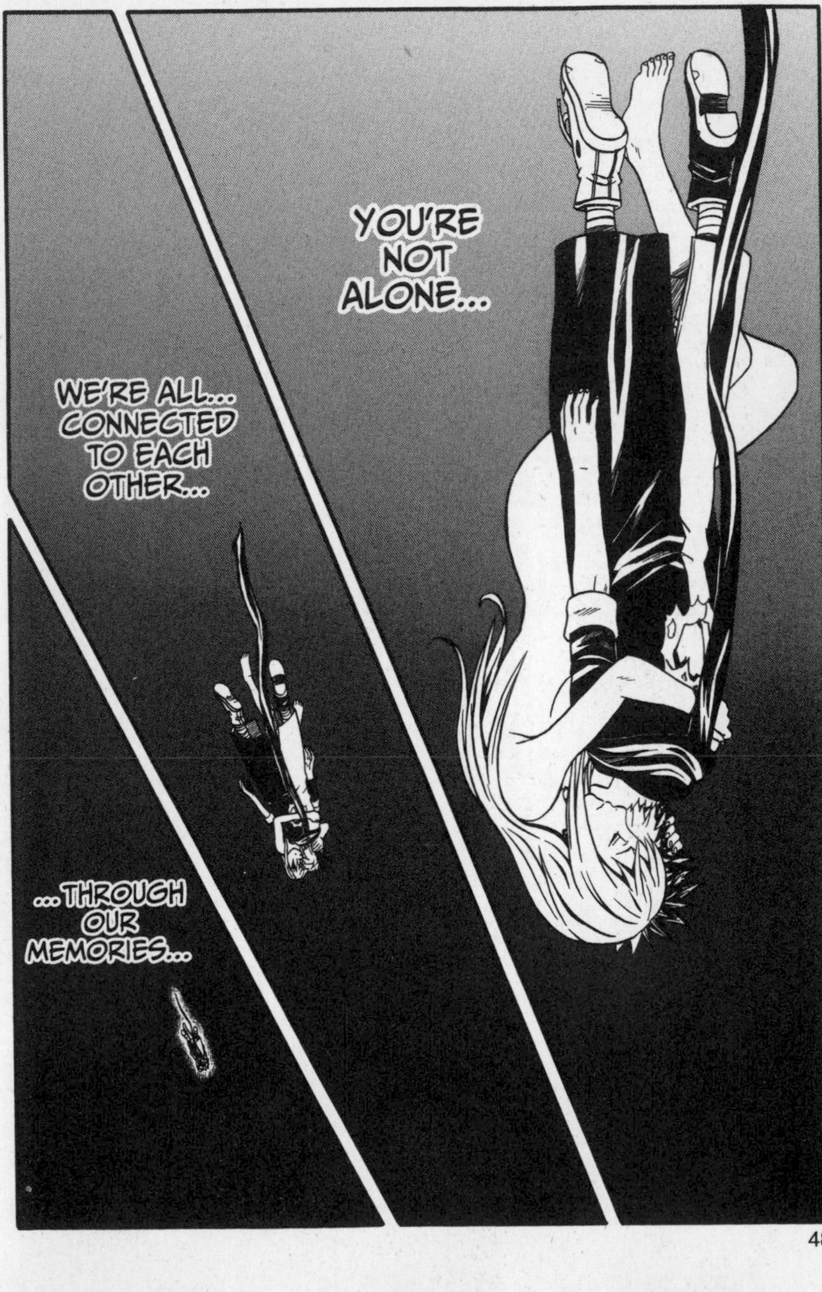
YOU'RE NOT ALONE...
WE'RE ALL... CONNECTED TO EACH OTHER...
...THROUGH OUR MEMORIES...

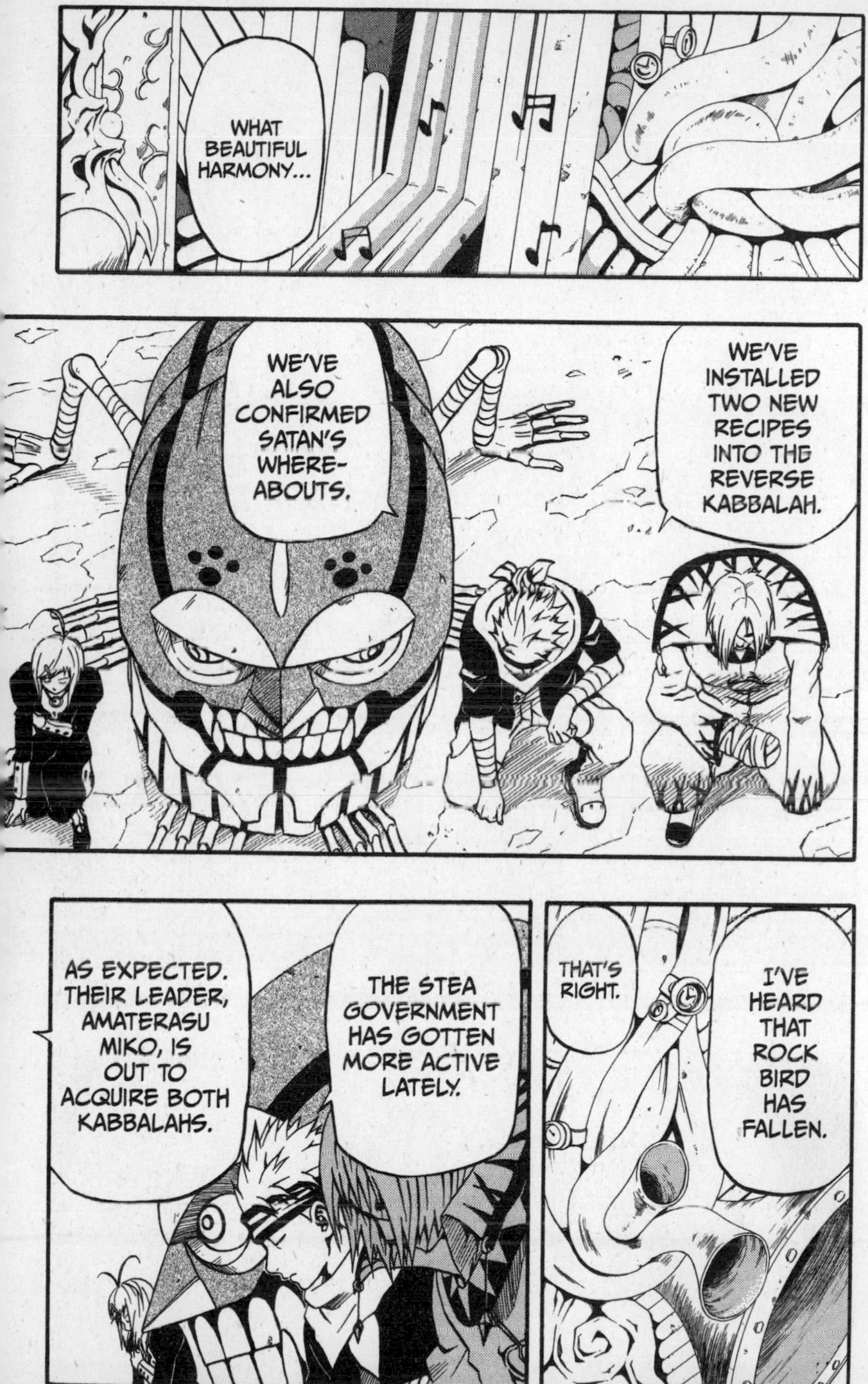
WHAT BEAUTIFUL HARMONY...
WE'VE INSTALLED TWO NEW RECIPES INTO THE REVERSE KABBALAH.
WE'VE ALSO CONFIRMED SATAN'S WHERE-ABOUTS.
I'VE HEARD THAT ROCK BIRD HAS FALLEN.
THAT'S RIGHT.
THE STEA GOVERNMENT HAS GOTTEN MORE ACTIVE LATELY.
AS EXPECTED. THEIR LEADER, AMATERASU MIKO, IS OUT TO ACQUIRE BOTH KABBALAHS.

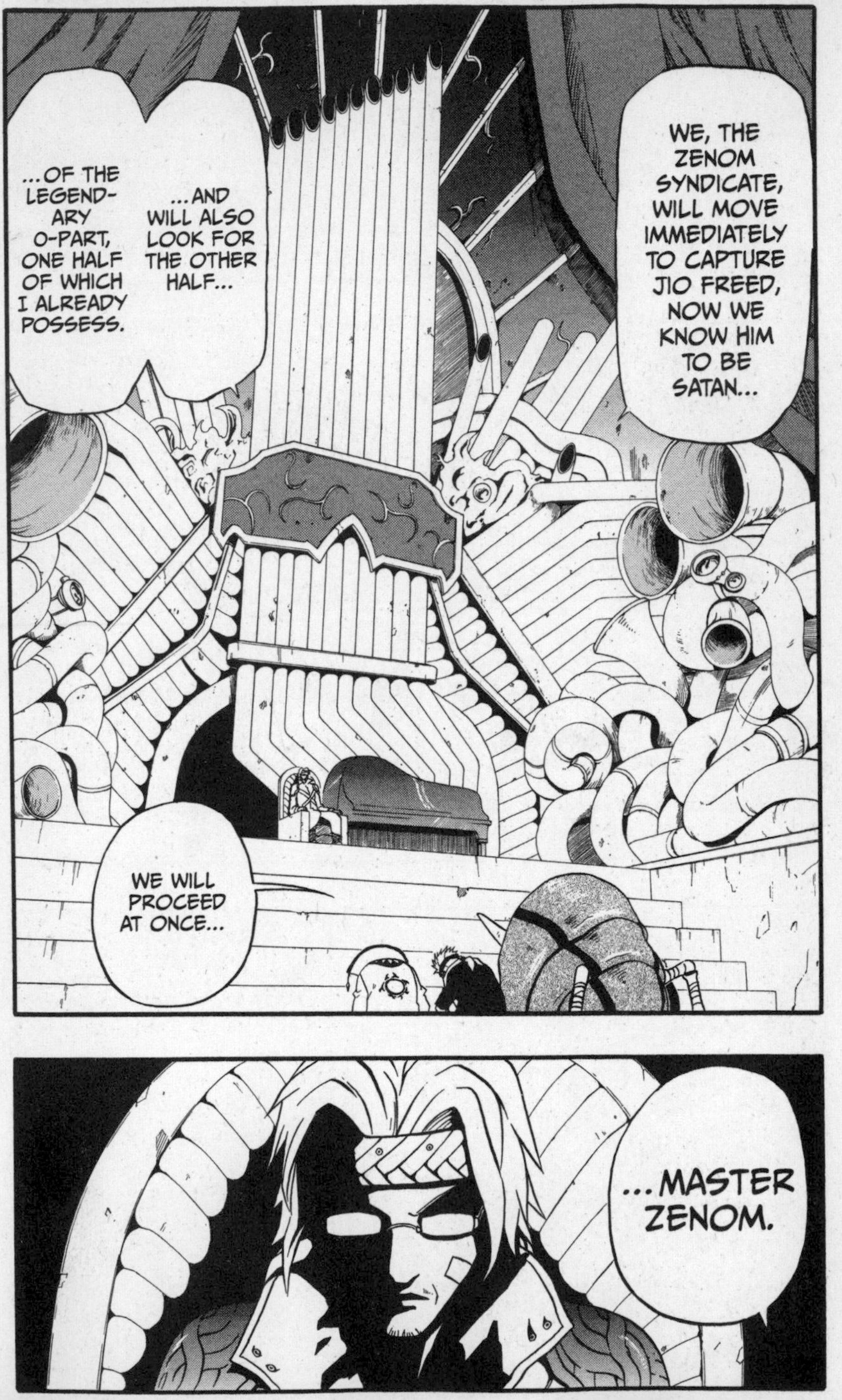
WE, THE ZENOM SYNDICATE, WILL MOVE IMMEDIATELY TO CAPTURE JIO FREED, NOW WE KNOW HIM TO BE SATAN...
...AND WILL ALSO LOOK FOR THE OTHER HALF...
...OF THE LEGENDARY O-PART, ONE HALF OF WHICH I ALREADY POSSESS.
WE WILL PROCEED AT ONCE...
...MASTER ZENOM.

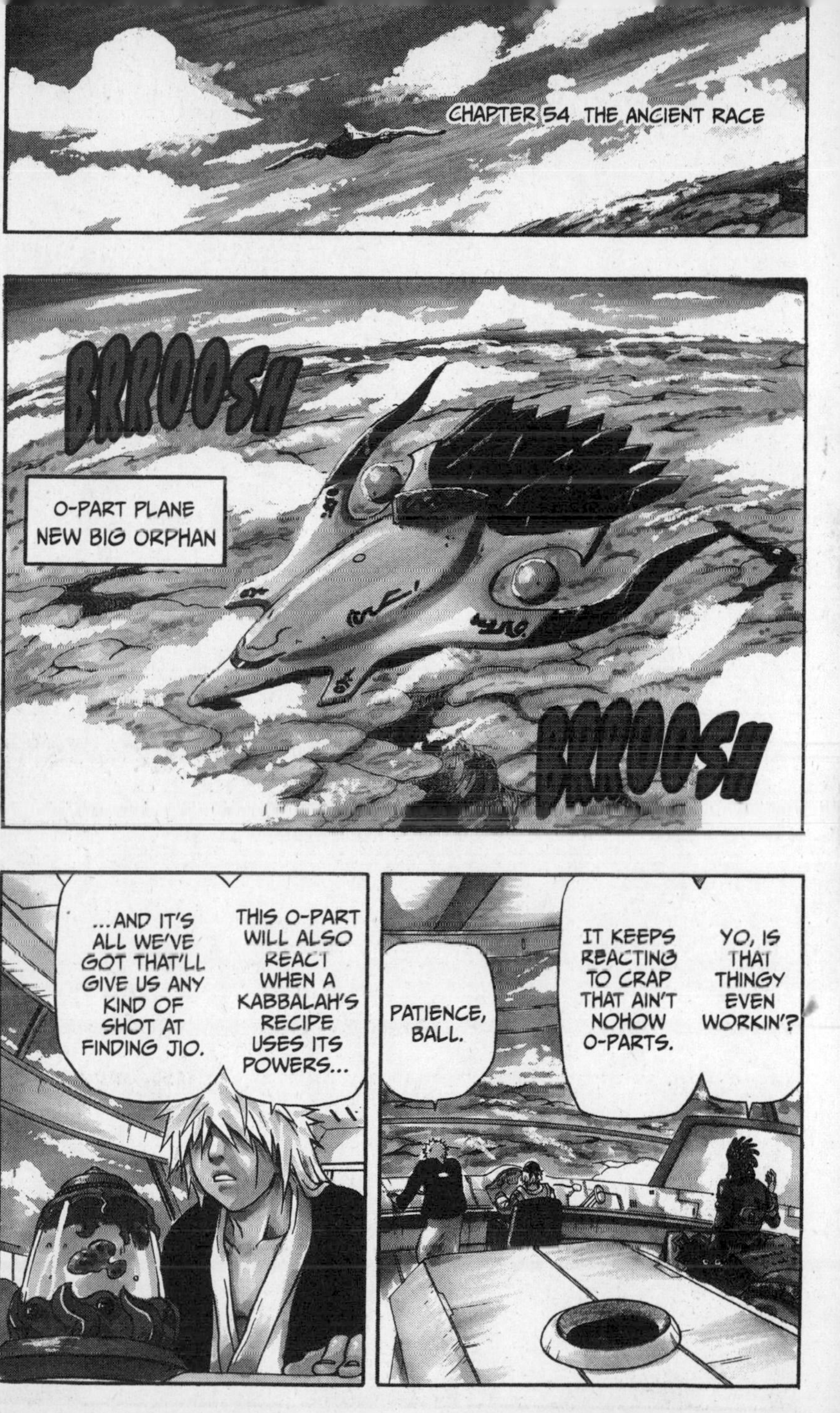
CHAPTER 54 THE ANCIENT RACE
BRROOSH
O-PART PLANE NEW BIG ORPHAN
BRROOSH
YO, IS THAT THINGY EVEN WORKIN'?
IT KEEPS REACTING TO CRAP THAT AIN'T NOHOW O-PARTS.
PATIENCE, BALL.
THIS O-PART WILL ALSO REACT WHEN A KABBALAH'S RECIPE USES ITS POWERS...
...AND IT'S ALL WE'VE GOT THAT'LL GIVE US ANY KIND OF SHOT AT FINDING JIO.

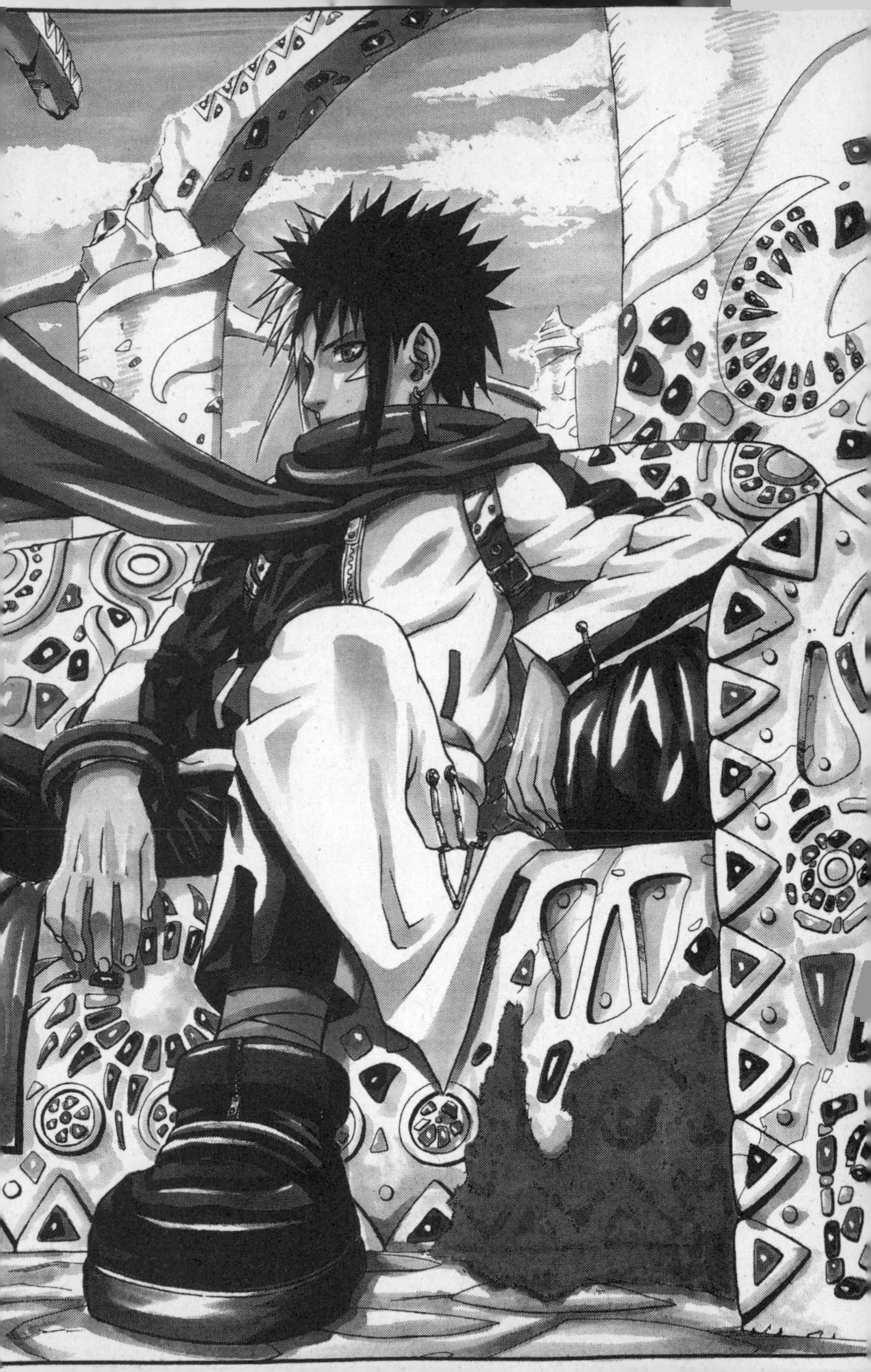

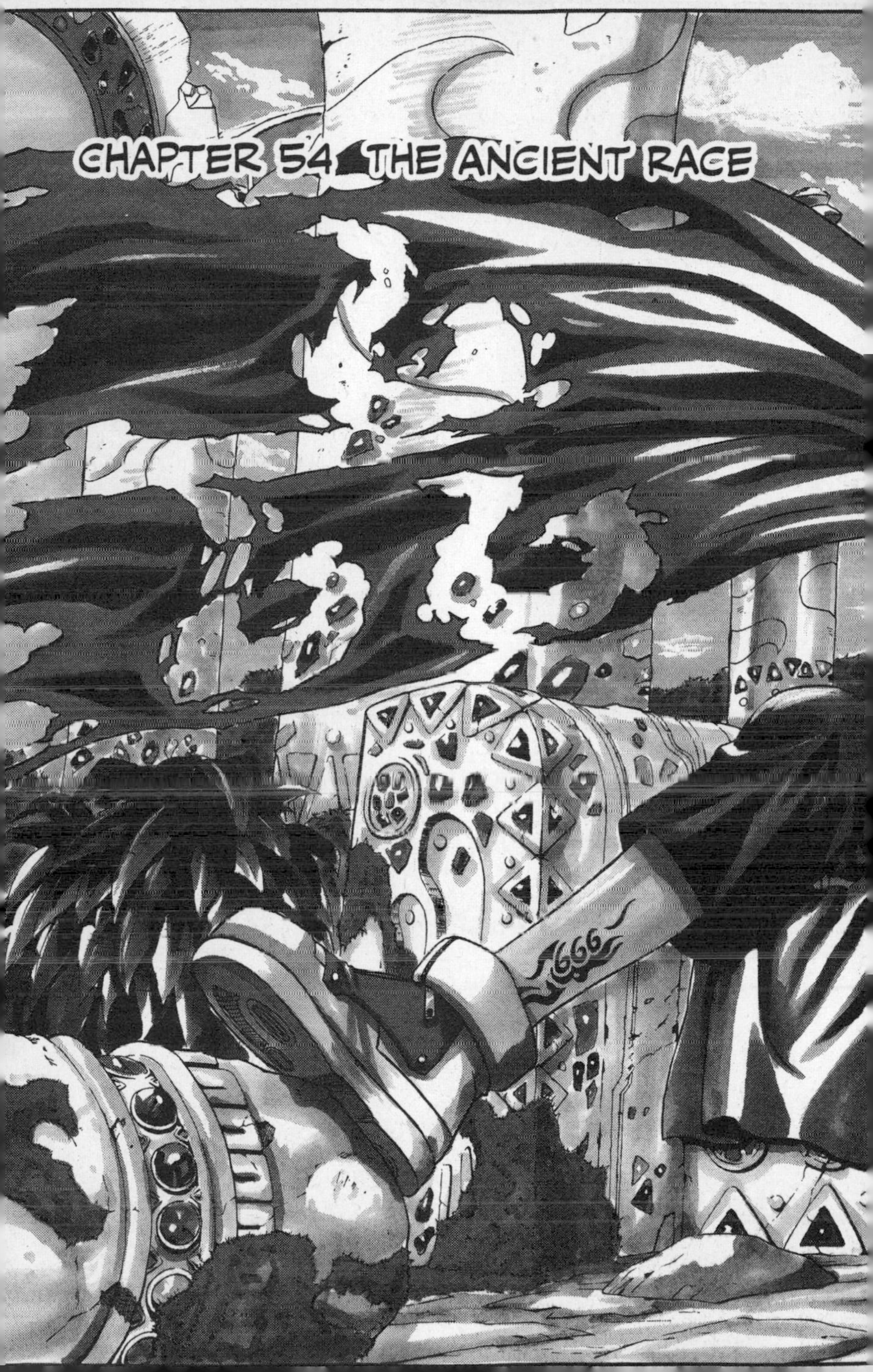
CHAPTER 54 THE ANCIENT RACE
666

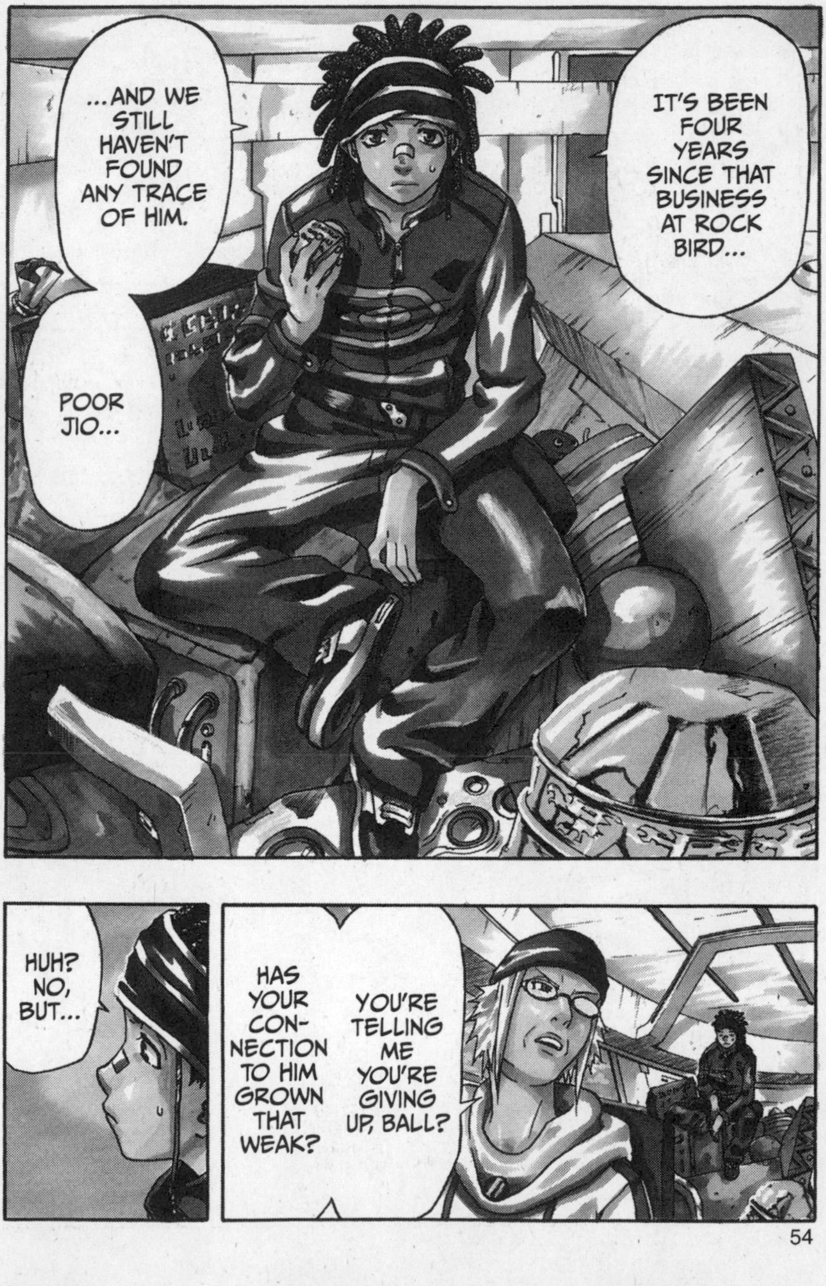
IT'S BEEN FOUR YEARS SINCE THAT BUSINESS AT ROCK BIRD...
...AND WE STILL HAVEN'T FOUND ANY TRACE OF HIM.
POOR JIO...
YOU'RE TELLING ME YOU'RE GIVING UP, BALL?
HAS YOUR CON-NECTION TO HIM GROWN THAT WEAK?
HUH? NO, BUT...

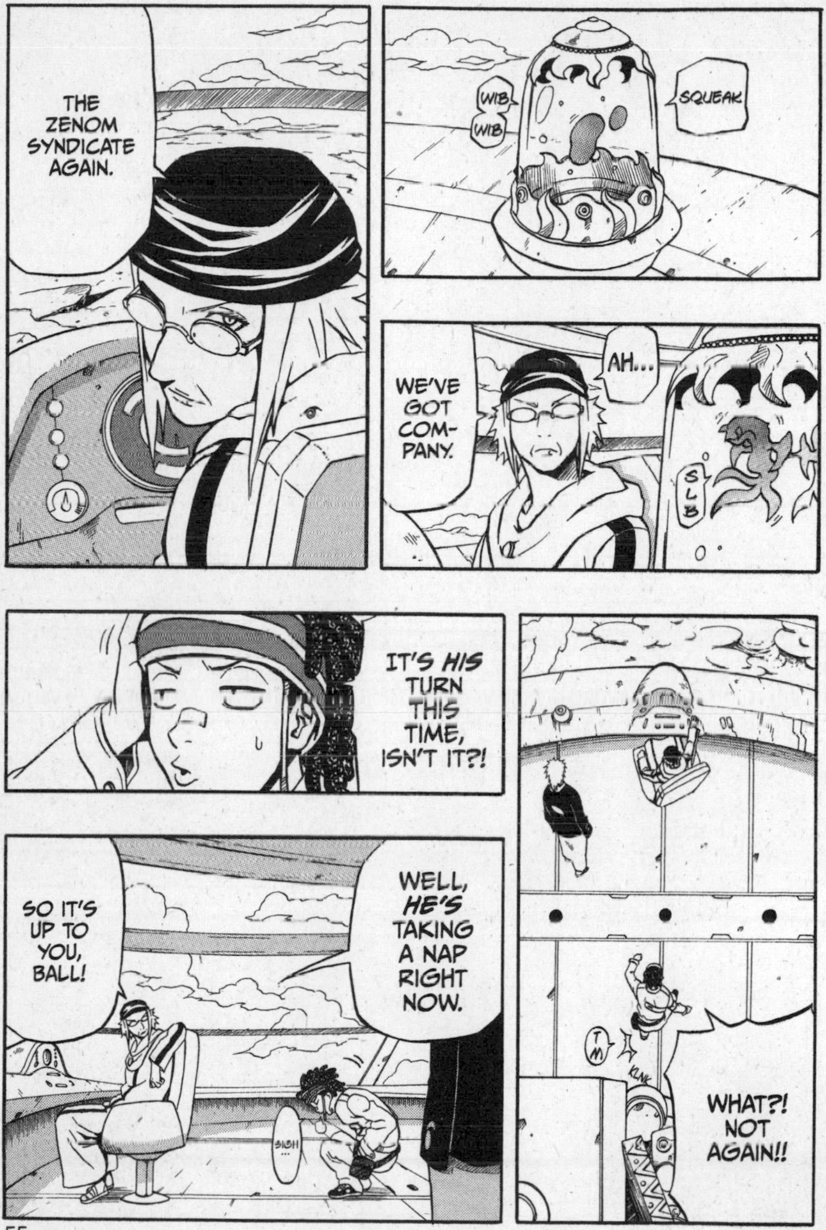
SQUEAK
WIB
WIB
AH...
SLB
WE'VE GOT COM-PANY.
THE ZENOM SYNDICATE AGAIN.
WHAT?! NOT AGAIN!!
TM
KLNK
IT'S HIS TURN THIS TIME, ISN'T IT?!
WELL, HE'S TAKING A NAP RIGHT NOW.
SO IT'S UP TO YOU, BALL!
SIGH...

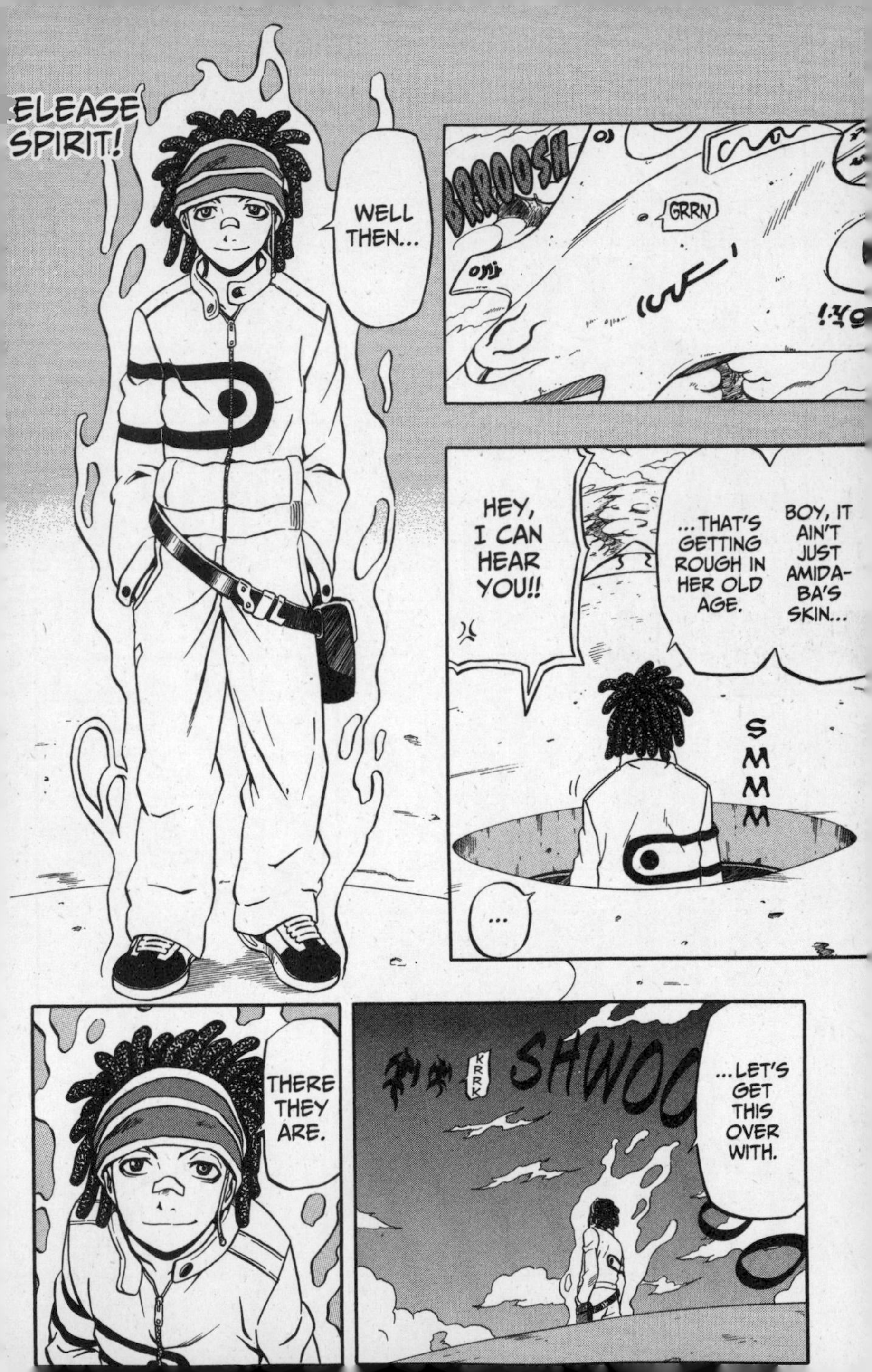
BRROOSH
GRRN
BOY, IT AIN'T JUST AMIDABA'S SKIN...
...THAT'S GETTING ROUGH IN HER OLD AGE.
HEY, I CAN HEAR YOU!!
SMMM
...
WELL THEN...
ELEASE SPIRIT!
SHWOO
KRRK
...LET'S GET THIS OVER WITH.
THERE THEY ARE.

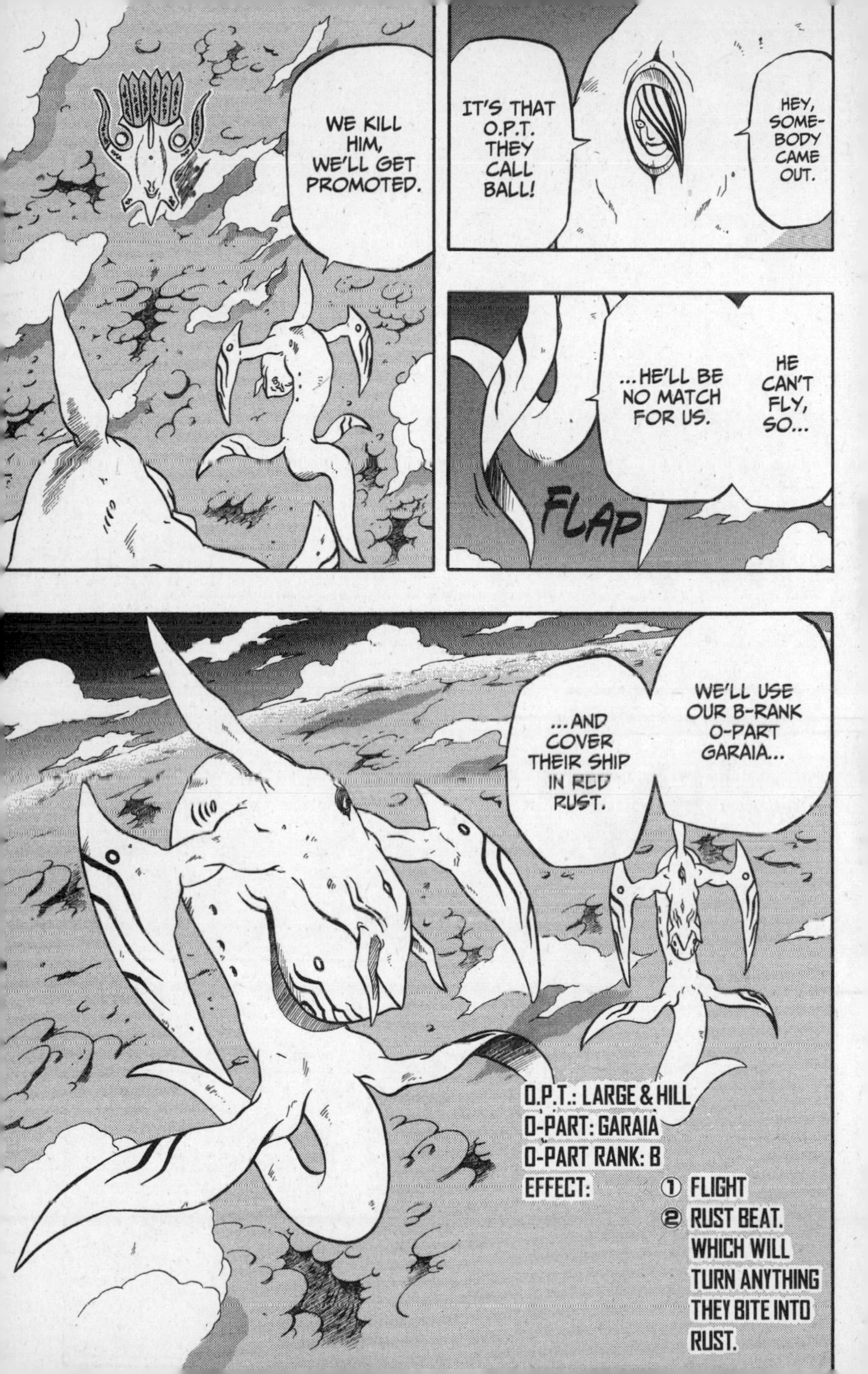
HEY, SOMEBODY CAME OUT.
IT'S THAT O.P.T. THEY CALL BALL!
HE CAN'T FLY, SO...
...HE'LL BE NO MATCH FOR US.
FLAP
WE KILL HIM, WE'LL GET PROMOTED.
WE'LL USE OUR B-RANK O-PART GARAIA...
...AND COVER THEIR SHIP IN RED RUST.
O.P.T.: LARGE & HILL
O-PART: GARAIA
O-PART RANK: B
EFFECT: ① FLIGHT
② RUST BEAT. WHICH WILL TURN ANYTHING THEY BITE INTO RUST.

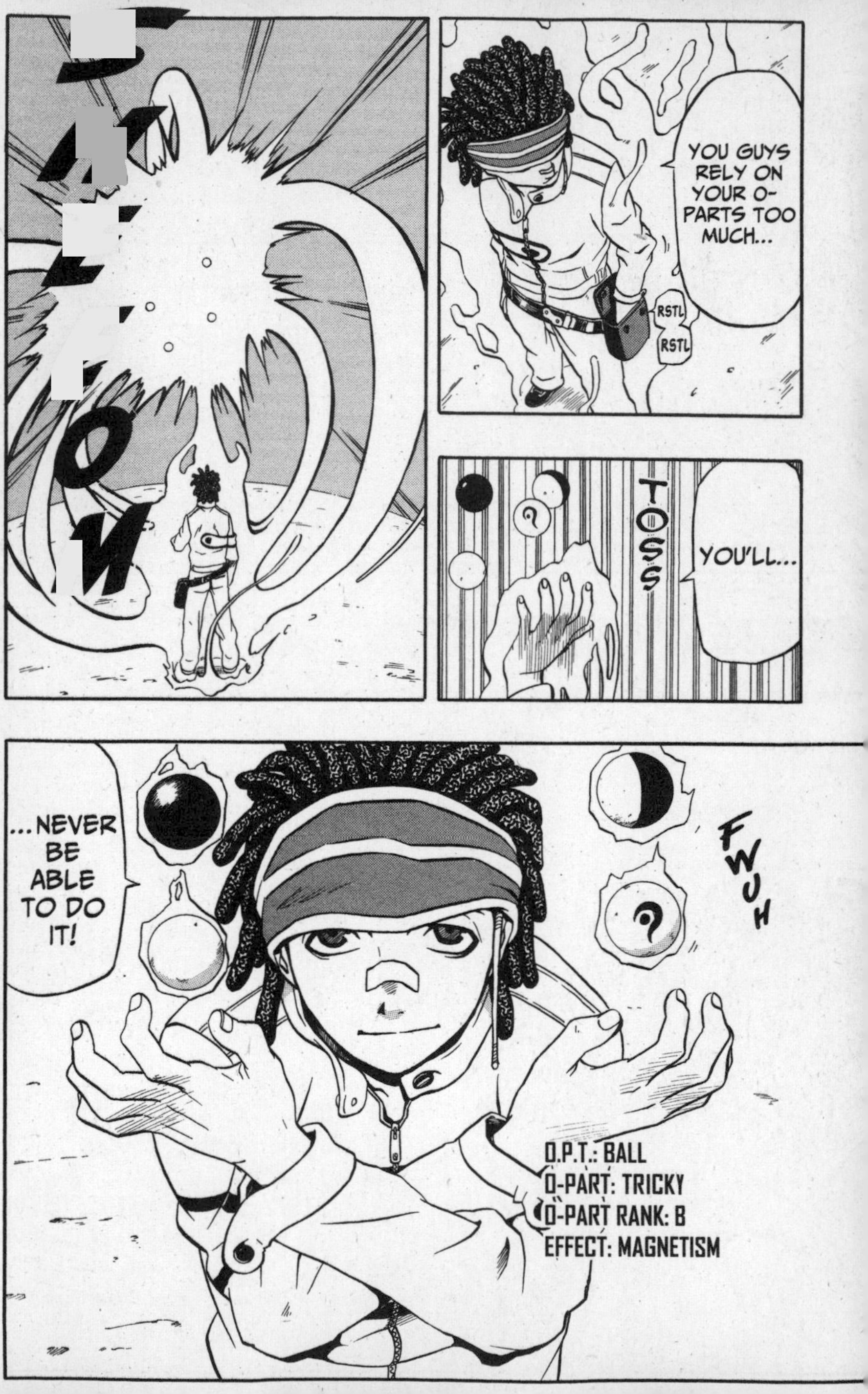
YOU GUYS RELY ON YOUR O-PARTS TOO MUCH...
RSTL
RSTL
TOSS
YOU'LL...
...NEVER BE ABLE TO DO IT!
FWUH
O.P.T.: BALL
O-PART: TRICKY
O-PART RANK: B
EFFECT: MAGNETISM

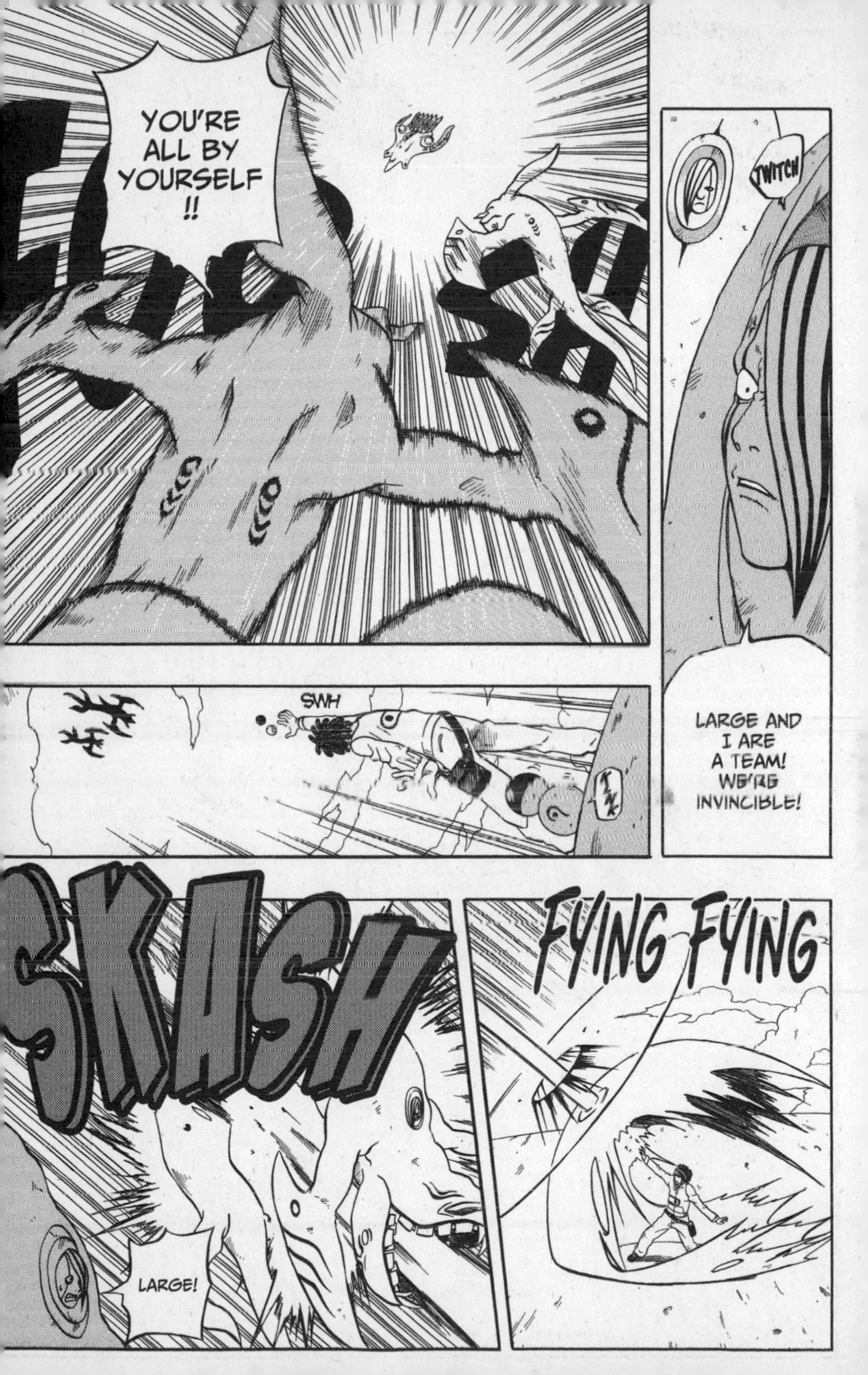
TWITCH
LARGE AND I ARE A TEAM! WE'RE INVINCIBLE!
YOU'RE ALL BY YOURSELF !!
SWH
TINK
FYING FYING
SMASH
LARGE!

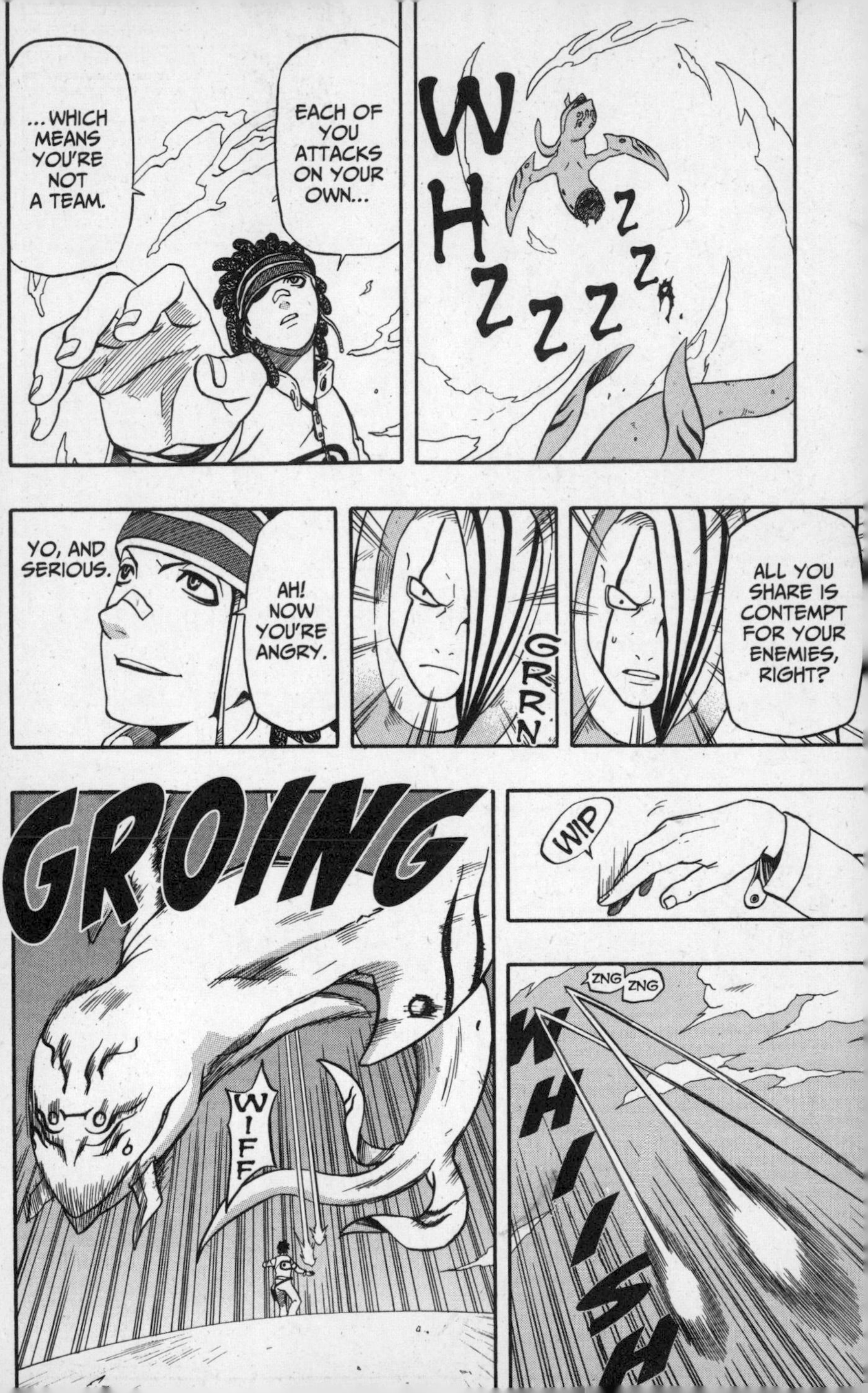
WHZZZZZ
EACH OF YOU ATTACKS ON YOUR OWN...
...WHICH MEANS YOU'RE NOT A TEAM.
ALL YOU SHARE IS CONTEMPT FOR YOUR ENEMIES, RIGHT?
GRRN
AH! NOW YOU'RE ANGRY.
YO, AND SERIOUS.
WIP
ZNG
ZNG
WHISH
GROING
WIFF

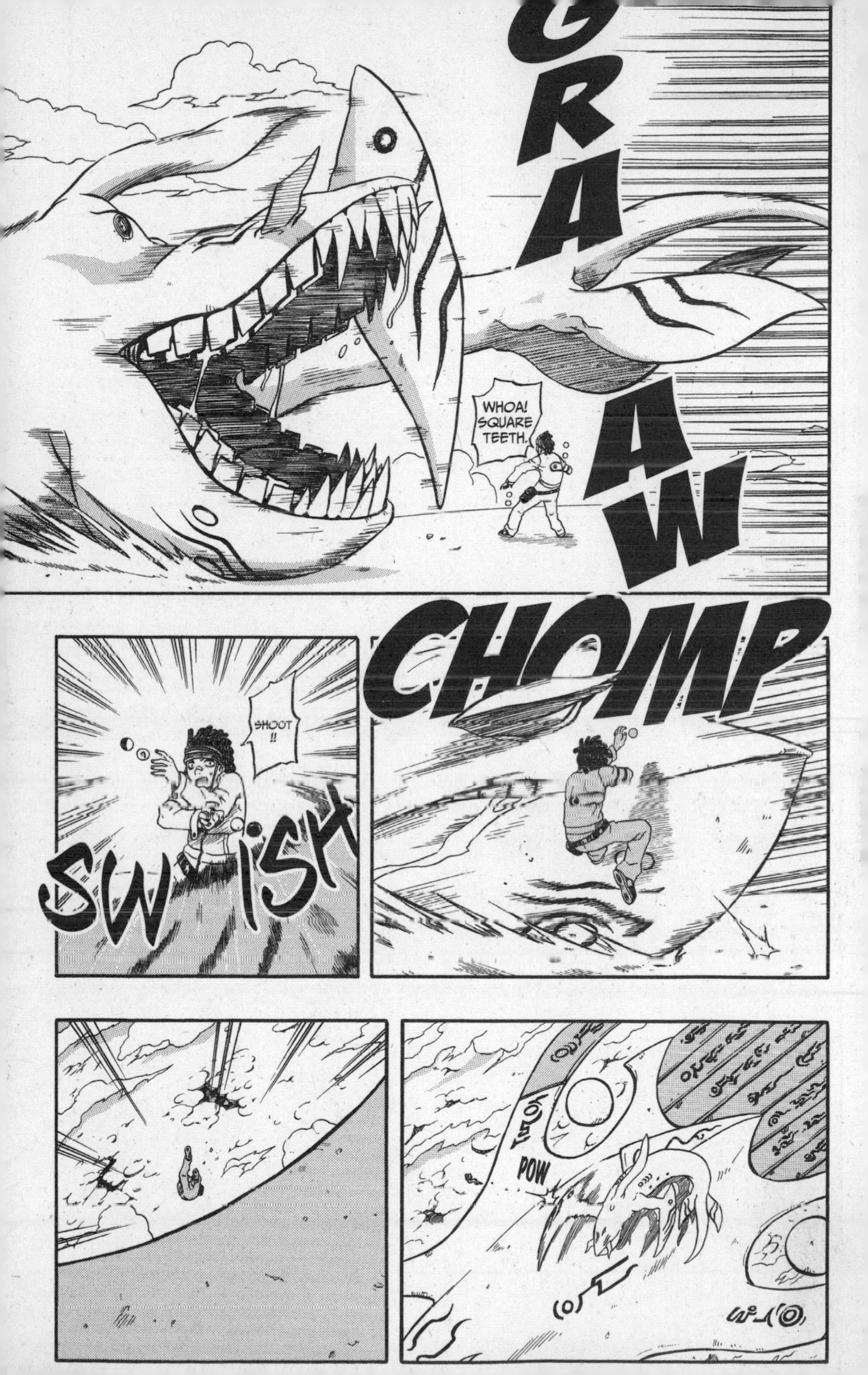
RAAW
WHOA! SQUARE TEETH.
CHOMP
SHOOT !!
SWISH
POW

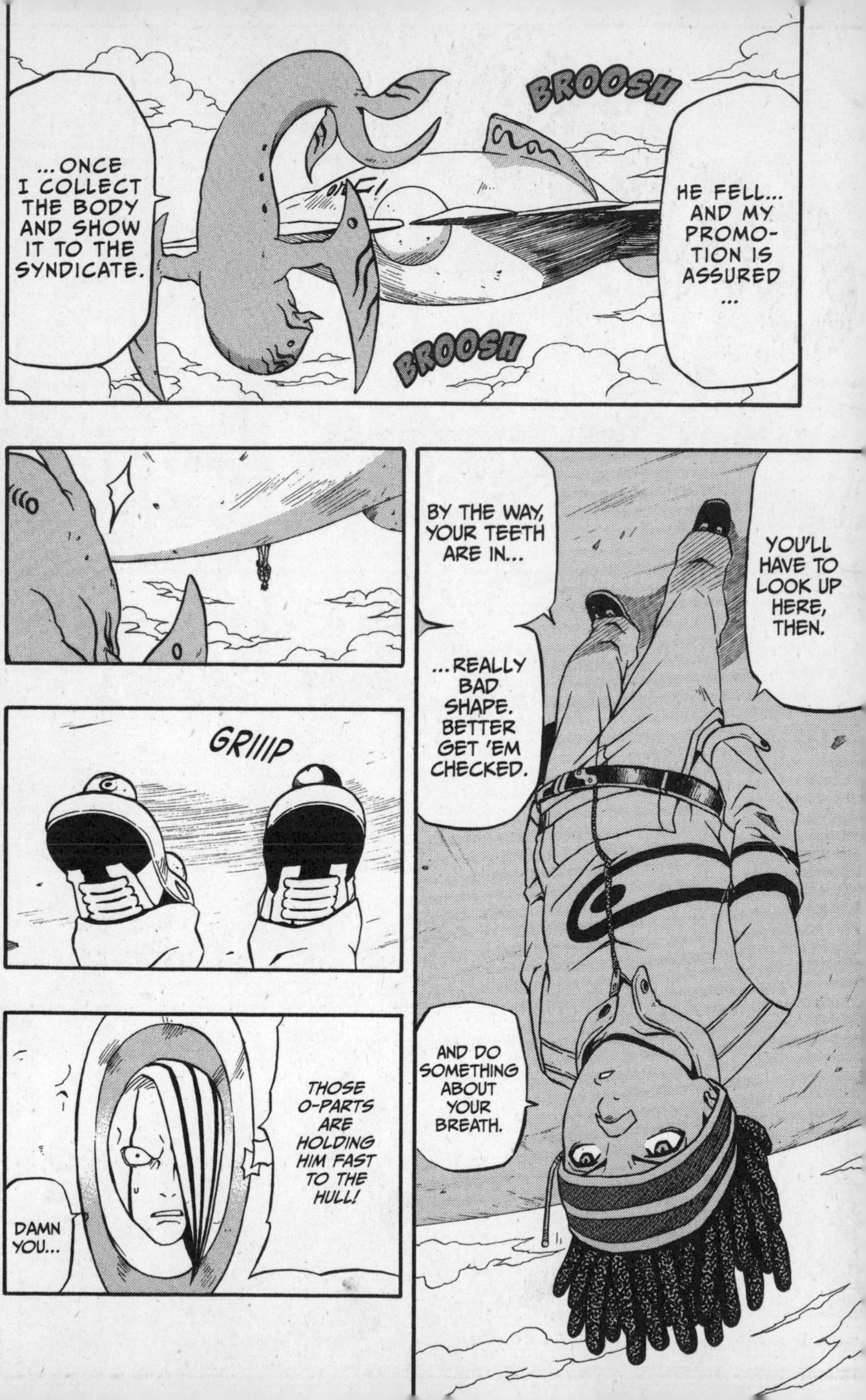
BROOSH
HE FELL... AND MY PROMOTION IS ASSURED ...
...ONCE I COLLECT THE BODY AND SHOW IT TO THE SYNDICATE.
BROOSH
YOU'LL HAVE TO LOOK UP HERE, THEN.
BY THE WAY, YOUR TEETH ARE IN...
...REALLY BAD SHAPE. BETTER GET 'EM CHECKED.
AND DO SOMETHING ABOUT YOUR BREATH.
GRIIIP
THOSE O-PARTS ARE HOLDING HIM FAST TO THE HULL!
DAMN YOU...

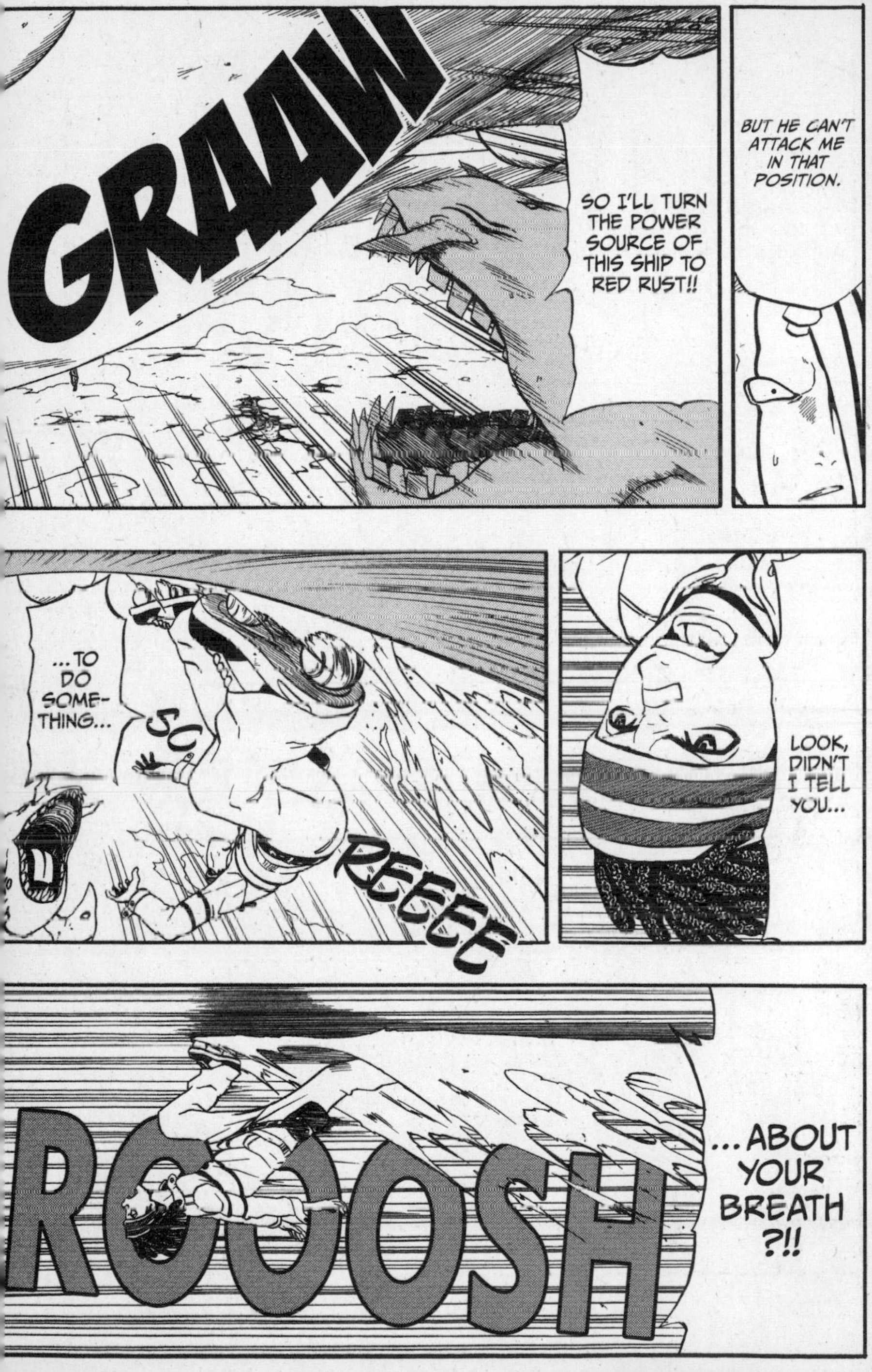
BUT HE CAN'T ATTACK ME IN THAT POSITION.
SO I'LL TURN THE POWER SOURCE OF THIS SHIP TO RED RUST!!
GRAAAW
LOOK, DIDN'T I TELL YOU...
...TO DO SOME-THING...
REEEE
...ABOUT YOUR BREATH ?!!
ROOOSH

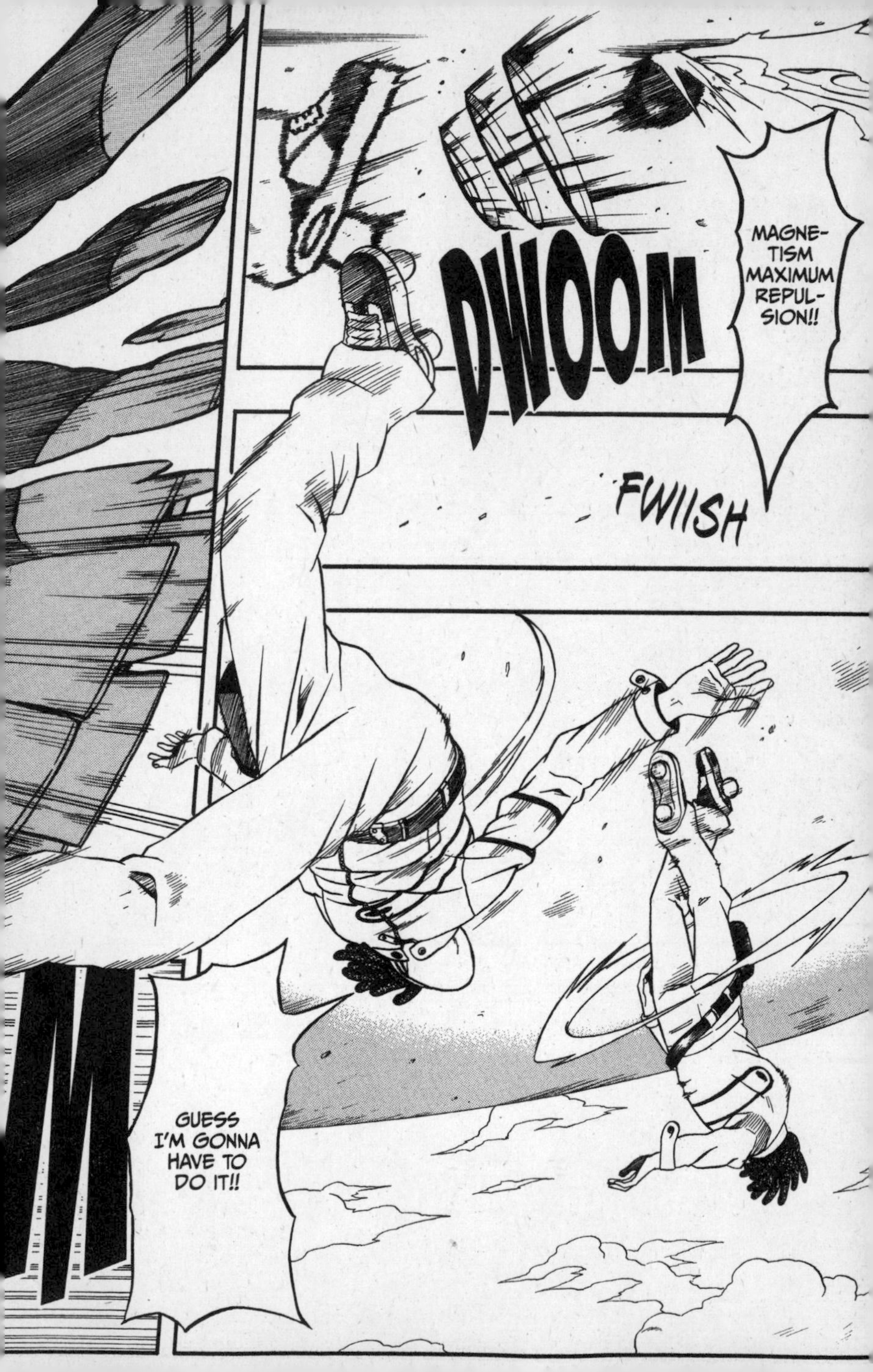
MAGNETISM MAXIMUM REPULSION!!
DWOOM
FWIISH
GUESS I'M GONNA HAVE TO DO IT!!

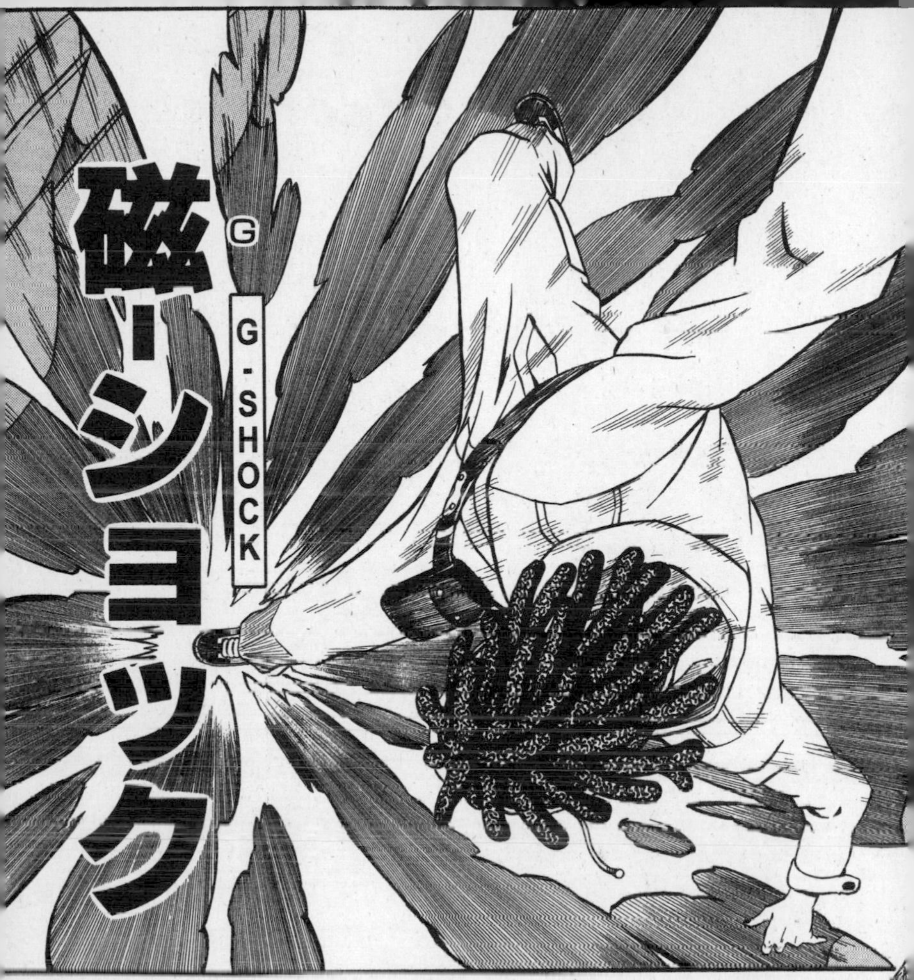
磁ーショック
G
G-SHOCK

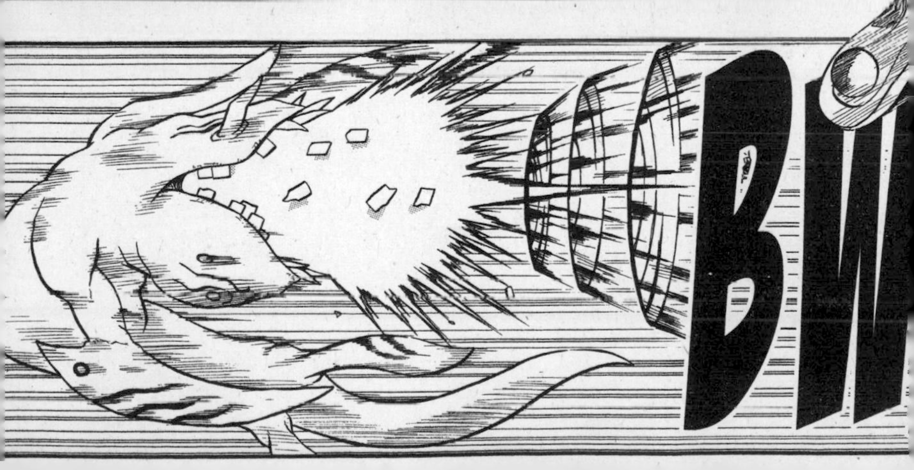
BW

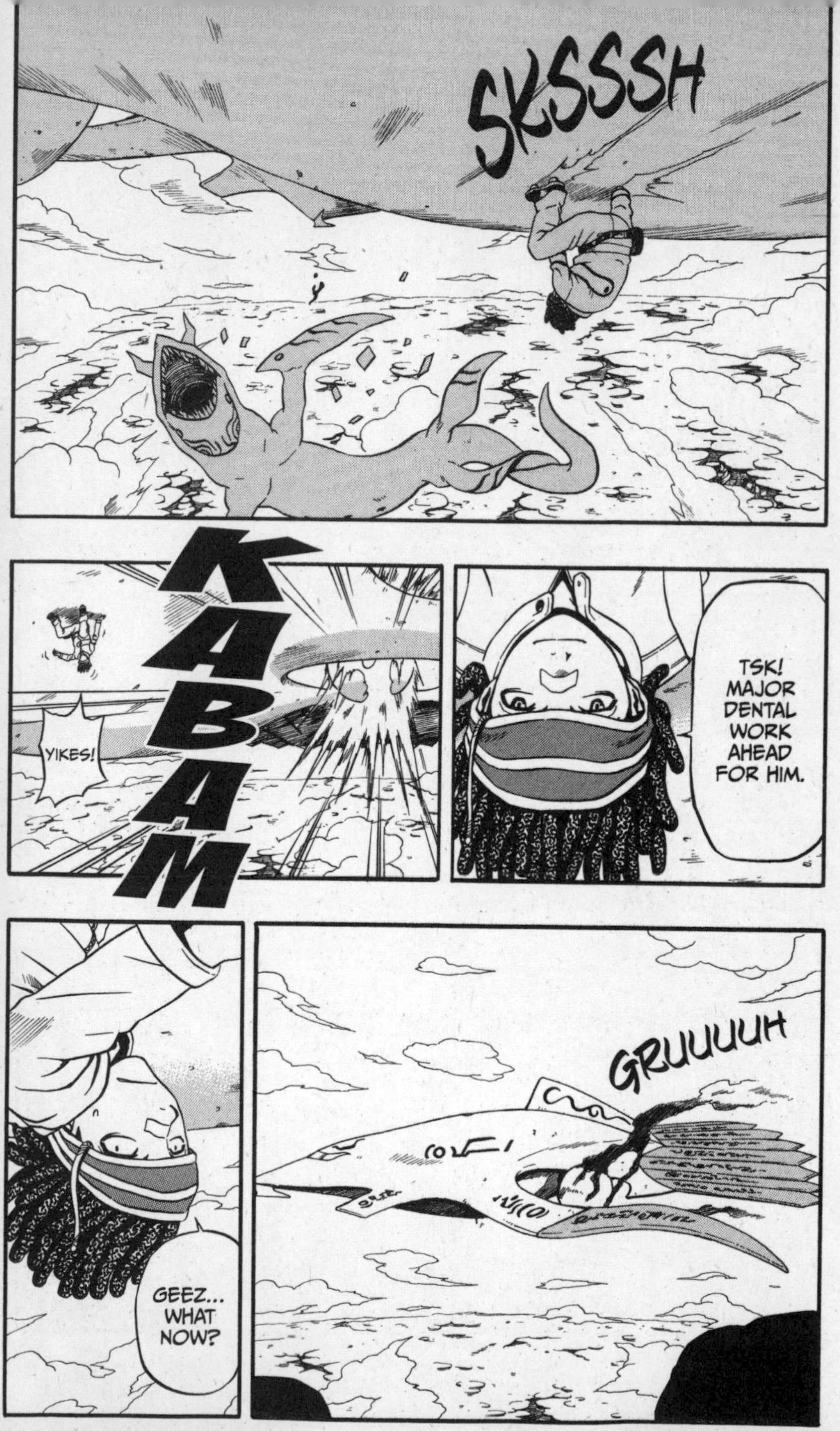
SKSSSH
TSK! MAJOR DENTAL WORK AHEAD FOR HIM.
KABAM
YIKES!
GRUUUUH
GEEZ... WHAT NOW?

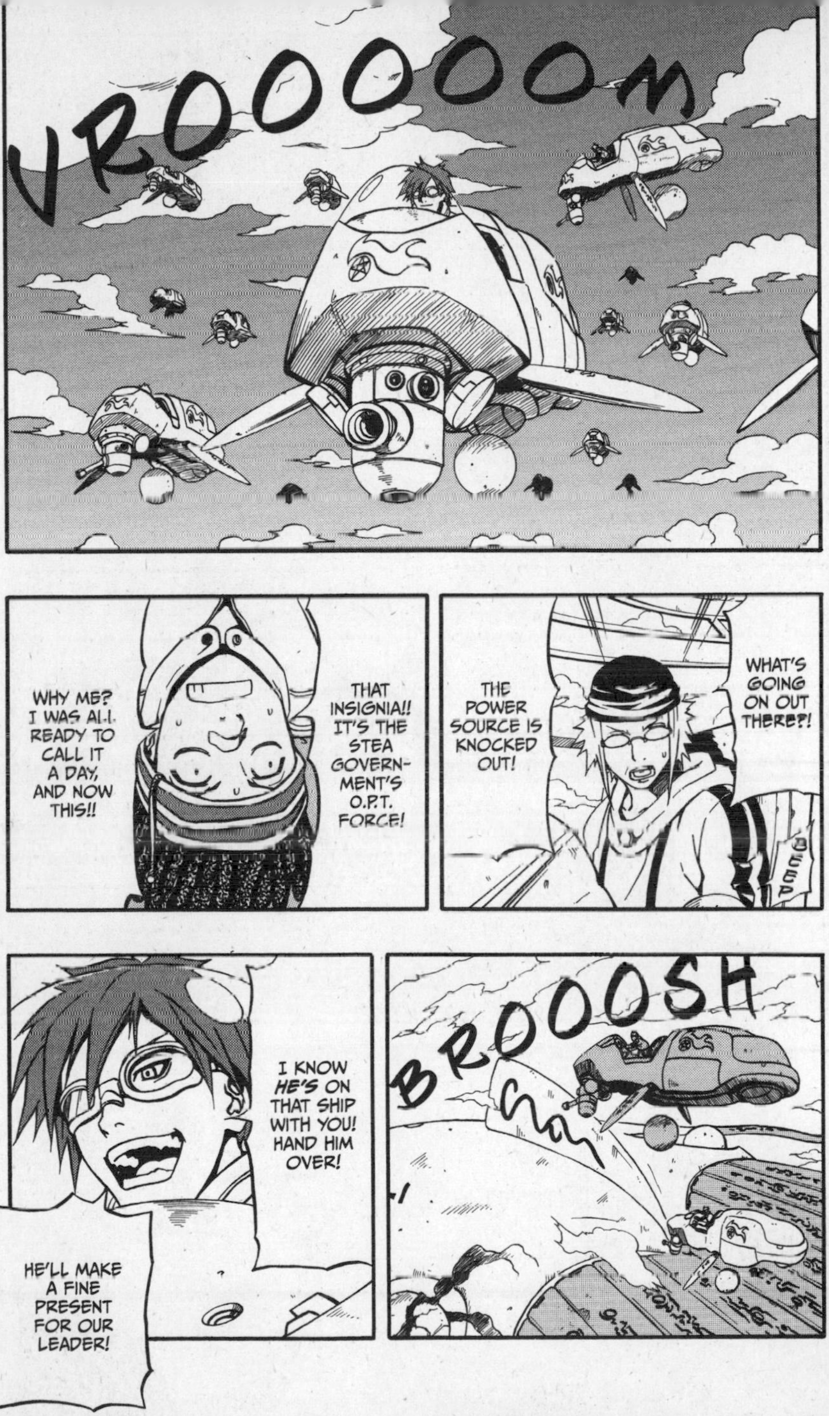
VROOOOOM
WHAT'S GOING ON OUT THERE?!
THE POWER SOURCE IS KNOCKED OUT!
THAT INSIGNIA!! IT'S THE STEA GOVERNMENT'S O.P.T. FORCE!
WHY ME? I WAS ALL READY TO CALL IT A DAY, AND NOW THIS!!
BROOOSH
I KNOW HE'S ON THAT SHIP WITH YOU! HAND HIM OVER!
HE'LL MAKE A FINE PRESENT FOR OUR LEADER!

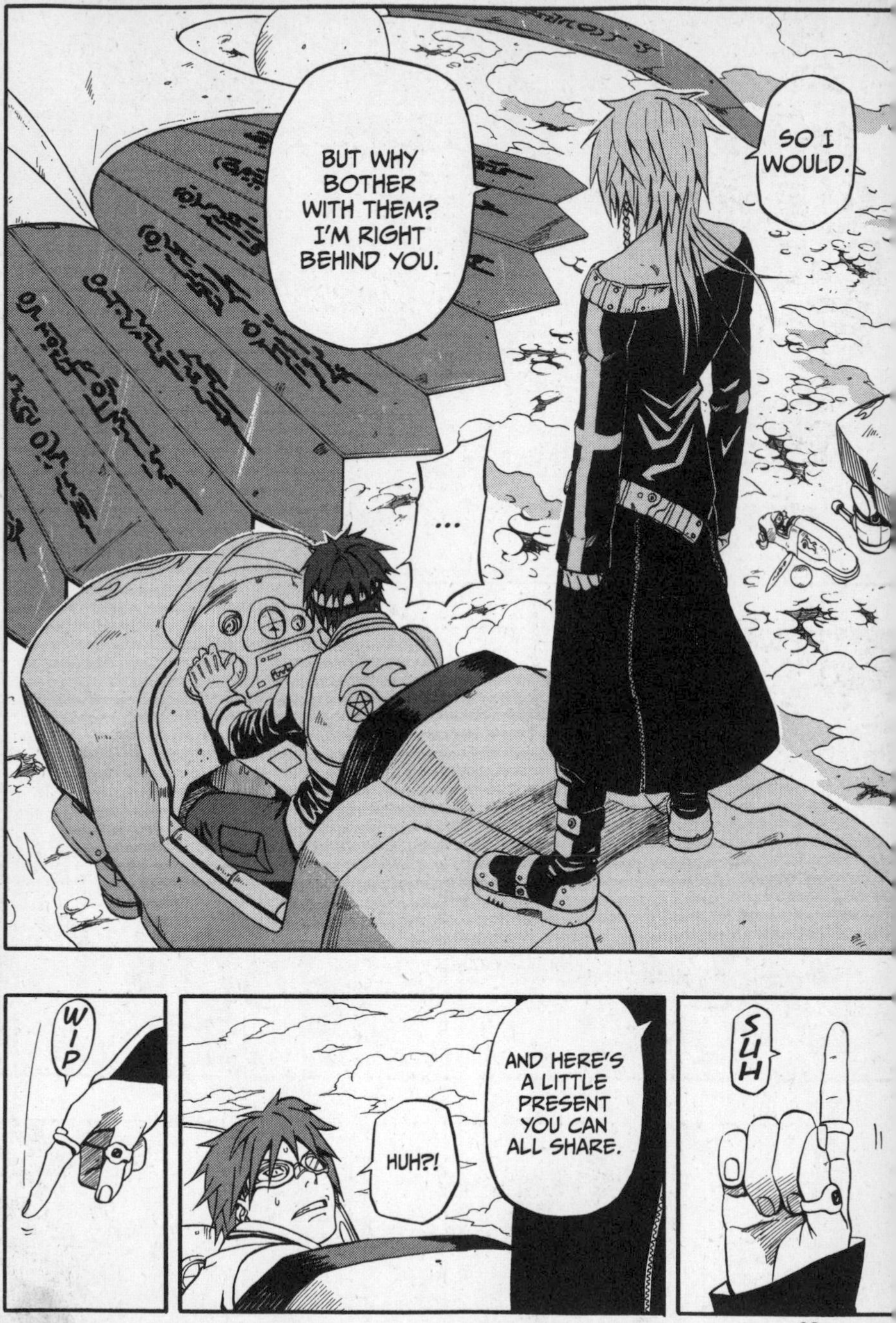
SO I WOULD.
BUT WHY BOTHER WITH THEM? I'M RIGHT BEHIND YOU.
...
SUH
AND HERE'S A LITTLE PRESENT YOU CAN ALL SHARE.
HUH?!
WIP

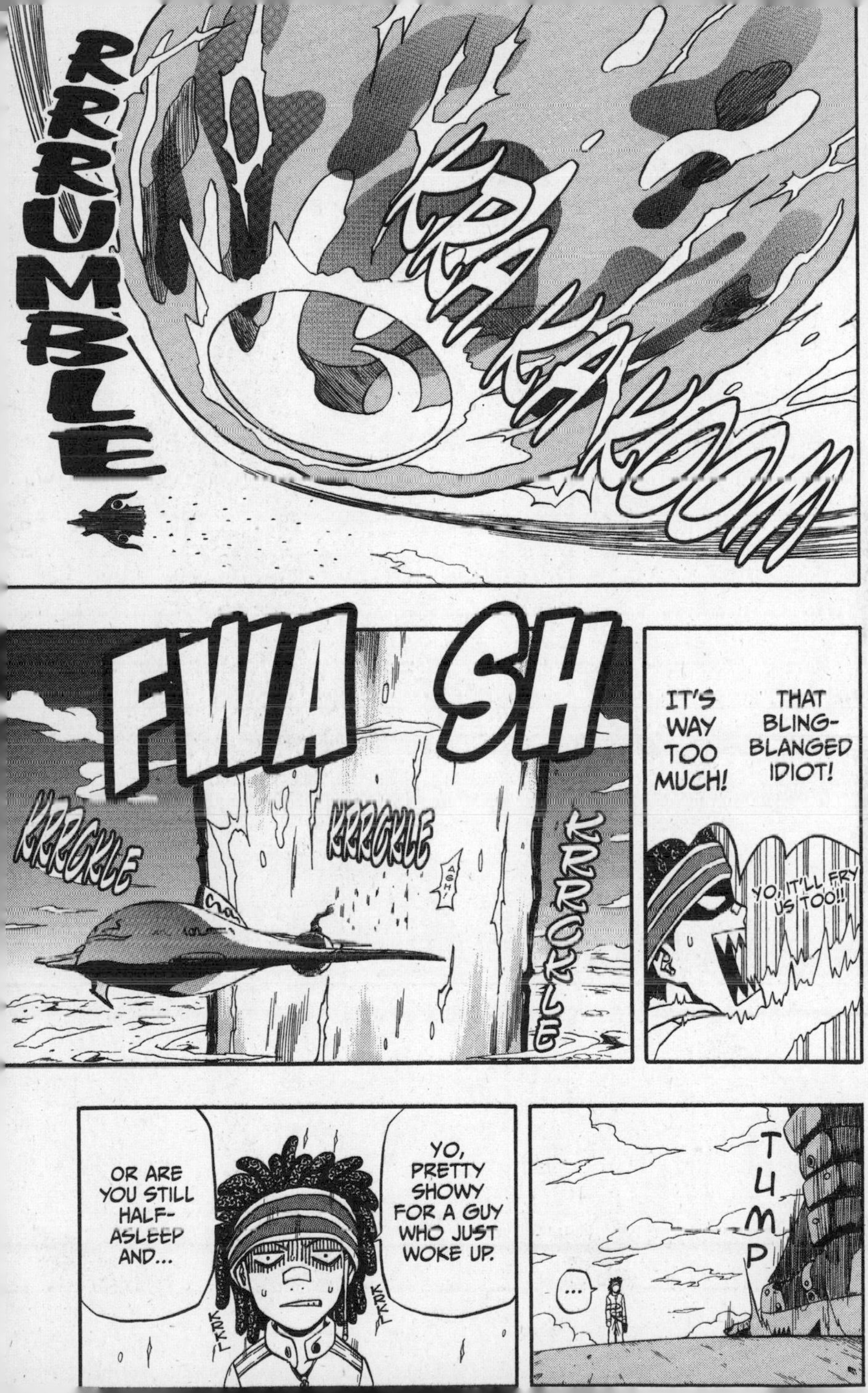
RRRUMBLE
KRAKAKOOM
THAT BLING-BLANGED IDIOT!
IT'S WAY TOO MUCH!
YO, IT'LL FRY US TOO!!
FWA SH
KRRACKLE
KRRACKLE
AGH!
KRRACKLE
TUMP
...
YO, PRETTY SHOWY FOR A GUY WHO JUST WOKE UP.
OR ARE YOU STILL HALF-ASLEEP AND...
KRKL
KRKL

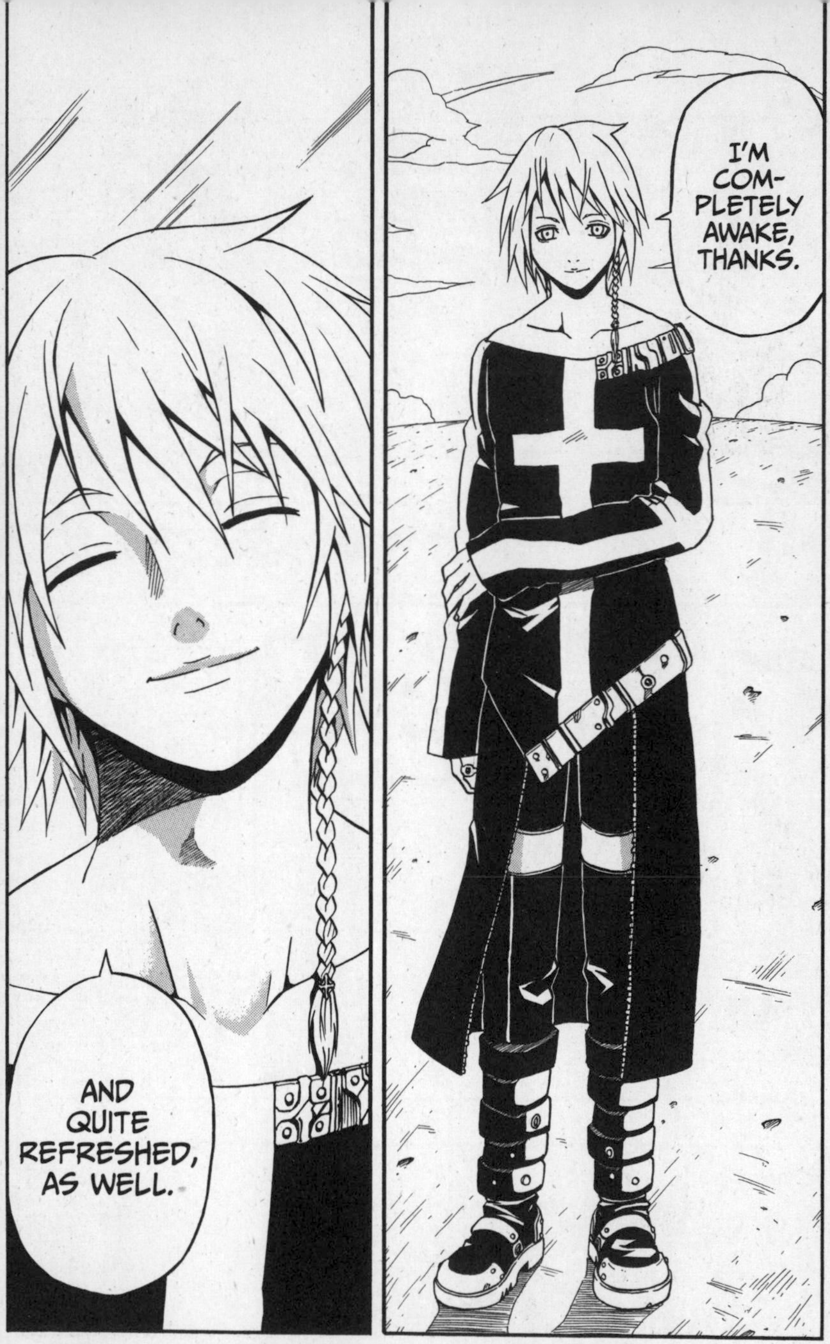
I'M COM- PLETELY AWAKE, THANKS.
AND QUITE REFRESHED, AS WELL.

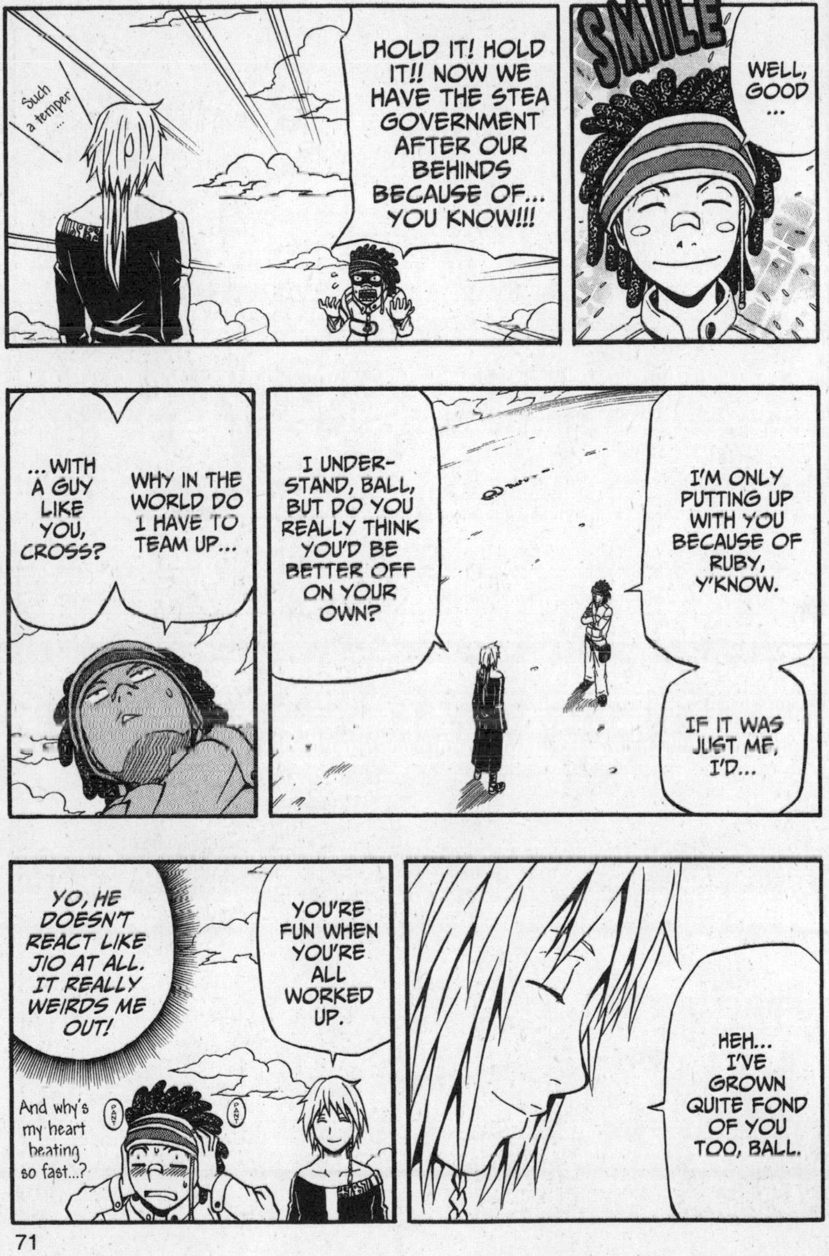
SMILE
WELL, GOOD ...
HOLD IT! HOLD IT!! NOW WE HAVE THE STEA GOVERNMENT AFTER OUR BEHINDS BECAUSE OF... YOU KNOW!!!
Such a temper ...
I'M ONLY PUTTING UP WITH YOU BECAUSE OF RUBY, Y'KNOW.
IF IT WAS JUST ME, I'D...
I UNDER-STAND, BALL, BUT DO YOU REALLY THINK YOU'D BE BETTER OFF ON YOUR OWN?
WHY IN THE WORLD DO I HAVE TO TEAM UP...
...WITH A GUY LIKE YOU, CROSS?
HEH... I'VE GROWN QUITE FOND OF YOU TOO, BALL.
YOU'RE FUN WHEN YOU'RE ALL WORKED UP.
YO, HE DOESN'T REACT LIKE JIO AT ALL. IT REALLY WEIRDS ME OUT!
PANT
PANT
And why's my heart beating so fast...?

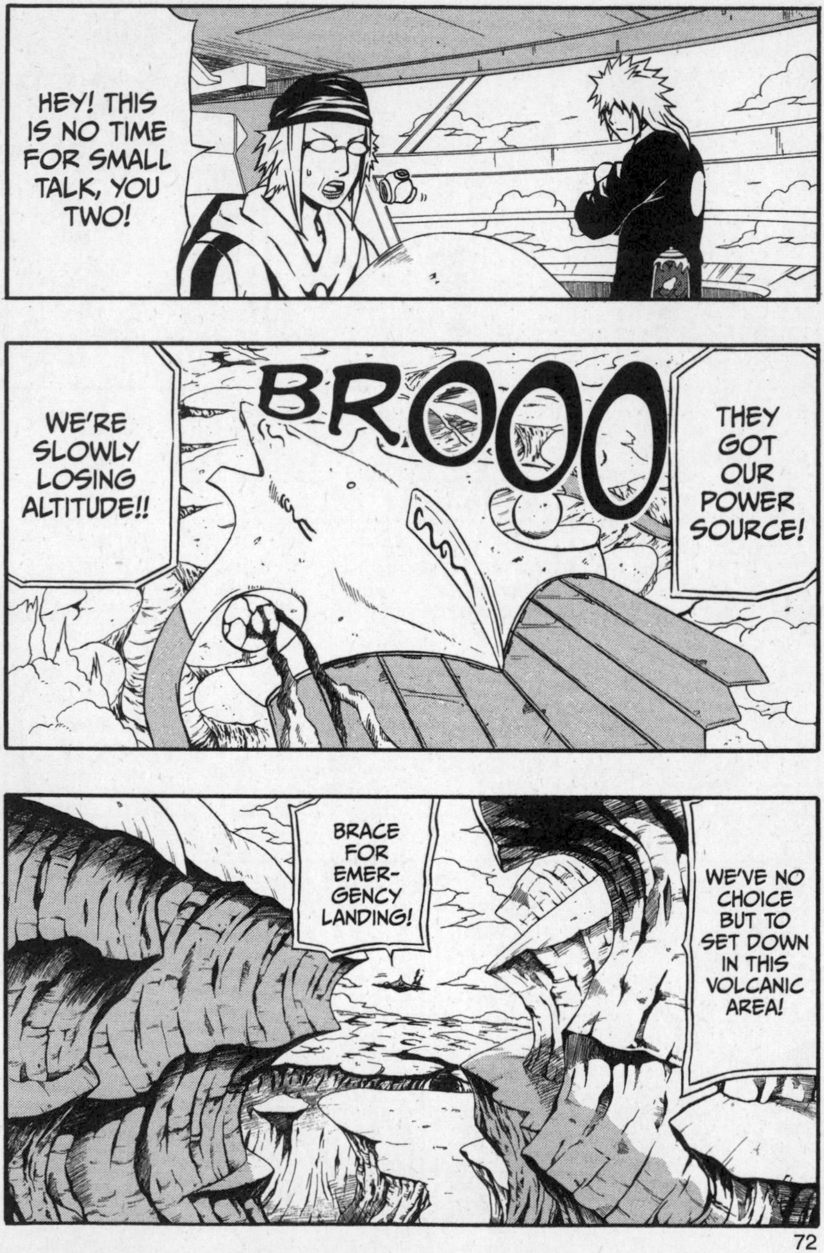
HEY! THIS IS NO TIME FOR SMALL TALK, YOU TWO!
THEY GOT OUR POWER SOURCE!
BROOO
WE'RE SLOWLY LOSING ALTITUDE!!
WE'VE NO CHOICE BUT TO SET DOWN IN THIS VOLCANIC AREA!
BRACE FOR EMER-GENCY LANDING!

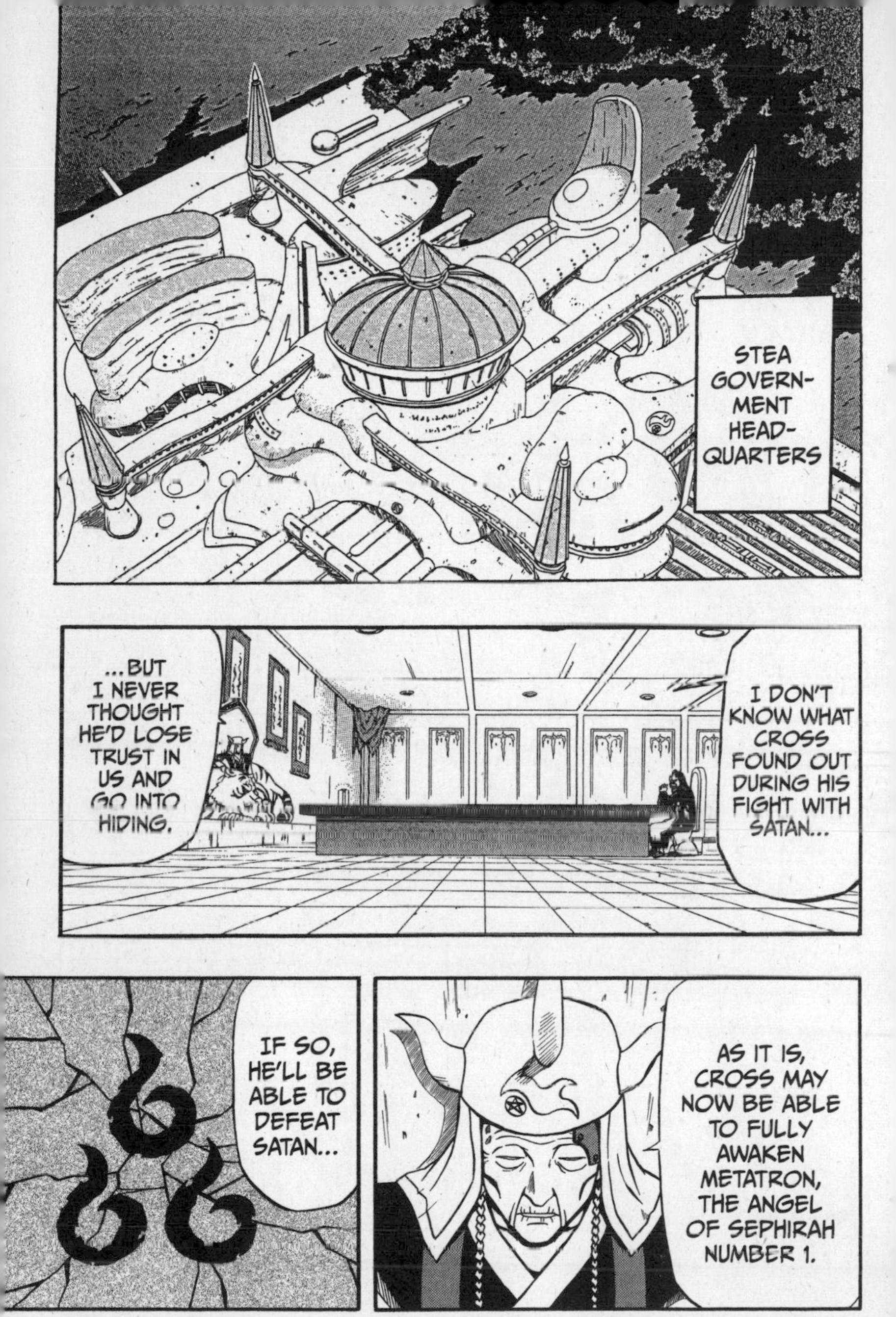
STEA GOVERNMENT HEADQUARTERS
I DON'T KNOW WHAT CROSS FOUND OUT DURING HIS FIGHT WITH SATAN...
...BUT I NEVER THOUGHT HE'D LOSE TRUST IN US AND GO INTO HIDING.
AS IT IS, CROSS MAY NOW BE ABLE TO FULLY AWAKEN METATRON, THE ANGEL OF SEPHIRAH NUMBER 1.
IF SO, HE'LL BE ABLE TO DEFEAT SATAN...

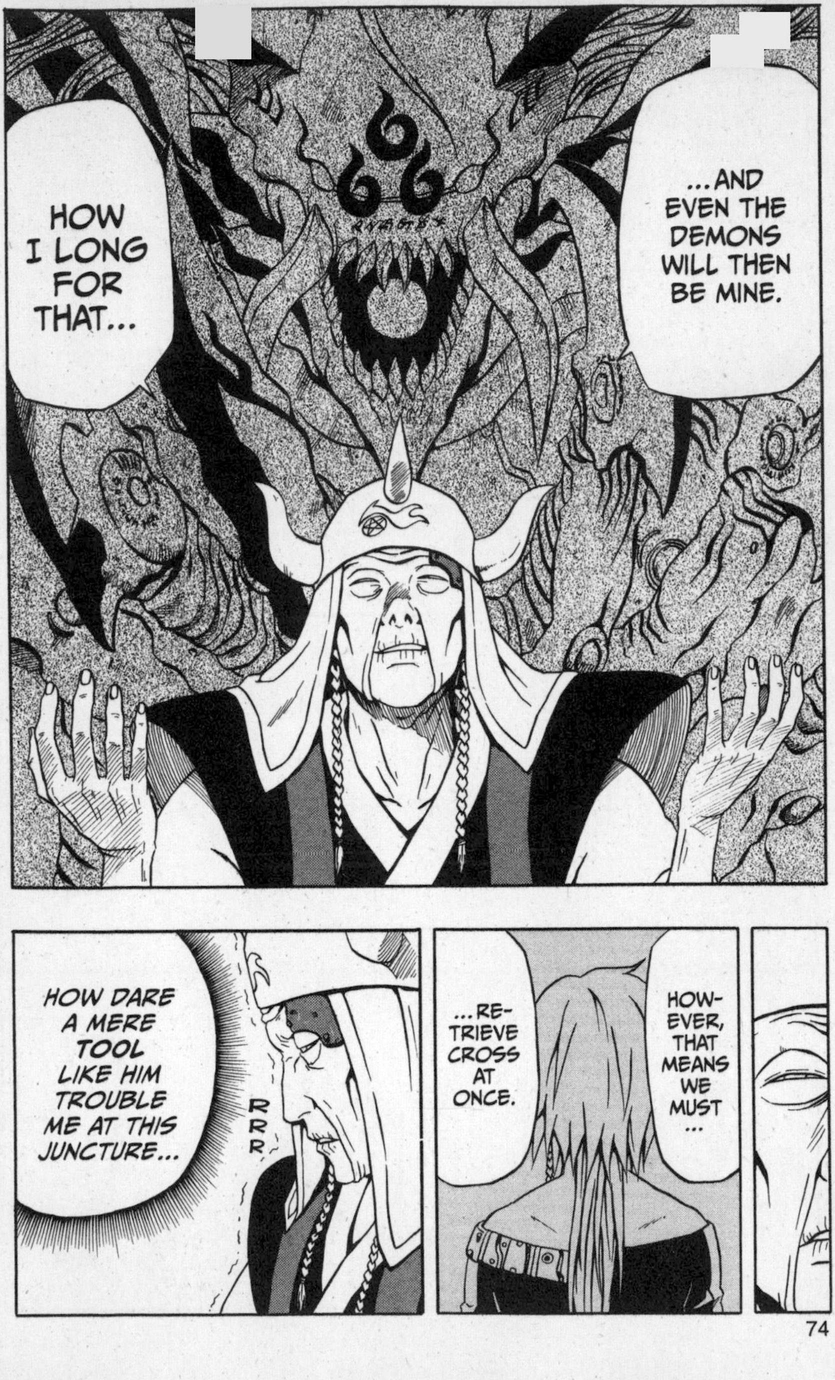
...AND EVEN THE DEMONS WILL THEN BE MINE.
HOW I LONG FOR THAT...
HOW-EVER, THAT MEANS WE MUST ...
...RE-TRIEVE CROSS AT ONCE.
HOW DARE A MERE TOOL LIKE HIM TROUBLE ME AT THIS JUNCTURE...
RRR

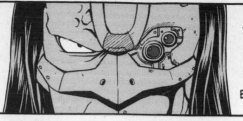

THE OLDER SHE GETS, THE MORE CHILDISH SHE BECOMES...
IS THERE TRULY NO END TO HER CRAVING FOR POWER?
WE MUST POSSESS BOTH KABBALAHS. UNLESS I HAVE THEM BOTH...
...MY DREAM, WITH ALL THAT I HAVE INVESTED IN IT, WILL NOT BE FULFILLED. I WILL NOT ALLOW THAT TO HAPPEN.
WHAT IS THERE IN IT...
...FOR US MERE HUMANS, MILADY?!
ONE KABBALAH IS ENOUGH TO DESTROY THIS PLANET. TO WIELD BOTH... IS MADNESS!

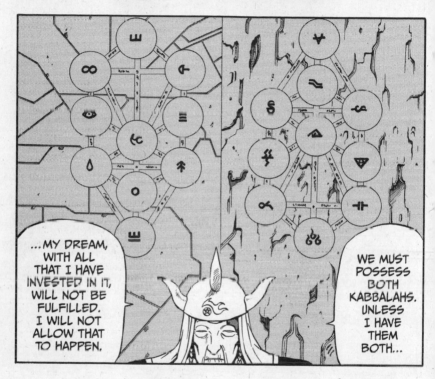

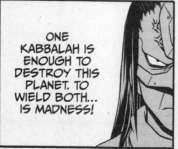

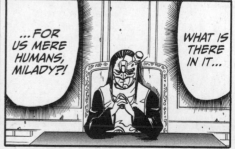

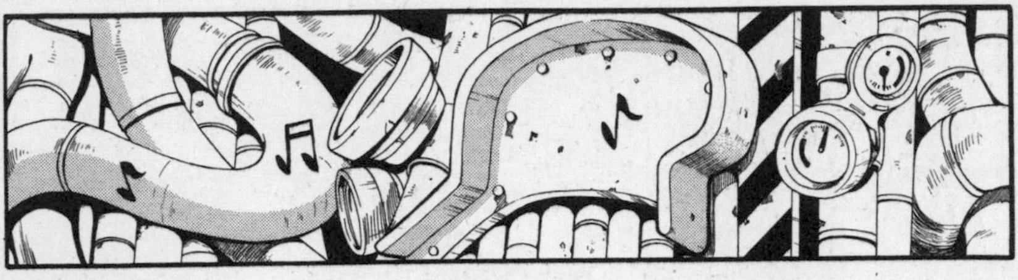

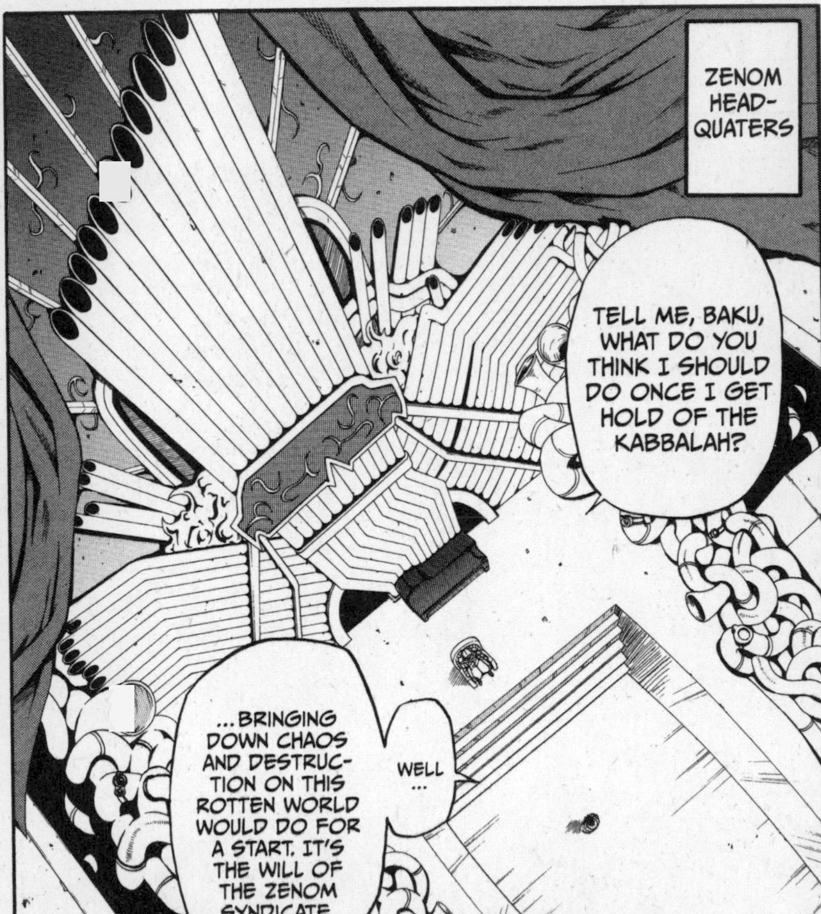
ZENOM HEAD-QUATERS
TELL ME, BAKU, WHAT DO YOU THINK I SHOULD DO ONCE I GET HOLD OF THE KABBALAH?
WELL ...
...BRINGING DOWN CHAOS AND DESTRUCTION ON THIS ROTTEN WORLD WOULD DO FOR A START. IT'S THE WILL OF THE ZENOM SYNDICATE.

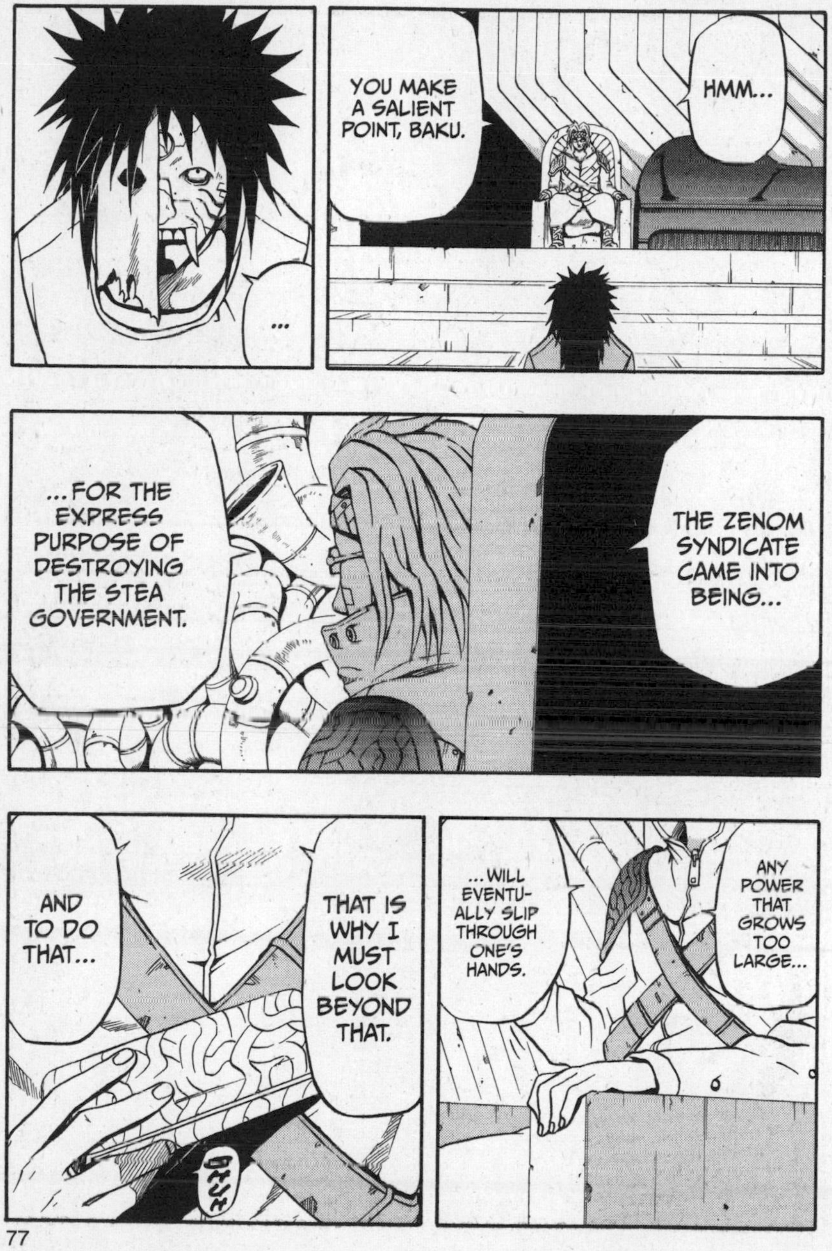
HMM...
YOU MAKE A SALIENT POINT, BAKU.
...
THE ZENOM SYNDICATE CAME INTO BEING...
...FOR THE EXPRESS PURPOSE OF DESTROYING THE STEA GOVERNMENT.
ANY POWER THAT GROWS TOO LARGE...
...WILL EVENTU-ALLY SLIP THROUGH ONE'S HANDS.
THAT IS WHY I MUST LOOK BEYOND THAT.
AND TO DO THAT...

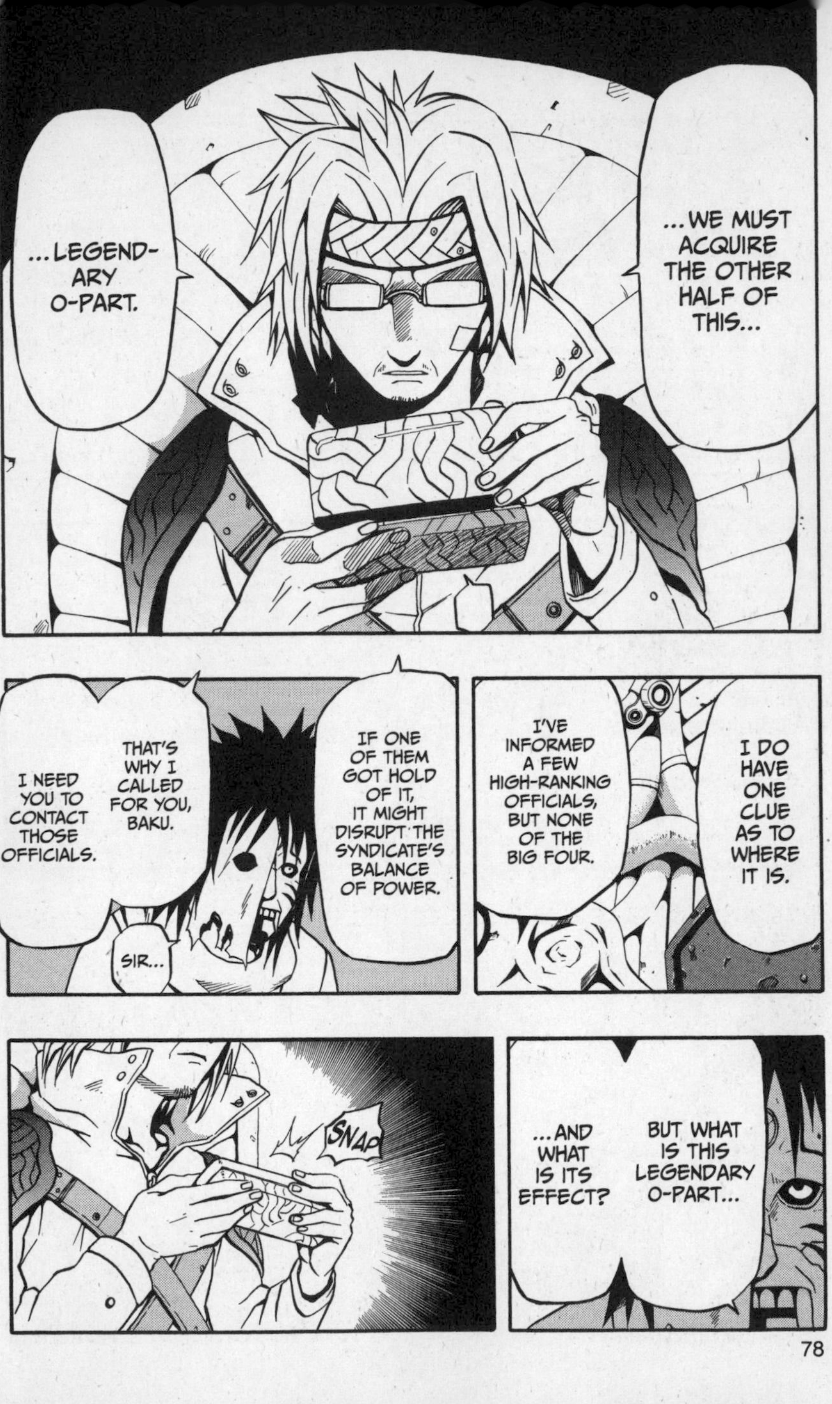
...WE MUST ACQUIRE THE OTHER HALF OF THIS...
...LEGEND-ARY O-PART.
I DO HAVE ONE CLUE AS TO WHERE IT IS.
I'VE INFORMED A FEW HIGH-RANKING OFFICIALS, BUT NONE OF THE BIG FOUR.
IF ONE OF THEM GOT HOLD OF IT, IT MIGHT DISRUPT THE SYNDICATE'S BALANCE OF POWER.
THAT'S WHY I CALLED FOR YOU, BAKU.
I NEED YOU TO CONTACT THOSE OFFICIALS.
SIR...
BUT WHAT IS THIS LEGENDARY O-PART...
...AND WHAT IS ITS EFFECT?
SNAP

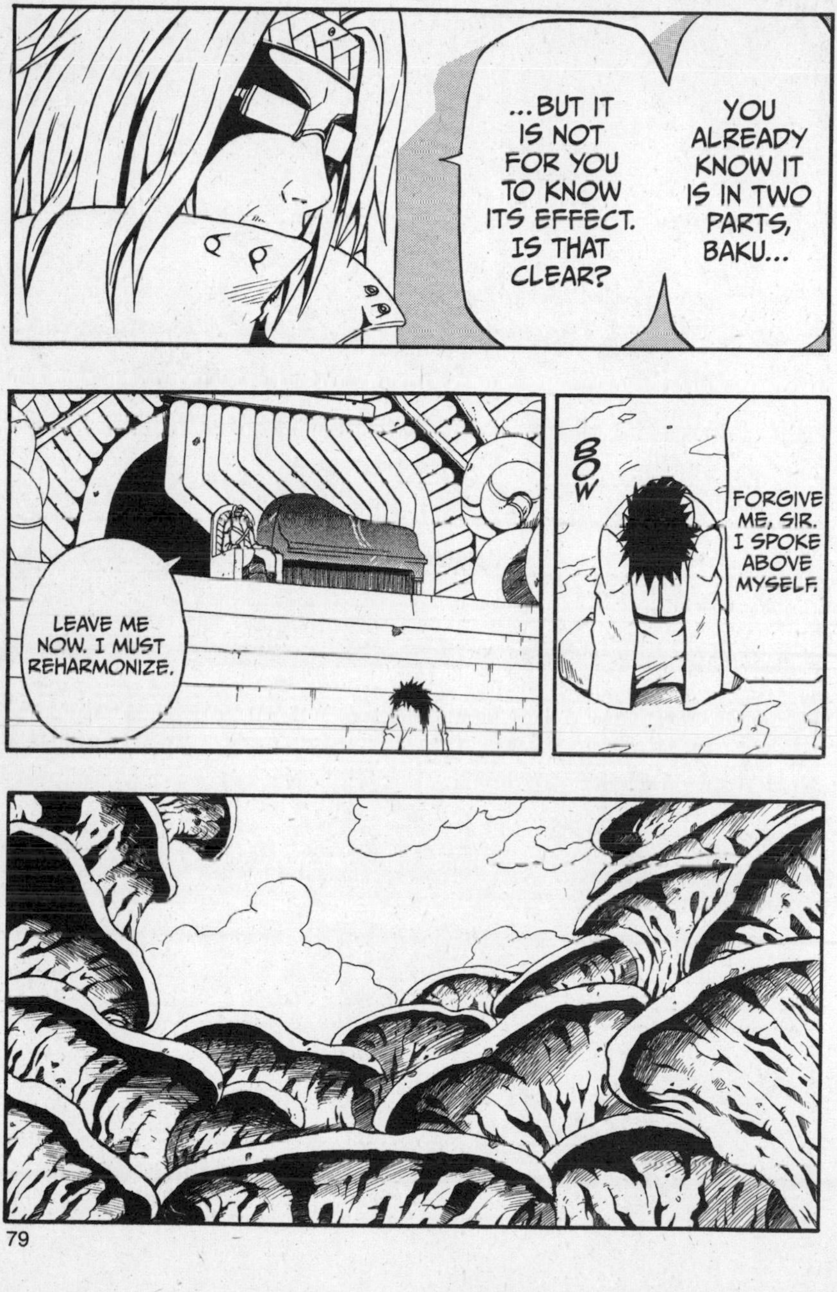
YOU ALREADY KNOW IT IS IN TWO PARTS, BAKU...
...BUT IT IS NOT FOR YOU TO KNOW ITS EFFECT. IS THAT CLEAR?
BOW
FORGIVE ME, SIR. I SPOKE ABOVE MYSELF.
LEAVE ME NOW. I MUST REHARMONIZE.

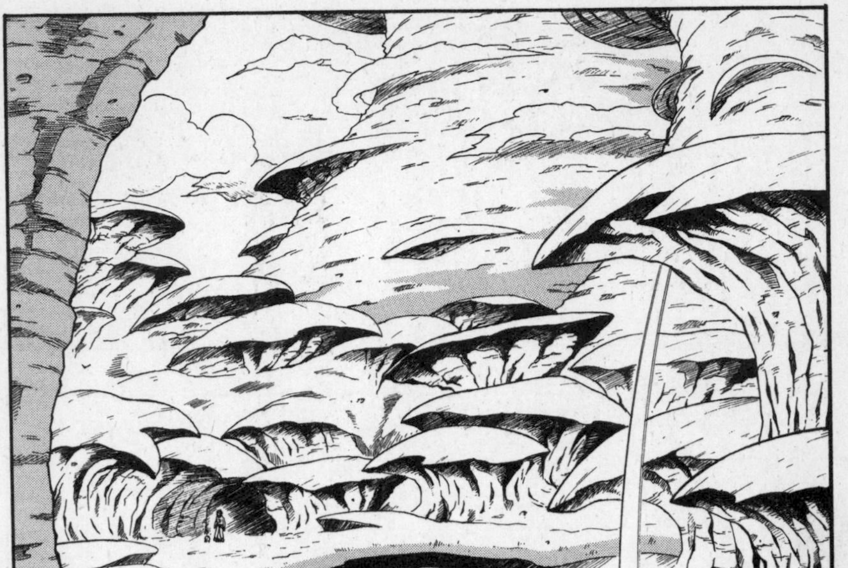
SPSSSSSH
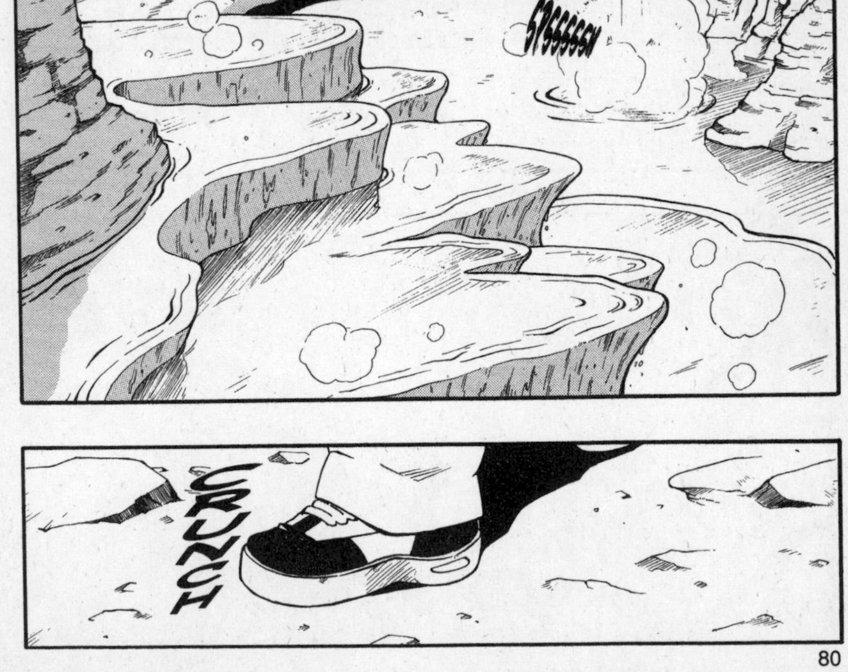
CRUNCH

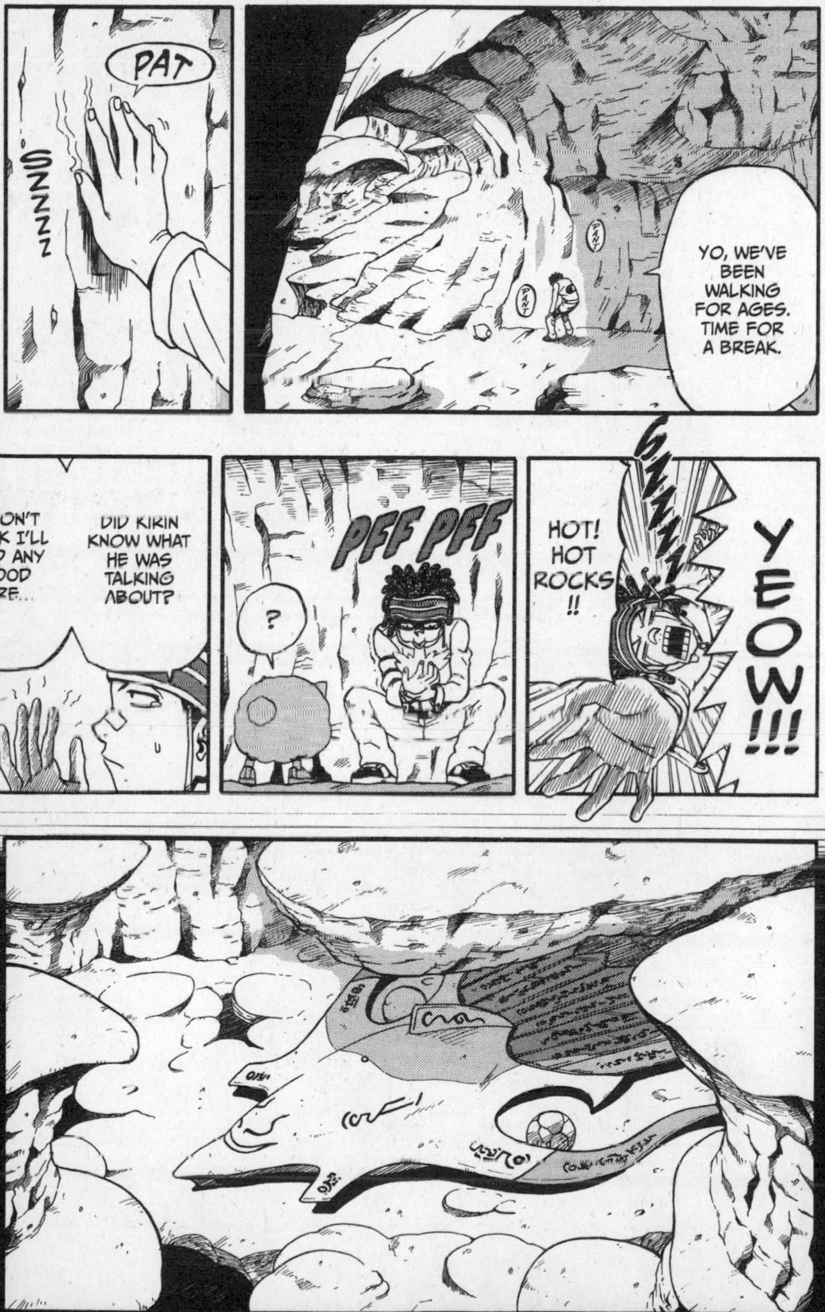
YO, WE'VE BEEN WALKING FOR AGES. TIME FOR A BREAK.
PAT
SZZZZ
YEOW!!!
HOT! HOT ROCKS!!
PFF PFF
?
DID KIRIN KNOW WHAT HE WAS TALKING ABOUT?
I DON'T THINK I'LL FIND ANY FOOD HERE...

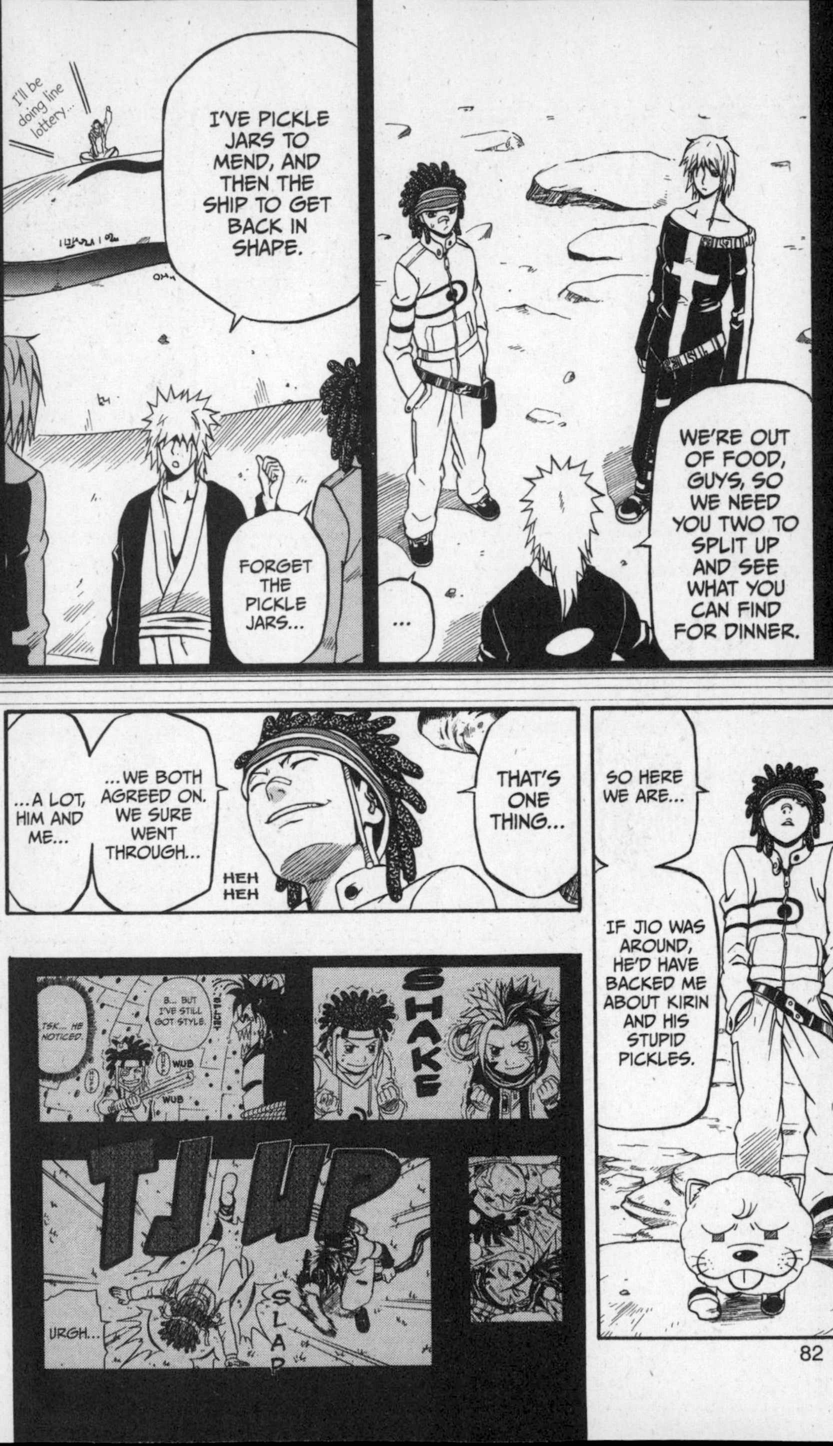
WE'RE OUT OF FOOD, GUYS, SO WE NEED YOU TWO TO SPLIT UP AND SEE WHAT YOU CAN FIND FOR DINNER.
...
I'VE PICKLE JARS TO MEND, AND THEN THE SHIP TO GET BACK IN SHAPE.
I'll be doing line lottery...
FORGET THE PICKLE JARS...
SO HERE WE ARE...
IF JIO WAS AROUND, HE'D HAVE BACKED ME ABOUT KIRIN AND HIS STUPID PICKLES.
THAT'S ONE THING...
...WE BOTH AGREED ON. WE SURE WENT THROUGH...
HEH HEH
...A LOT, HIM AND ME...
SHAKE
B... BUT I'VE STILL GOT STYLE.
TSK... HE NOTICED.
WUB
WUB
THUP
SLAP
URGH...

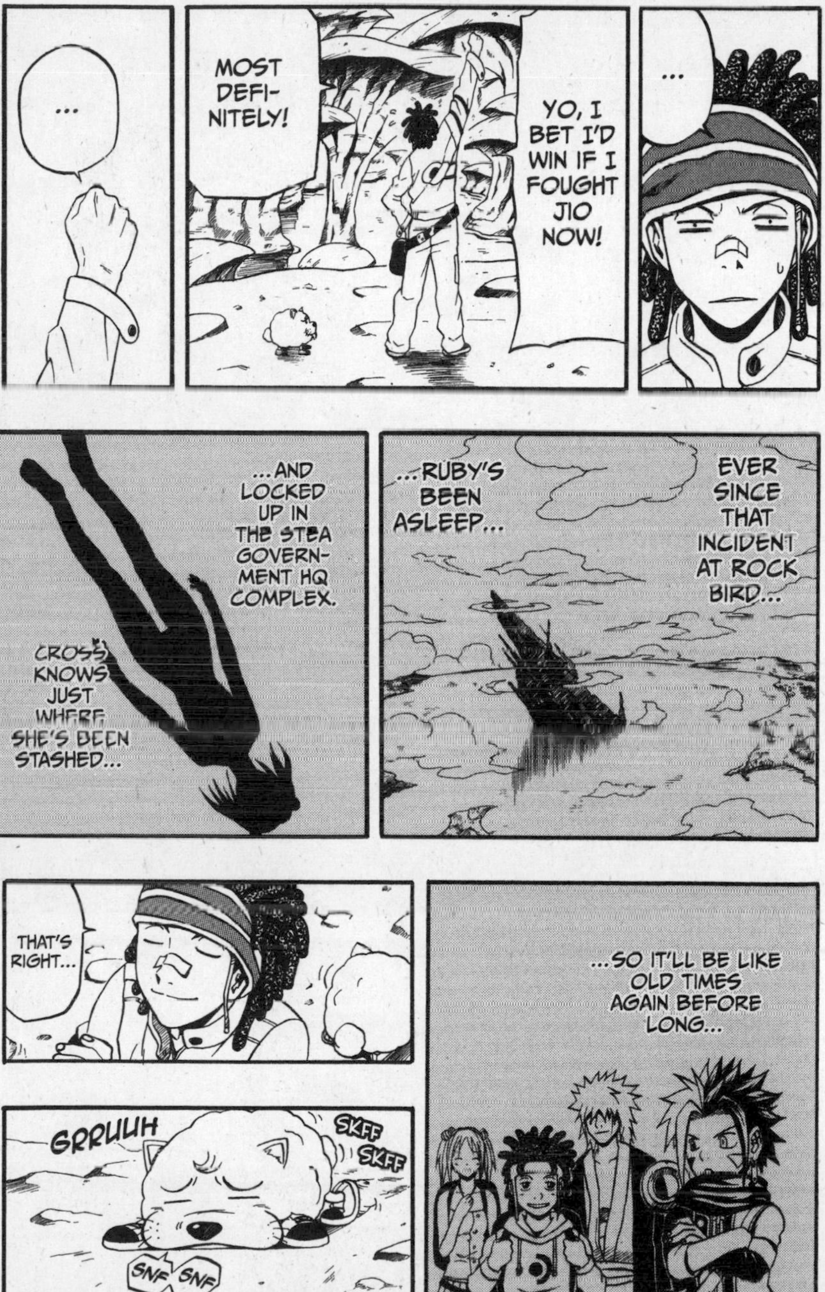
...
YO, I BET I'D WIN IF I FOUGHT JIO NOW!
MOST DEFI-NITELY!
...
EVER SINCE THAT INCIDENT AT ROCK BIRD...
...RUBY'S BEEN ASLEEP...
...AND LOCKED UP IN THE STEA GOVERN-MENT HQ COMPLEX.
CROSS KNOWS JUST WHERE SHE'S BEEN STASHED...
THAT'S RIGHT...
GRRUUH
SKFF SKFF
SNF SNF
...SO IT'LL BE LIKE OLD TIMES AGAIN BEFORE LONG...

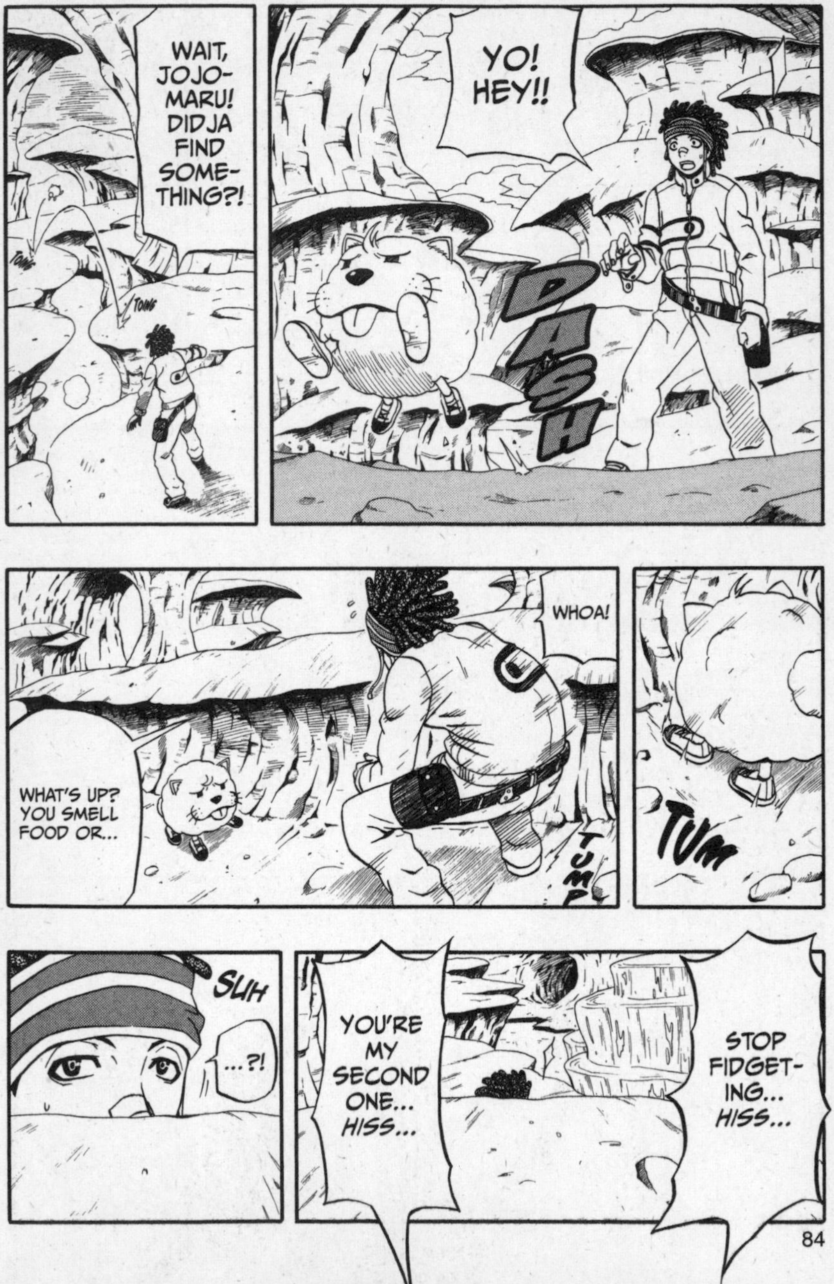
YO! HEY!!
DASH
WAIT, JOJO-MARU! DIDJA FIND SOME-THING?!
TOING
TOING
TUM
WHOA!
WHAT'S UP? YOU SMELL FOOD OR...
TUMP
STOP FIDGET-ING... HISS...
YOU'RE MY SECOND ONE... HISS...
SUH
...?!

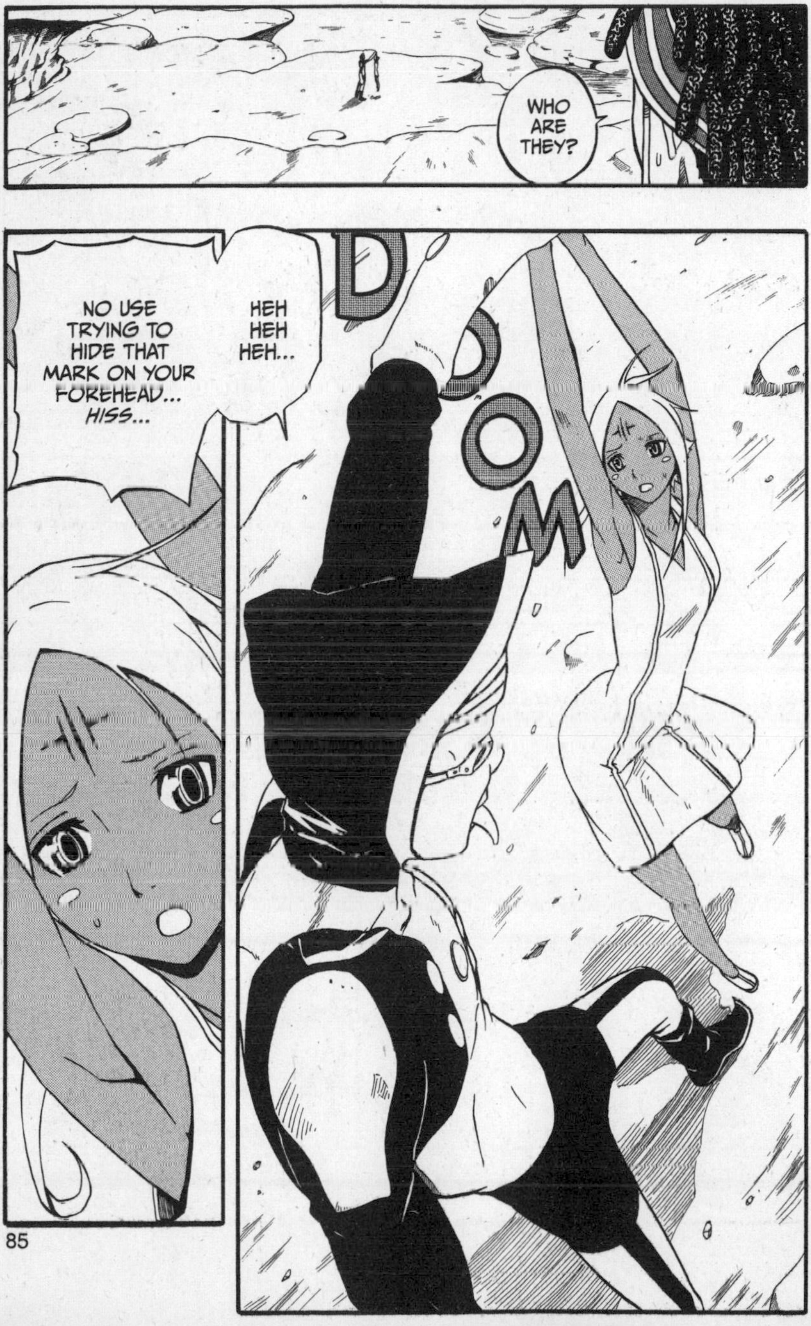
WHO ARE THEY?
DOOM
HEH HEH HEH...
NO USE TRYING TO HIDE THAT MARK ON YOUR FOREHEAD... *HISS*...

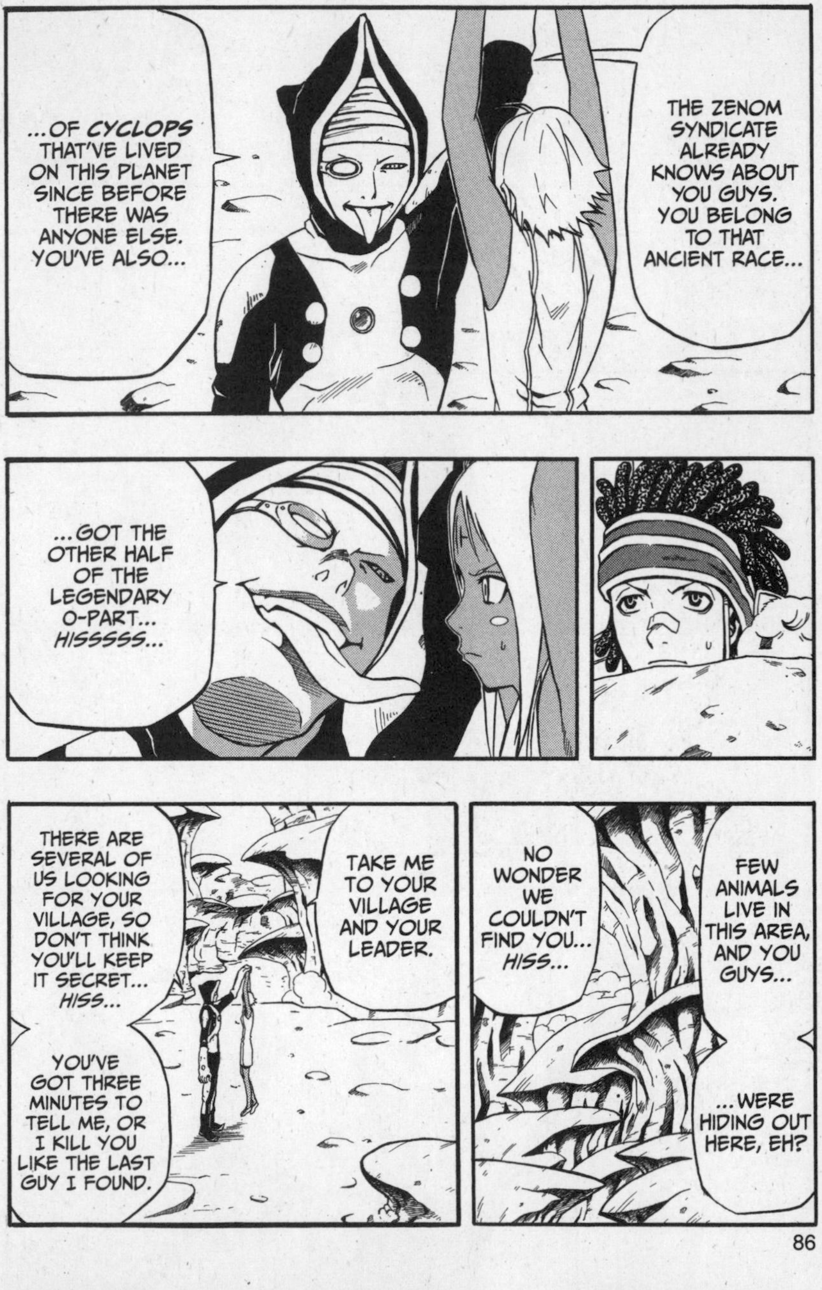
THE ZENOM SYNDICATE ALREADY KNOWS ABOUT YOU GUYS. YOU BELONG TO THAT ANCIENT RACE...
...OF *CYCLOPS* THAT'VE LIVED ON THIS PLANET SINCE BEFORE THERE WAS ANYONE ELSE. YOU'VE ALSO...
...GOT THE OTHER HALF OF THE LEGENDARY O-PART... *HISSSSS...*
FEW ANIMALS LIVE IN THIS AREA, AND YOU GUYS...
...WERE HIDING OUT HERE, EH?
NO WONDER WE COULDN'T FIND YOU... *HISS...*
TAKE ME TO YOUR VILLAGE AND YOUR LEADER.
THERE ARE SEVERAL OF US LOOKING FOR YOUR VILLAGE, SO DON'T THINK YOU'LL KEEP IT SECRET... *HISS...*
YOU'VE GOT THREE MINUTES TO TELL ME, OR I KILL YOU LIKE THE LAST GUY I FOUND.

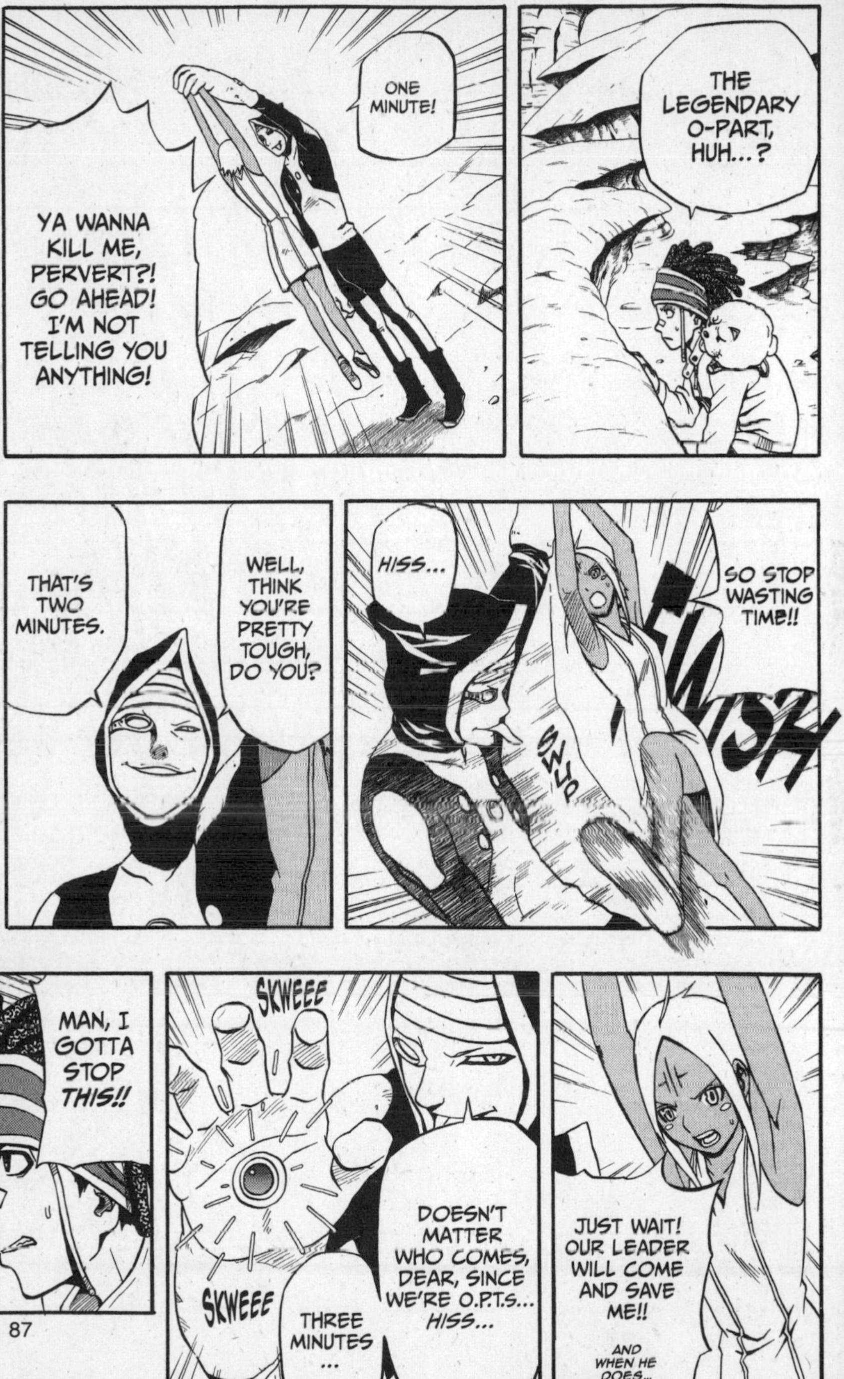
THE LEGENDARY O-PART, HUH...?
ONE MINUTE!
YA WANNA KILL ME, PERVERT?! GO AHEAD! I'M NOT TELLING YOU ANYTHING!
SO STOP WASTING TIME!!
SWISH
HISS...
SWUP
WELL, THINK YOU'RE PRETTY TOUGH, DO YOU?
THAT'S TWO MINUTES.
JUST WAIT! OUR LEADER WILL COME AND SAVE ME!!
AND WHEN HE DOES...
SKWEEE
DOESN'T MATTER WHO COMES, DEAR, SINCE WE'RE O.P.T.S... HISS...
SKWEEE
THREE MINUTES ...
MAN, I GOTTA STOP THIS!!

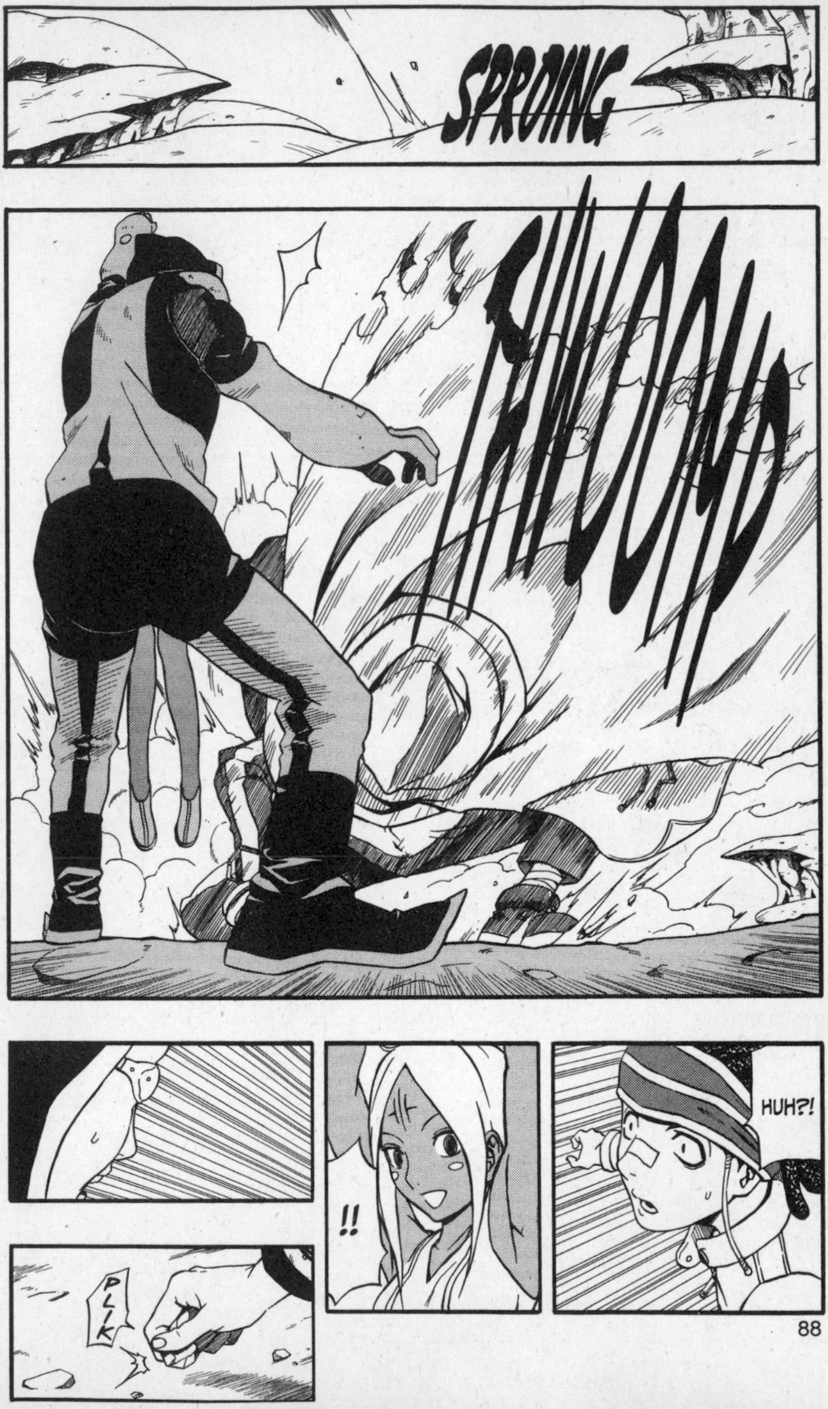
SPROING
THWOMP
HUH?!
!!
PLIK

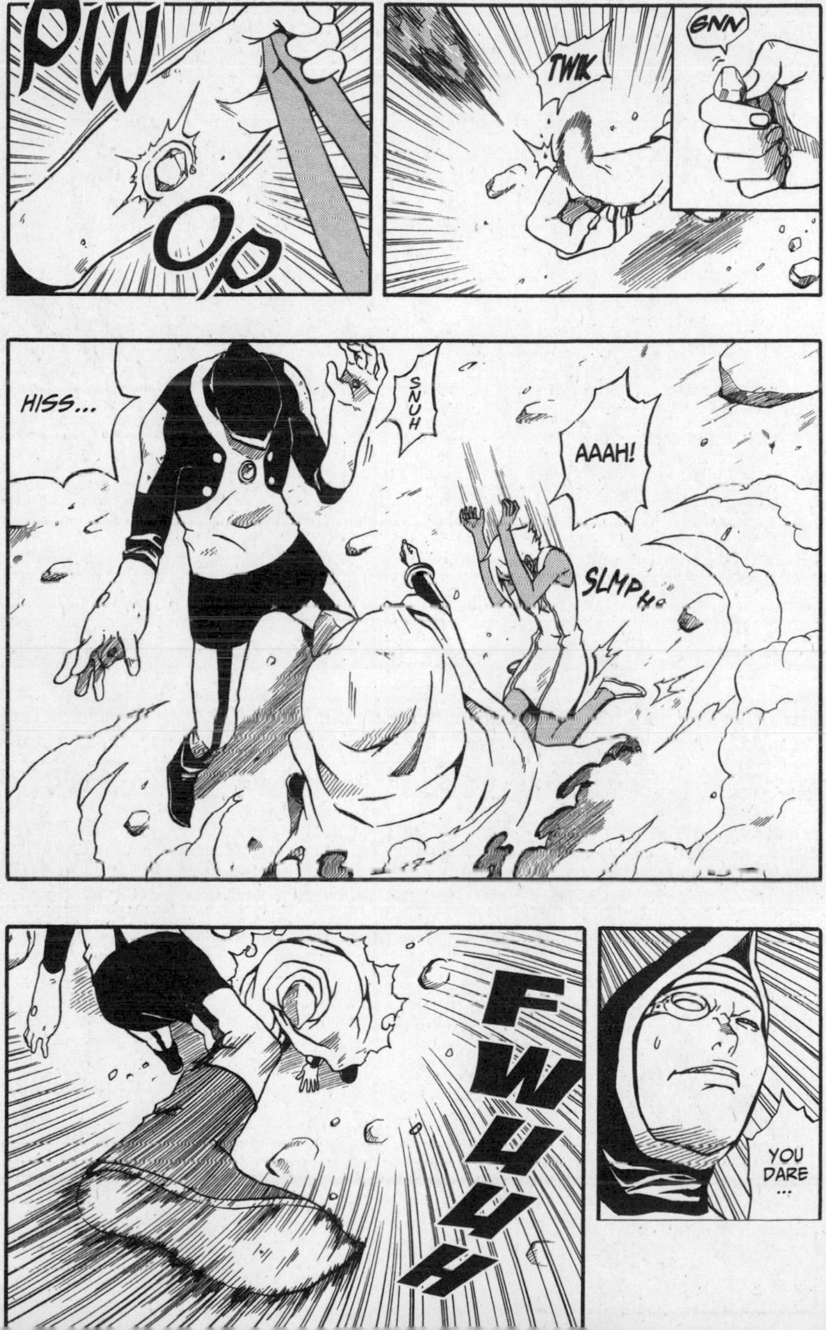
GNN
TWIK
PW
OOP
AAAH!
SLMPH
SNUH
HISS...
YOU DARE...
FWUUH

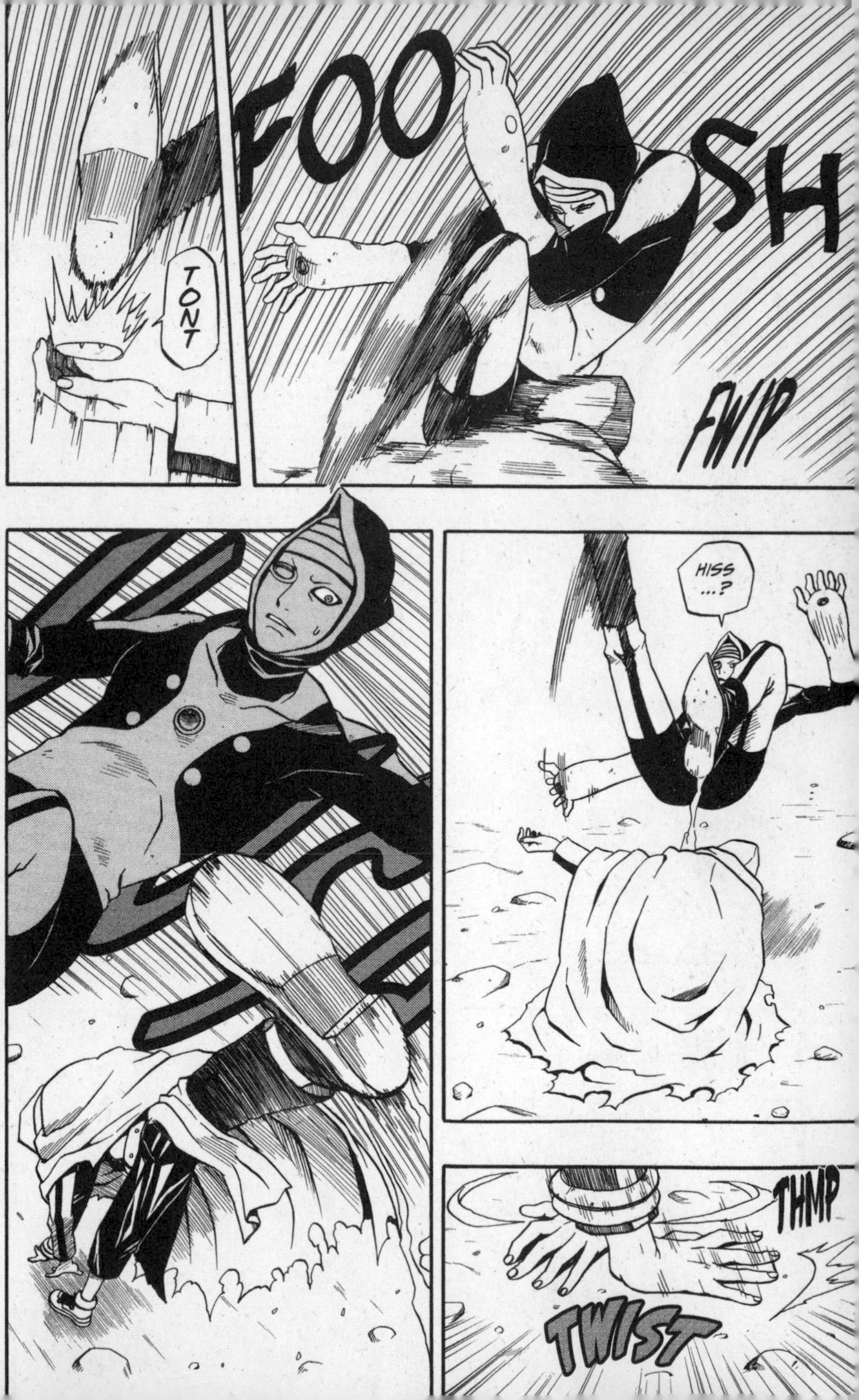
FOOOSH
FWIP
TONT
HISS ...?
THMP
TWIST

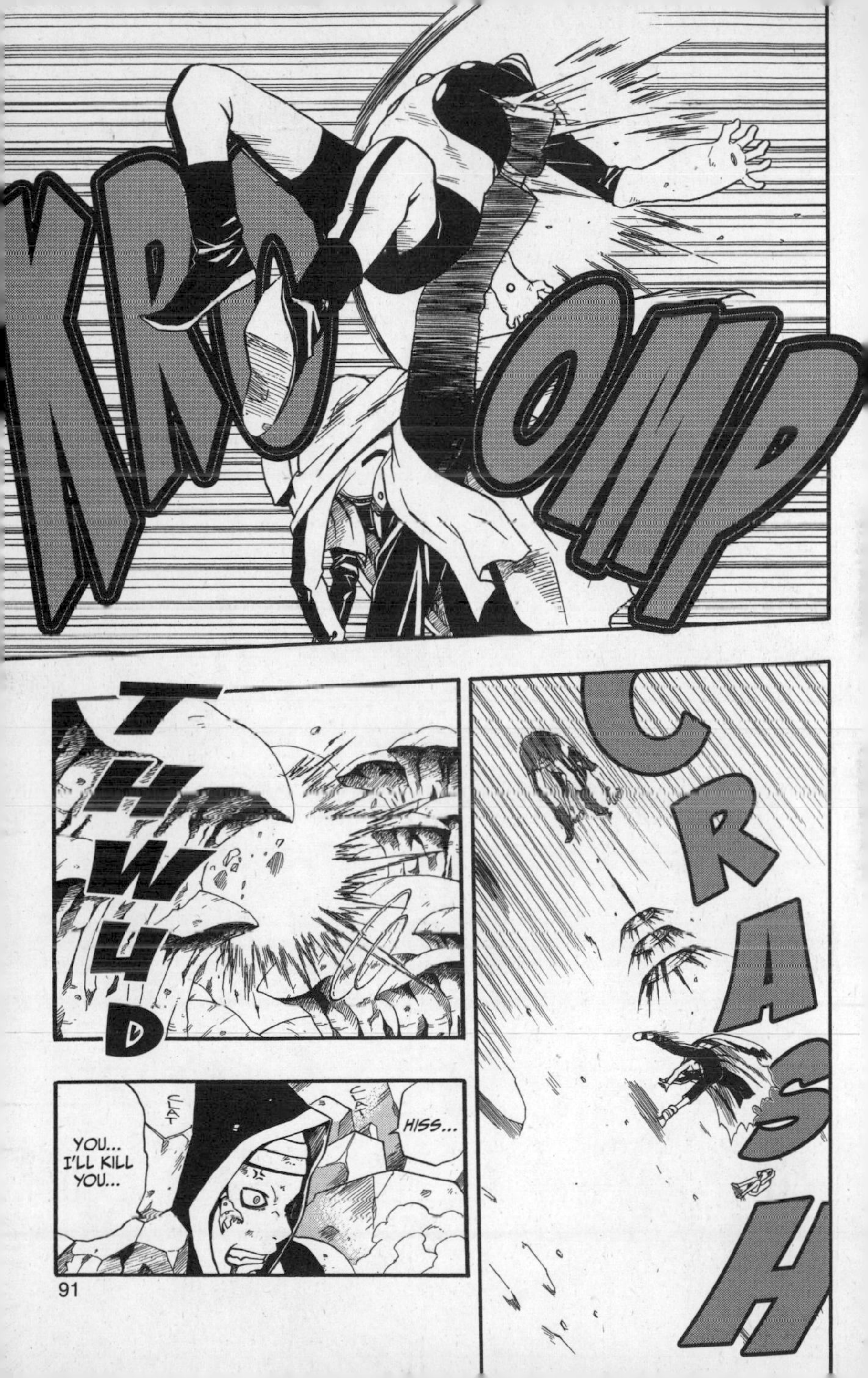
CRASH
THWUD
CLAT
HISS...
CLAT
YOU... I'LL KILL YOU...

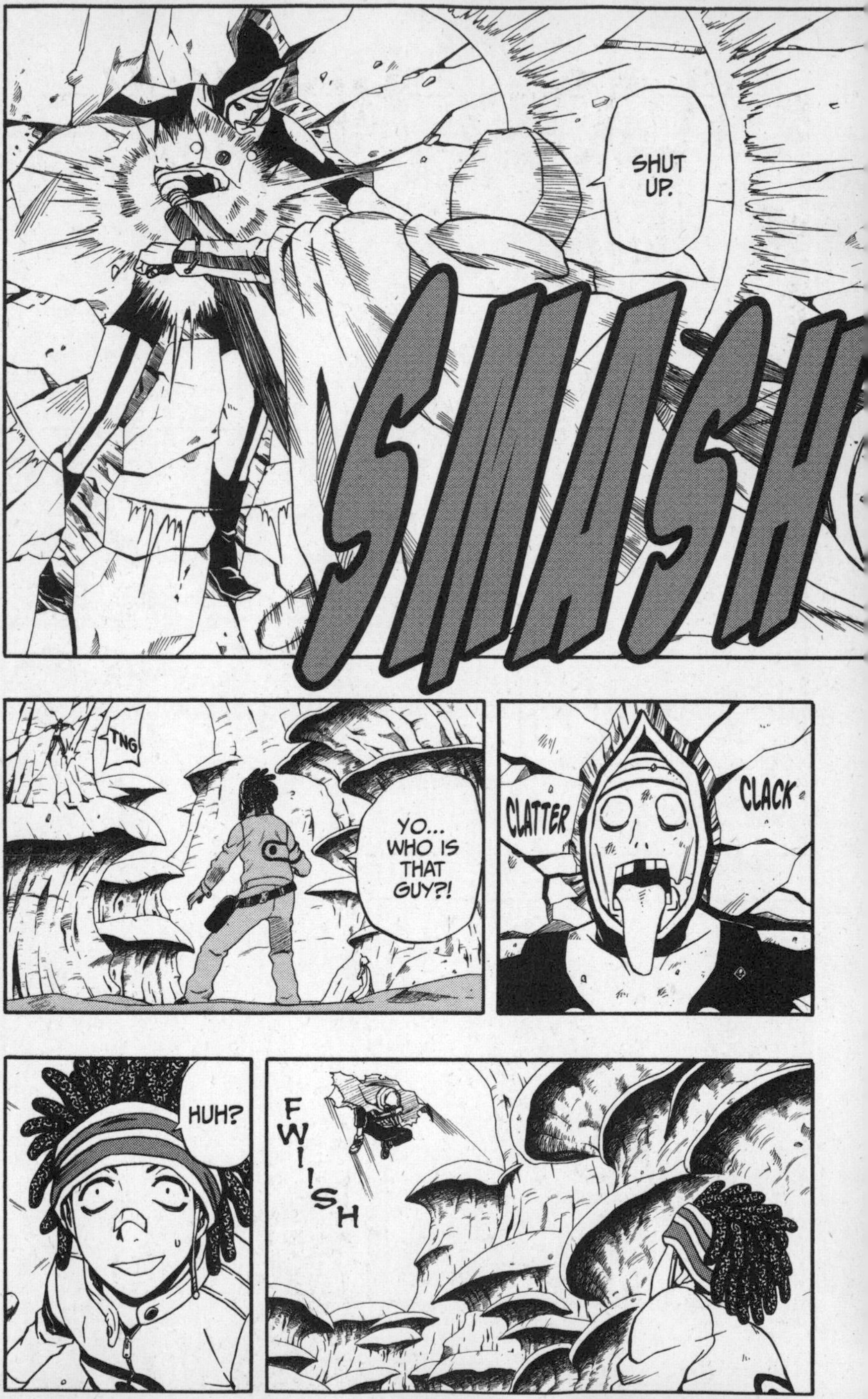
SHUT UP.
SMASH
CLACK
CLATTER
TNG
YO... WHO IS THAT GUY?!
FWISH
HUH?

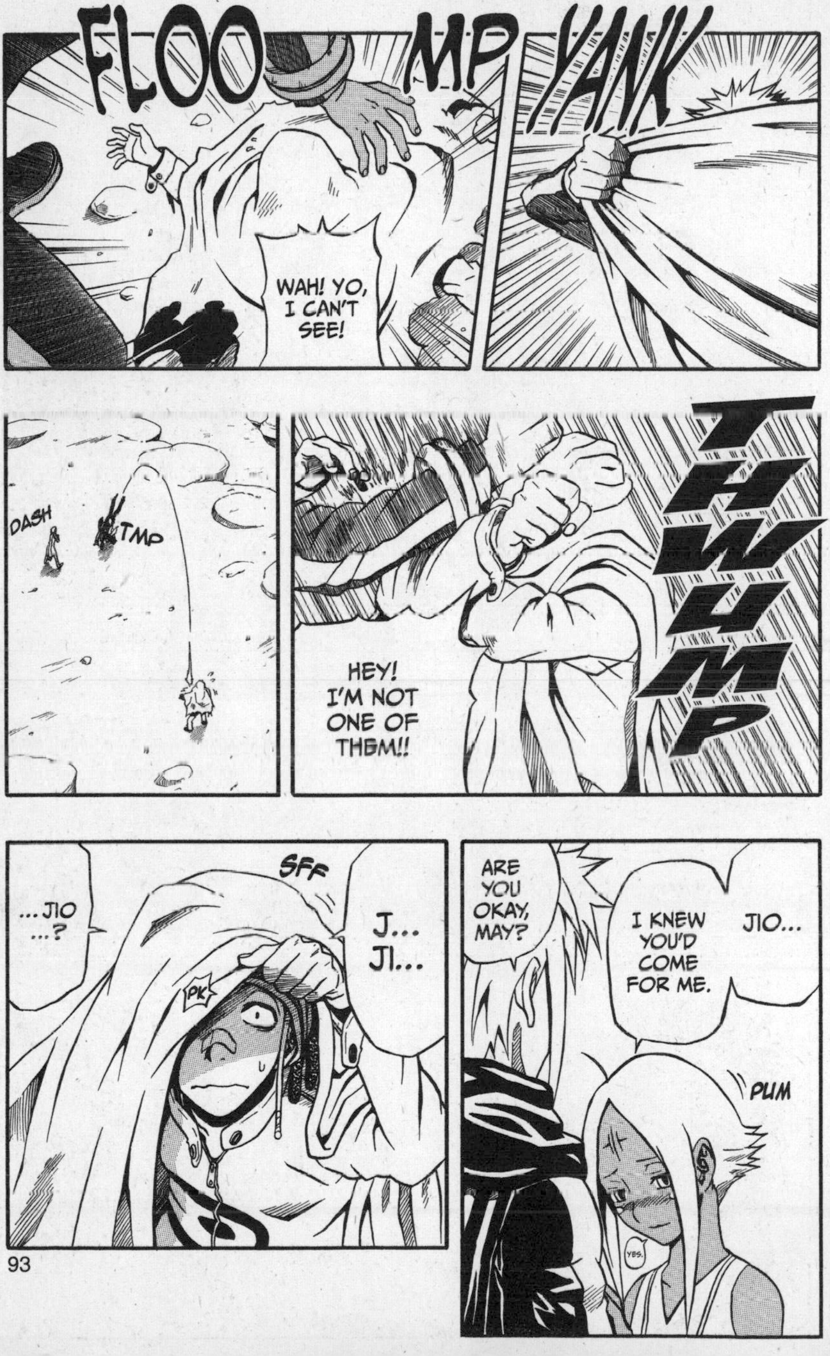
YANK
FLOOMP
WAH! YO, I CAN'T SEE!
THWUMP
HEY! I'M NOT ONE OF THEM!!
DASH
TMP
JIO... I KNEW YOU'D COME FOR ME.
ARE YOU OKAY, MAY?
PUM
YES.
SFF
J... JI...
...JIO ...?
PK

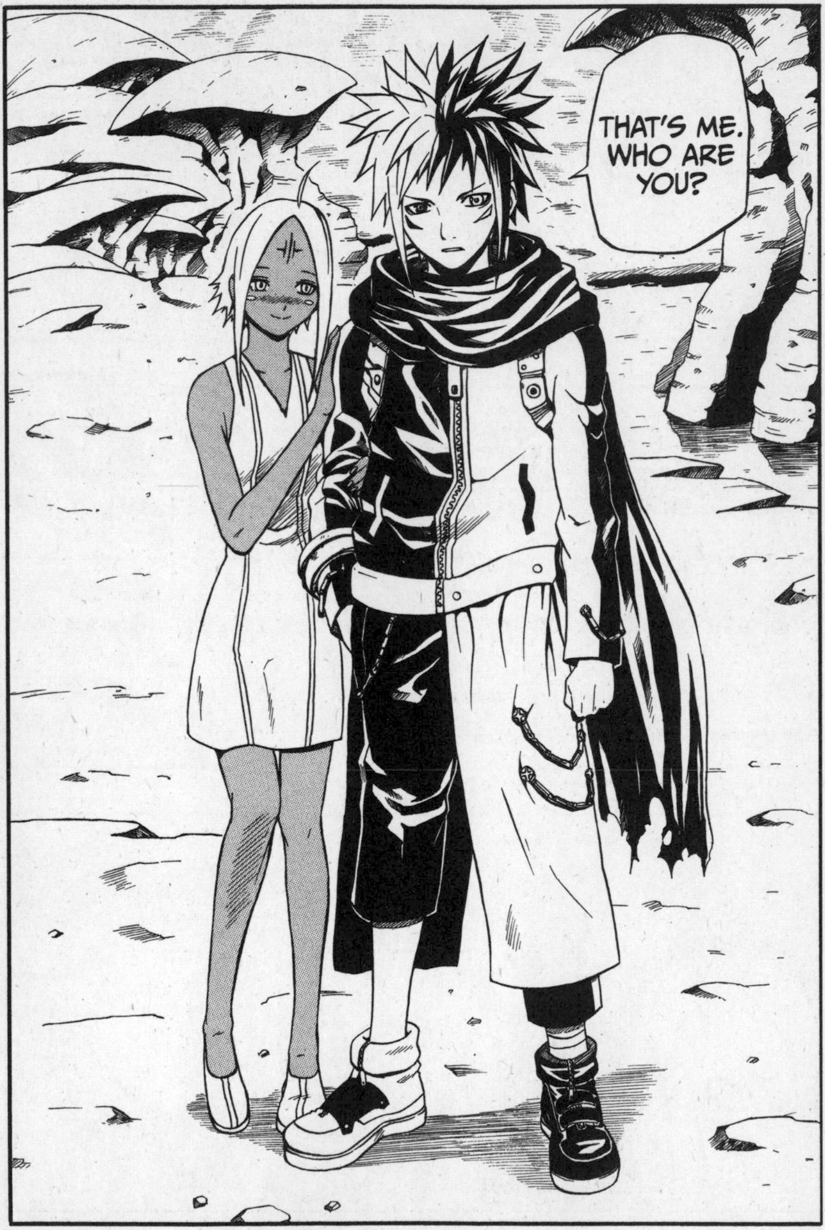
THAT'S ME. WHO ARE YOU?

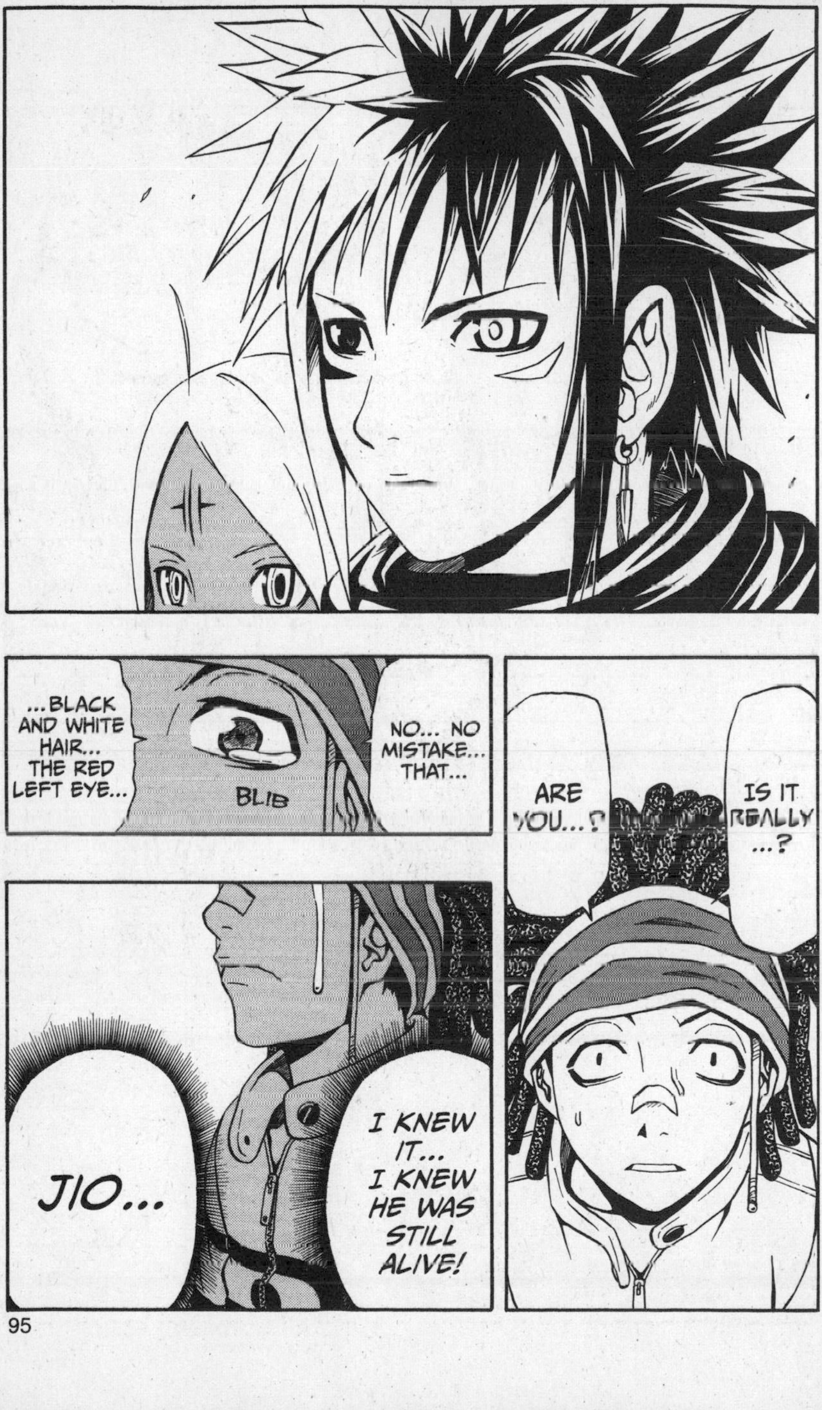

IS IT REALLY ...?
ARE YOU...?
NO... NO MISTAKE... THAT...
BLIB
...BLACK AND WHITE HAIR... THE RED LEFT EYE...
I KNEW IT... I KNEW HE WAS STILL ALIVE!
JIO...

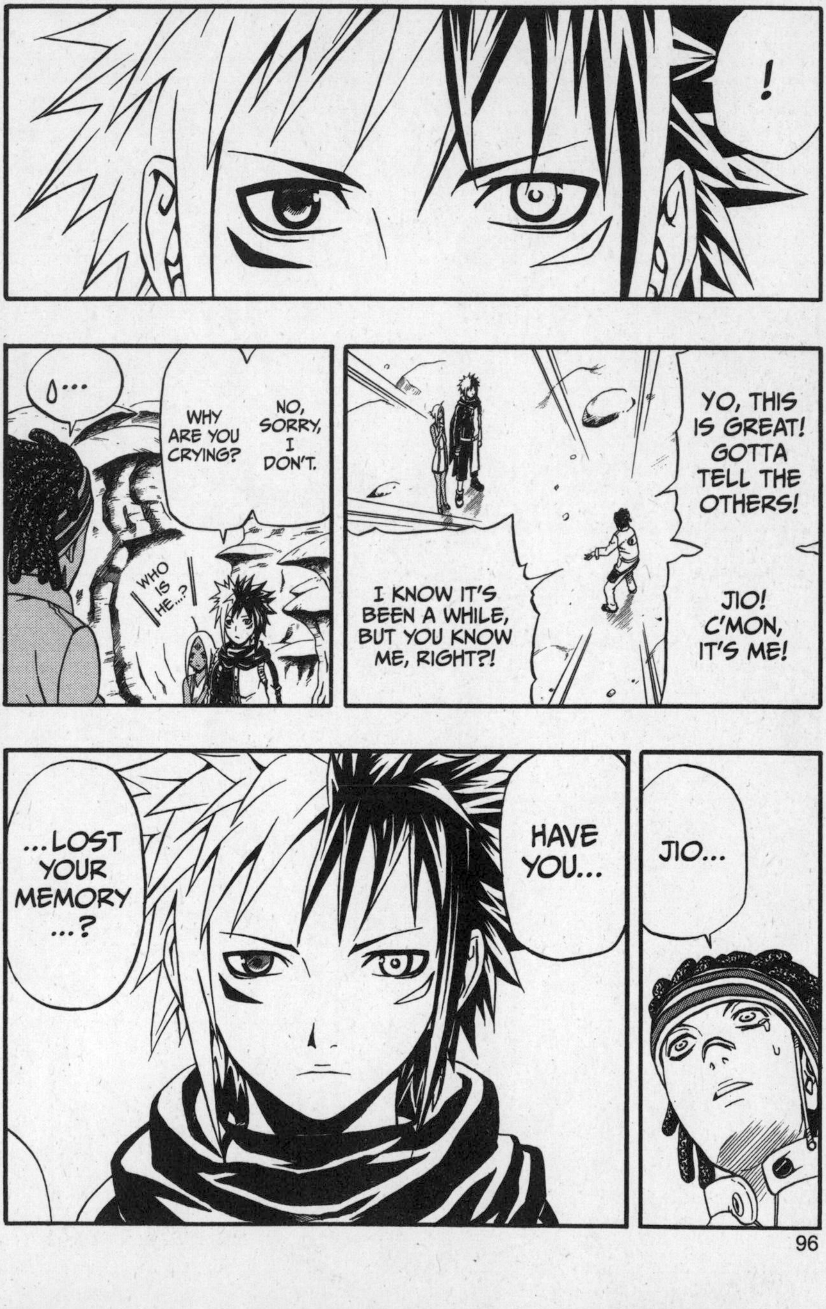
!
YO, THIS IS GREAT! GOTTA TELL THE OTHERS!
JIO! C'MON, IT'S ME!
I KNOW IT'S BEEN A WHILE, BUT YOU KNOW ME, RIGHT?!
NO, SORRY, I DON'T.
WHY ARE YOU CRYING?
WHO IS HE...?
JIO...
HAVE YOU...
...LOST YOUR MEMORY ...?

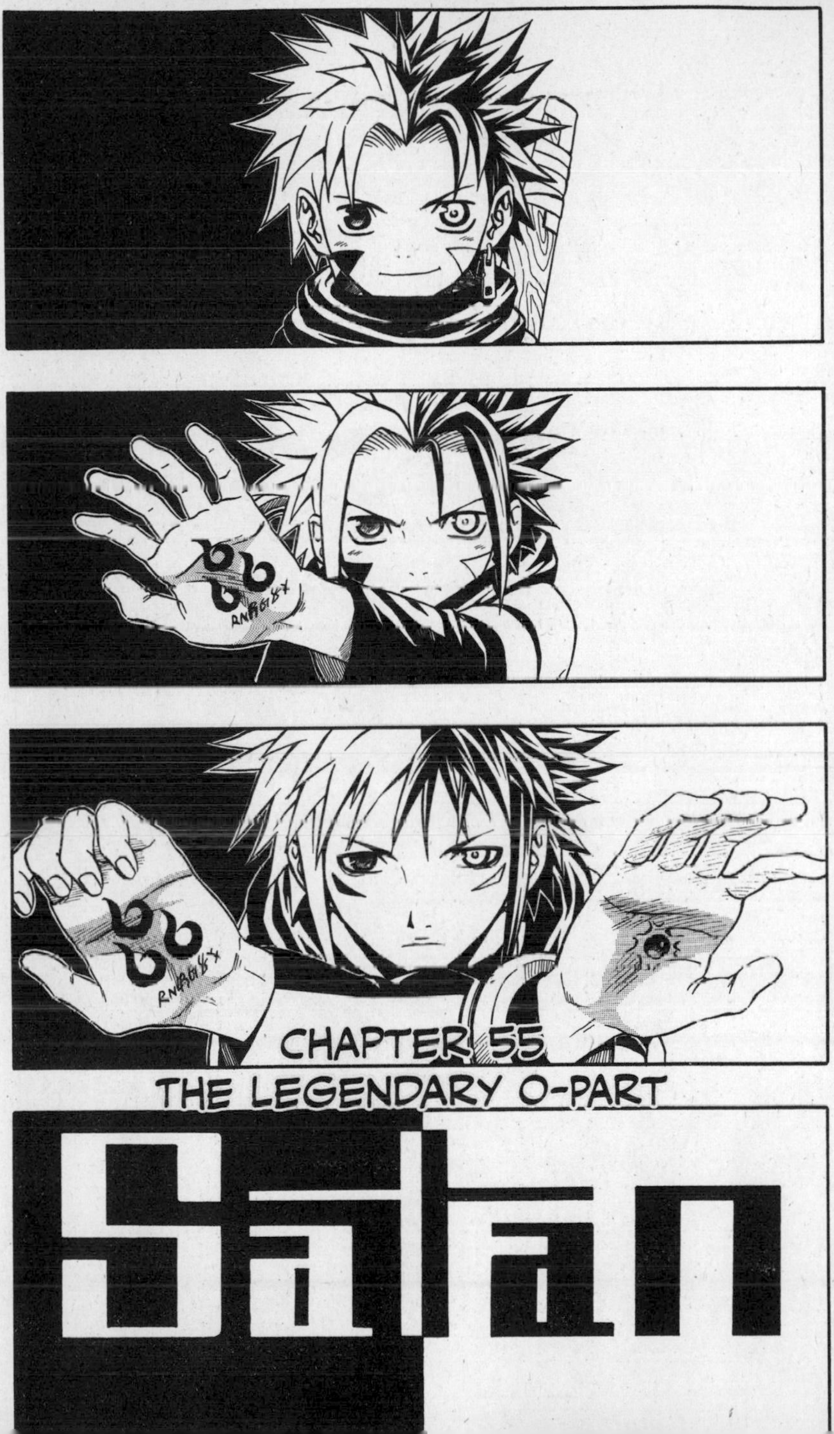
CHAPTER 55
THE LEGENDARY O-PART
Satan

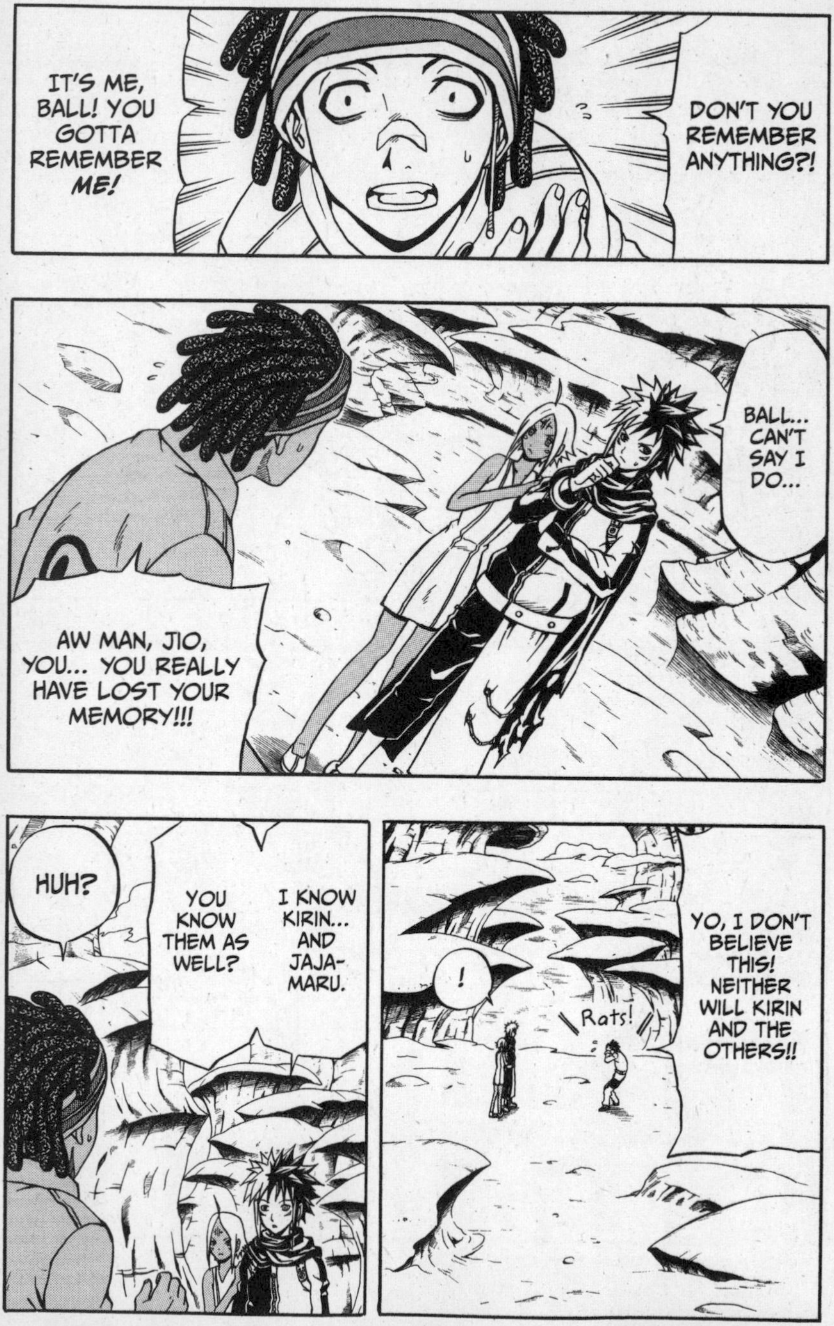
DON'T YOU REMEMBER ANYTHING?!
IT'S ME, BALL! YOU GOTTA REMEMBER *ME!*
BALL... CAN'T SAY I DO...
AW MAN, JIO, YOU... YOU REALLY HAVE LOST YOUR MEMORY!!!
YO, I DON'T BELIEVE THIS! NEITHER WILL KIRIN AND THE OTHERS!!
!
Rats!
I KNOW KIRIN... AND JAJA-MARU.
YOU KNOW THEM AS WELL?
HUH?

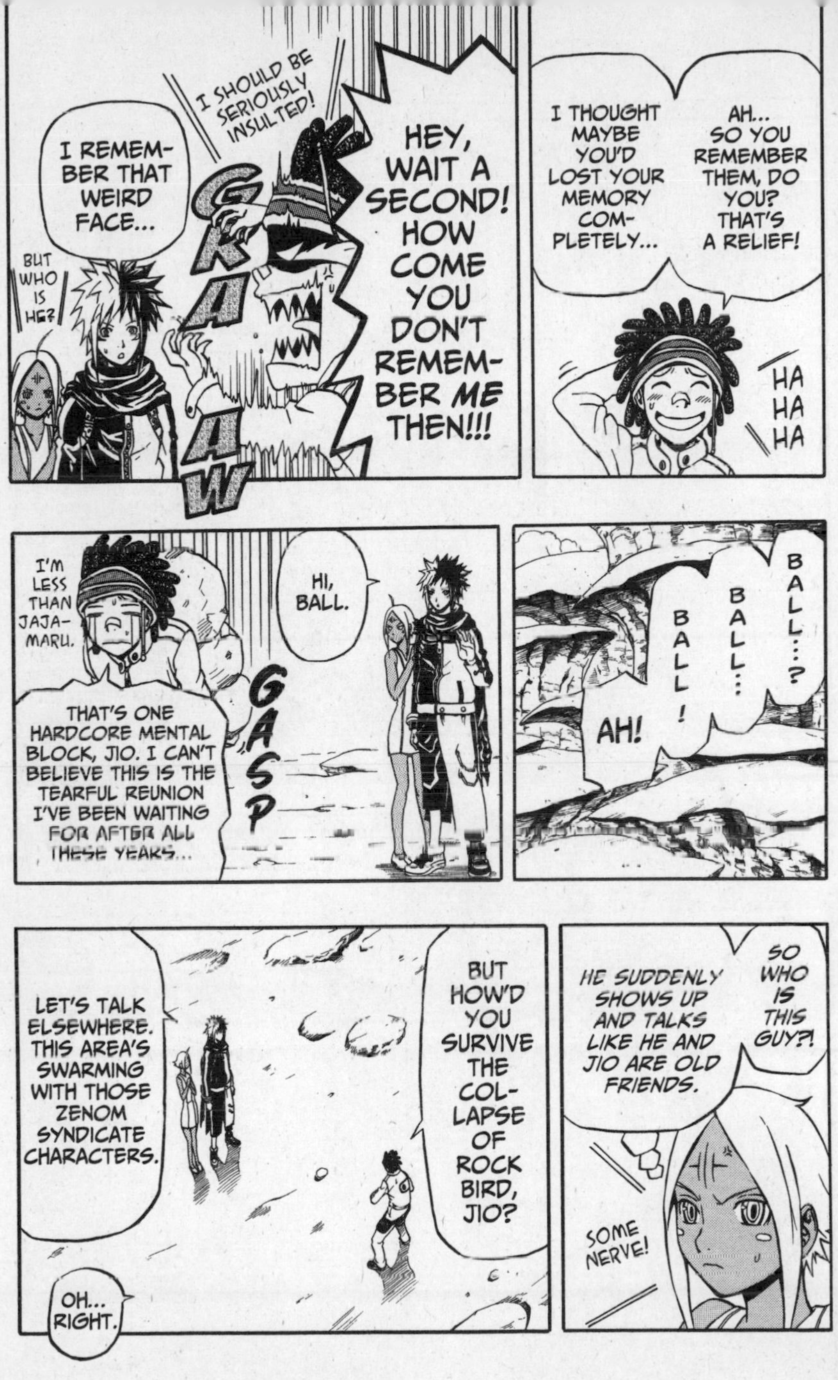
AH... SO YOU REMEMBER THEM, DO YOU? THAT'S A RELIEF!
I THOUGHT MAYBE YOU'D LOST YOUR MEMORY COMPLETELY...
HA HA HA
HEY, WAIT A SECOND! HOW COME YOU DON'T REMEMBER ME THEN!!!
I SHOULD BE SERIOUSLY INSULTED!
GKAAW
I REMEMBER THAT WEIRD FACE...
BUT WHO IS HE?
BALL...?
BALL...
BALL!
AH!
HI, BALL.
GASP
I'M LESS THAN JAJAMARU.
THAT'S ONE HARDCORE MENTAL BLOCK, JIO. I CAN'T BELIEVE THIS IS THE TEARFUL REUNION I'VE BEEN WAITING FOR AFTER ALL THESE YEARS...
SO WHO IS THIS GUY?!
HE SUDDENLY SHOWS UP AND TALKS LIKE HE AND JIO ARE OLD FRIENDS.
SOME NERVE!
BUT HOW'D YOU SURVIVE THE COLLAPSE OF ROCK BIRD, JIO?
LET'S TALK ELSEWHERE. THIS AREA'S SWARMING WITH THOSE ZENOM SYNDICATE CHARACTERS.
OH... RIGHT.

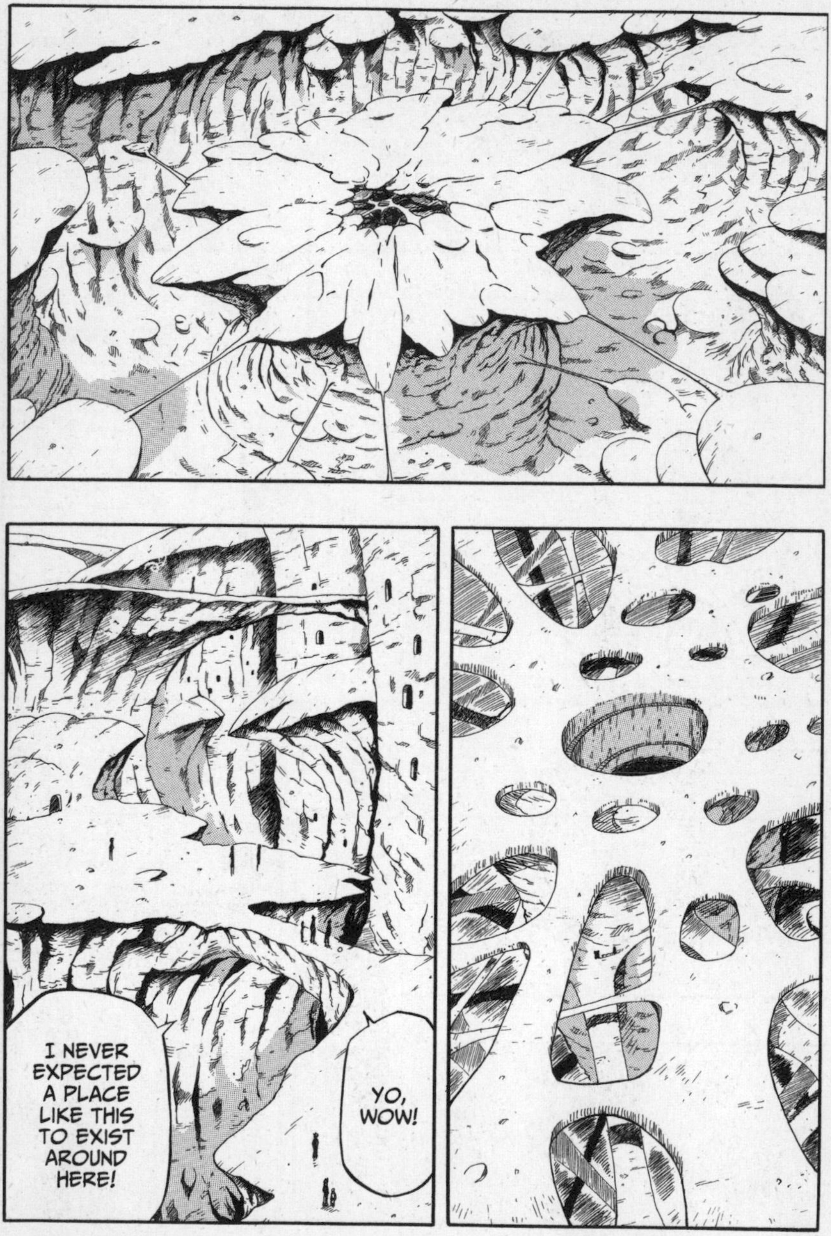
YO, WOW!
I NEVER EXPECTED A PLACE LIKE THIS TO EXIST AROUND HERE!

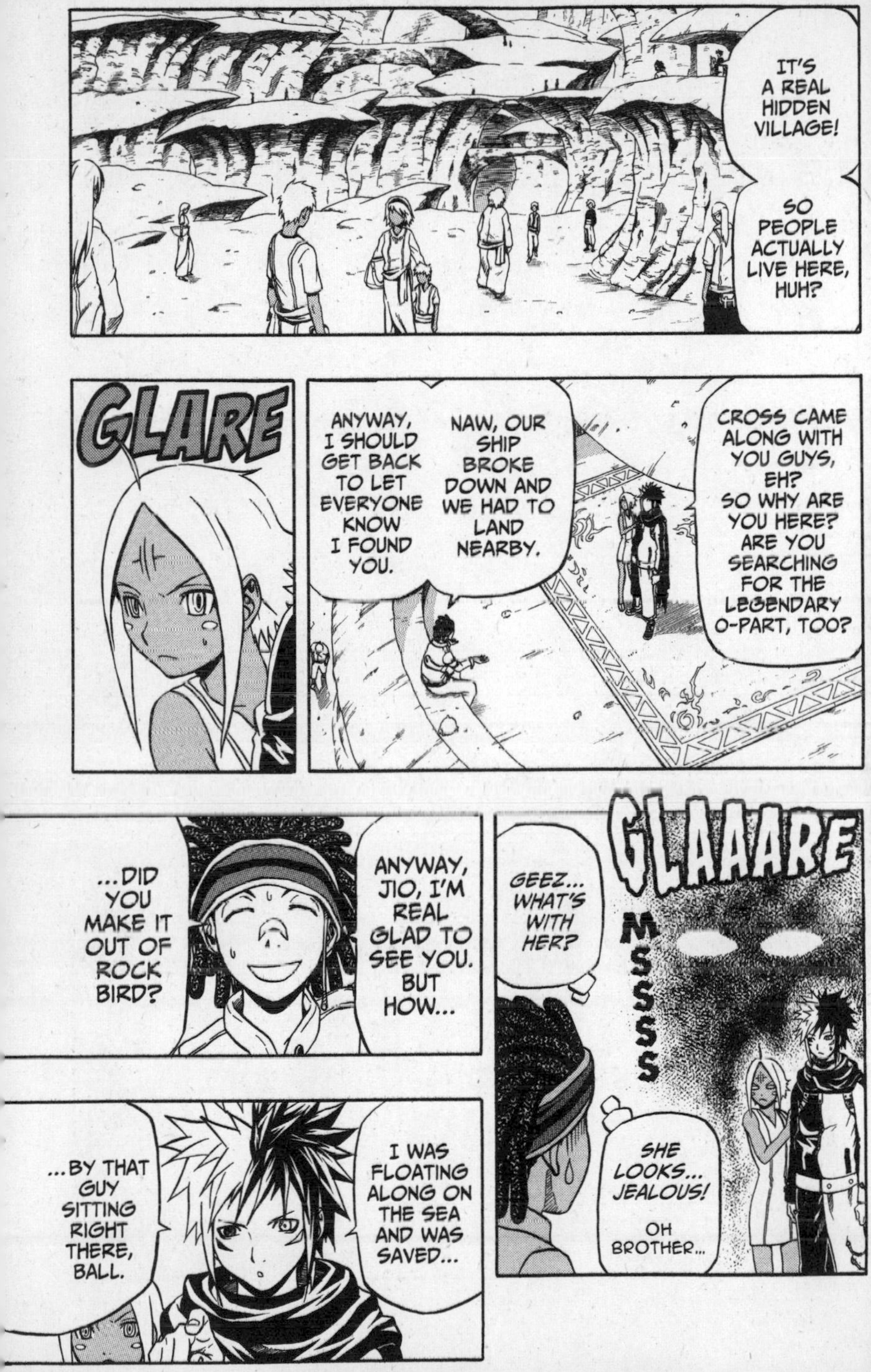

IT'S A REAL HIDDEN VILLAGE!
SO PEOPLE ACTUALLY LIVE HERE, HUH?
CROSS CAME ALONG WITH YOU GUYS, EH? SO WHY ARE YOU HERE? ARE YOU SEARCHING FOR THE LEGENDARY O-PART, TOO?
NAW, OUR SHIP BROKE DOWN AND WE HAD TO LAND NEARBY.
ANYWAY, I SHOULD GET BACK TO LET EVERYONE KNOW I FOUND YOU.
GLARE
GLAAARE
GEEZ... WHAT'S WITH HER?
MSSSS
SHE LOOKS... JEALOUS!
OH BROTHER...
ANYWAY, JIO, I'M REAL GLAD TO SEE YOU. BUT HOW...
...DID YOU MAKE IT OUT OF ROCK BIRD?
I WAS FLOATING ALONG ON THE SEA AND WAS SAVED...
...BY THAT GUY SITTING RIGHT THERE, BALL.

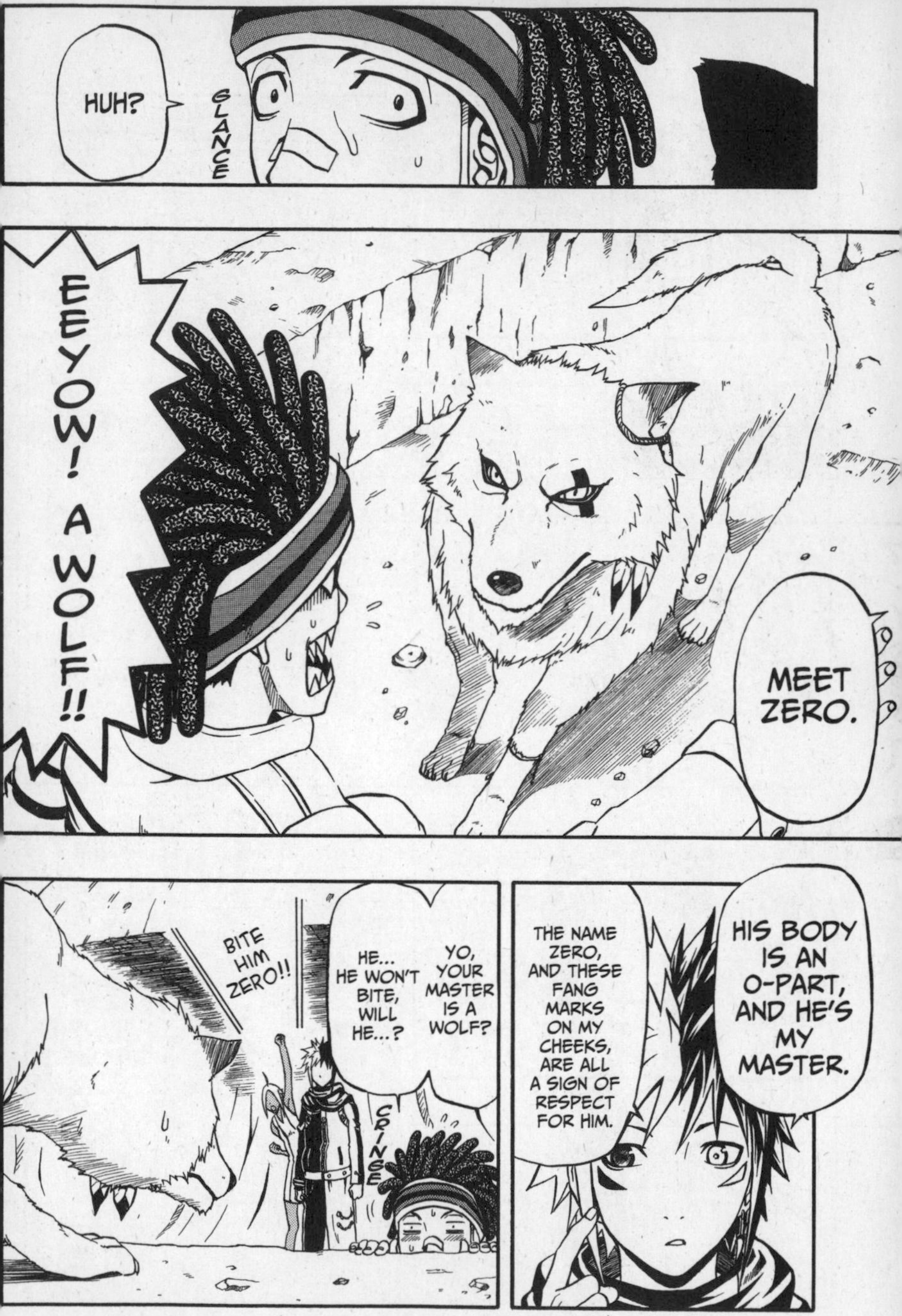
HUH?
GLANCE
MEET ZERO.
EEYOW! A WOLF!!
HIS BODY IS AN O-PART, AND HE'S MY MASTER.
THE NAME ZERO, AND THESE FANG MARKS ON MY CHEEKS, ARE ALL A SIGN OF RESPECT FOR HIM.
YO, YOUR MASTER IS A WOLF?
HE... HE WON'T BITE, WILL HE...?
BITE HIM ZERO!!
CRINGE

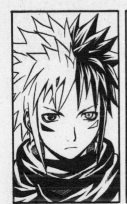

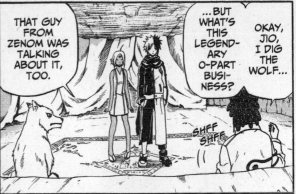

OKAY, JIO, I DIG THE WOLF...
...BUT WHAT'S THIS LEGENDARY O-PART BUSINESS?
SHFF SHFF
THAT GUY FROM ZENOM WAS TALKING ABOUT IT, TOO.
IT'S HERE IN THIS VILLAGE.
THE ZENOM SYNDICATE KNOWS THAT, BUT HAS NO IDEA JUST WHERE THE VILLAGE IS.
BUT IT'S ONLY A MATTER OF TIME UNTIL THEY FIND IT.
AS FOR ME, IT'S THANKS TO THESE PEOPLE THAT I SURVIVED.
NOT ONLY THAT, THEY'VE ACCEPTED ME, EVEN THOUGH I BRING BAD LUCK.
I'M OBLIGED, AND QUITE READY, TO PROTECT THEM FROM THE SYNDICATE.

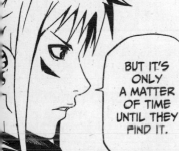

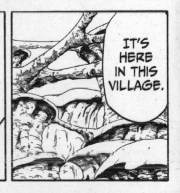

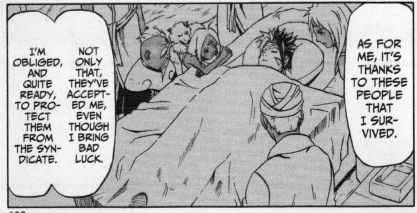

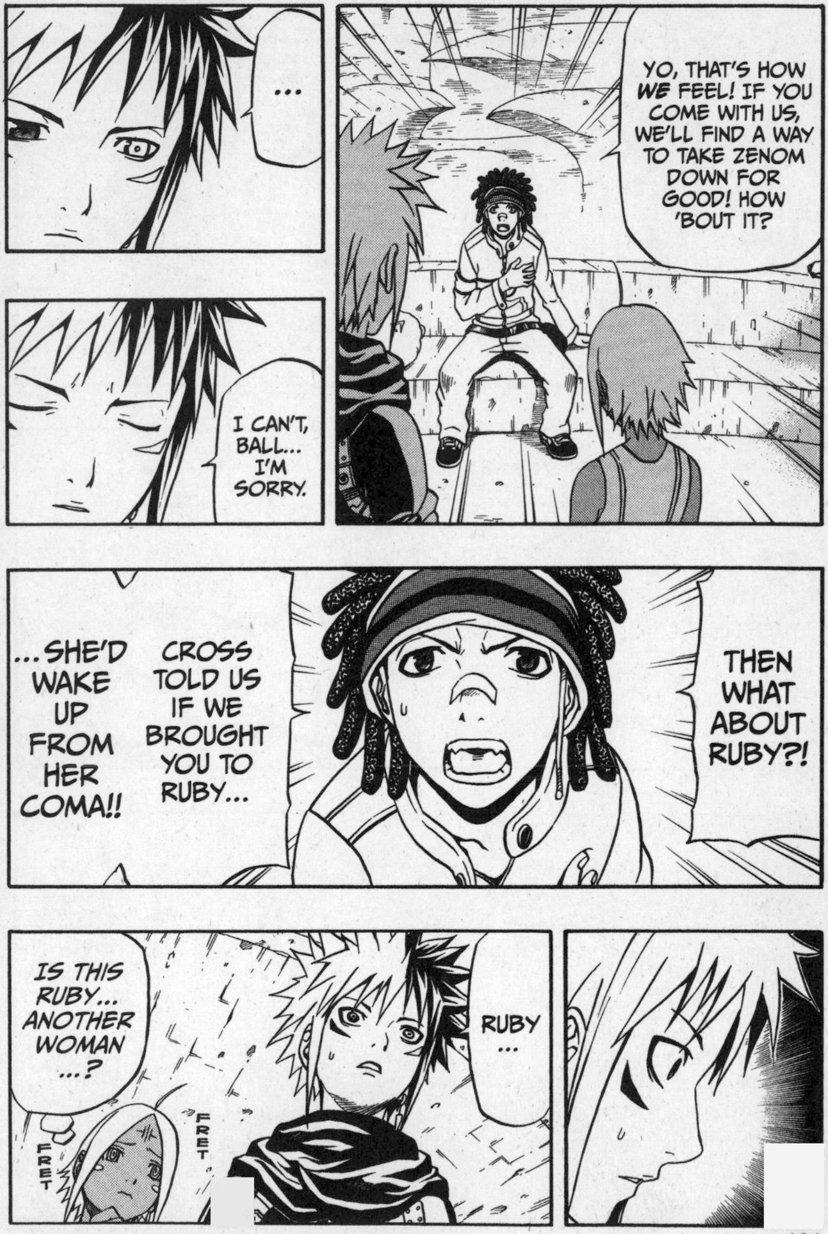
YO, THAT'S HOW WE FEEL! IF YOU COME WITH US, WE'LL FIND A WAY TO TAKE ZENOM DOWN FOR GOOD! HOW 'BOUT IT?
...
I CAN'T, BALL... I'M SORRY.
THEN WHAT ABOUT RUBY?!
CROSS TOLD US IF WE BROUGHT YOU TO RUBY...
...SHE'D WAKE UP FROM HER COMA!!
RUBY ...
IS THIS RUBY... ANOTHER WOMAN ...?
FRET
FRET

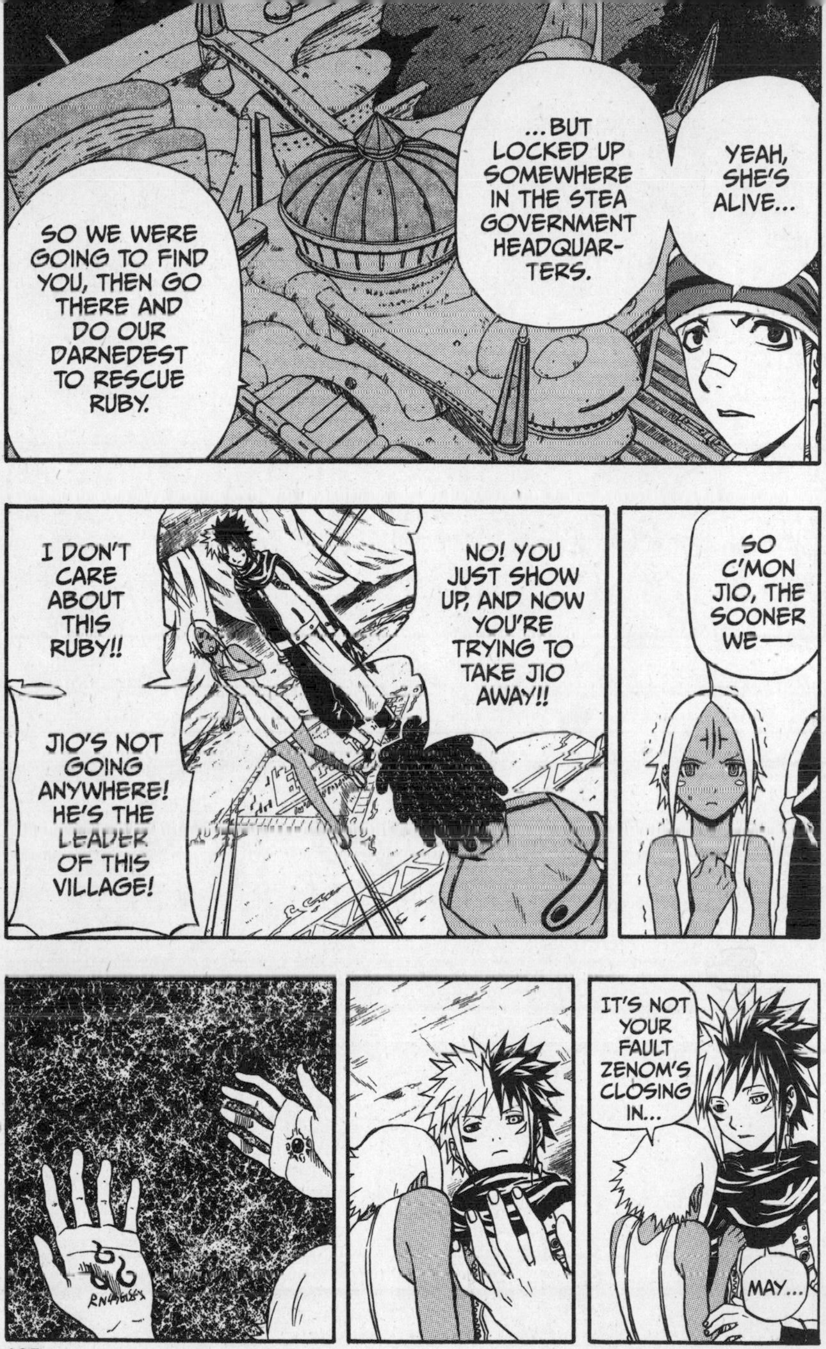
YEAH, SHE'S ALIVE...
...BUT LOCKED UP SOMEWHERE IN THE STEA GOVERNMENT HEADQUAR-TERS.
SO WE WERE GOING TO FIND YOU, THEN GO THERE AND DO OUR DARNEDEST TO RESCUE RUBY.
SO C'MON JIO, THE SOONER WE—
NO! YOU JUST SHOW UP, AND NOW YOU'RE TRYING TO TAKE JIO AWAY!!
I DON'T CARE ABOUT THIS RUBY!!
JIO'S NOT GOING ANYWHERE! HE'S THE LEADER OF THIS VILLAGE!
IT'S NOT YOUR FAULT ZENOM'S CLOSING IN...
MAY...

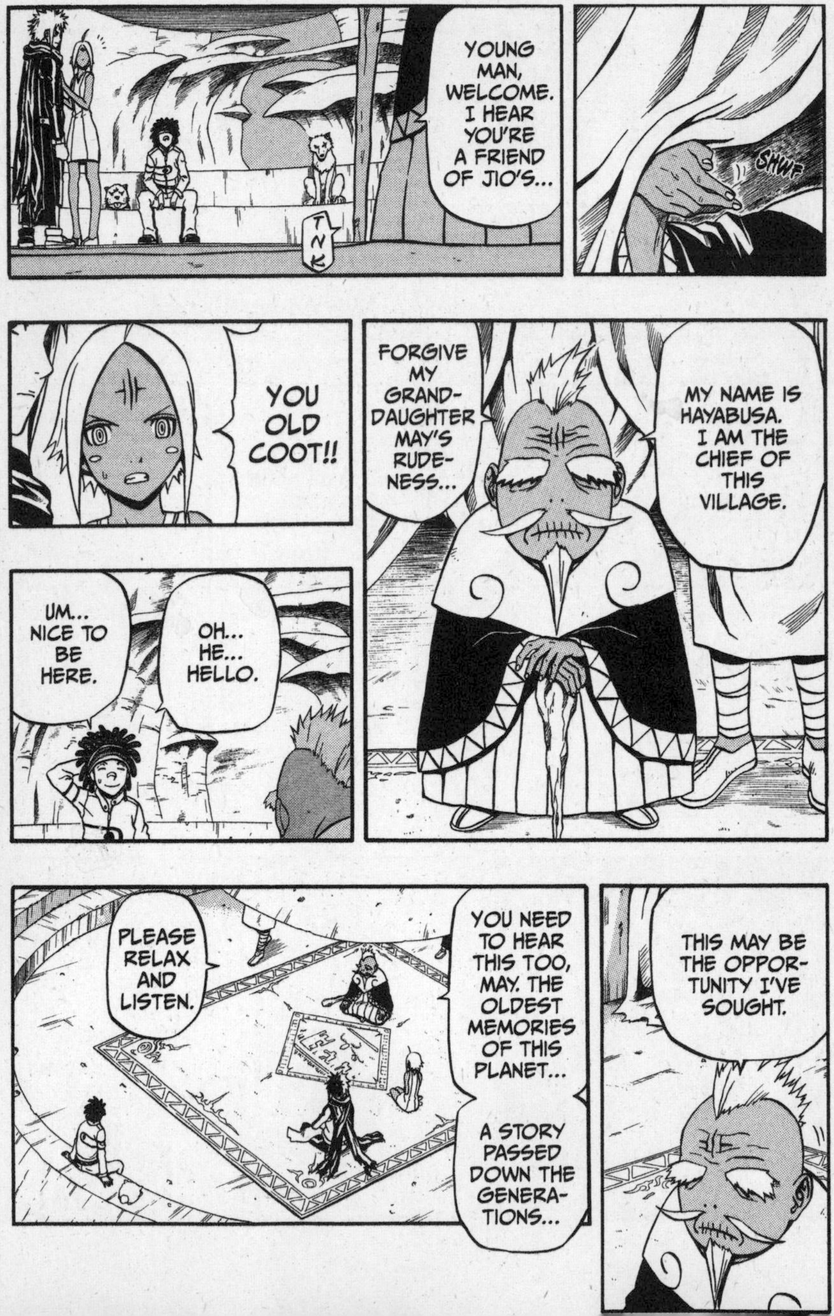
SHWF
YOUNG MAN, WELCOME. I HEAR YOU'RE A FRIEND OF JIO'S...
TNK
MY NAME IS HAYABUSA. I AM THE CHIEF OF THIS VILLAGE.
FORGIVE MY GRAND-DAUGHTER MAY'S RUDE-NESS...
YOU OLD COOT!!
OH... HE... HELLO.
UM... NICE TO BE HERE.
THIS MAY BE THE OPPOR-TUNITY I'VE SOUGHT.
YOU NEED TO HEAR THIS TOO, MAY. THE OLDEST MEMORIES OF THIS PLANET...
A STORY PASSED DOWN THE GENERA-TIONS...
PLEASE RELAX AND LISTEN.

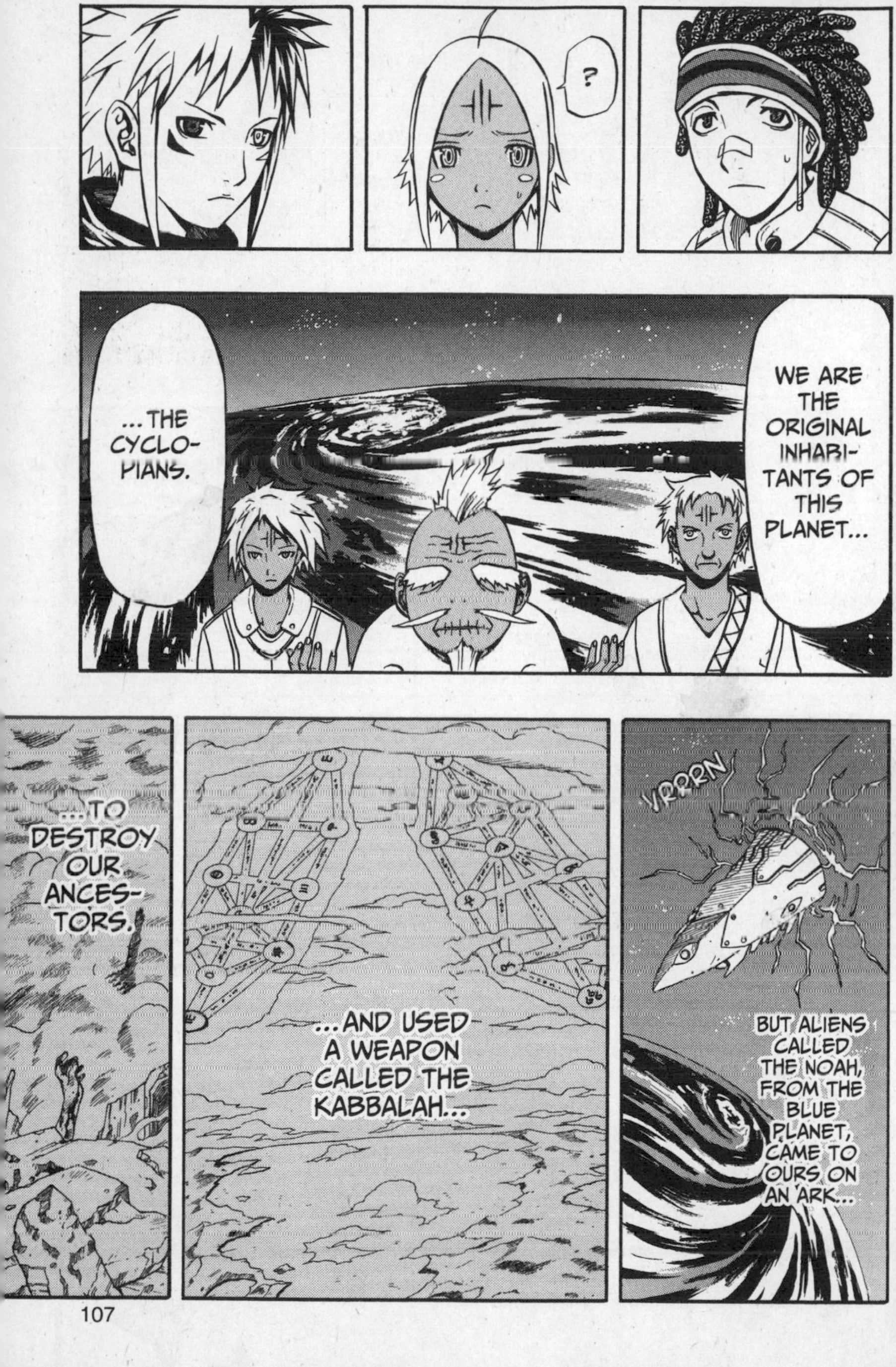
?
WE ARE THE ORIGINAL INHABI-TANTS OF THIS PLANET...
...THE CYCLO-PIANS.
VRRRN
BUT ALIENS CALLED THE NOAH, FROM THE BLUE PLANET, CAME TO OURS ON AN ARK...
...AND USED A WEAPON CALLED THE KABBALAH...
...TO DESTROY OUR ANCES-TORS.

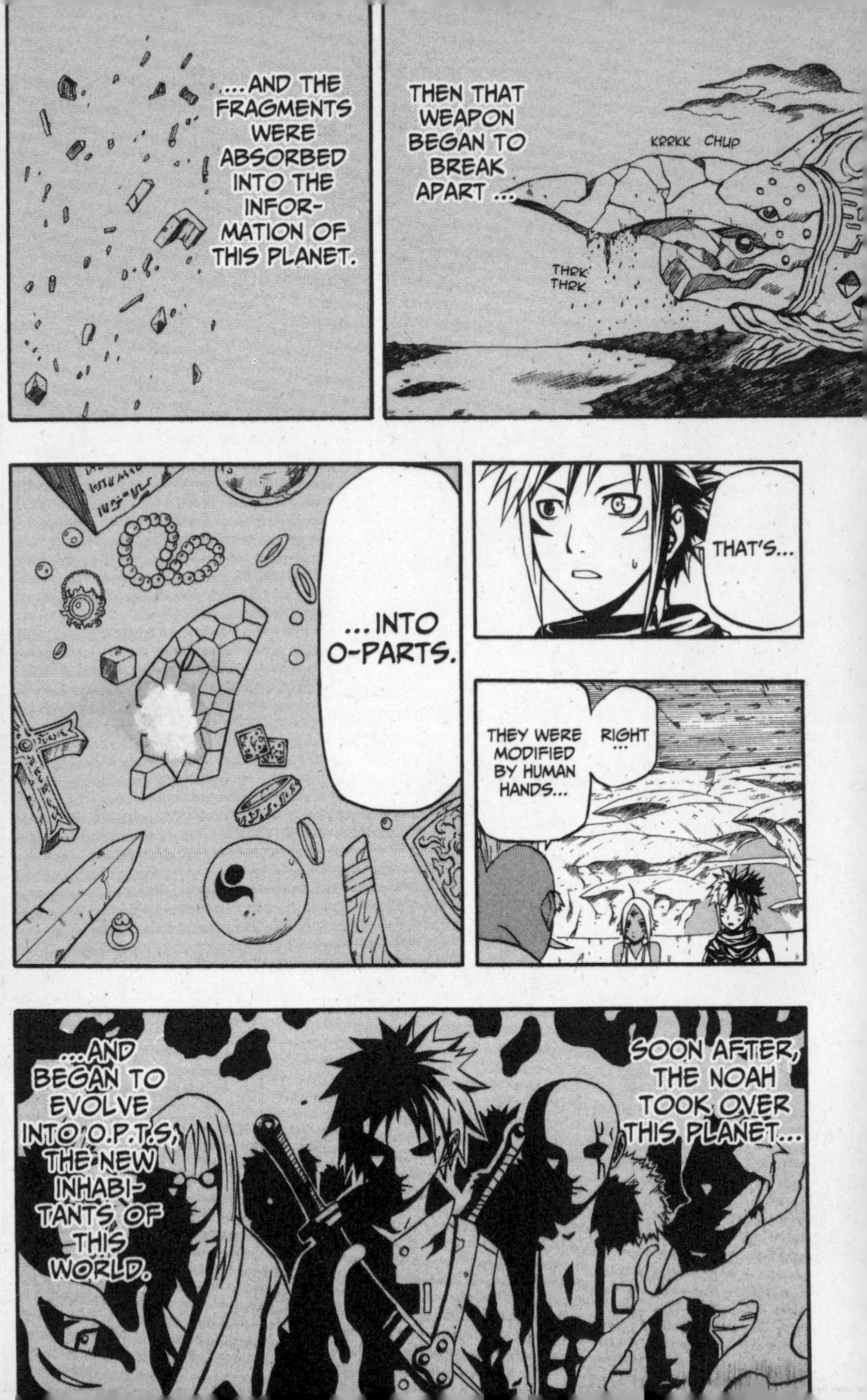
THEN THAT WEAPON BEGAN TO BREAK APART ...
KRRKK CHUP
THRK THRK
...AND THE FRAGMENTS WERE ABSORBED INTO THE INFOR-MATION OF THIS PLANET.
THAT'S...
RIGHT ...
THEY WERE MODIFIED BY HUMAN HANDS...
...INTO O-PARTS.
SOON AFTER, THE NOAH TOOK OVER THIS PLANET...
...AND BEGAN TO EVOLVE INTO O.P.T.S, THE NEW INHABI-TANTS OF THIS WORLD.

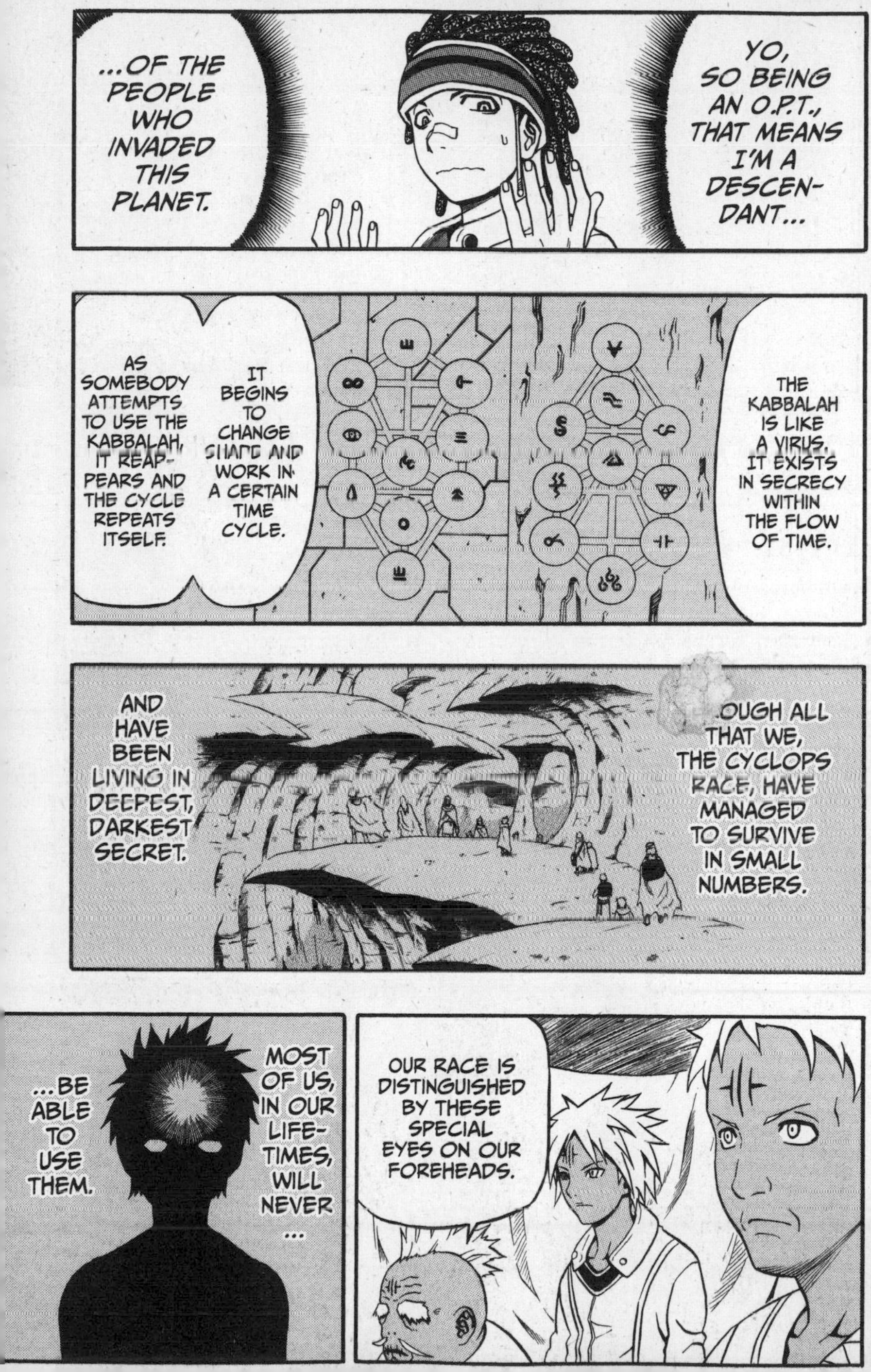

YO, SO BEING AN O.P.T., THAT MEANS I'M A DESCENDANT...
...OF THE PEOPLE WHO INVADED THIS PLANET.
THE KABBALAH IS LIKE A VIRUS. IT EXISTS IN SECRECY WITHIN THE FLOW OF TIME.
IT BEGINS TO CHANGE SHAPE AND WORK IN A CERTAIN TIME CYCLE.
AS SOMEBODY ATTEMPTS TO USE THE KABBALAH, IT REAPPEARS AND THE CYCLE REPEATS ITSELF.
...OUGH ALL THAT WE, THE CYCLOPS RACE, HAVE MANAGED TO SURVIVE IN SMALL NUMBERS.
AND HAVE BEEN LIVING IN DEEPEST, DARKEST SECRET.
OUR RACE IS DISTINGUISHED BY THESE SPECIAL EYES ON OUR FOREHEADS.
MOST OF US, IN OUR LIFETIMES, WILL NEVER...
...BE ABLE TO USE THEM.

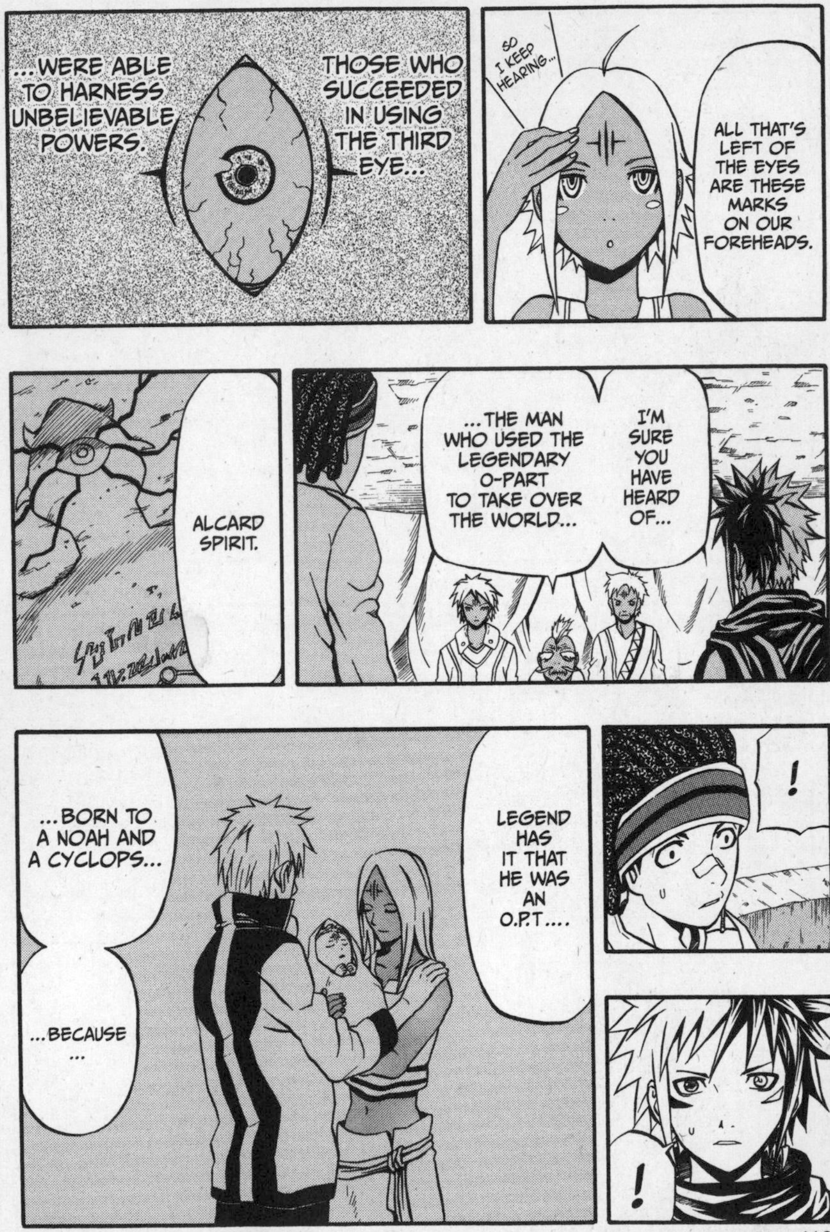
ALL THAT'S LEFT OF THE EYES ARE THESE MARKS ON OUR FOREHEADS.
SO I KEEP HEARING...
THOSE WHO SUCCEEDED IN USING THE THIRD EYE...
...WERE ABLE TO HARNESS UNBELIEVABLE POWERS.
I'M SURE YOU HAVE HEARD OF...
...THE MAN WHO USED THE LEGENDARY O-PART TO TAKE OVER THE WORLD...
ALCARD SPIRIT.
!
!
LEGEND HAS IT THAT HE WAS AN O.P.T....
...BORN TO A NOAH AND A CYCLOPS...
...BECAUSE ...

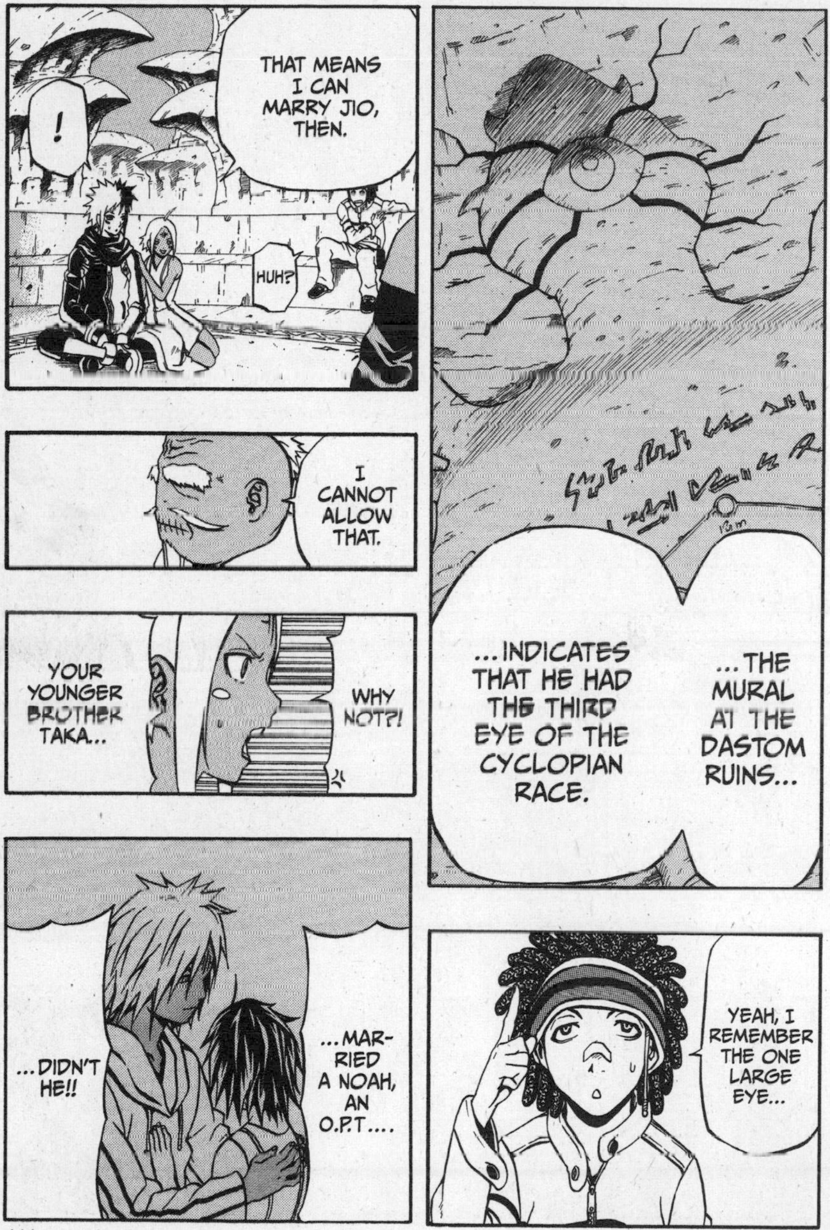
...THE MURAL AT THE DASTOM RUINS...
...INDICATES THAT HE HAD THE THIRD EYE OF THE CYCLOPIAN RACE.
THAT MEANS I CAN MARRY JIO, THEN.
!
HUH?
I CANNOT ALLOW THAT.
WHY NOT?!
YOUR YOUNGER BROTHER TAKA...
YEAH, I REMEMBER THE ONE LARGE EYE...
...MAR-RIED A NOAH, AN O.P.T....
...DIDN'T HE!!

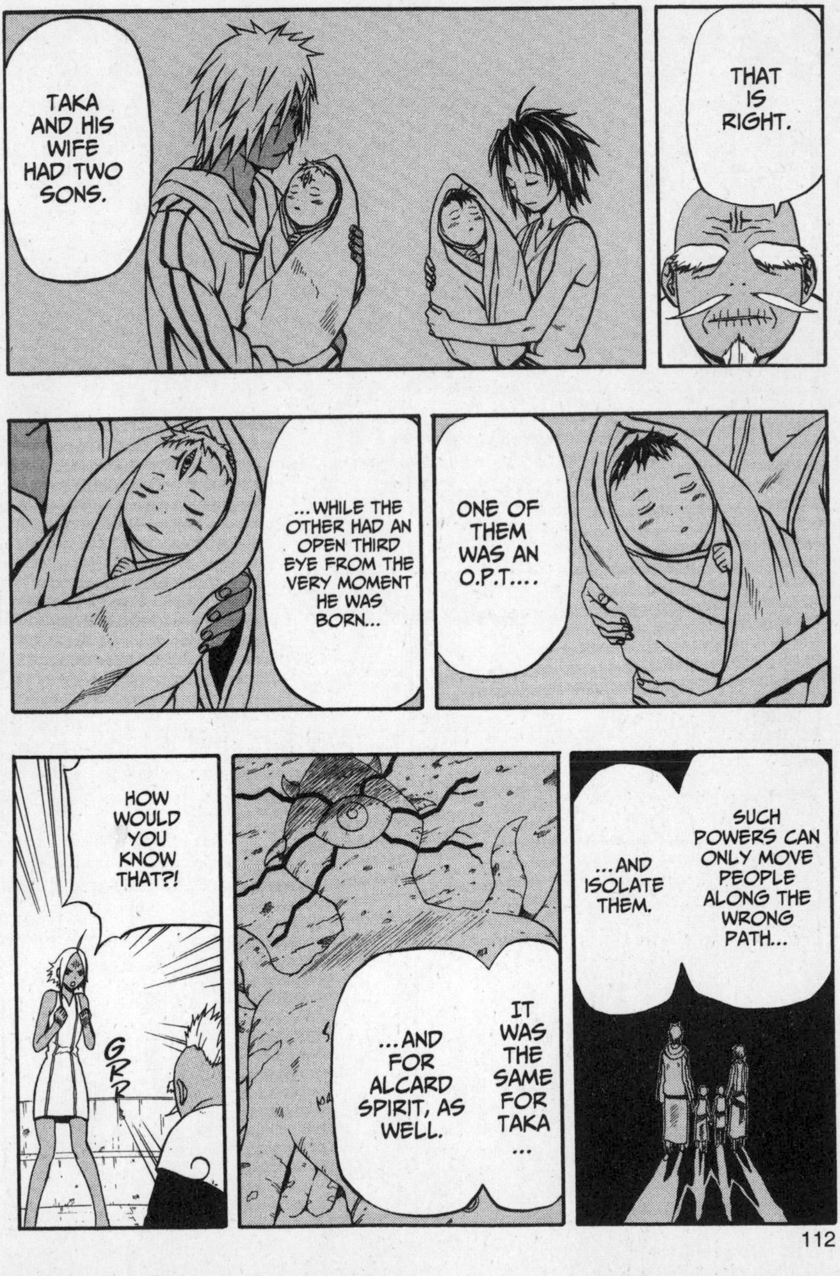
THAT IS RIGHT.
TAKA AND HIS WIFE HAD TWO SONS.
ONE OF THEM WAS AN O.P.T....
...WHILE THE OTHER HAD AN OPEN THIRD EYE FROM THE VERY MOMENT HE WAS BORN...
SUCH POWERS CAN ONLY MOVE PEOPLE ALONG THE WRONG PATH...
...AND ISOLATE THEM.
IT WAS THE SAME FOR TAKA...
...AND FOR ALCARD SPIRIT, AS WELL.
HOW WOULD YOU KNOW THAT?!
GRR

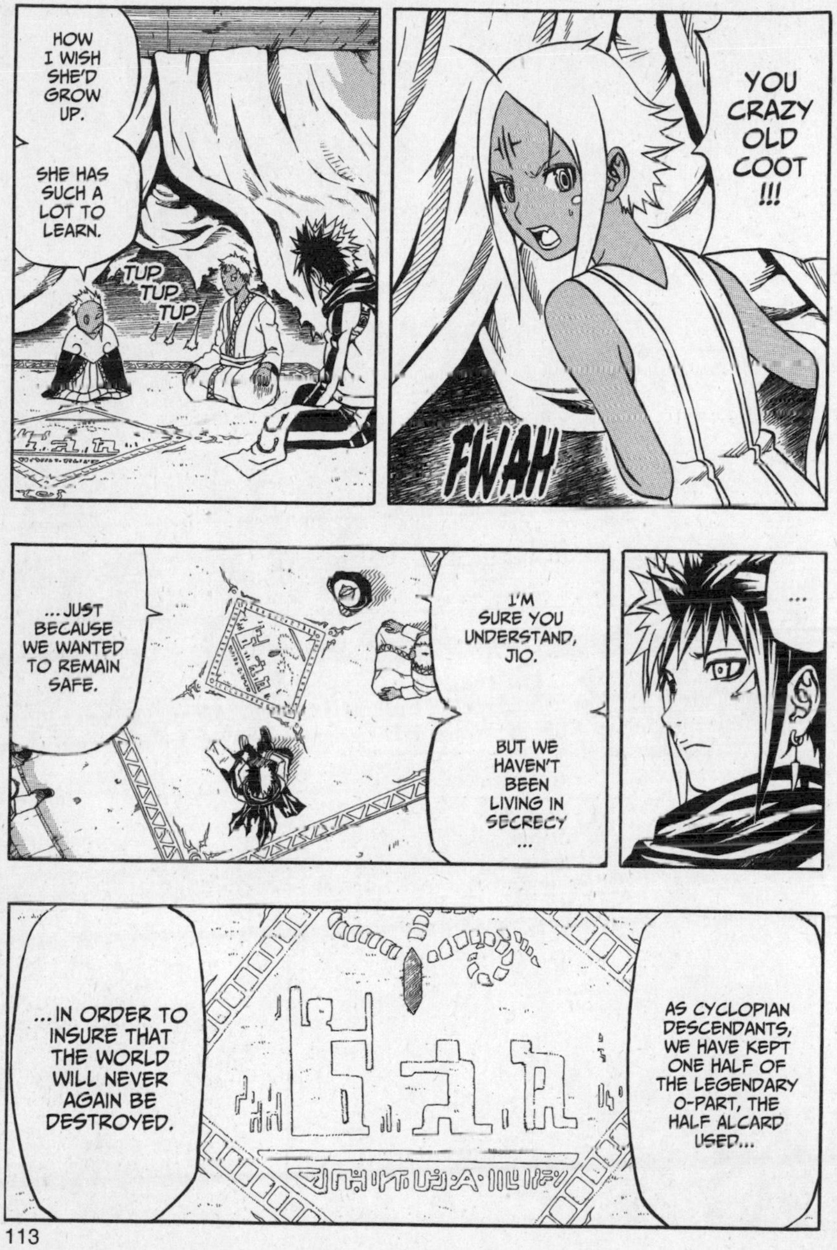
YOU CRAZY OLD COOT!!!
FWAH
HOW I WISH SHE'D GROW UP.
SHE HAS SUCH A LOT TO LEARN.
TUP TUP TUP
...
I'M SURE YOU UNDERSTAND, JIO.
BUT WE HAVEN'T BEEN LIVING IN SECRECY...
...JUST BECAUSE WE WANTED TO REMAIN SAFE.
AS CYCLOPIAN DESCENDANTS, WE HAVE KEPT ONE HALF OF THE LEGENDARY O-PART, THE HALF ALCARD USED...
...IN ORDER TO INSURE THAT THE WORLD WILL NEVER AGAIN BE DESTROYED.

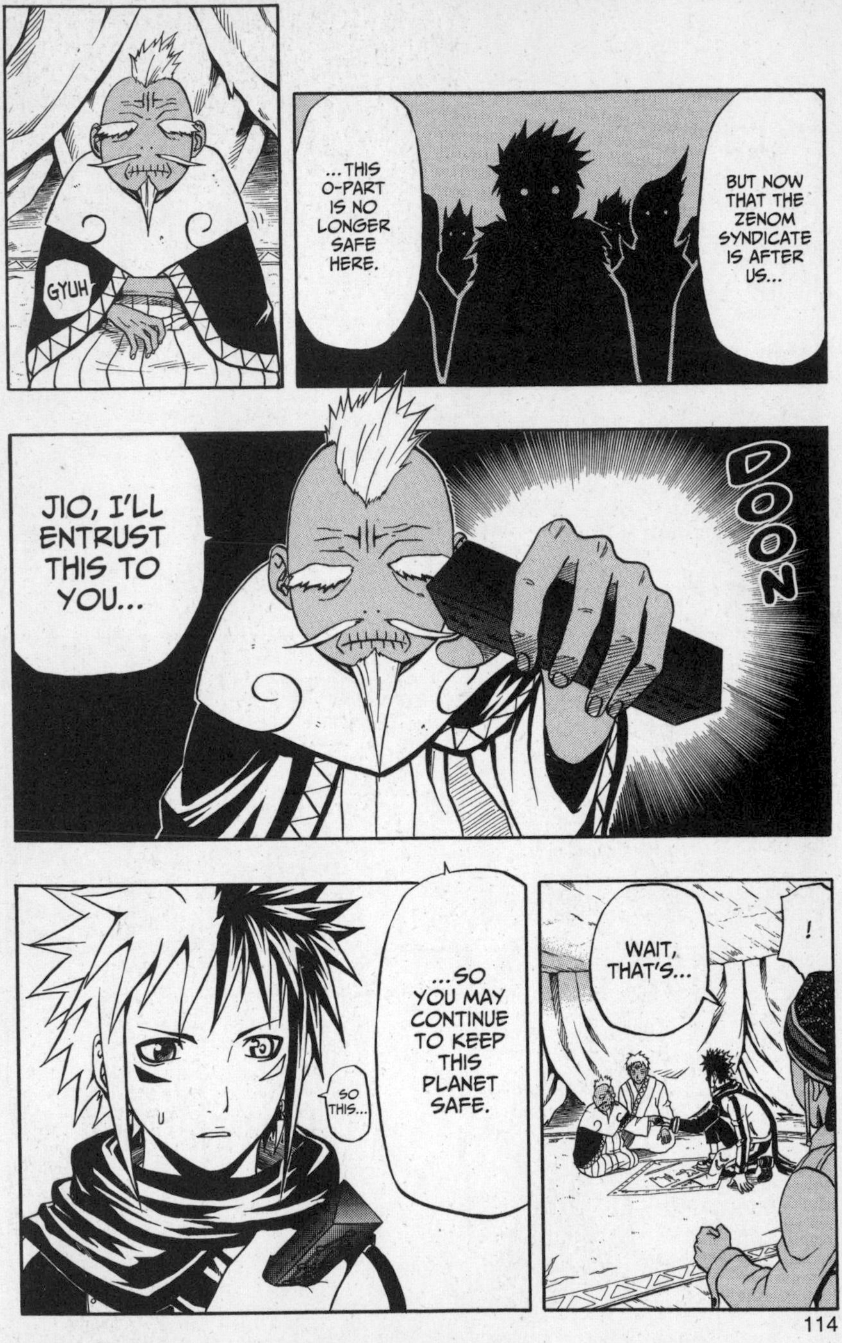
BUT NOW THAT THE ZENOM SYNDICATE IS AFTER US...
...THIS O-PART IS NO LONGER SAFE HERE.
GYUH
DOON
JIO, I'LL ENTRUST THIS TO YOU...
!
WAIT, THAT'S...
...SO YOU MAY CONTINUE TO KEEP THIS PLANET SAFE.
SO THIS...

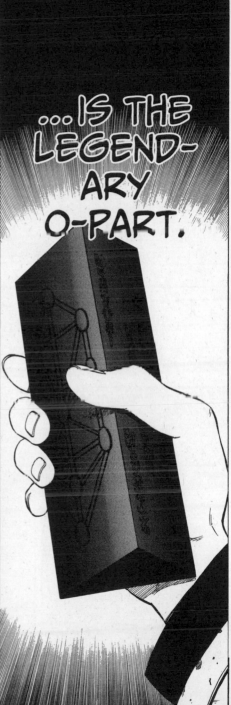

...IS THE LEGEND-ARY O-PART.

CHIEF !!!

CH... CHIEF !!

FWOM

WHAT'S WRONG ?!

IT...IT'S ABOUT YOUR GRAND-DAUGHTER!

MAY !!

!

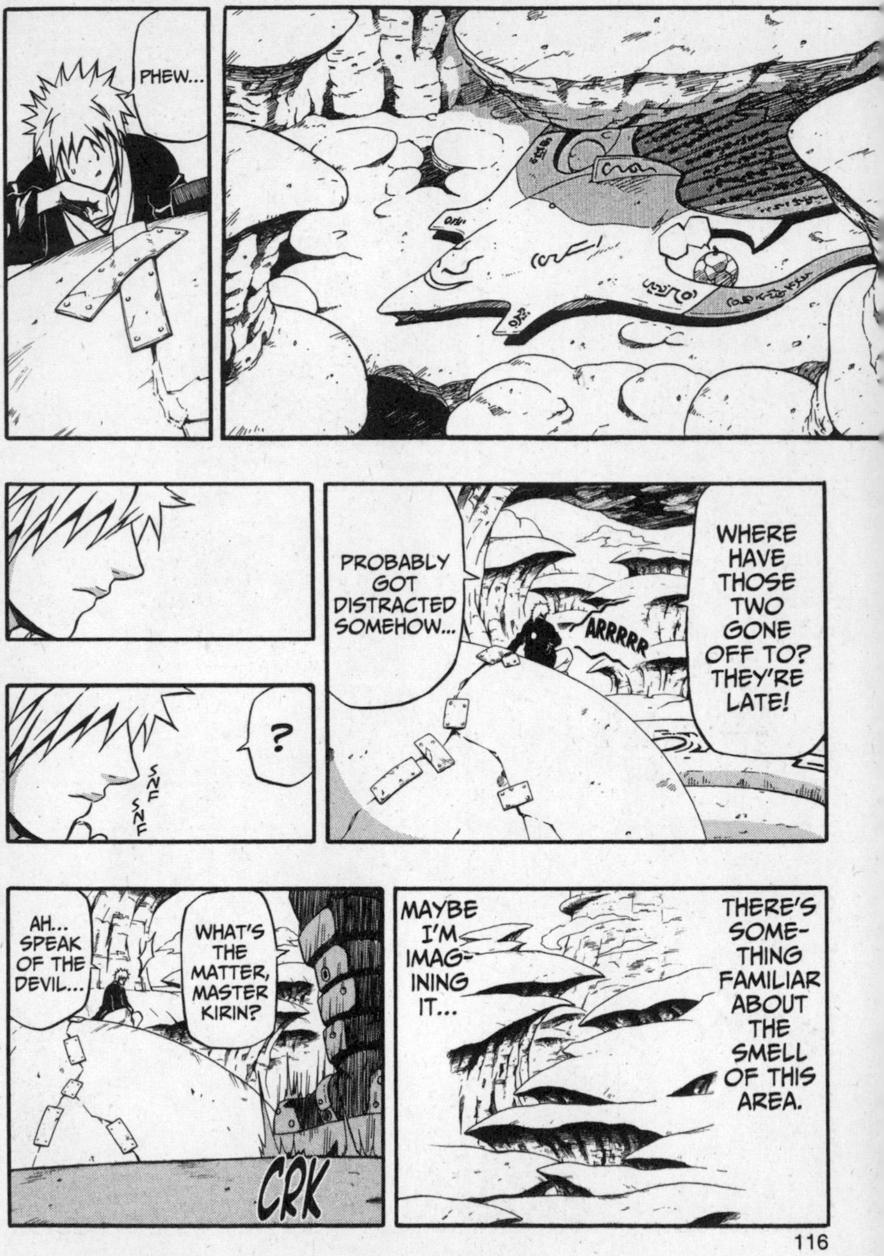
PHEW...
WHERE HAVE THOSE TWO GONE OFF TO? THEY'RE LATE!
PROBABLY GOT DISTRACTED SOMEHOW...
ARRRRR
?
SNF SNF
THERE'S SOME-THING FAMILIAR ABOUT THE SMELL OF THIS AREA.
MAYBE I'M IMAG-INING IT...
WHAT'S THE MATTER, MASTER KIRIN?
AH... SPEAK OF THE DEVIL...
CRK

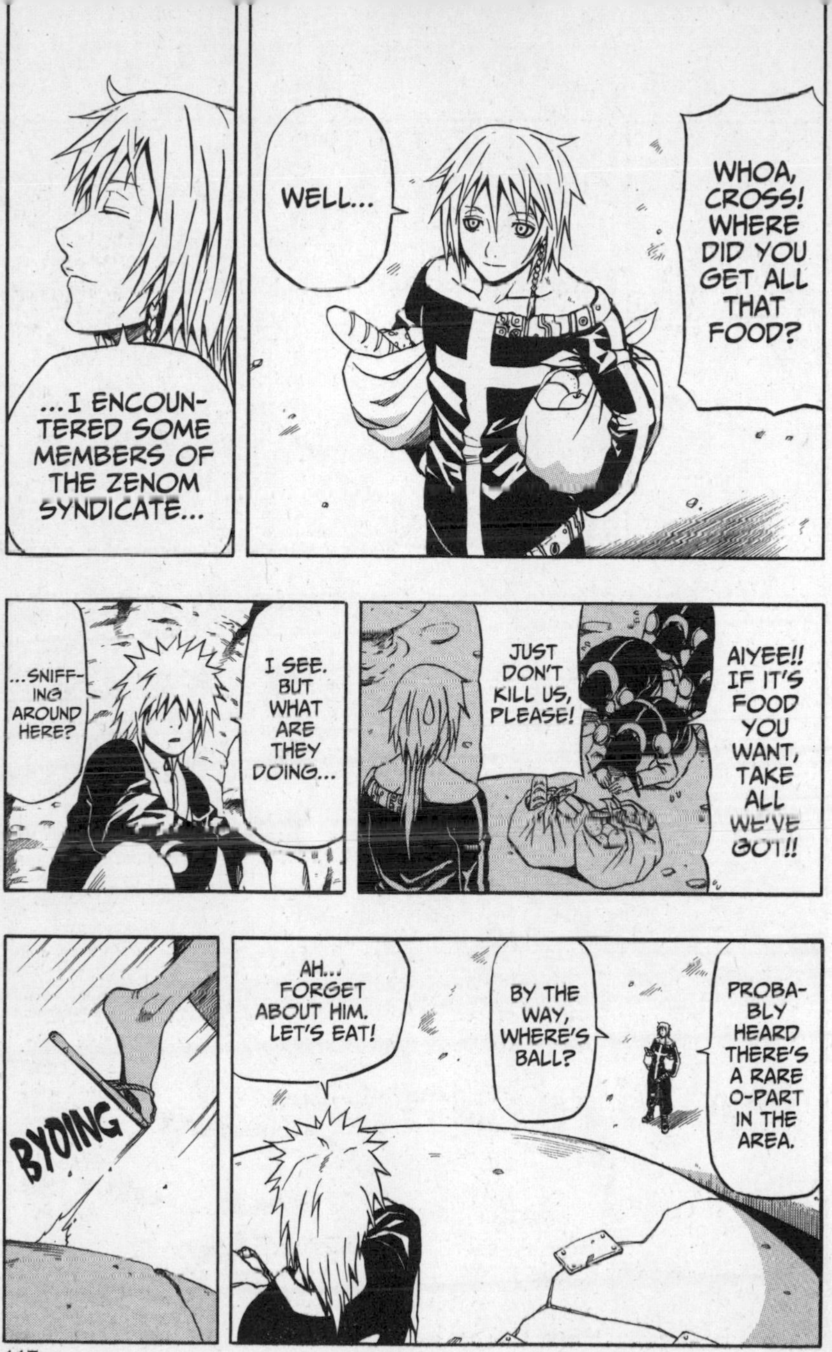
WHOA, CROSS! WHERE DID YOU GET ALL THAT FOOD?
WELL...
...I ENCOUNTERED SOME MEMBERS OF THE ZENOM SYNDICATE...
AIYEE!! IF IT'S FOOD YOU WANT, TAKE ALL WE'VE GOT!!
JUST DON'T KILL US, PLEASE!
I SEE. BUT WHAT ARE THEY DOING...
...SNIFFING AROUND HERE?
PROBABLY HEARD THERE'S A RARE O-PART IN THE AREA.
BY THE WAY, WHERE'S BALL?
AH... FORGET ABOUT HIM. LET'S EAT!
BYOING

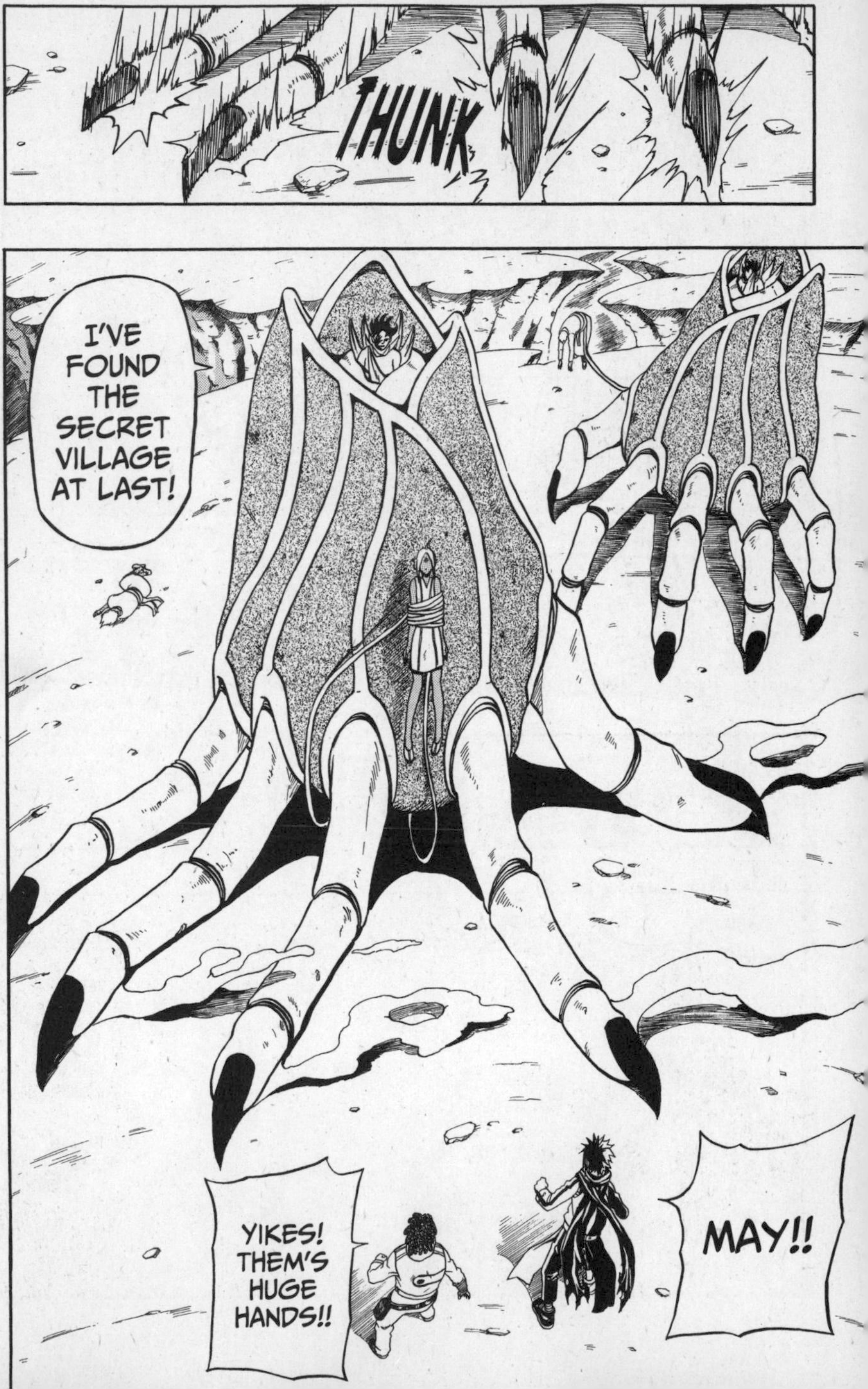
THUNK
I'VE FOUND THE SECRET VILLAGE AT LAST!
MAY!!
YIKES! THEM'S HUGE HANDS!!

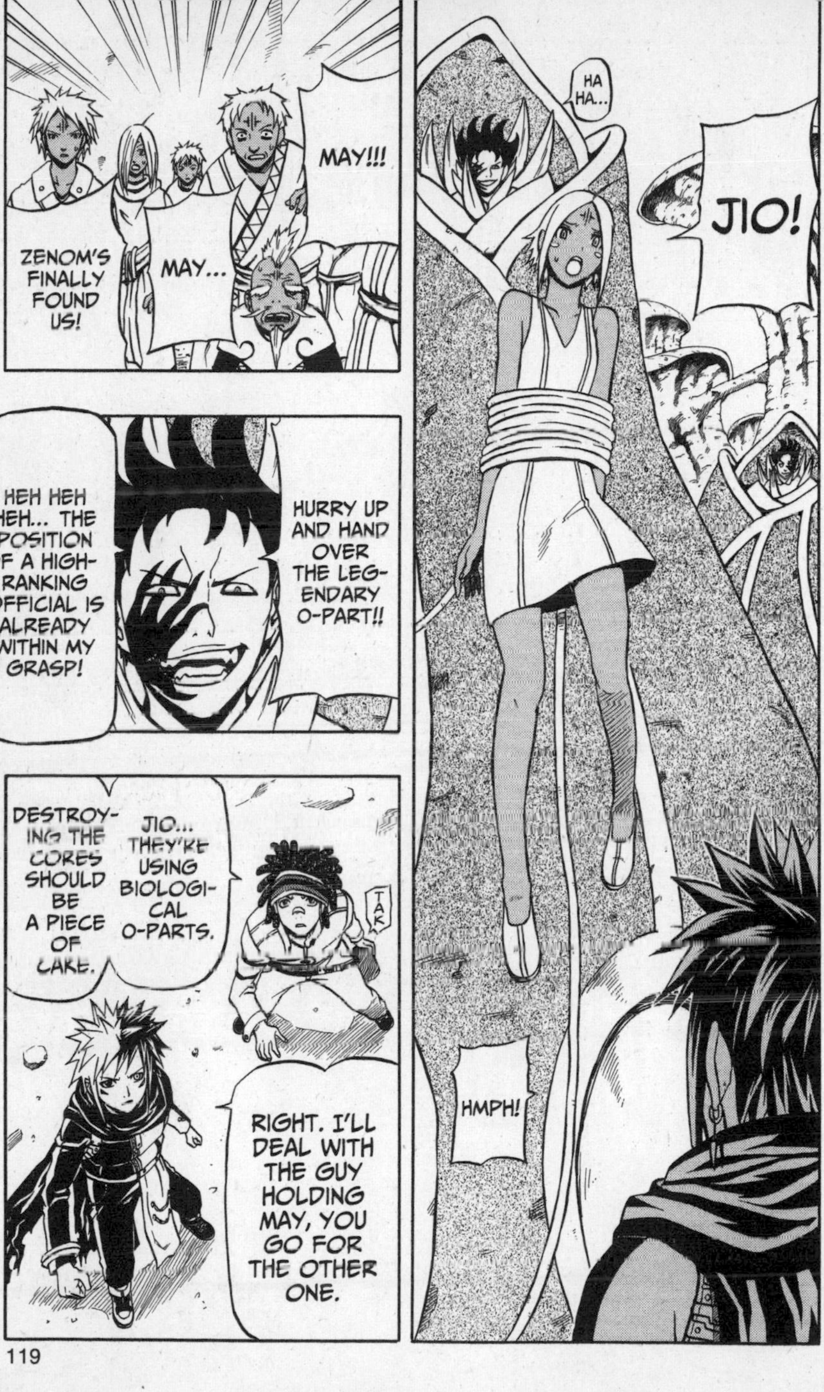
HA HA...
JIO!
HMPH!
MAY!!!
MAY...
ZENOM'S FINALLY FOUND US!
HURRY UP AND HAND OVER THE LEG-ENDARY O-PART!!
HEH HEH HEH... THE POSITION OF A HIGH-RANKING OFFICIAL IS ALREADY WITHIN MY GRASP!
JIO... THEY'RE USING BIOLOGI-CAL O-PARTS.
TAK
DESTROY-ING THE CORES SHOULD BE A PIECE OF CAKE.
RIGHT. I'LL DEAL WITH THE GUY HOLDING MAY, YOU GO FOR THE OTHER ONE.

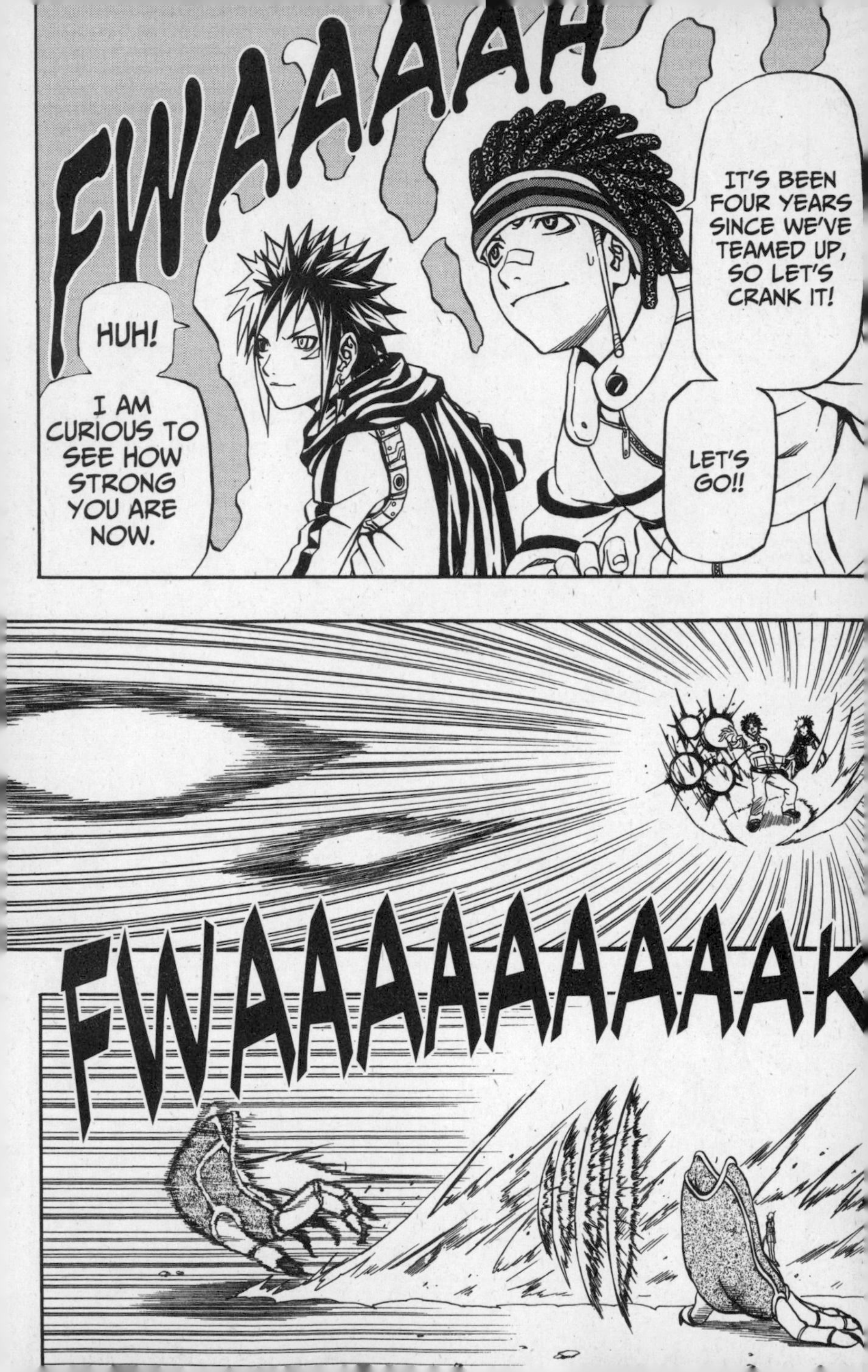
FWAAAAAH
IT'S BEEN FOUR YEARS SINCE WE'VE TEAMED UP, SO LET'S CRANK IT!
LET'S GO!!
HUH!
I AM CURIOUS TO SEE HOW STRONG YOU ARE NOW.
FWAAAAAAAAAK

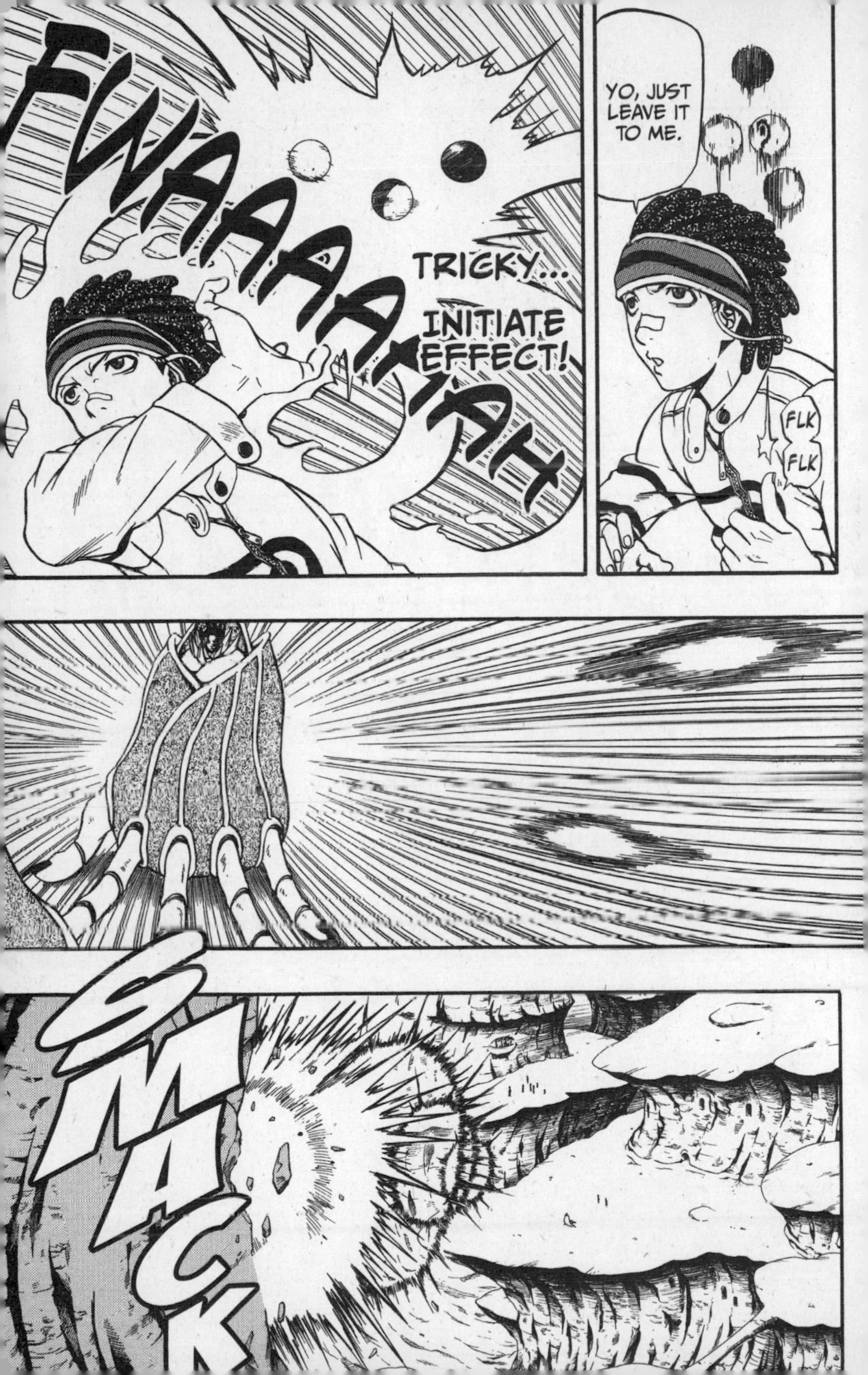
YO, JUST LEAVE IT TO ME.
FLK FLK
FWAAAAAAAH
TRICKY...
INITIATE EFFECT!
SMACK

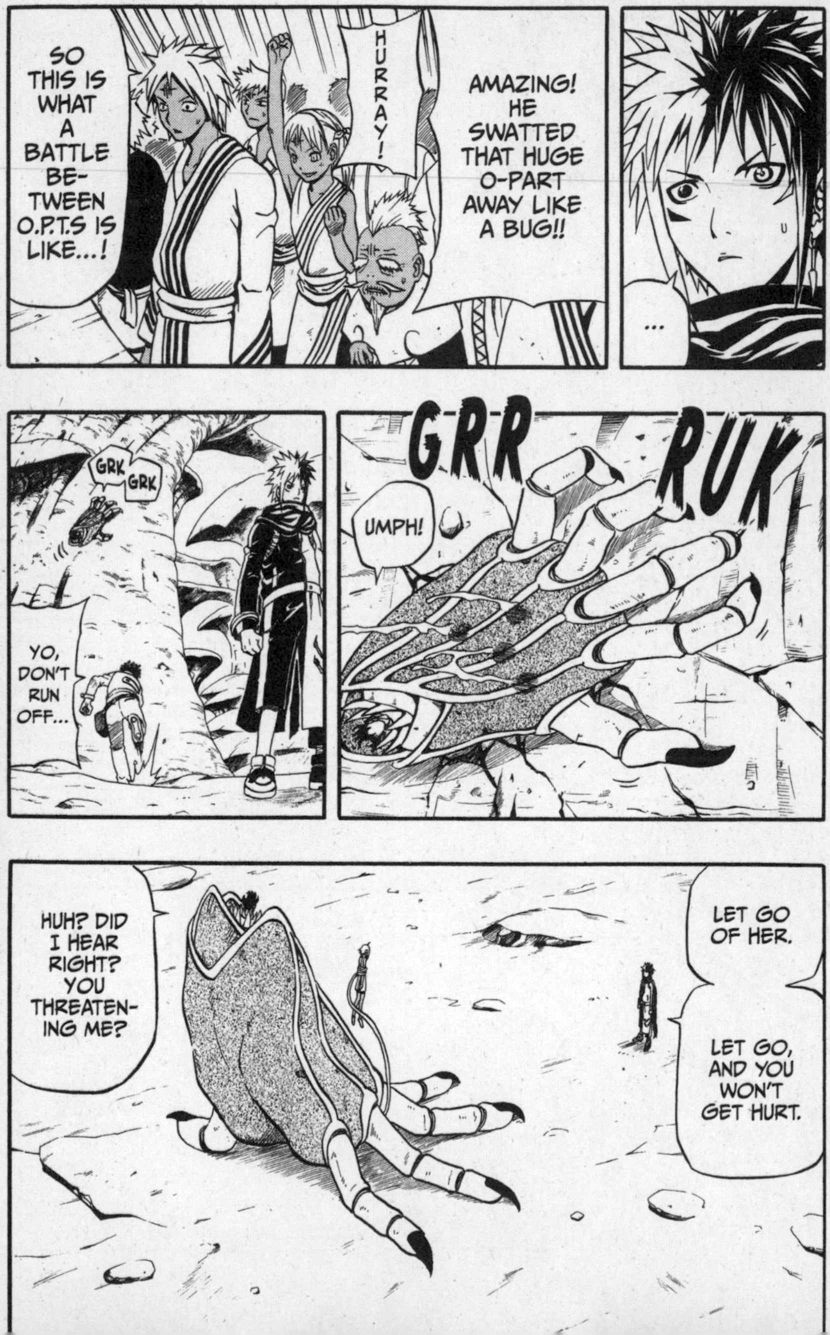
...
AMAZING! HE SWATTED THAT HUGE O-PART AWAY LIKE A BUG!!
HURRAY!
SO THIS IS WHAT A BATTLE BE-TWEEN O.P.T.S IS LIKE...!
GRR RUK
UMPH!
GRK
GRK
YO, DON'T RUN OFF...
LET GO OF HER.
LET GO, AND YOU WON'T GET HURT.
HUH? DID I HEAR RIGHT? YOU THREATEN-ING ME?

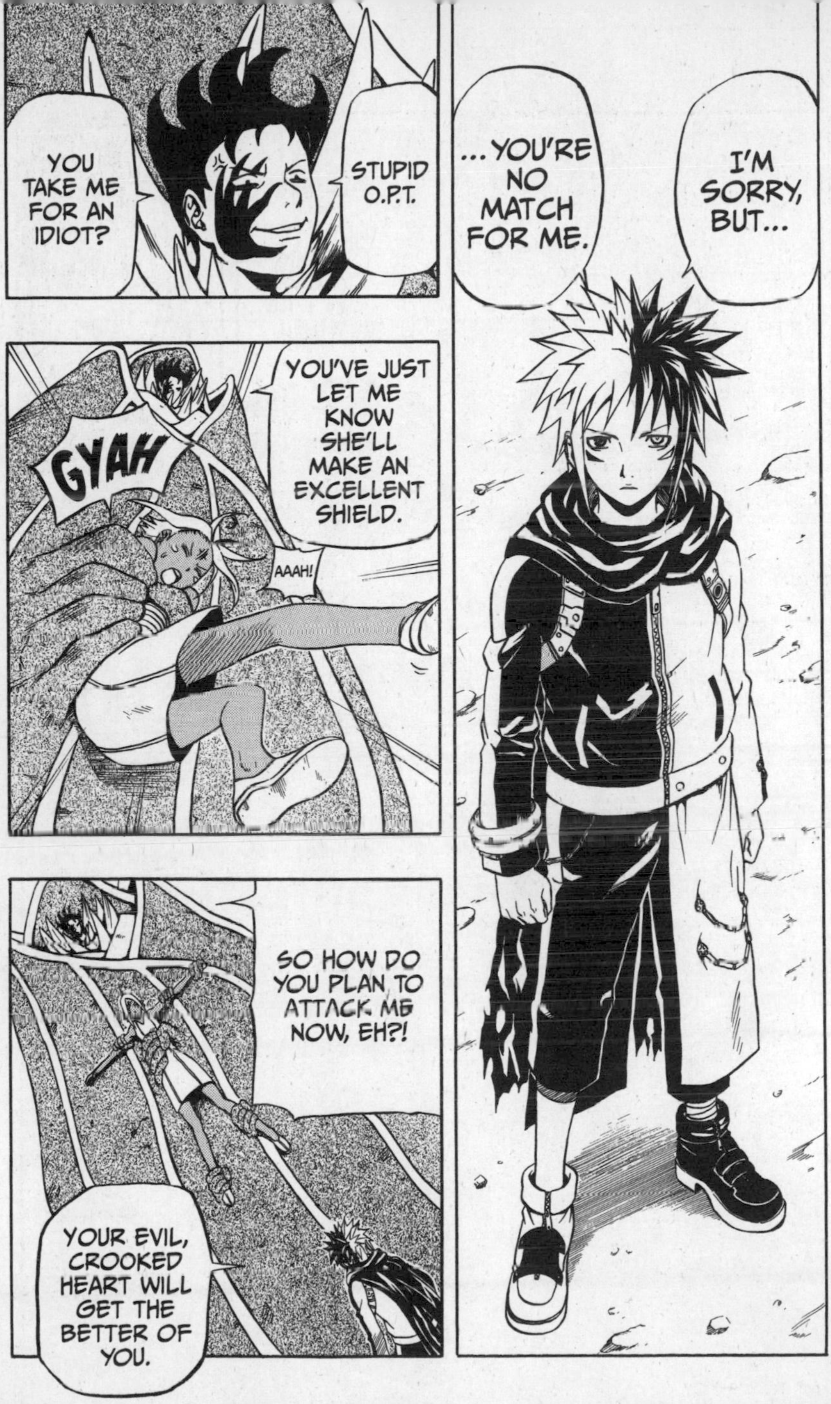
I'M SORRY, BUT...
...YOU'RE NO MATCH FOR ME.
STUPID O.P.T.
YOU TAKE ME FOR AN IDIOT?
YOU'VE JUST LET ME KNOW SHE'LL MAKE AN EXCELLENT SHIELD.
GYAH
AAAH!
SO HOW DO YOU PLAN TO ATTACK ME NOW, EH?!
YOUR EVIL, CROOKED HEART WILL GET THE BETTER OF YOU.

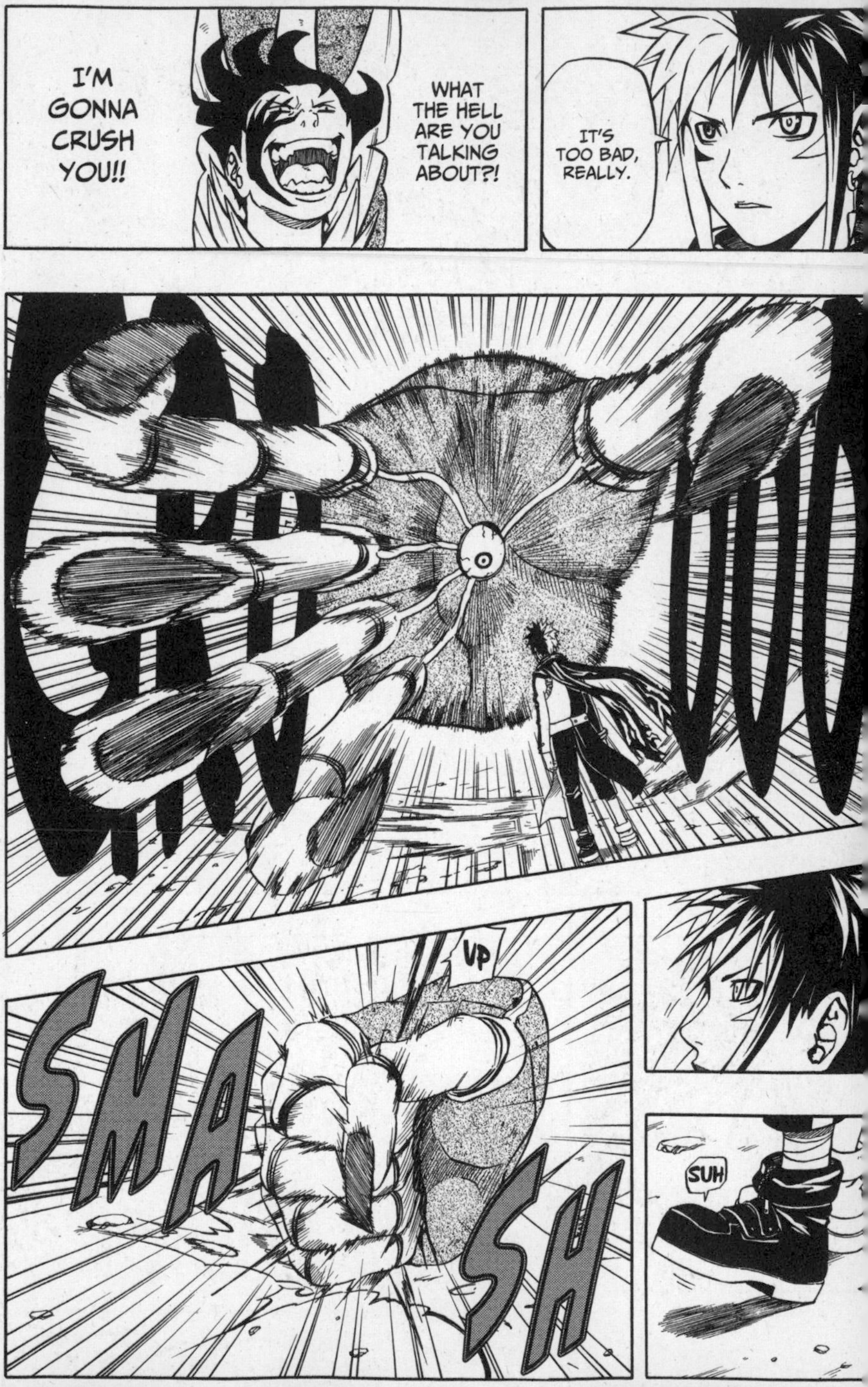
IT'S TOO BAD, REALLY.
WHAT THE HELL ARE YOU TALKING ABOUT?!
I'M GONNA CRUSH YOU!!
SUH
UP
SMASH

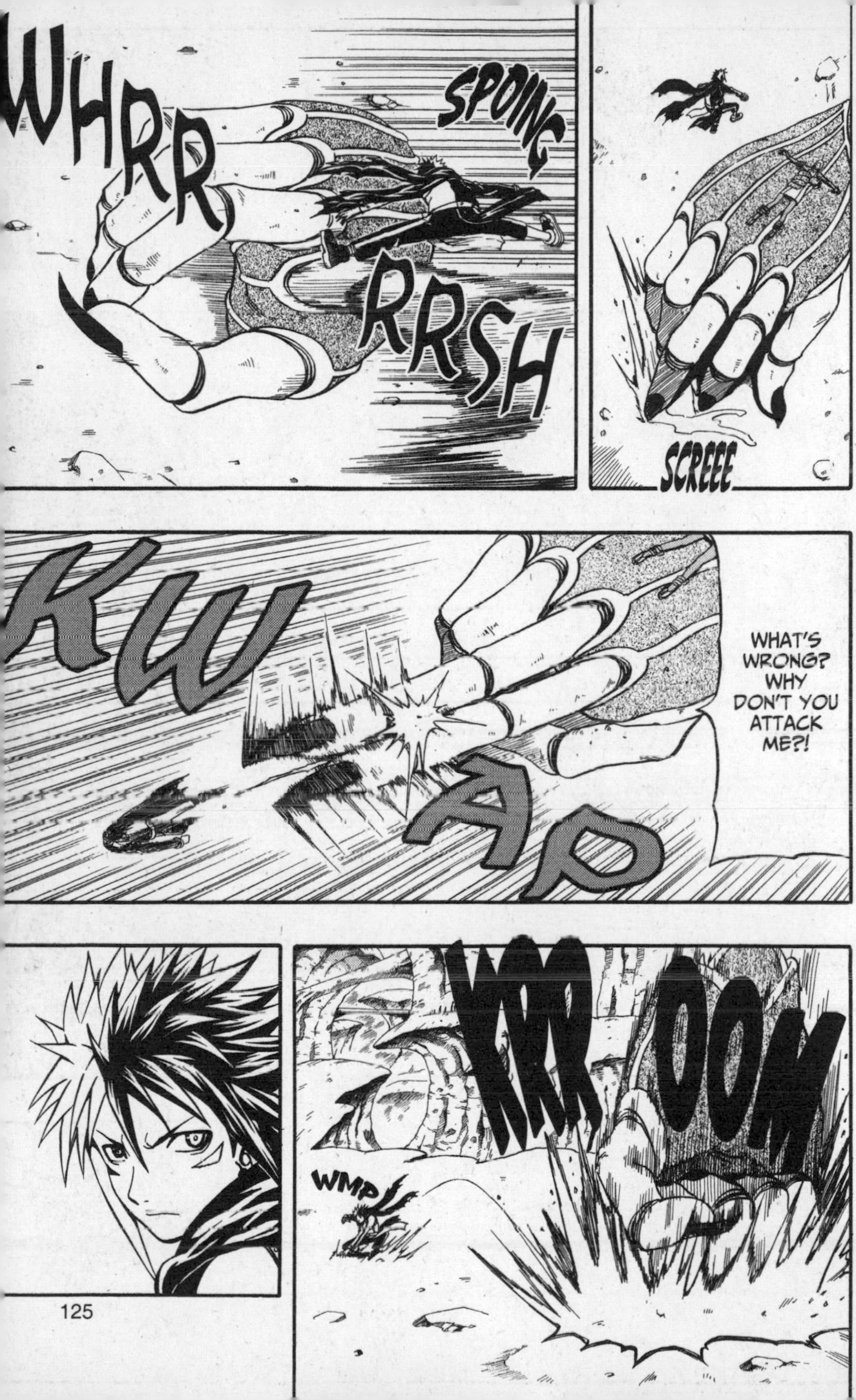
SCREEE
SPOING
WHRR
RRSH
WHAT'S WRONG? WHY DON'T YOU ATTACK ME?!
KWAP
KRR OOM
WMP

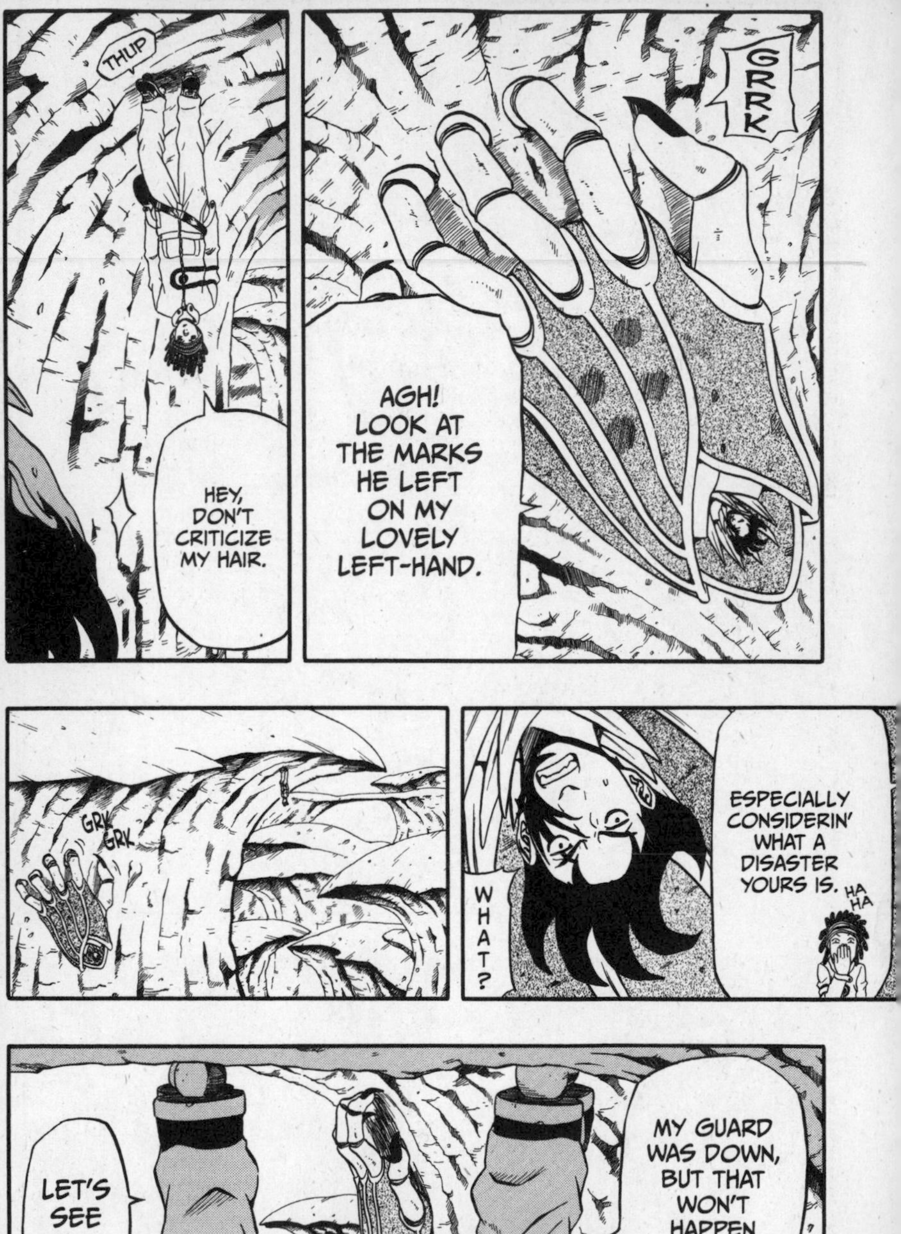
GRRK
AGH! LOOK AT THE MARKS HE LEFT ON MY LOVELY LEFT-HAND.
THUP
HEY, DON'T CRITICIZE MY HAIR.
ESPECIALLY CONSIDERIN' WHAT A DISASTER YOURS IS.
HA HA
WHAT?
GRK GRK
MY GUARD WAS DOWN, BUT THAT WON'T HAPPEN TWICE.
LET'S SEE IT.

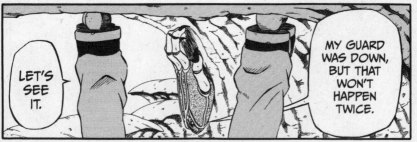

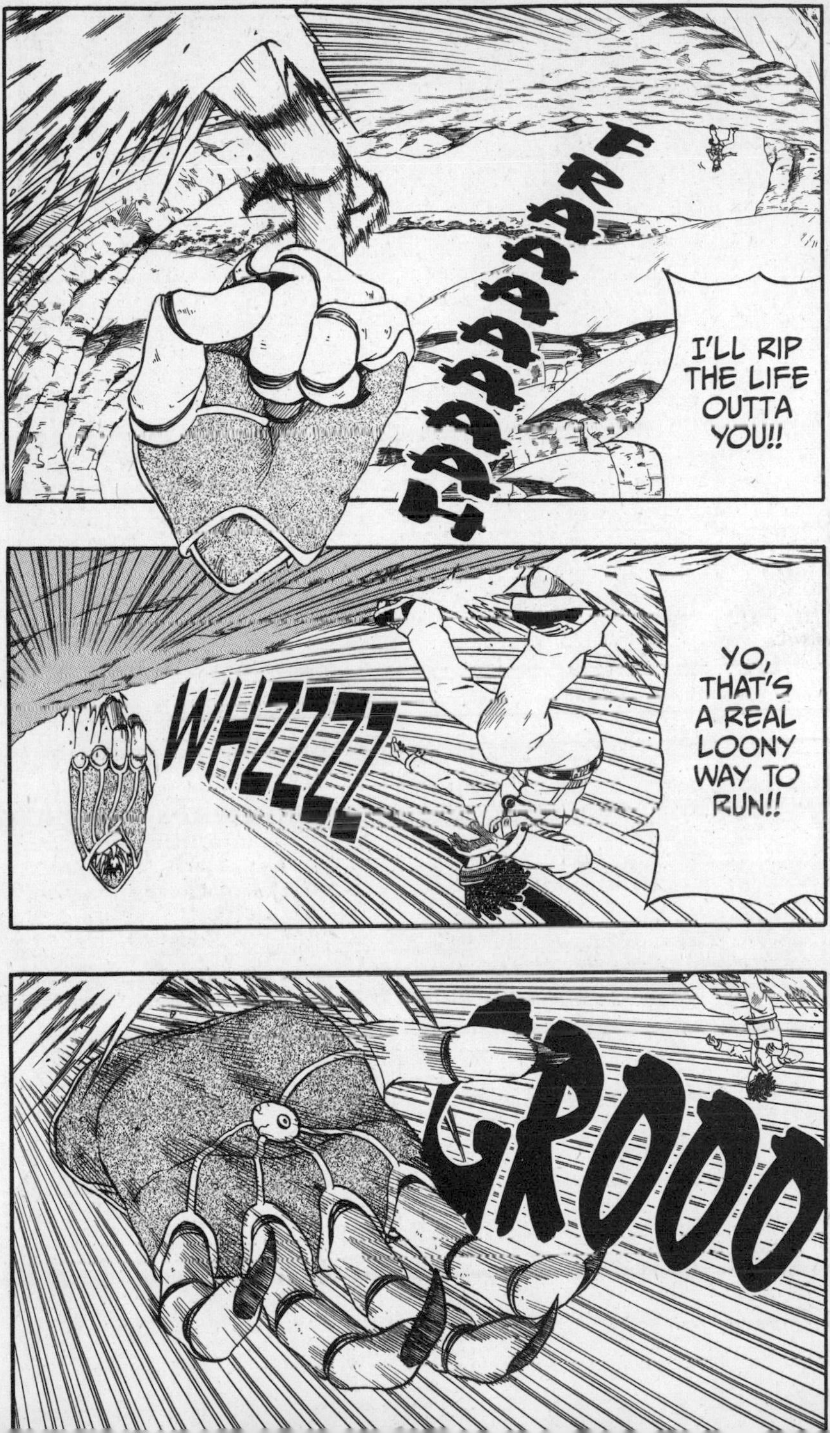
FRAAAAAAAGH
I'LL RIP THE LIFE OUTTA YOU!!
YO, THAT'S A REAL LOONY WAY TO RUN!!
WHZZZZ
GROOO

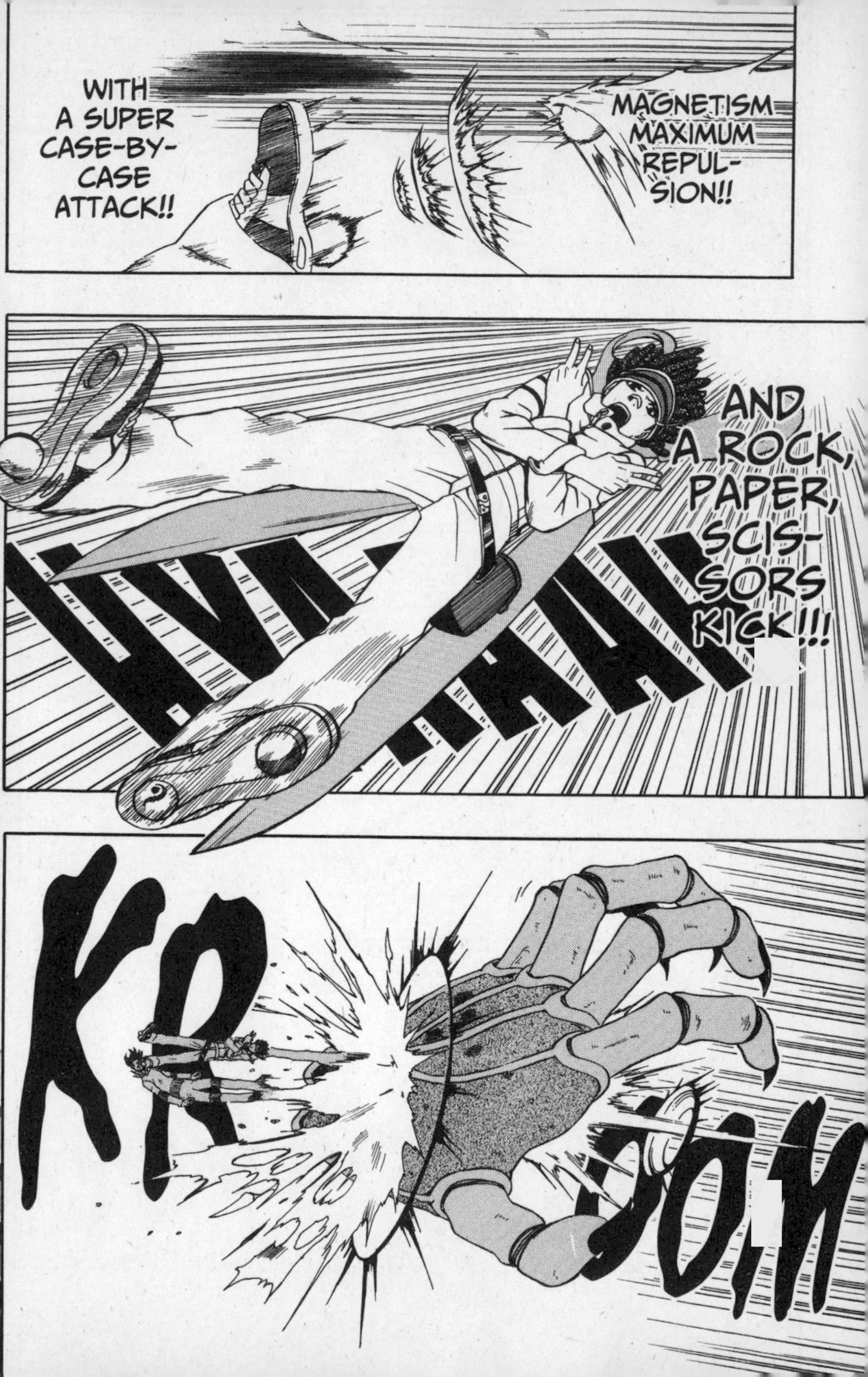
MAGNETISM MAXIMUM REPUL-SION!!
WITH A SUPER CASE-BY-CASE ATTACK!!
AND A ROCK, PAPER, SCIS-SORS KICK!!!

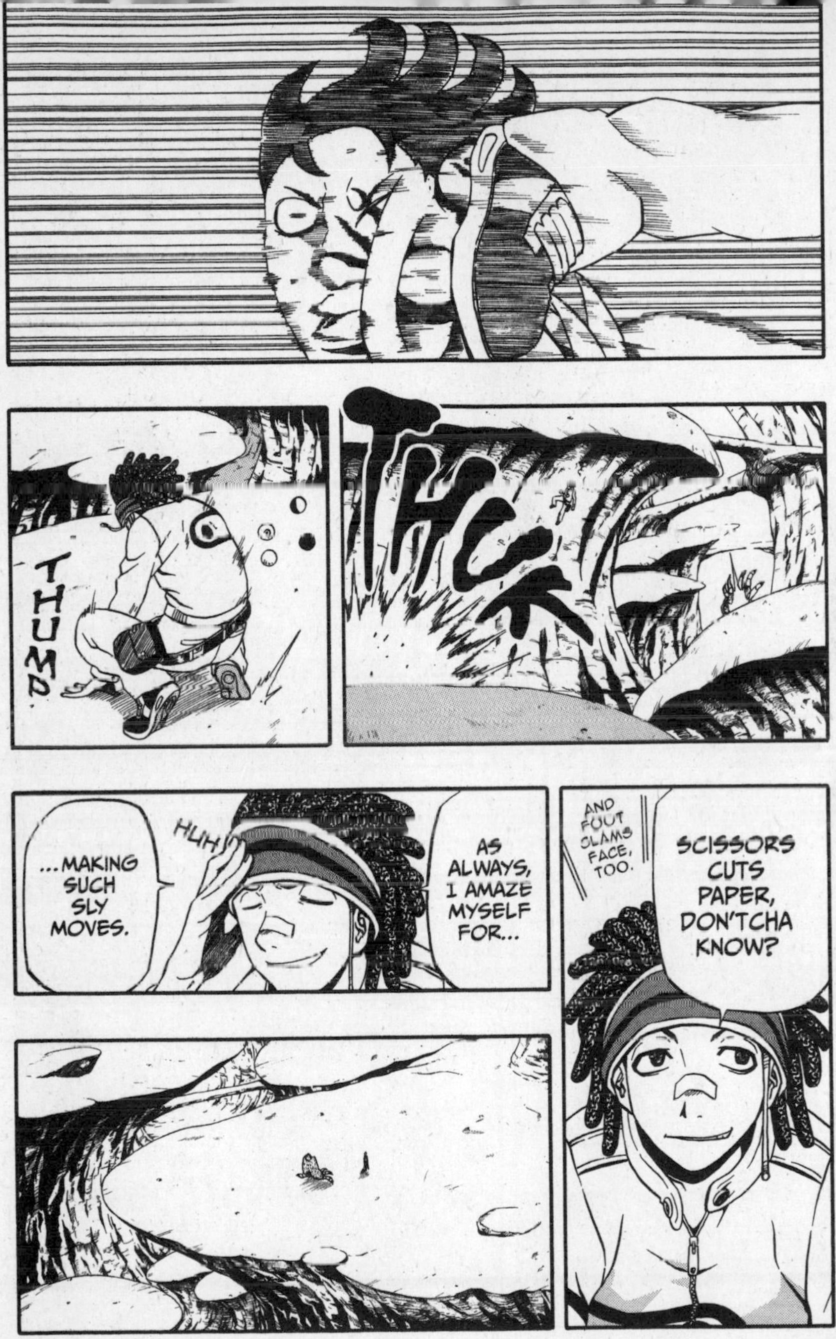
THUK
THUMP
SCISSORS CUTS PAPER, DON'TCHA KNOW?
AND FOUT SLAMS FACE, TOO.
AS ALWAYS, I AMAZE MYSELF FOR...
HUH
...MAKING SUCH SLY MOVES.

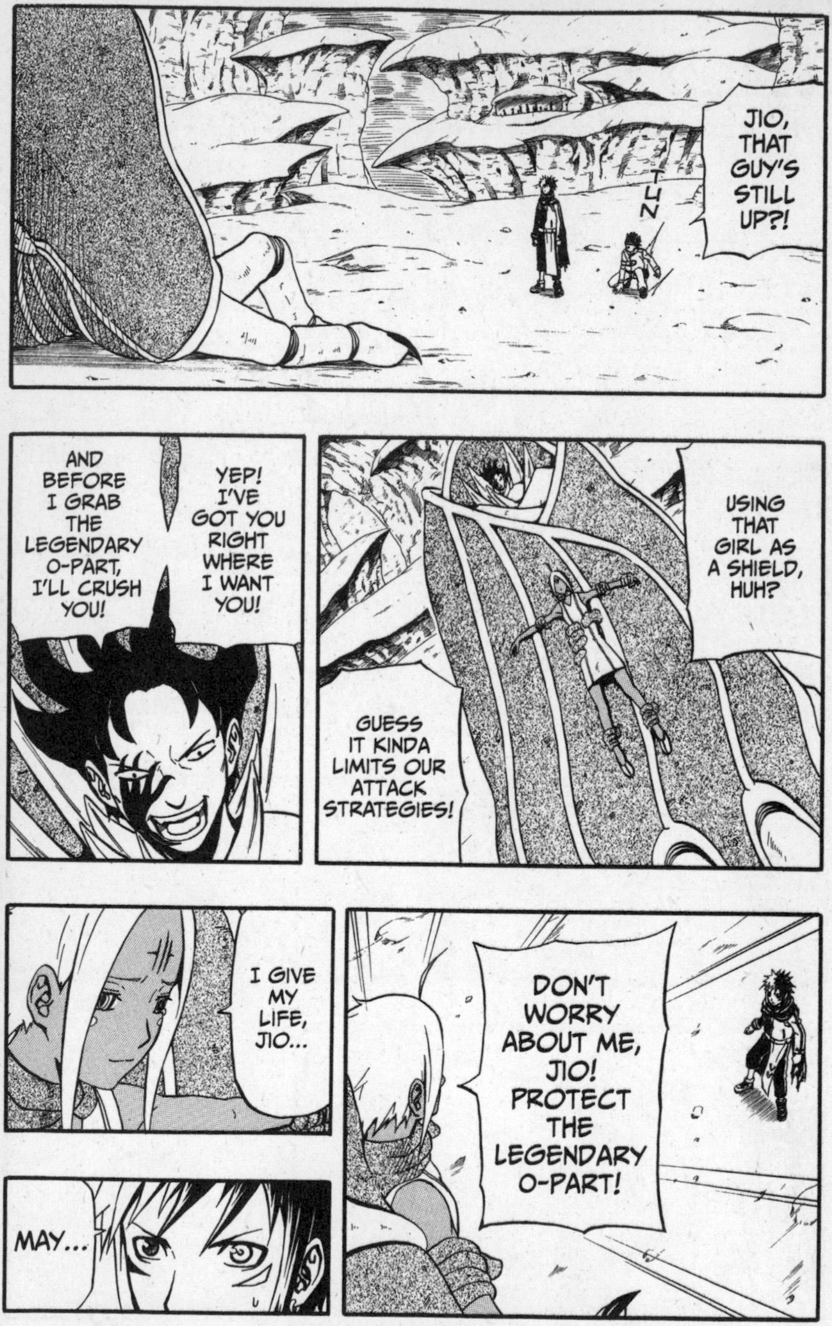
JIO, THAT GUY'S STILL UP?!
TUN
USING THAT GIRL AS A SHIELD, HUH?
GUESS IT KINDA LIMITS OUR ATTACK STRATEGIES!
YEP! I'VE GOT YOU RIGHT WHERE I WANT YOU!
AND BEFORE I GRAB THE LEGENDARY O-PART, I'LL CRUSH YOU!
DON'T WORRY ABOUT ME, JIO! PROTECT THE LEGENDARY O-PART!
I GIVE MY LIFE, JIO...
MAY...

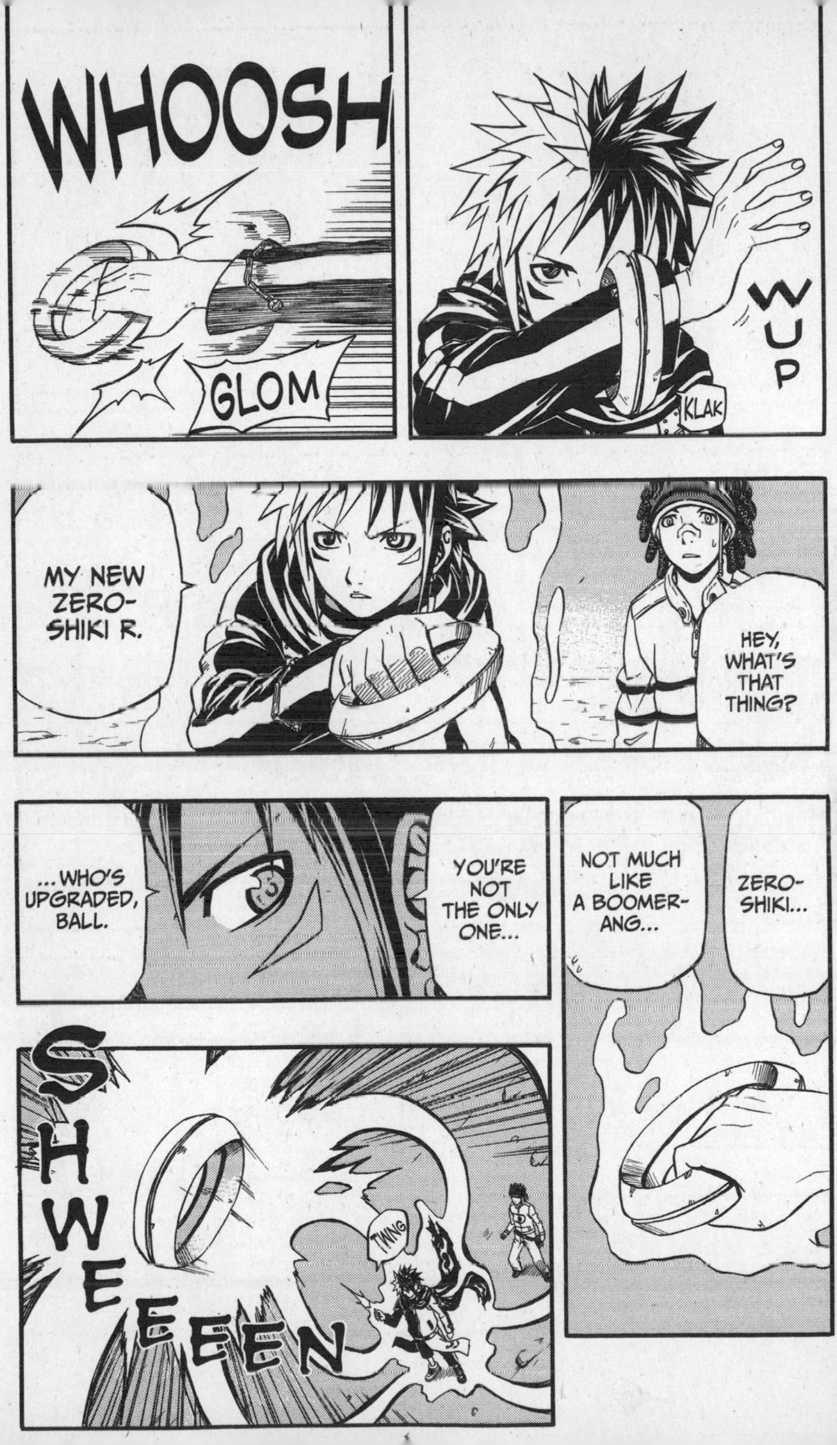
WUP
KLAK
WHOOSH
GLOM
HEY, WHAT'S THAT THING?
MY NEW ZERO-SHIKI R.
ZERO-SHIKI...
NOT MUCH LIKE A BOOMER-ANG...
YOU'RE NOT THE ONLY ONE...
...WHO'S UPGRADED, BALL.
SHWEEEEN
TWING

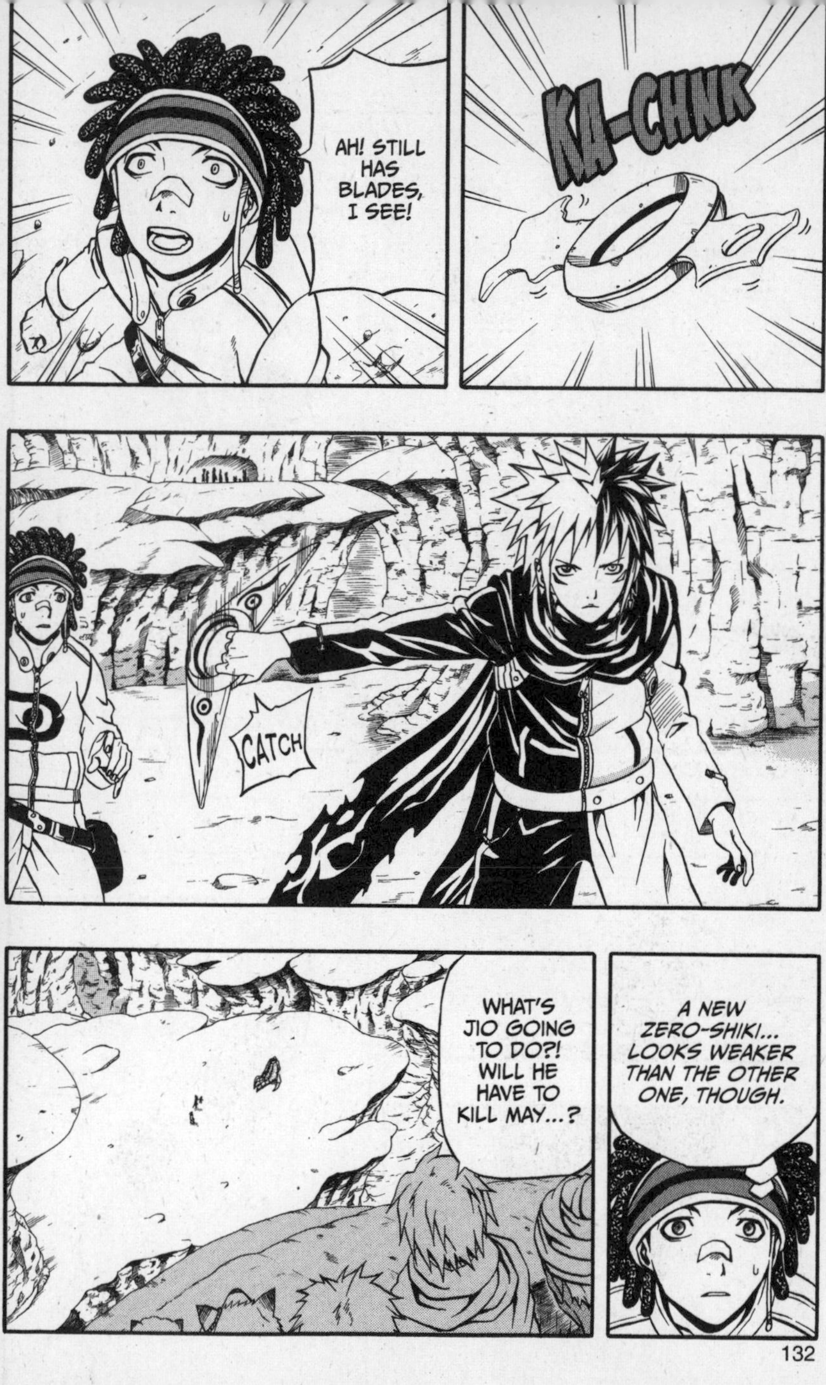
KA-CHNK
AH! STILL HAS BLADES, I SEE!
CATCH
A NEW ZERO-SHIKI... LOOKS WEAKER THAN THE OTHER ONE, THOUGH.
WHAT'S JIO GOING TO DO?! WILL HE HAVE TO KILL MAY...?

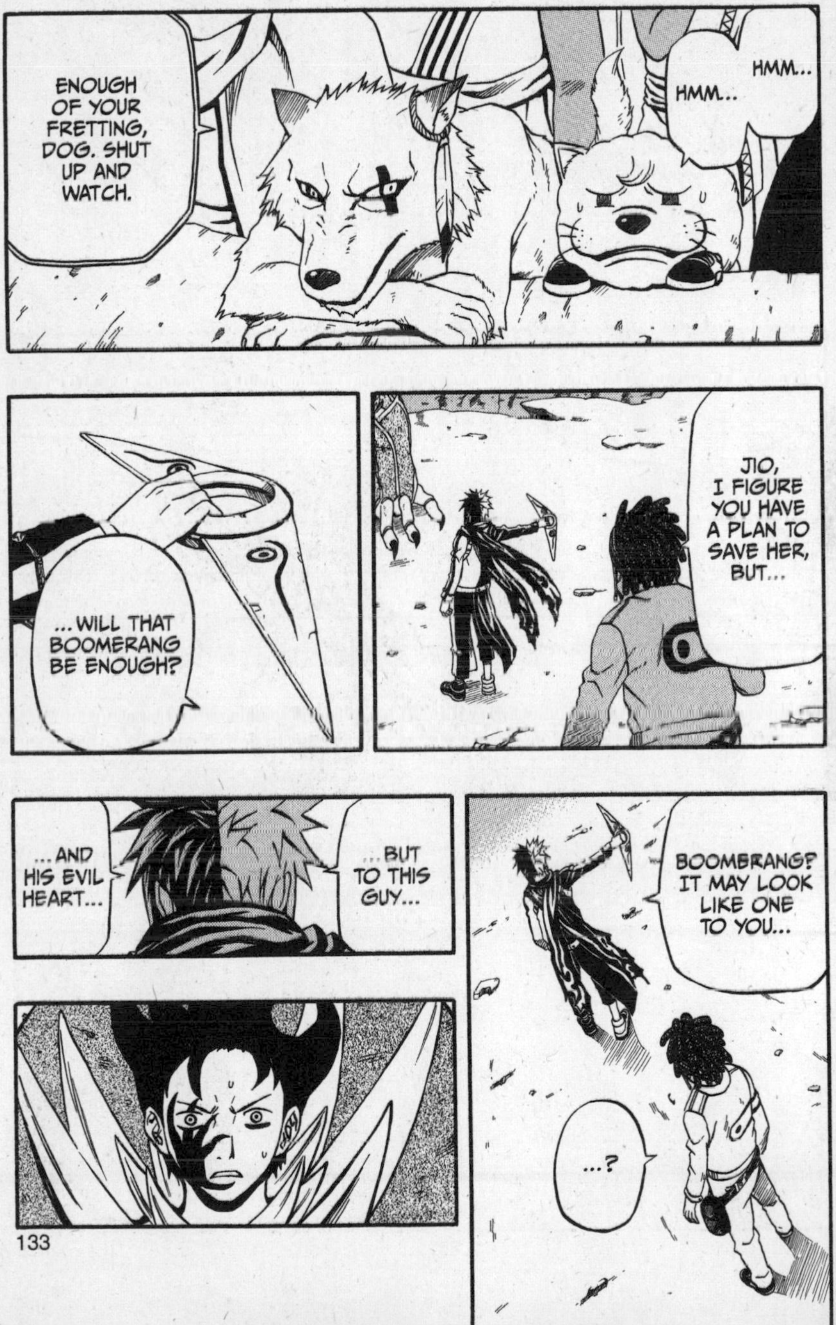
HMM...
HMM...
ENOUGH OF YOUR FRETTING, DOG. SHUT UP AND WATCH.
JIO, I FIGURE YOU HAVE A PLAN TO SAVE HER, BUT...
...WILL THAT BOOMERANG BE ENOUGH?
BOOMERANG? IT MAY LOOK LIKE ONE TO YOU...
...?
...BUT TO THIS GUY...
...AND HIS EVIL HEART...

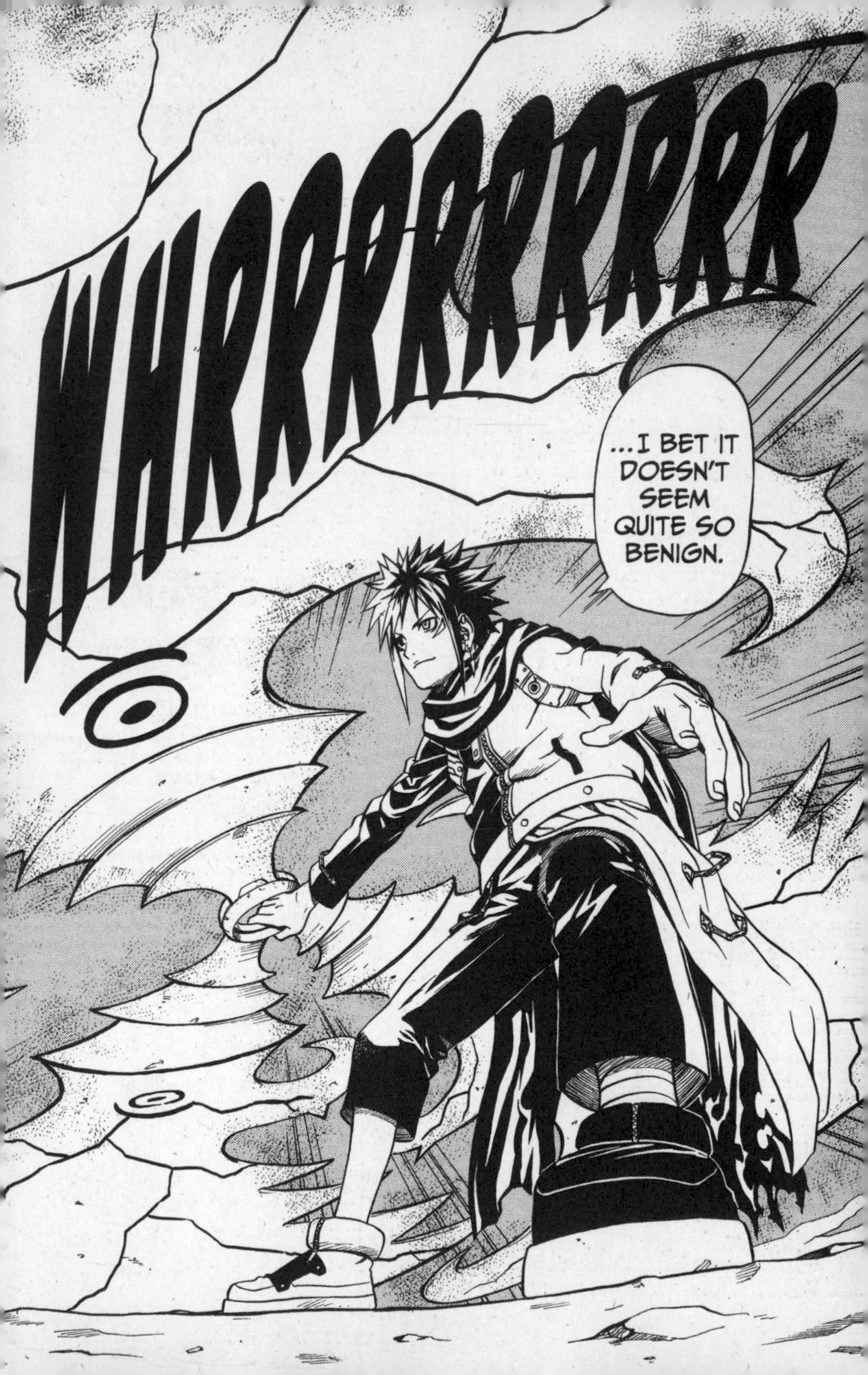
WHRRRRRRRRRRR
...I BET IT DOESN'T SEEM QUITE SO BENIGN.

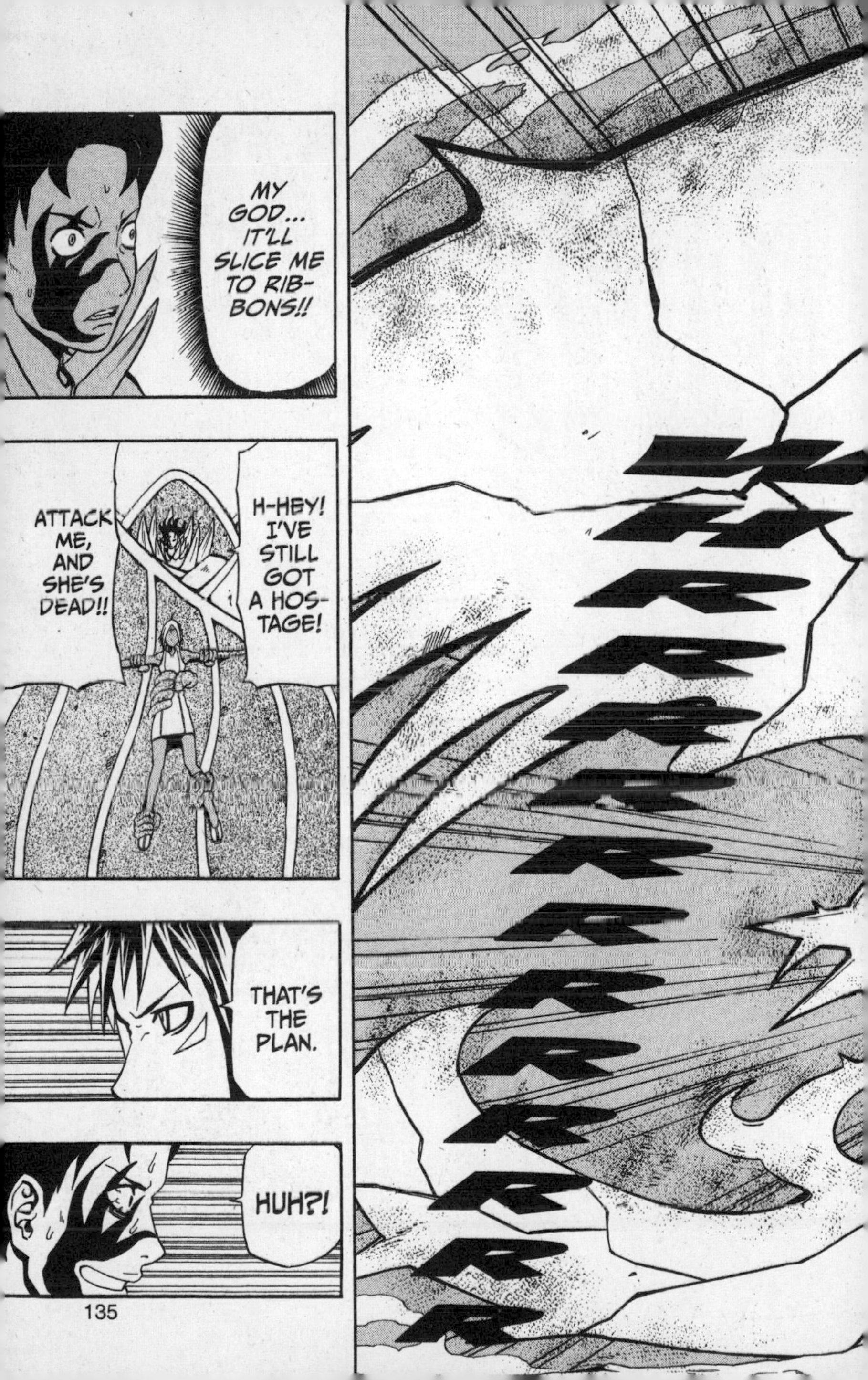
WHRRRRRRRRRRRR
MY GOD... IT'LL SLICE ME TO RIB-BONS!!
H-HEY! I'VE STILL GOT A HOS-TAGE!
ATTACK ME, AND SHE'S DEAD!!
THAT'S THE PLAN.
HUH?!

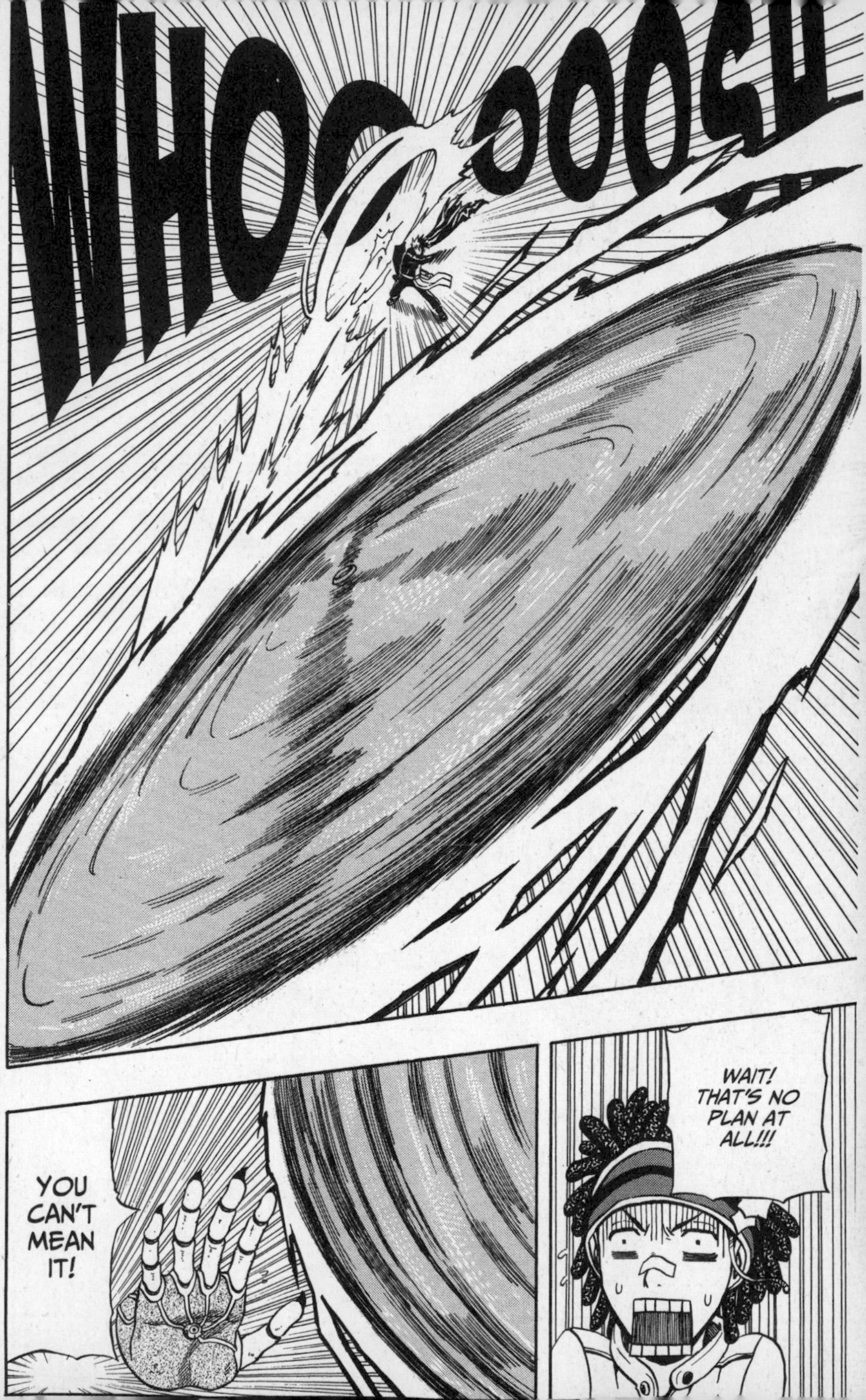
WHOOOOOSH
WAIT! THAT'S NO PLAN AT ALL!!!
YOU CAN'T MEAN IT!

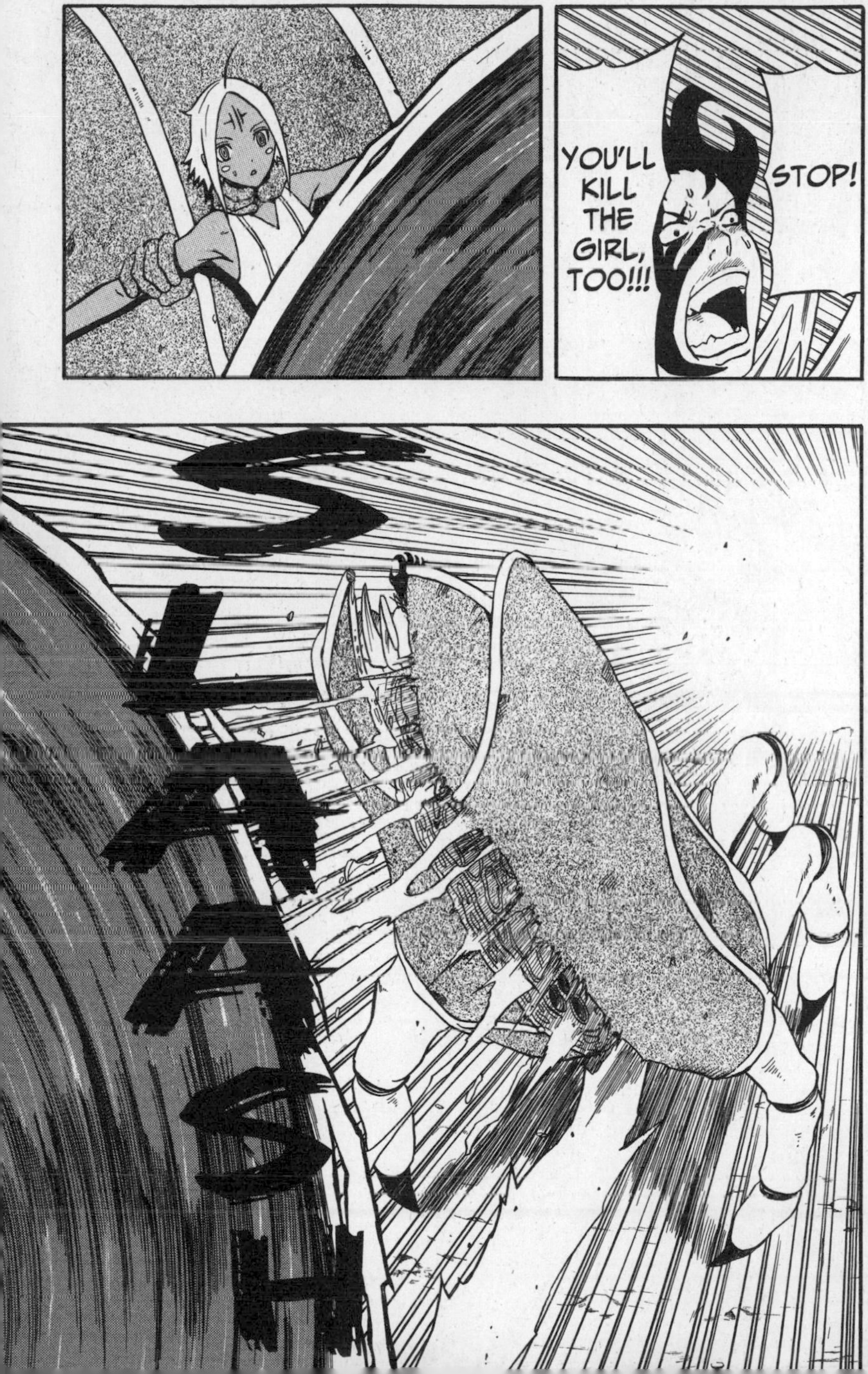
STOP!
YOU'LL KILL THE GIRL, TOO!!!
SMASH

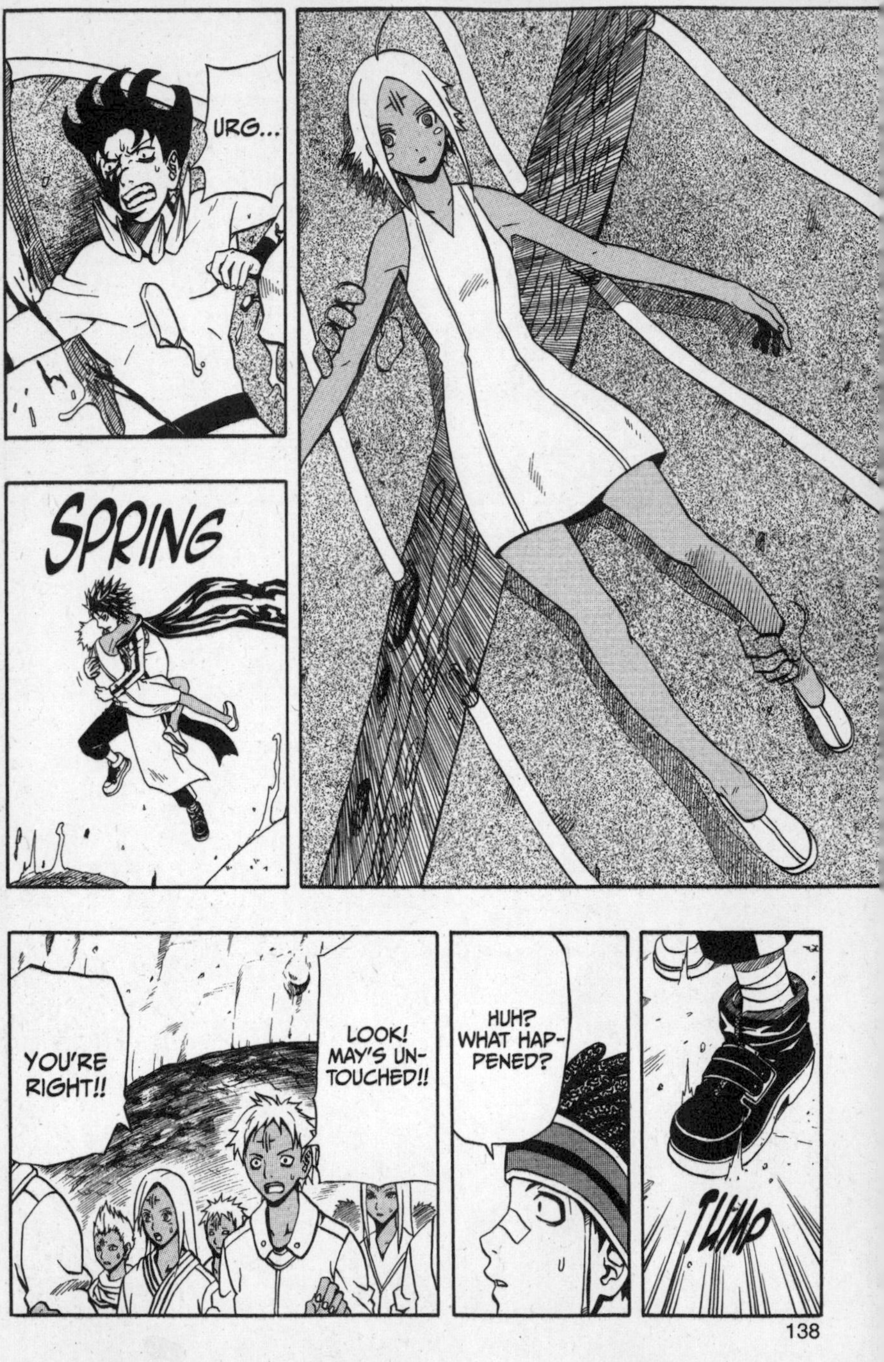
URG...
SPRING
TUMP
HUH? WHAT HAP-PENED?
LOOK! MAY'S UN-TOUCHED!!
YOU'RE RIGHT!!

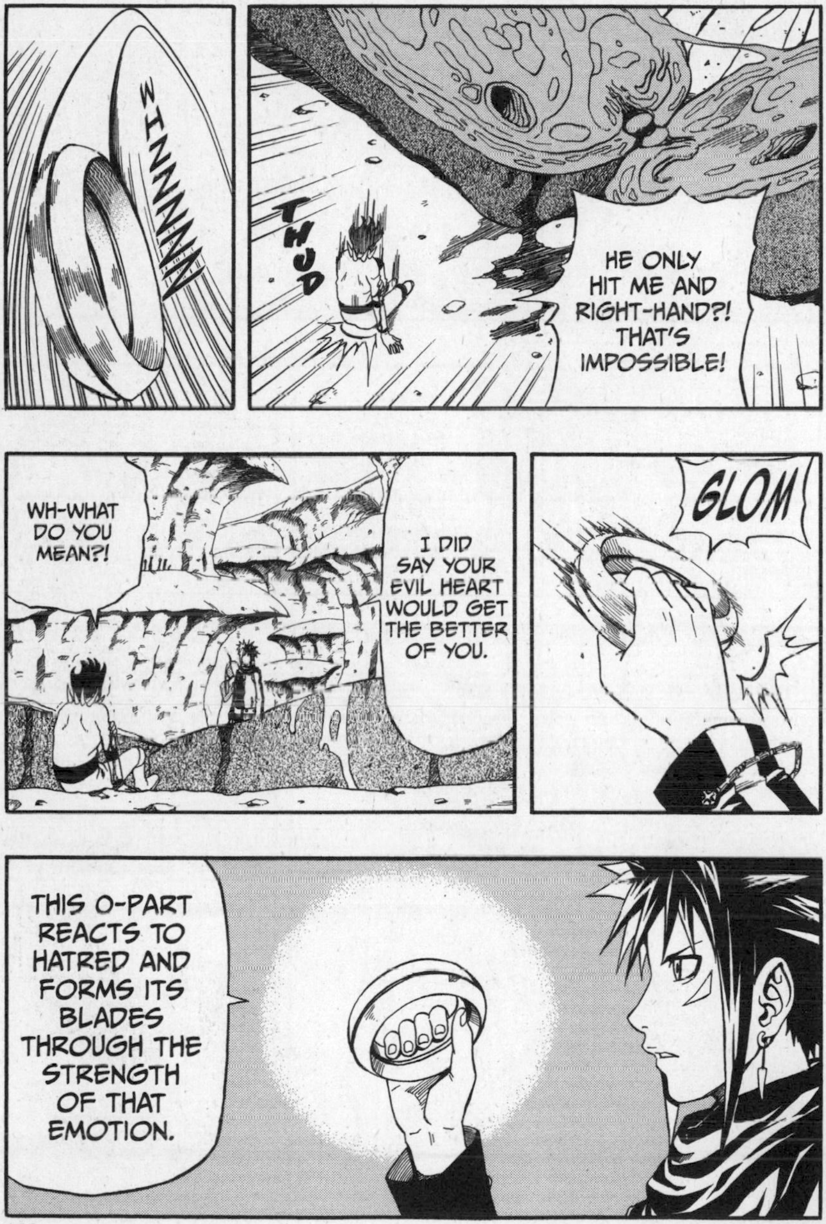
THUD
HE ONLY HIT ME AND RIGHT-HAND?! THAT'S IMPOSSIBLE!
WHNNNNN
GLOM
I DID SAY YOUR EVIL HEART WOULD GET THE BETTER OF YOU.
WH-WHAT DO YOU MEAN?!
THIS O-PART REACTS TO HATRED AND FORMS ITS BLADES THROUGH THE STRENGTH OF THAT EMOTION.

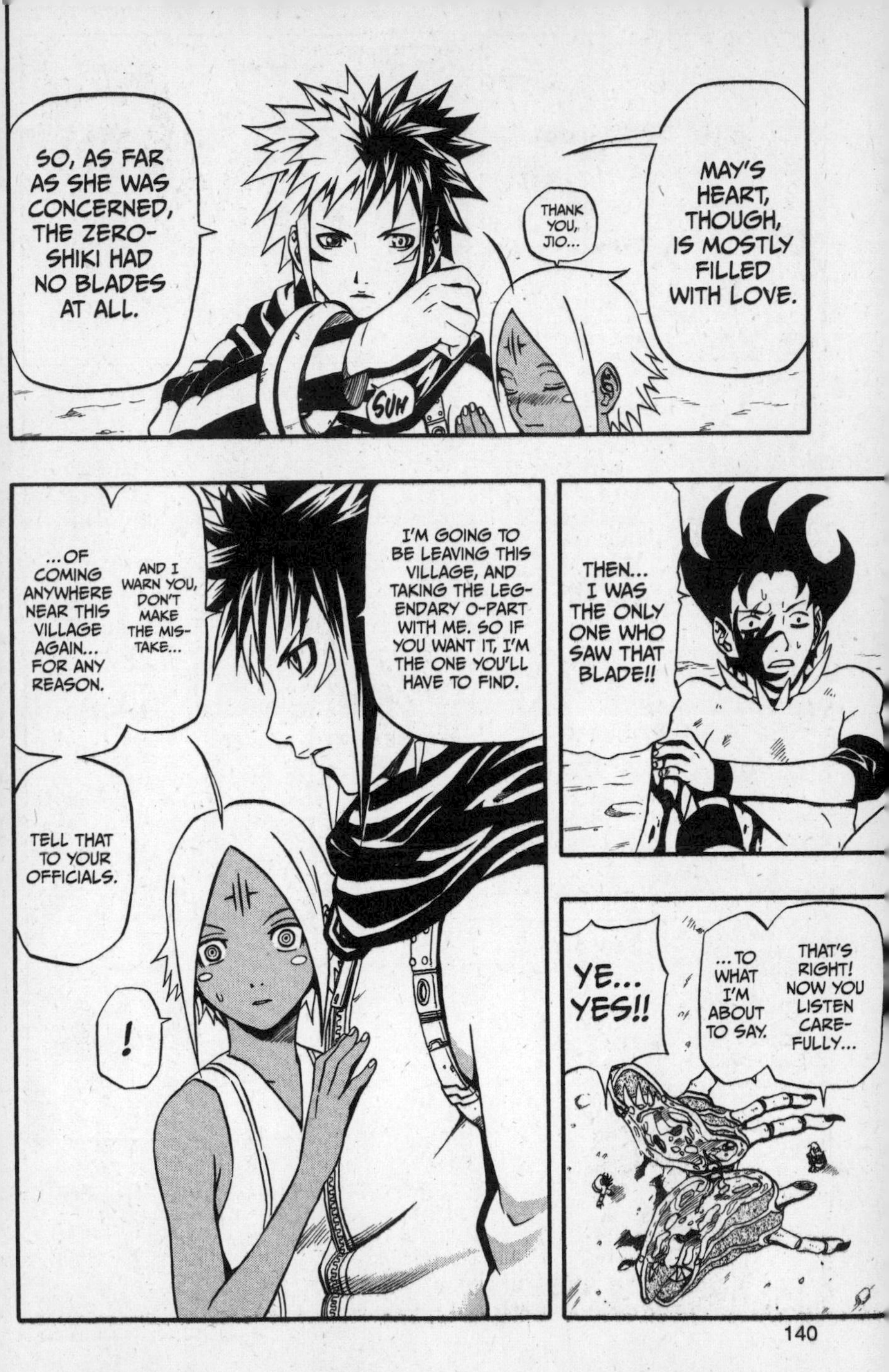
MAY'S HEART, THOUGH, IS MOSTLY FILLED WITH LOVE.
THANK YOU, JIO...
SO, AS FAR AS SHE WAS CONCERNED, THE ZERO-SHIKI HAD NO BLADES AT ALL.
SUH
THEN... I WAS THE ONLY ONE WHO SAW THAT BLADE!!
THAT'S RIGHT! NOW YOU LISTEN CAREFULLY...
...TO WHAT I'M ABOUT TO SAY.
YE... YES!!
I'M GOING TO BE LEAVING THIS VILLAGE, AND TAKING THE LEGENDARY O-PART WITH ME. SO IF YOU WANT IT, I'M THE ONE YOU'LL HAVE TO FIND.
AND I WARN YOU, DON'T MAKE THE MISTAKE...
...OF COMING ANYWHERE NEAR THIS VILLAGE AGAIN... FOR ANY REASON.
TELL THAT TO YOUR OFFICIALS.
!

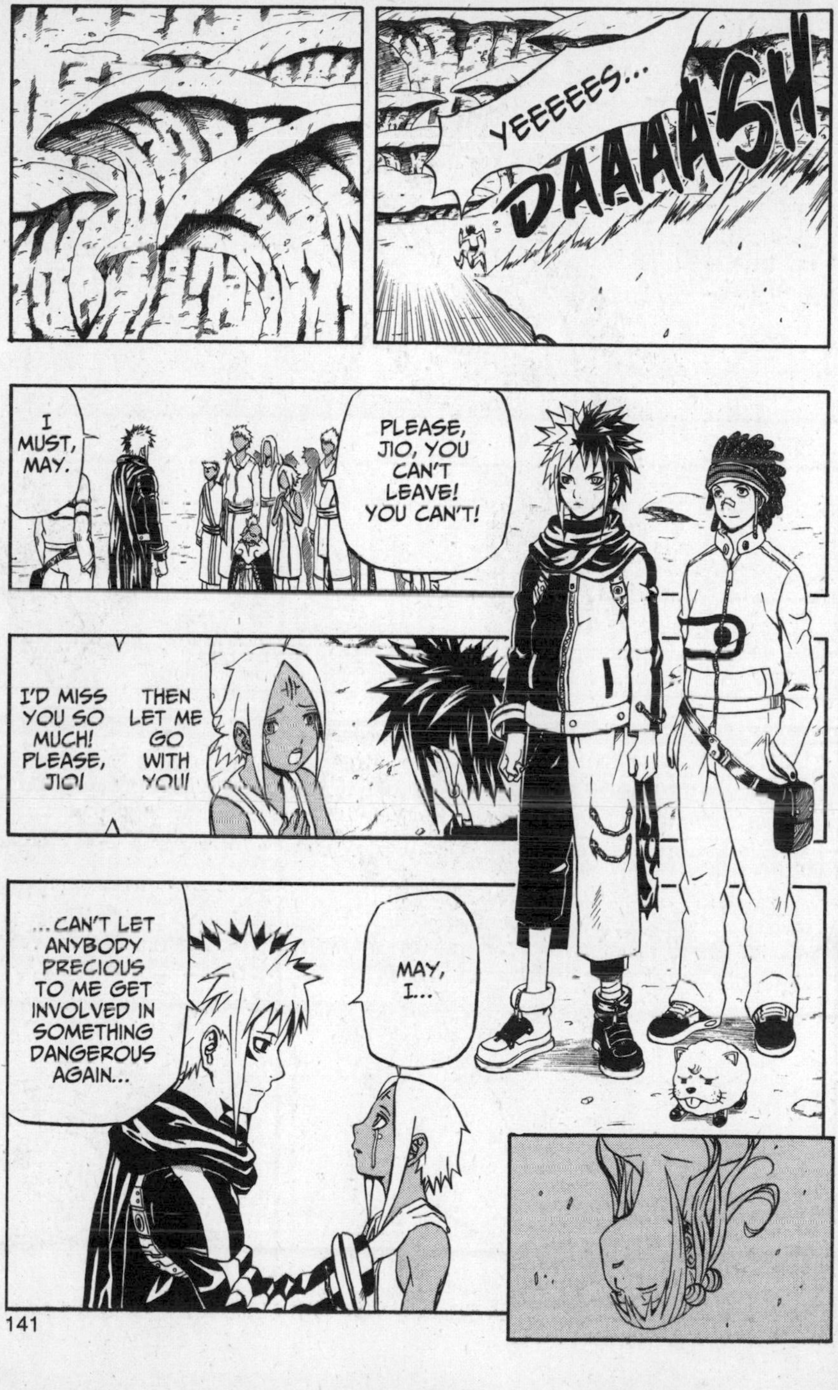
YEEEEES...
DAAAAASH
PLEASE, JIO, YOU CAN'T LEAVE! YOU CAN'T!
I MUST, MAY.
THEN LET ME GO WITH YOU!
I'D MISS YOU SO MUCH! PLEASE, JIO!
MAY, I...
...CAN'T LET ANYBODY PRECIOUS TO ME GET INVOLVED IN SOMETHING DANGEROUS AGAIN...

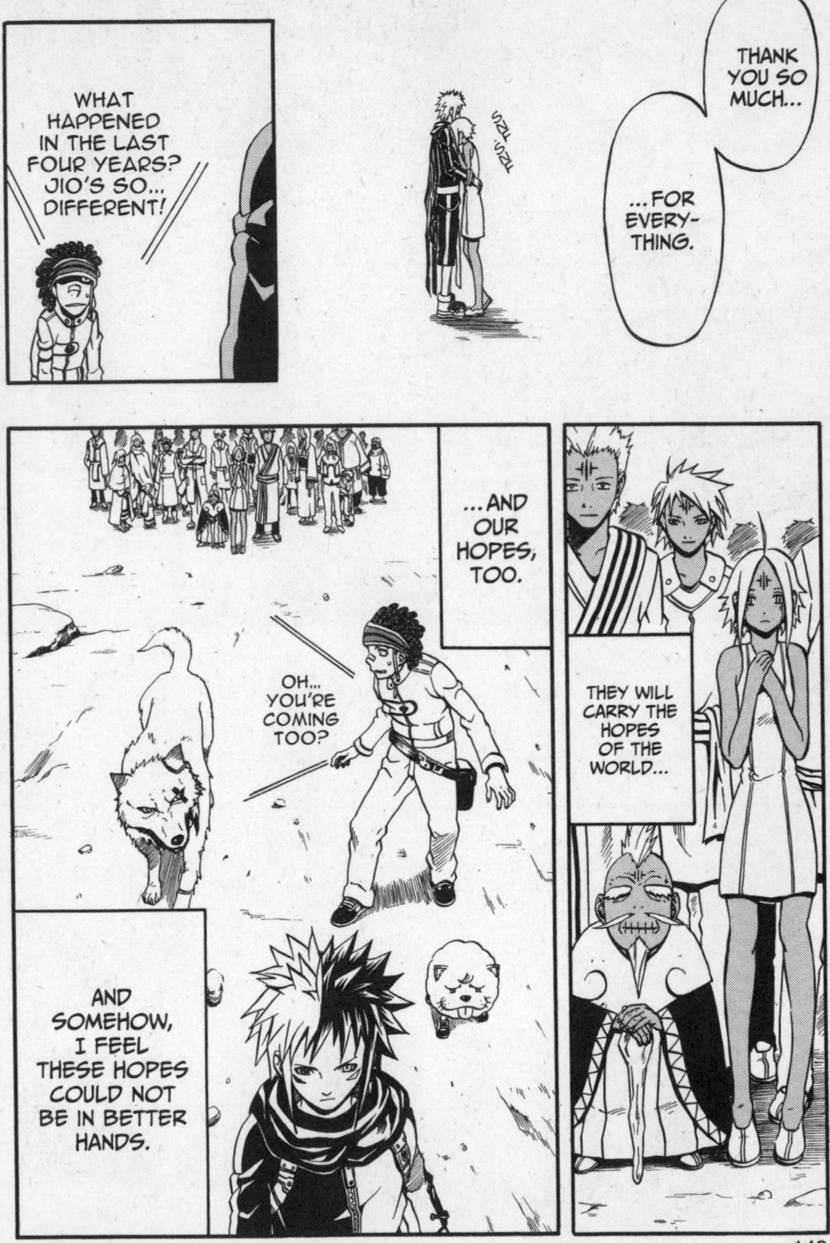
THANK YOU SO MUCH...
...FOR EVERY-THING.
WHAT HAPPENED IN THE LAST FOUR YEARS? JIO'S SO... DIFFERENT!
THEY WILL CARRY THE HOPES OF THE WORLD...
...AND OUR HOPES, TOO.
OH... YOU'RE COMING TOO?
AND SOMEHOW, I FEEL THESE HOPES COULD NOT BE IN BETTER HANDS.

CHAPTER 56 A NEW MEMBER

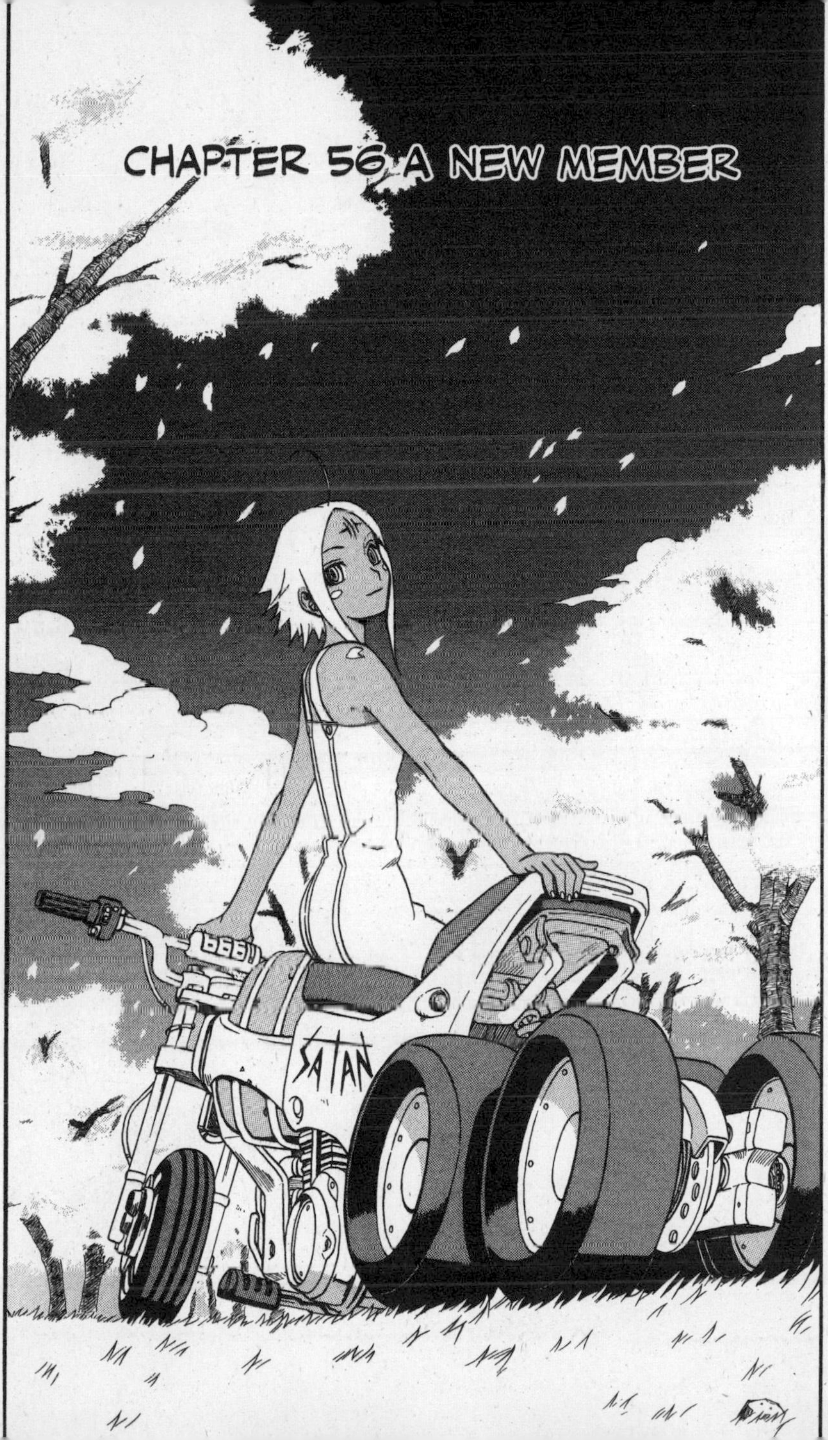
SATAN

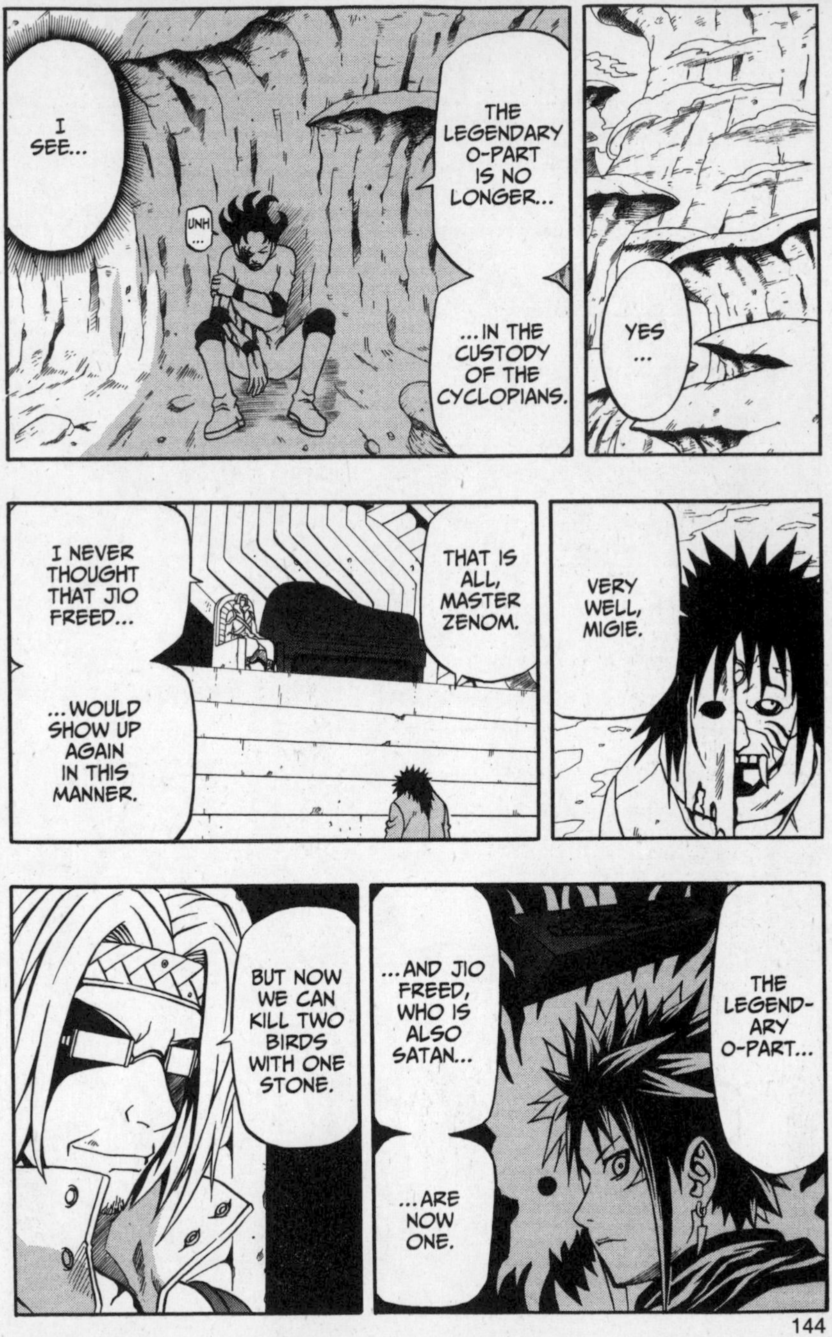
I SEE...
UNH ...
THE LEGENDARY O-PART IS NO LONGER...
...IN THE CUSTODY OF THE CYCLOPIANS.
YES ...
I NEVER THOUGHT THAT JIO FREED...
...WOULD SHOW UP AGAIN IN THIS MANNER.
THAT IS ALL, MASTER ZENOM.
VERY WELL, MIGIE.
BUT NOW WE CAN KILL TWO BIRDS WITH ONE STONE.
THE LEGEND-ARY O-PART...
...AND JIO FREED, WHO IS ALSO SATAN...
...ARE NOW ONE.

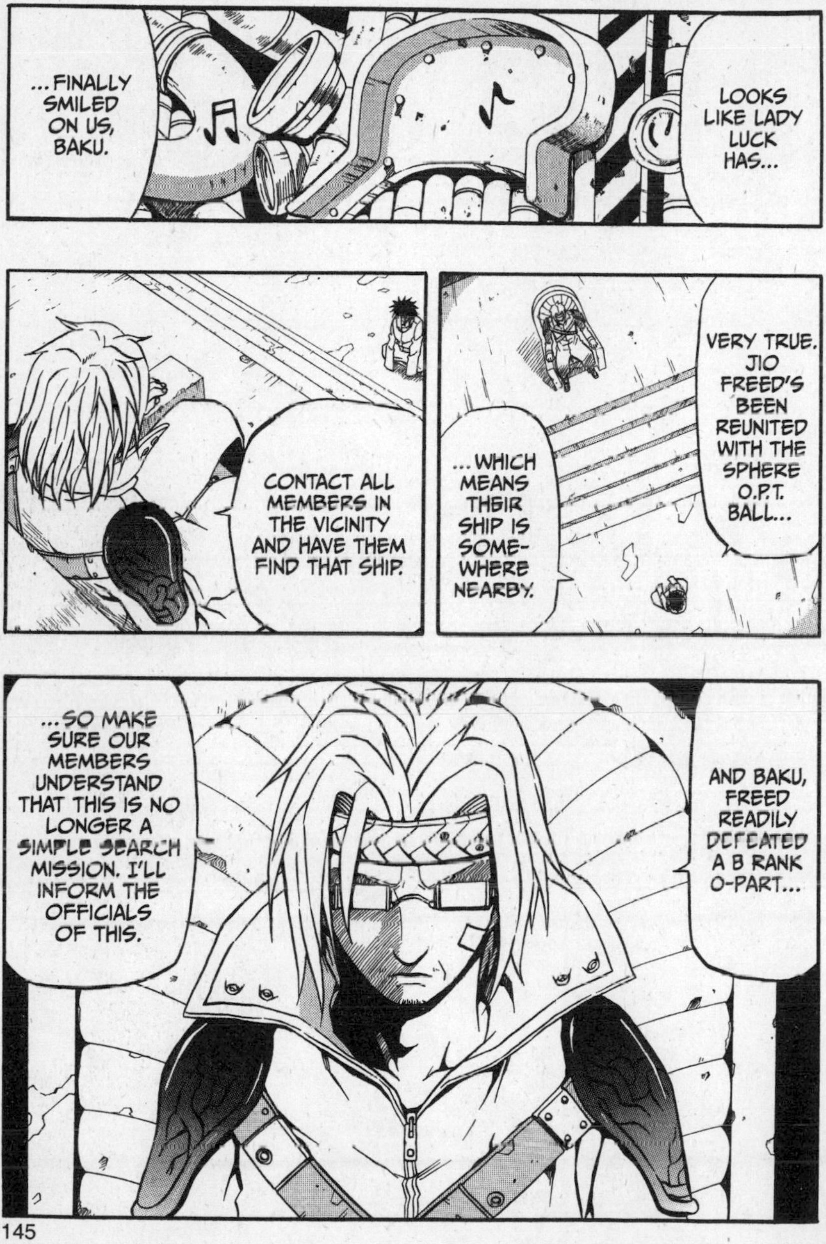
LOOKS LIKE LADY LUCK HAS...
...FINALLY SMILED ON US, BAKU.
VERY TRUE. JIO FREED'S BEEN REUNITED WITH THE SPHERE O.P.T. BALL...
...WHICH MEANS THEIR SHIP IS SOME-WHERE NEARBY.
CONTACT ALL MEMBERS IN THE VICINITY AND HAVE THEM FIND THAT SHIP.
AND BAKU, FREED READILY DEFEATED A B RANK O-PART...
...SO MAKE SURE OUR MEMBERS UNDERSTAND THAT THIS IS NO LONGER A SIMPLE SEARCH MISSION. I'LL INFORM THE OFFICIALS OF THIS.

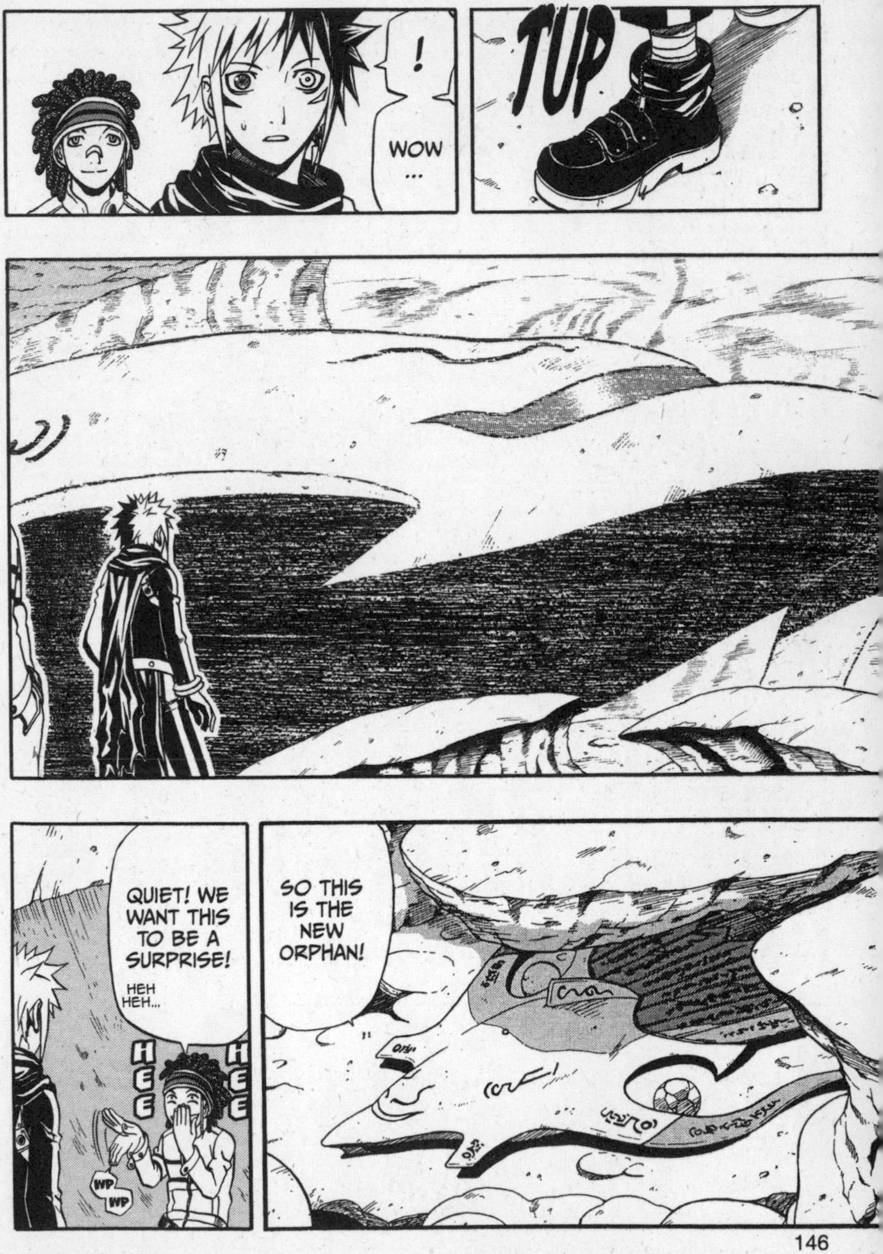
TUP
!
WOW ...
SO THIS IS THE NEW ORPHAN!
QUIET! WE WANT THIS TO BE A SURPRISE!
HEH HEH...
HEE
HEE
WP WP

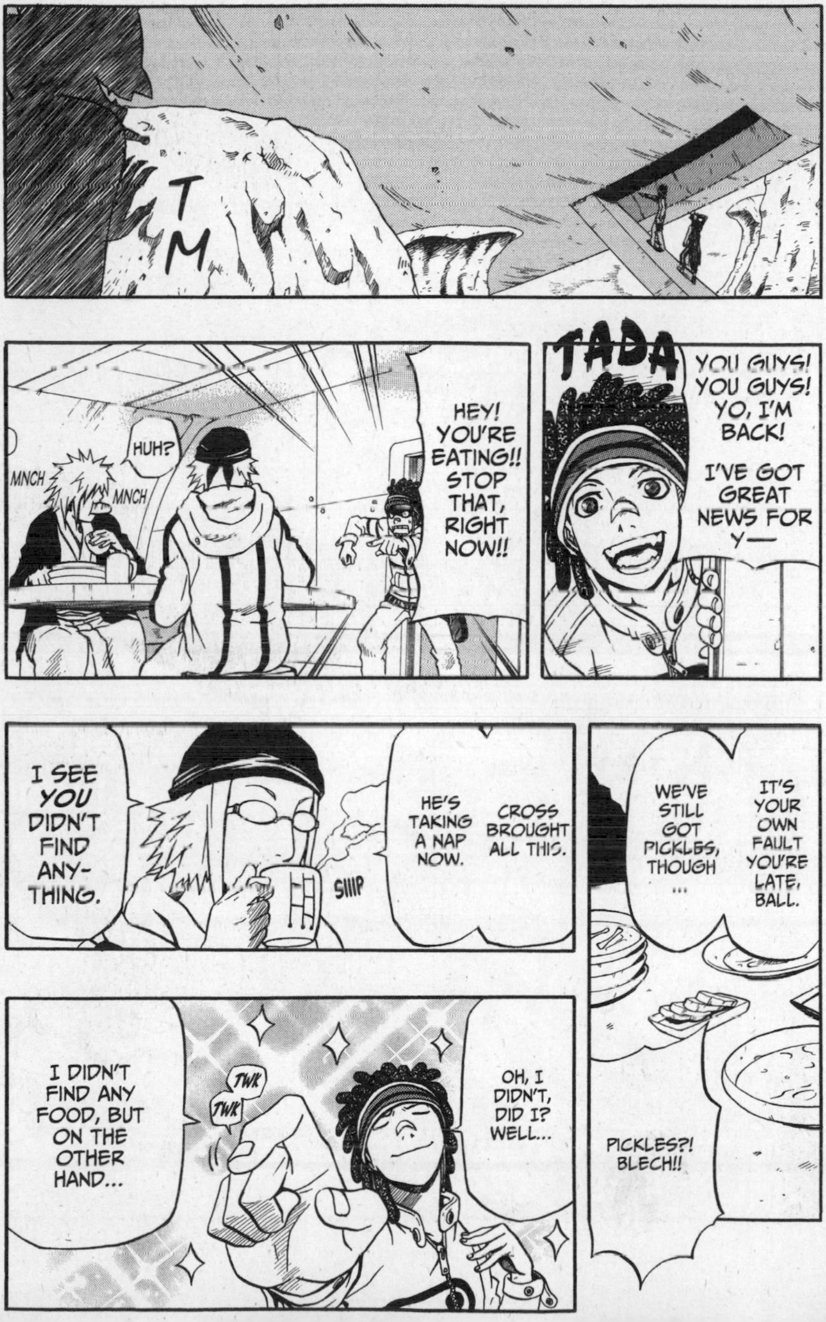
TM
TADA
YOU GUYS! YOU GUYS! YO, I'M BACK!
I'VE GOT GREAT NEWS FOR Y—
HEY! YOU'RE EATING!! STOP THAT, RIGHT NOW!!
HUH?
MNCH
MNCH
IT'S YOUR OWN FAULT YOU'RE LATE, BALL.
WE'VE STILL GOT PICKLES, THOUGH ...
PICKLES?! BLECH!!
CROSS BROUGHT ALL THIS.
HE'S TAKING A NAP NOW.
SIIIP
I SEE *YOU* DIDN'T FIND ANY-THING.
OH, I DIDN'T, DID I? WELL...
TWK
TWK
I DIDN'T FIND ANY FOOD, BUT ON THE OTHER HAND...

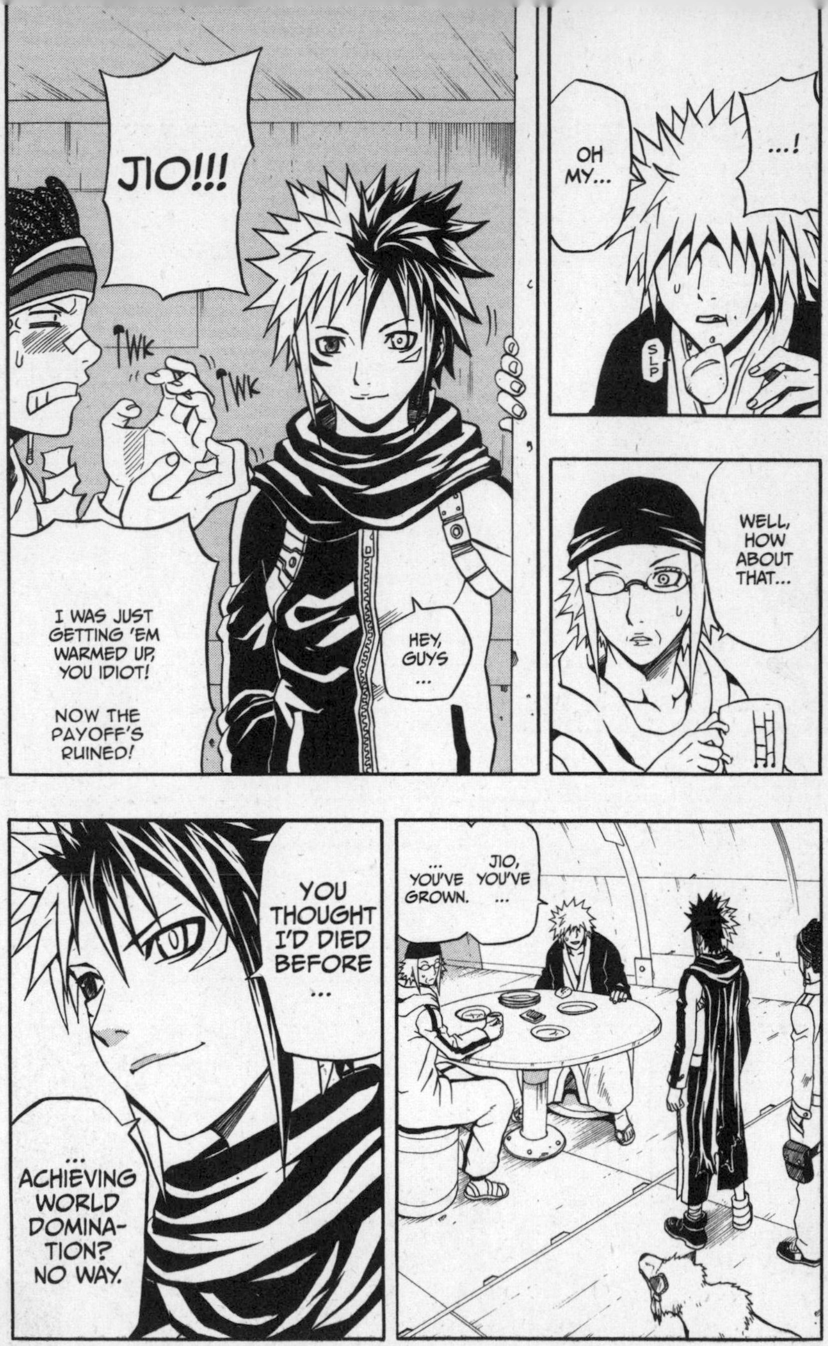
...!
OH MY...
SLP
WELL, HOW ABOUT THAT...
JIO!!!
TWK
TWK
HEY, GUYS ...
I WAS JUST GETTING 'EM WARMED UP, YOU IDIOT!
NOW THE PAYOFF'S RUINED!
JIO, YOU'VE ...
... YOU'VE GROWN.
YOU THOUGHT I'D DIED BEFORE ...
... ACHIEVING WORLD DOMINA-TION? NO WAY.

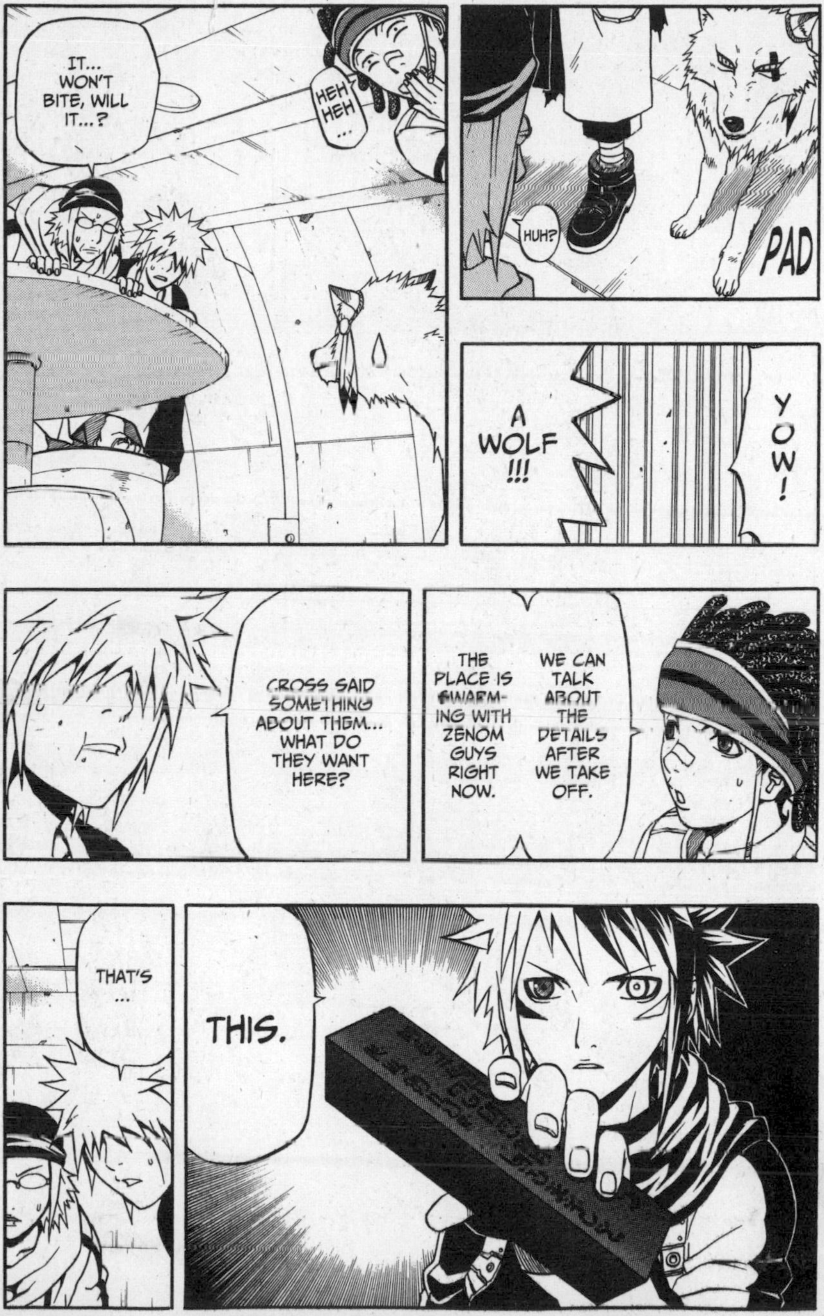
HUH?
PAD
YOW!
A WOLF!!!
HEH HEH ...
IT... WON'T BITE, WILL IT...?
WE CAN TALK ABOUT THE DETAILS AFTER WE TAKE OFF.
THE PLACE IS SWARMING WITH ZENOM GUYS RIGHT NOW.
CROSS SAID SOMETHING ABOUT THEM... WHAT DO THEY WANT HERE?
THIS.
THAT'S ...

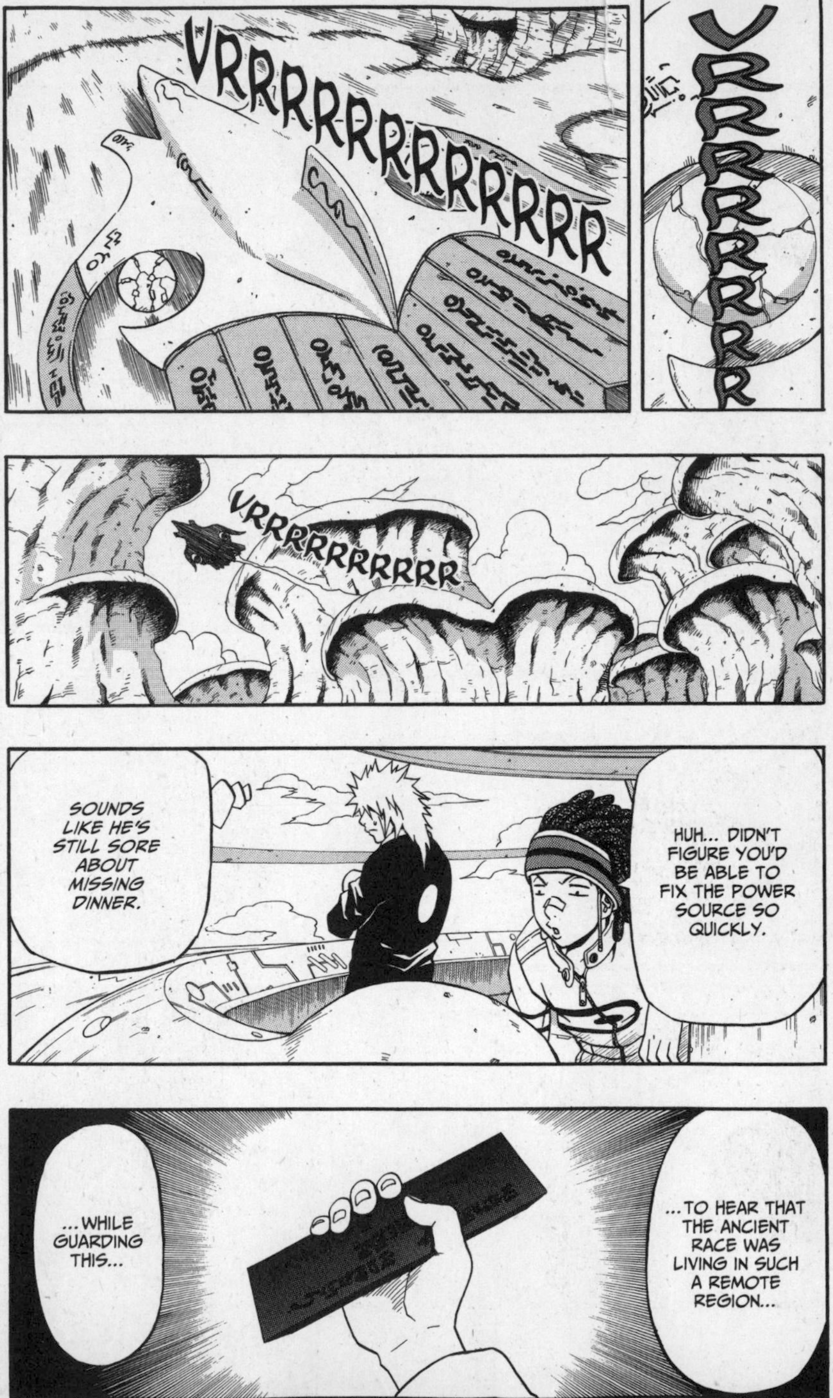
VRRRRRRRRR
VRRRRRRRRRRRRRR
VRRRRRRRRRRRR
HUH... DIDN'T FIGURE YOU'D BE ABLE TO FIX THE POWER SOURCE SO QUICKLY.
SOUNDS LIKE HE'S STILL SORE ABOUT MISSING DINNER.
...TO HEAR THAT THE ANCIENT RACE WAS LIVING IN SUCH A REMOTE REGION...
...WHILE GUARDING THIS...

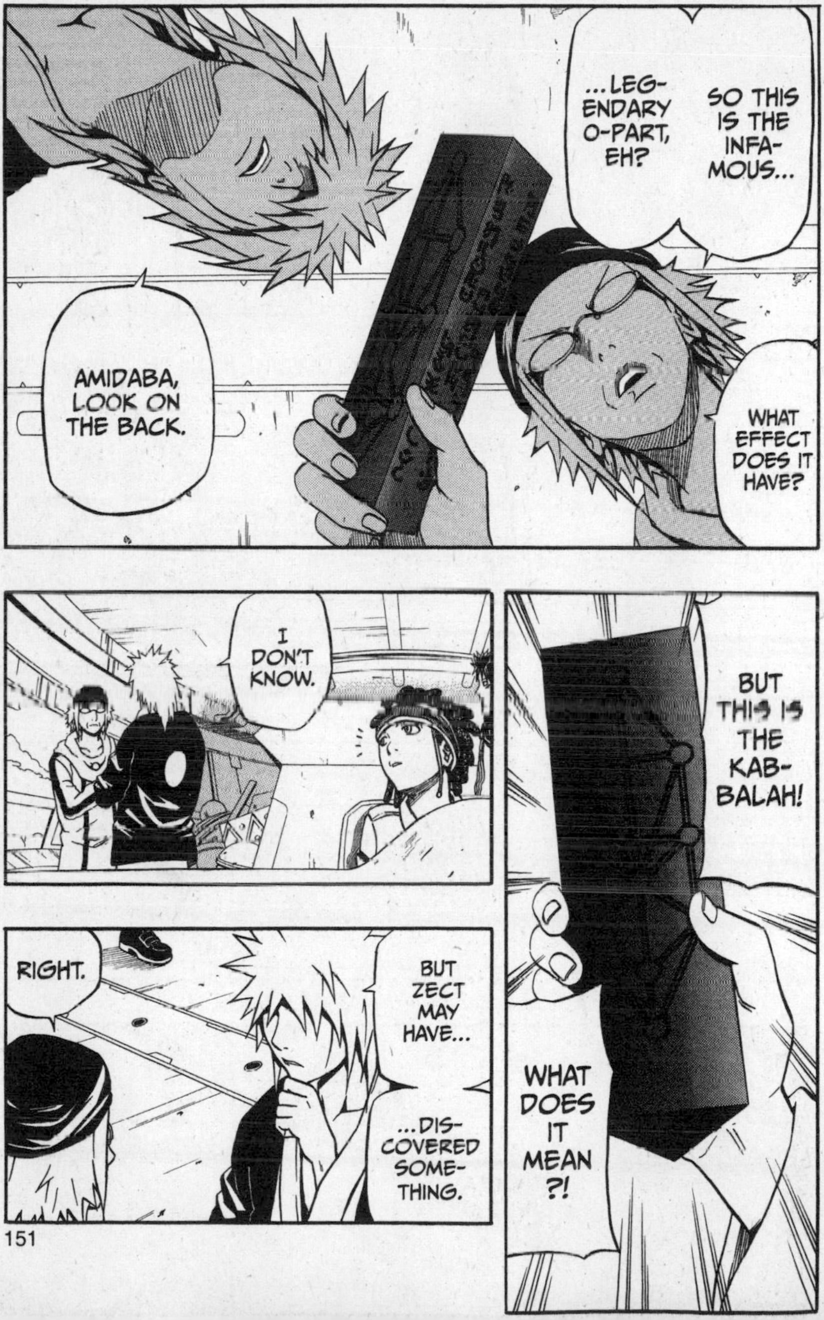
SO THIS IS THE INFAMOUS...
...LEGENDARY O-PART, EH?
WHAT EFFECT DOES IT HAVE?
AMIDABA, LOOK ON THE BACK.
BUT THIS IS THE KABBALAH!
WHAT DOES IT MEAN?!
I DON'T KNOW.
BUT ZECT MAY HAVE...
...DISCOVERED SOMETHING.
RIGHT.

AT THIS POINT I DON'T THINK THERE'S ANY DOUBT ABOUT IT. I BEGIN TO UNDERSTAND WHY...
...HE LEFT RUBY TO GO LOOKING FOR THIS.
HMM...
T M.
SPOING
KRRK
WIP
AH!!
SNATCH

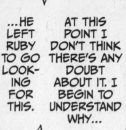

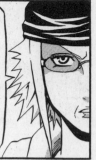

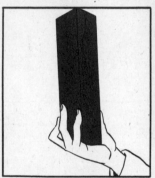

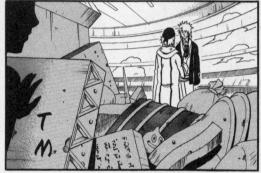

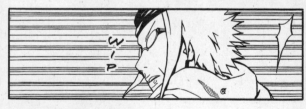

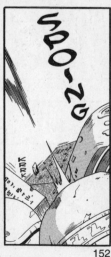

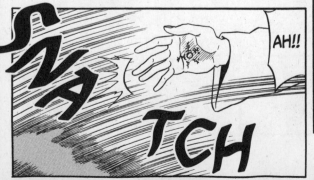

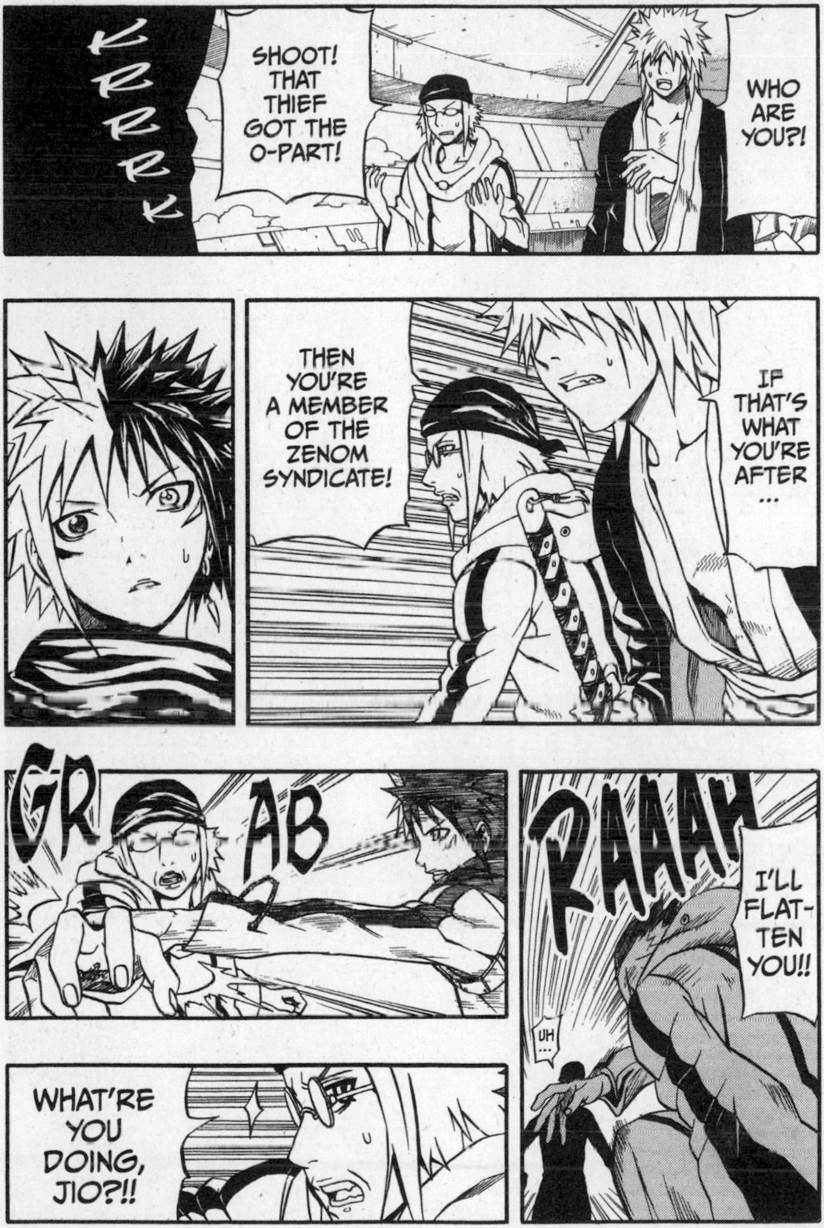
WHO ARE YOU?!
SHOOT! THAT THIEF GOT THE O-PART!
KRRRK
IF THAT'S WHAT YOU'RE AFTER...
THEN YOU'RE A MEMBER OF THE ZENOM SYNDICATE!
RAAAH
I'LL FLAT-TEN YOU!!
UH...
GRAB
WHAT'RE YOU DOING, JIO?!!

?!

HEEEEY...

JIO, IS THIS SOME FRIEND OF YOURS?

THIS O-PART WAS GIVEN TO JIO FOR SAFE-KEEPING.

IT'S HIS, NOT YOURS.

MAY!

MAY... WHAT ARE YOU DOING HERE?

AND END UP LIKE YOUR OLDER BROTHER...?

...BUT I MUST GO WITH YOU!

I'M SORRY, JIO...

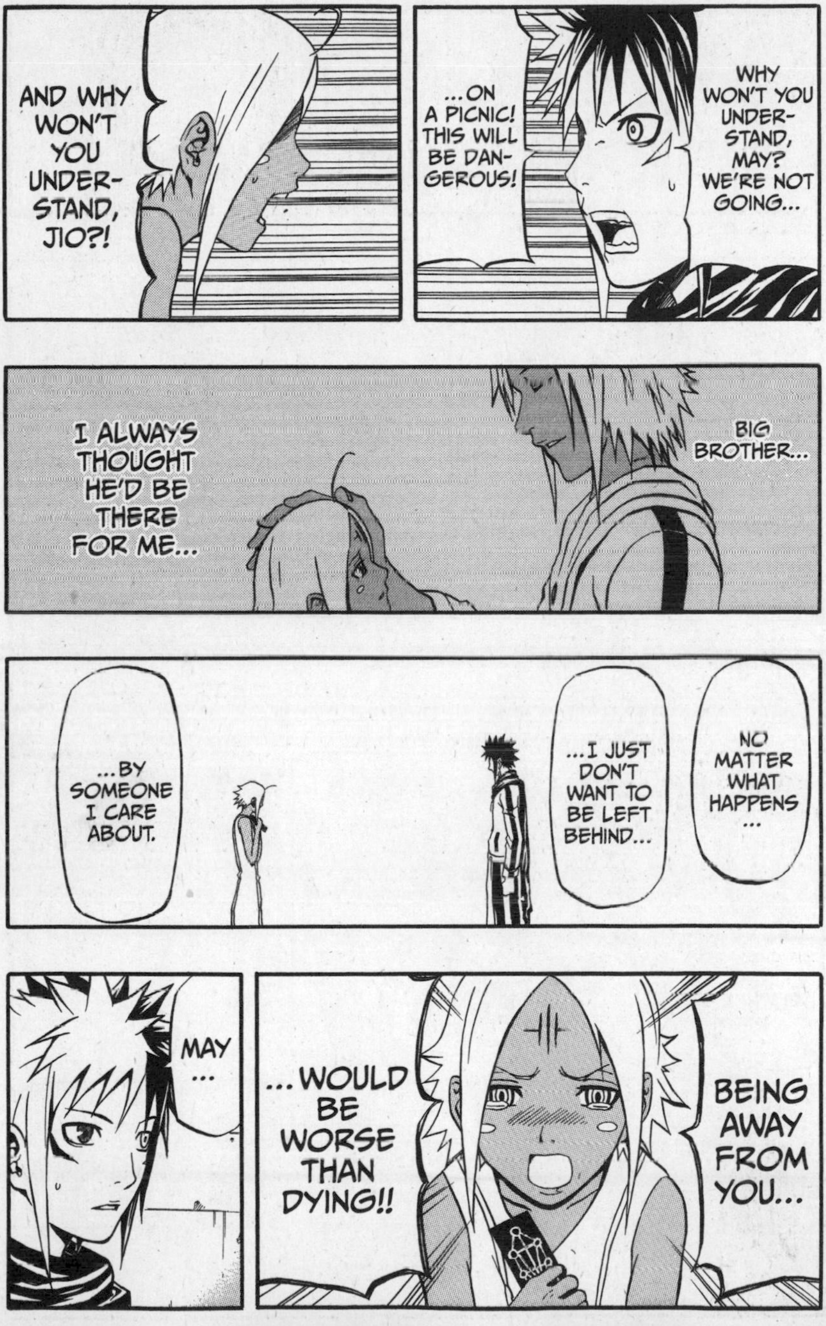
WHY WON'T YOU UNDER-STAND, MAY? WE'RE NOT GOING...
...ON A PICNIC! THIS WILL BE DAN-GEROUS!
AND WHY WON'T YOU UNDER-STAND, JIO?!
BIG BROTHER...
I ALWAYS THOUGHT HE'D BE THERE FOR ME...
NO MATTER WHAT HAPPENS...
...I JUST DON'T WANT TO BE LEFT BEHIND...
...BY SOMEONE I CARE ABOUT.
BEING AWAY FROM YOU...
...WOULD BE WORSE THAN DYING!!
MAY...

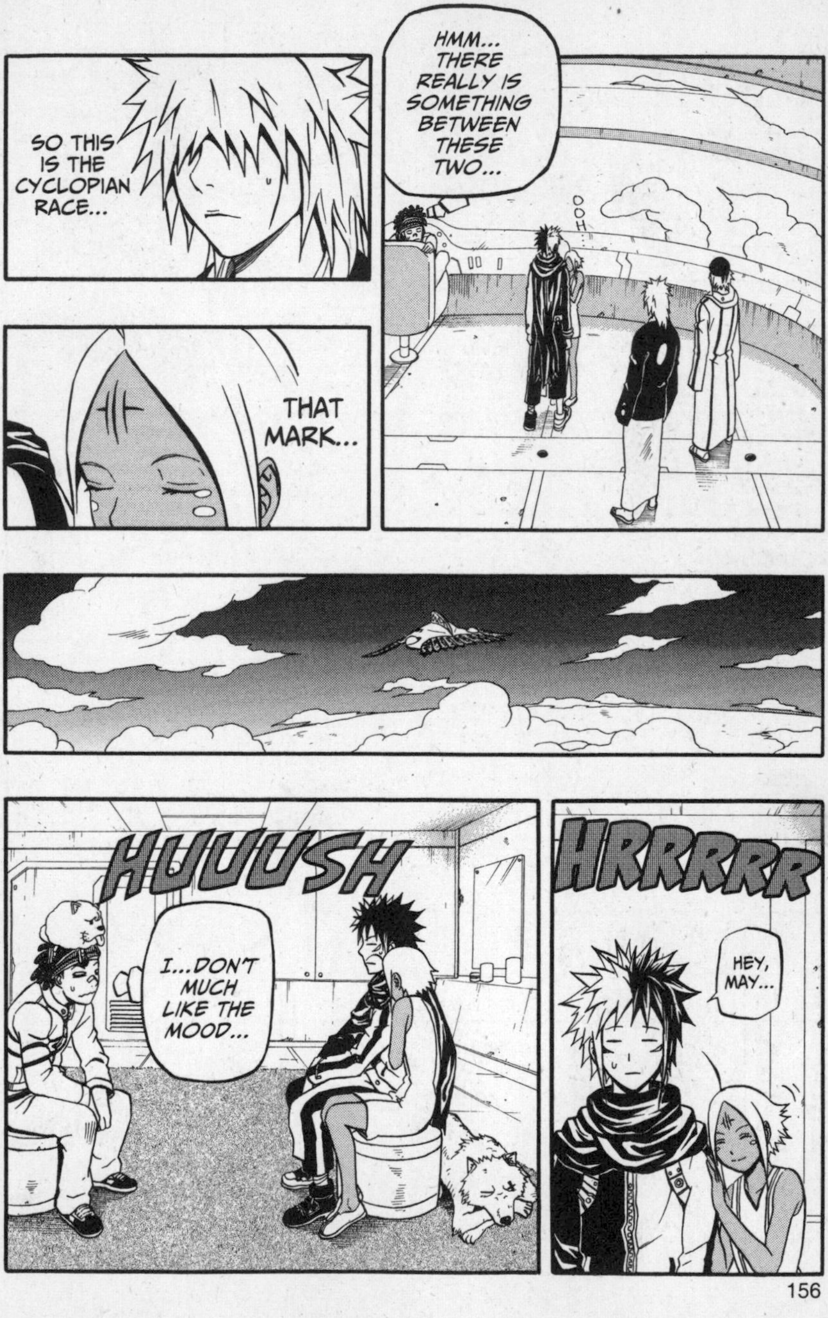
HMM... THERE REALLY IS SOMETHING BETWEEN THESE TWO...
OOH...
SO THIS IS THE CYCLOPIAN RACE...
THAT MARK...
HRRRRRR
HEY, MAY...
HUUUSH
I...DON'T MUCH LIKE THE MOOD...

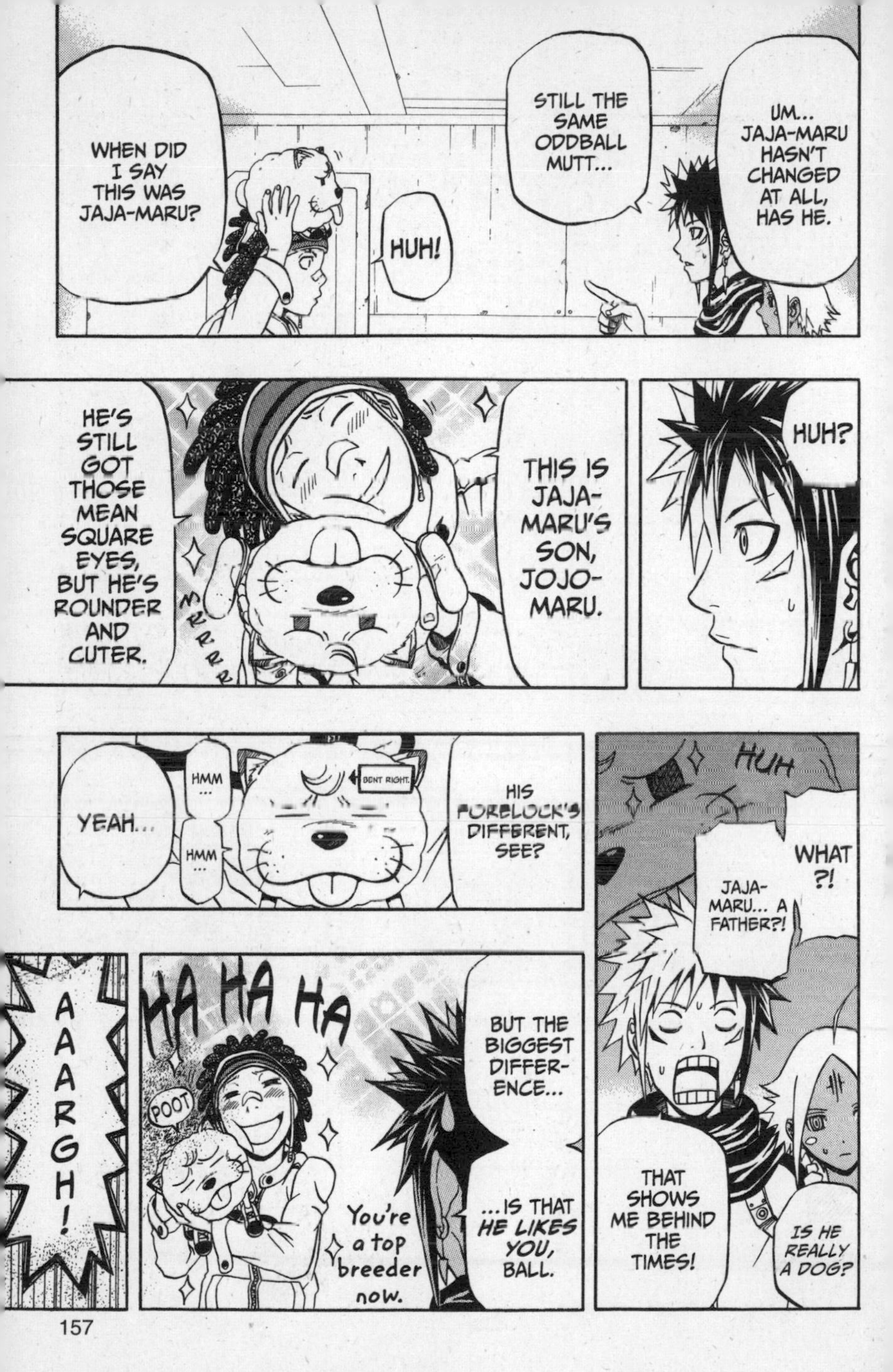
UM... JAJA-MARU HASN'T CHANGED AT ALL, HAS HE.
STILL THE SAME ODDBALL MUTT...
HUH!
WHEN DID I SAY THIS WAS JAJA-MARU?
HUH?
THIS IS JAJA-MARU'S SON, JOJO-MARU.
HE'S STILL GOT THOSE MEAN SQUARE EYES, BUT HE'S ROUNDER AND CUTER.
MRRRR
HUH
WHAT?!
JAJA-MARU... A FATHER?!
THAT SHOWS ME BEHIND THE TIMES!
IS HE REALLY A DOG?
HIS FORELOCK'S DIFFERENT, SEE?
BENT RIGHT.
HMM...
HMM...
YEAH...
BUT THE BIGGEST DIFFERENCE...
...IS THAT HE LIKES YOU, BALL.
You're a top breeder now.
HA HA HA
POOT
AAARGH!

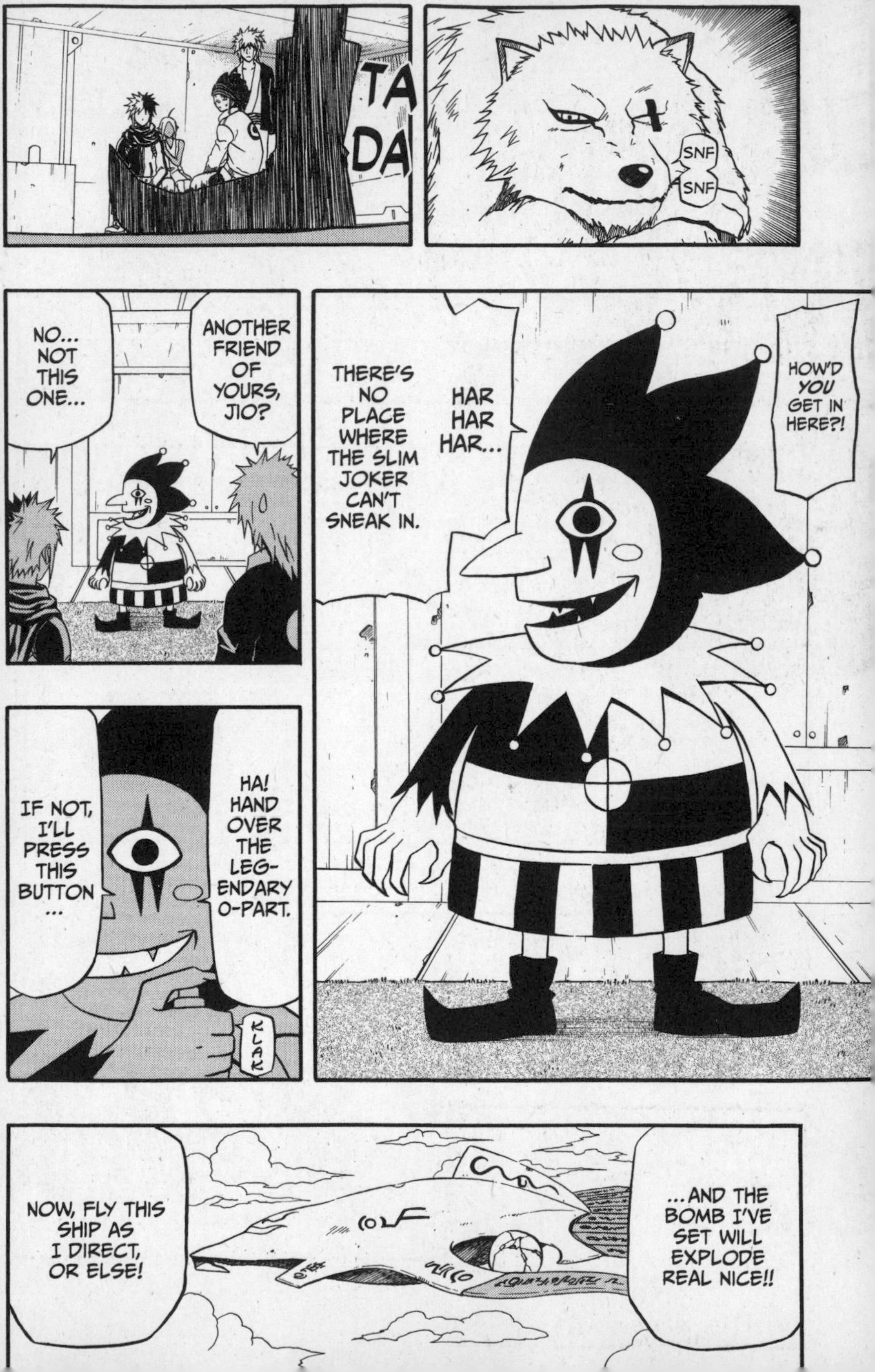
SNF
SNF
TA DA
HOW'D YOU GET IN HERE?!
HAR HAR HAR...
THERE'S NO PLACE WHERE THE SLIM JOKER CAN'T SNEAK IN.
ANOTHER FRIEND OF YOURS, JIO?
NO... NOT THIS ONE...
HA! HAND OVER THE LEG-ENDARY O-PART.
KLAK
IF NOT, I'LL PRESS THIS BUTTON ...
...AND THE BOMB I'VE SET WILL EXPLODE REAL NICE!!
NOW, FLY THIS SHIP AS I DIRECT, OR ELSE!

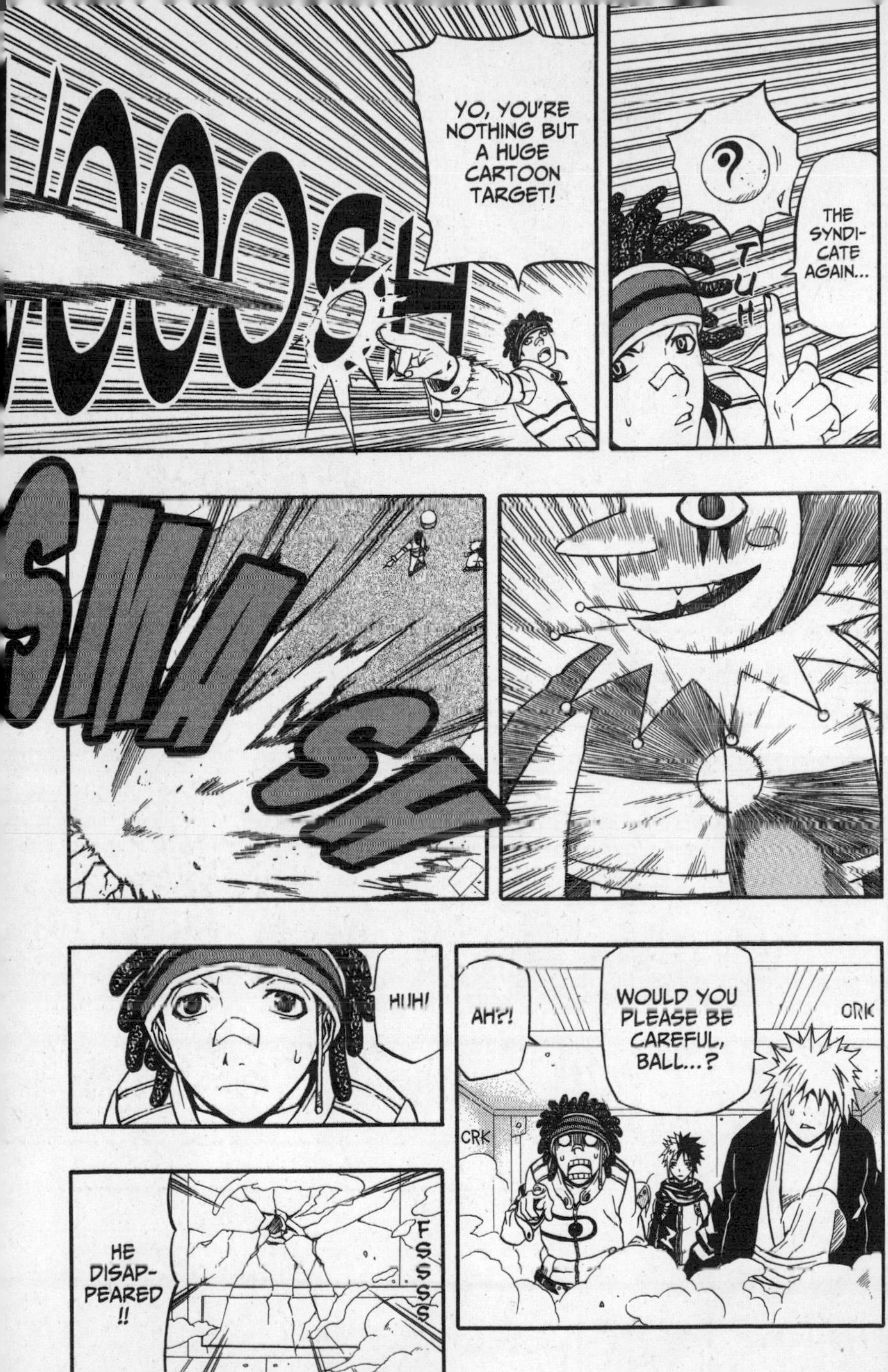
?
THE SYNDICATE AGAIN...
TUH
YO, YOU'RE NOTHING BUT A HUGE CARTOON TARGET!
WOOOSH
SMASH
ORK
WOULD YOU PLEASE BE CAREFUL, BALL...?
AH?!
CRK
HUH!
HE DISAP-PEARED!!
FSSSS

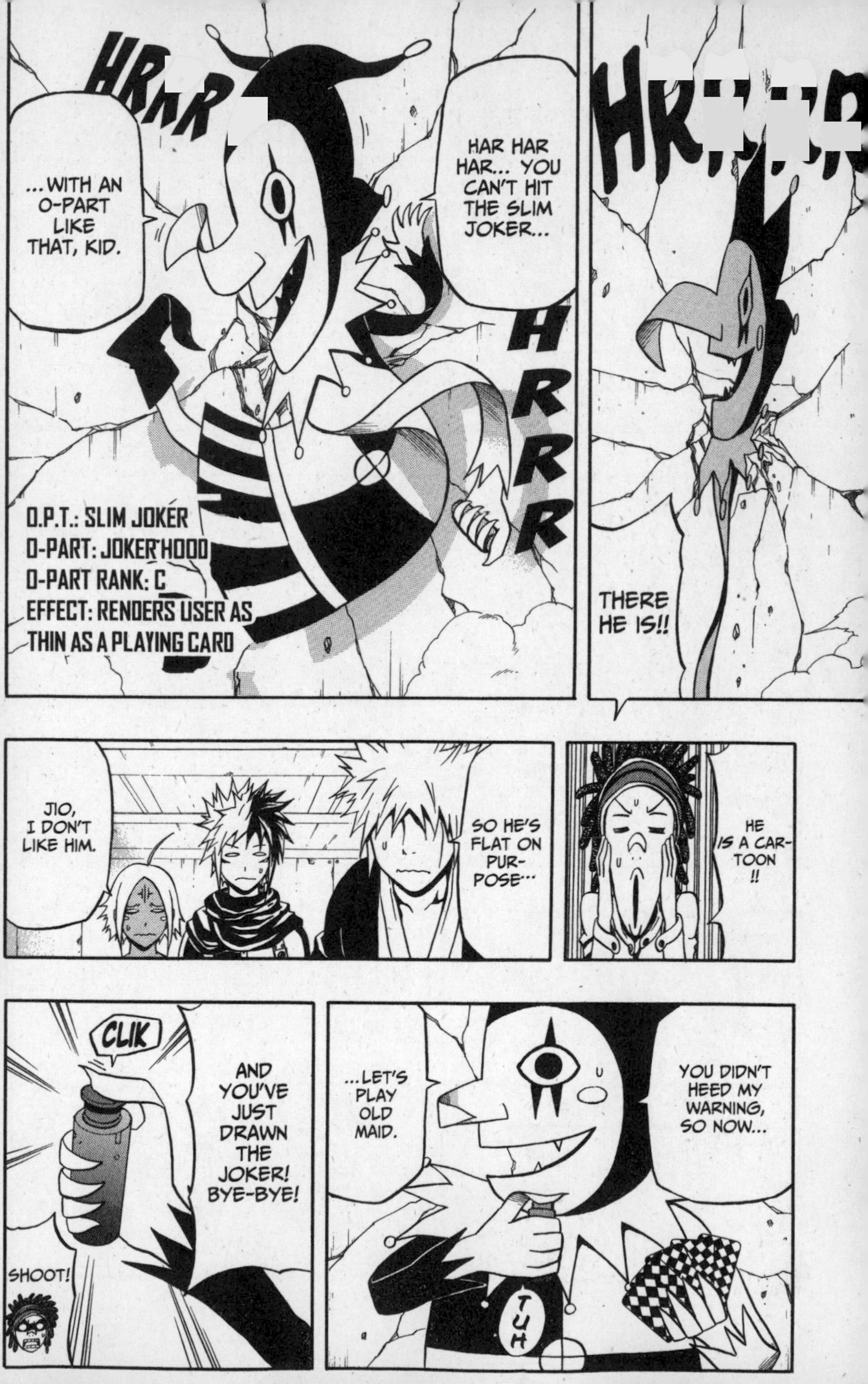
HR
THERE HE IS!!
HAR HAR HAR... YOU CAN'T HIT THE SLIM JOKER...
HRRR
...WITH AN O-PART LIKE THAT, KID.
O.P.T.: SLIM JOKER
O-PART: JOKER HOOD
O-PART RANK: C
EFFECT: RENDERS USER AS THIN AS A PLAYING CARD
HRRR
HE IS A CARTOON!!
SO HE'S FLAT ON PURPOSE...
JIO, I DON'T LIKE HIM.
YOU DIDN'T HEED MY WARNING, SO NOW...
...LET'S PLAY OLD MAID.
TUH
CLIK
AND YOU'VE JUST DRAWN THE JOKER! BYE-BYE!
SHOOT!

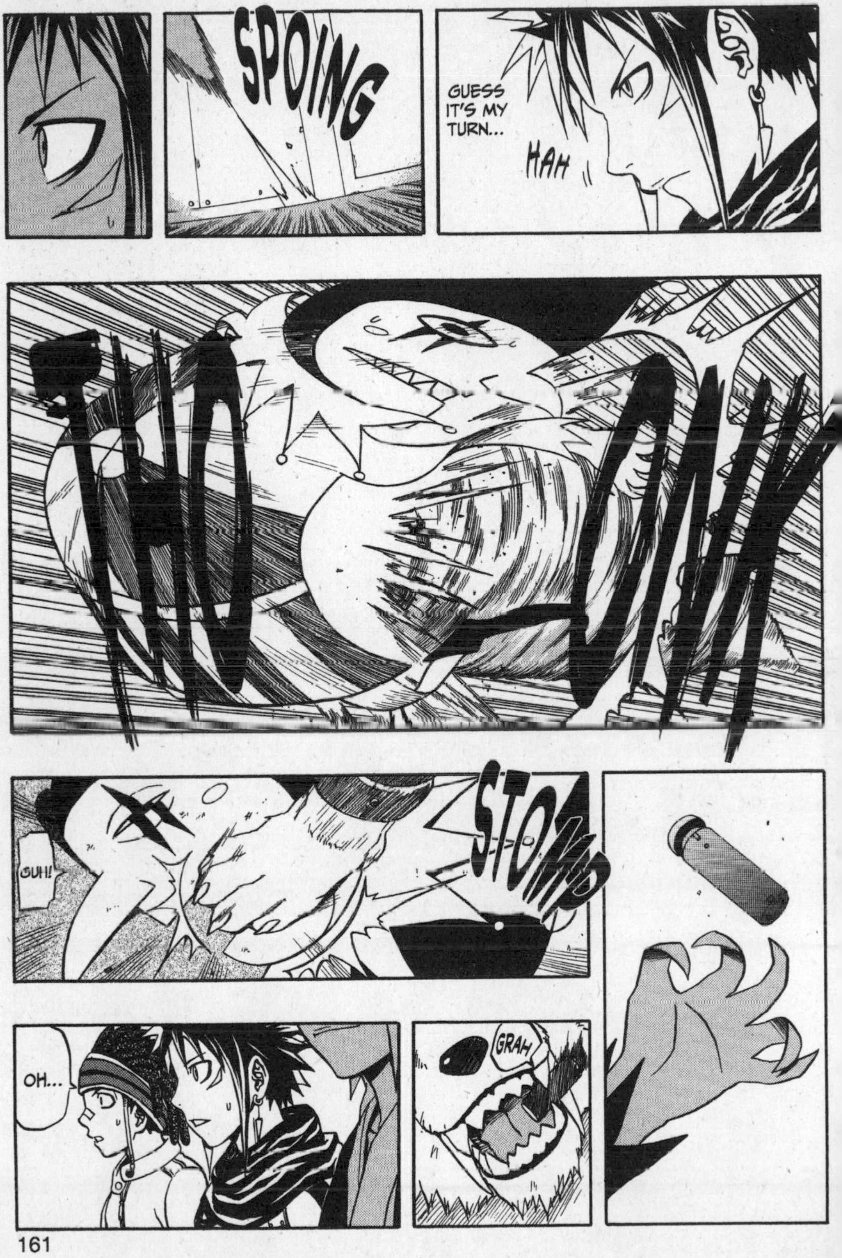
GUESS IT'S MY TURN...
HAH
SPOING
STOMP
GUH!
GRAH
OH...

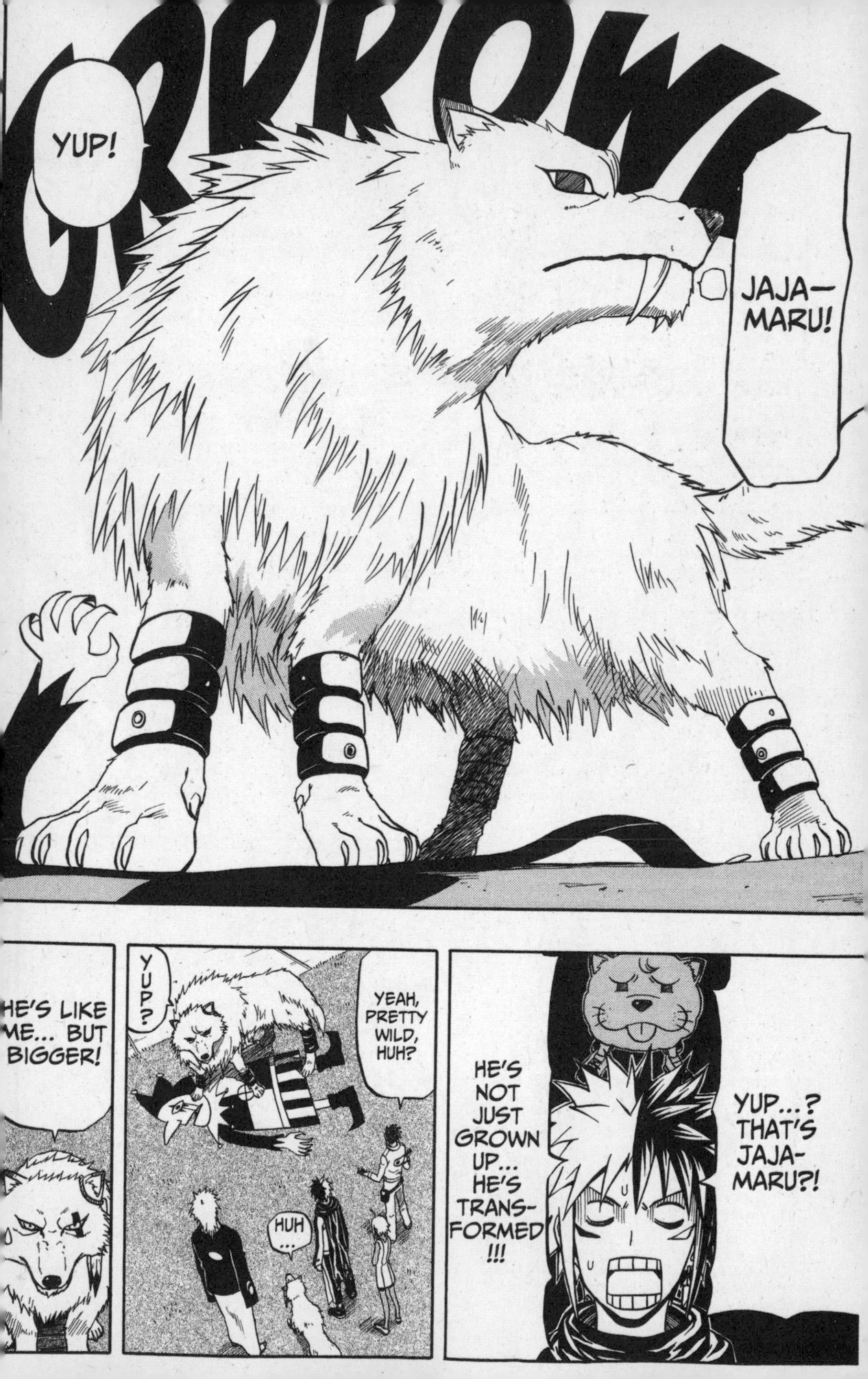
JAJA-
MARU!
YUP!
YUP...?
THAT'S
JAJA-
MARU?!
HE'S
NOT
JUST
GROWN
UP...
HE'S
TRANS-
FORMED
!!!
YEAH,
PRETTY
WILD,
HUH?
YUP?
HUH
...
HE'S LIKE
ME... BUT
BIGGER!

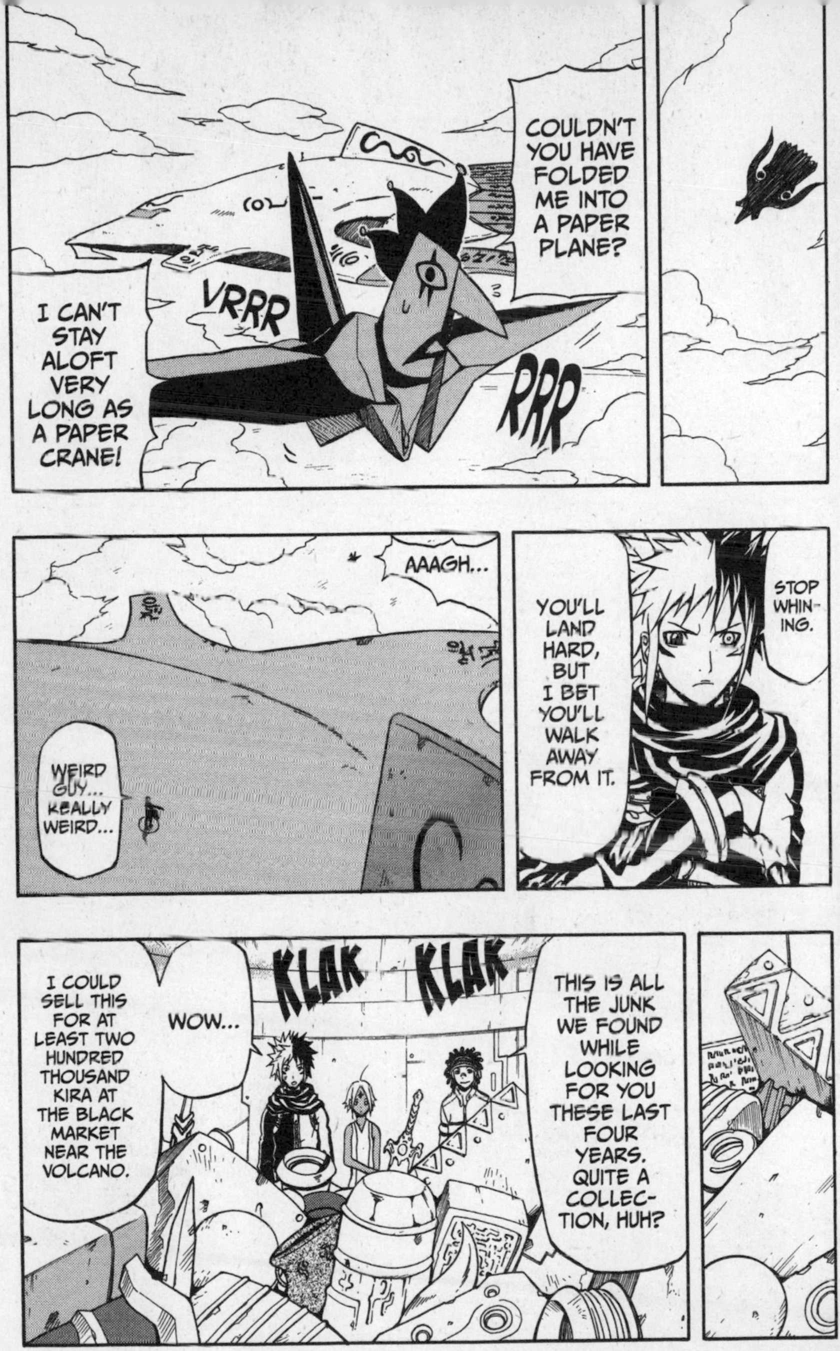
COULDN'T YOU HAVE FOLDED ME INTO A PAPER PLANE?
VRRR
RRR
I CAN'T STAY ALOFT VERY LONG AS A PAPER CRANE!
STOP WHINING.
YOU'LL LAND HARD, BUT I BET YOU'LL WALK AWAY FROM IT.
AAAGH...
WEIRD GUY... REALLY WEIRD...
THIS IS ALL THE JUNK WE FOUND WHILE LOOKING FOR YOU THESE LAST FOUR YEARS. QUITE A COLLECTION, HUH?
KLAK KLAK
WOW...
I COULD SELL THIS FOR AT LEAST TWO HUNDRED THOUSAND KIRA AT THE BLACK MARKET NEAR THE VOLCANO.

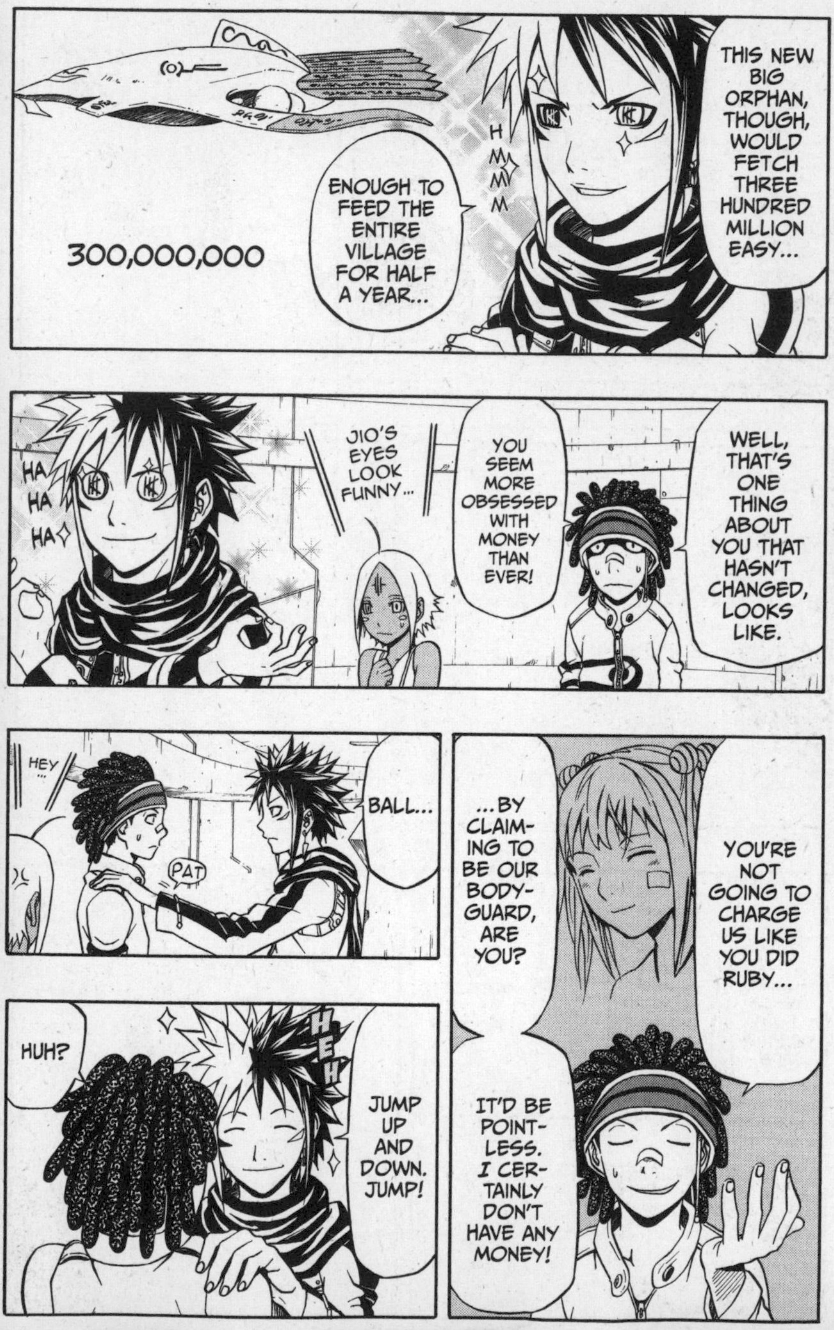
THIS NEW BIG ORPHAN, THOUGH, WOULD FETCH THREE HUNDRED MILLION EASY...
HMMM
ENOUGH TO FEED THE ENTIRE VILLAGE FOR HALF A YEAR...
300,000,000
WELL, THAT'S ONE THING ABOUT YOU THAT HASN'T CHANGED, LOOKS LIKE.
YOU SEEM MORE OBSESSED WITH MONEY THAN EVER!
JIO'S EYES LOOK FUNNY...
HA HA HA
YOU'RE NOT GOING TO CHARGE US LIKE YOU DID RUBY...
...BY CLAIMING TO BE OUR BODYGUARD, ARE YOU?
IT'D BE POINTLESS. I CERTAINLY DON'T HAVE ANY MONEY!
BALL...
HEY...
PAT
HEH
JUMP UP AND DOWN. JUMP!
HUH?

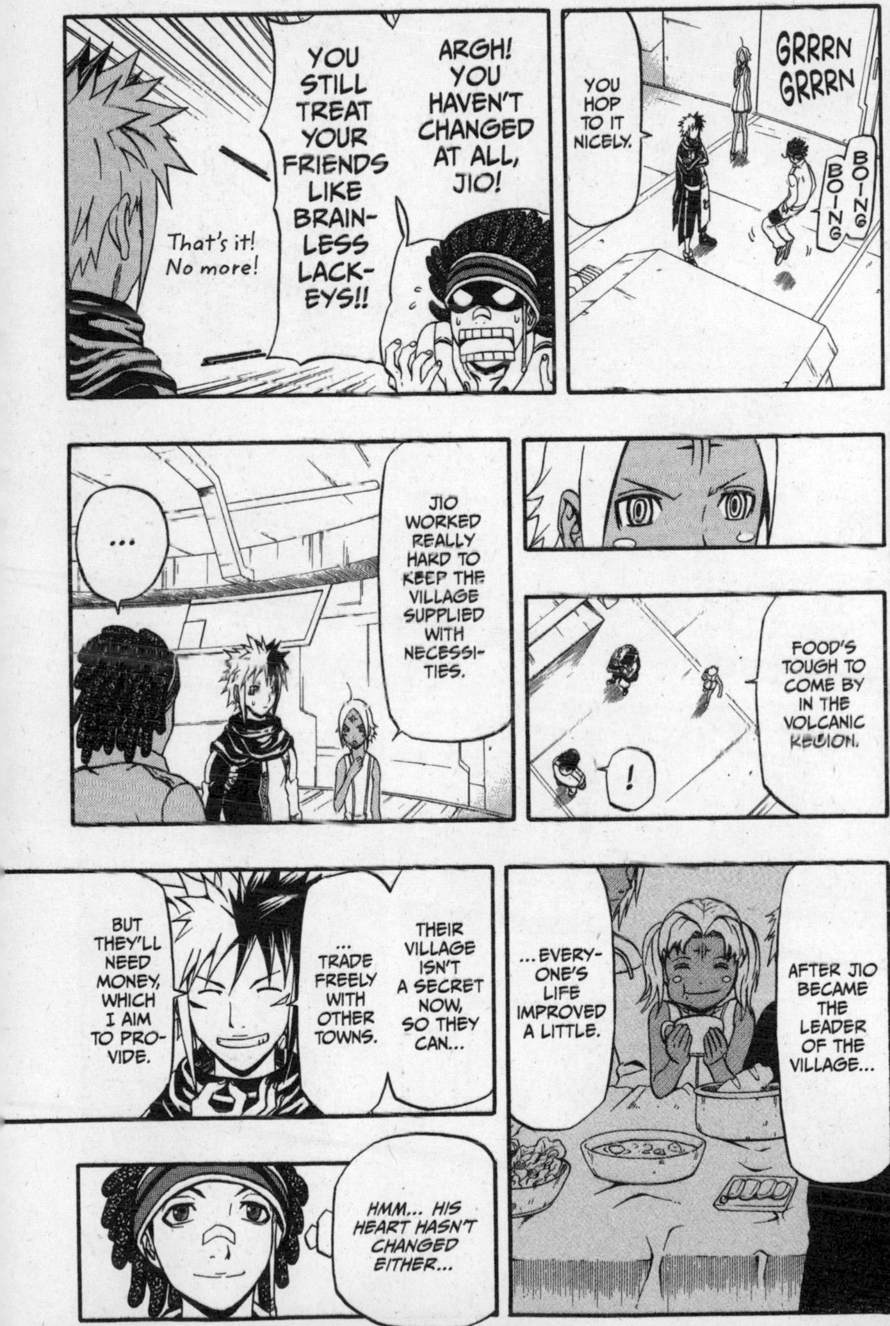
GRRRN GRRRN
YOU HOP TO IT NICELY.
BOING BOING
ARGH! YOU HAVEN'T CHANGED AT ALL, JIO!
YOU STILL TREAT YOUR FRIENDS LIKE BRAIN-LESS LACK-EYS!!
That's it! No more!
FOOD'S TOUGH TO COME BY IN THE VOLCANIC REGION.
!
JIO WORKED REALLY HARD TO KEEP THE VILLAGE SUPPLIED WITH NECESSI-TIES.
...
AFTER JIO BECAME THE LEADER OF THE VILLAGE...
...EVERY-ONE'S LIFE IMPROVED A LITTLE.
THEIR VILLAGE ISN'T A SECRET NOW, SO THEY CAN...
...TRADE FREELY WITH OTHER TOWNS.
BUT THEY'LL NEED MONEY, WHICH I AIM TO PRO-VIDE.
HMM... HIS HEART HASN'T CHANGED EITHER...

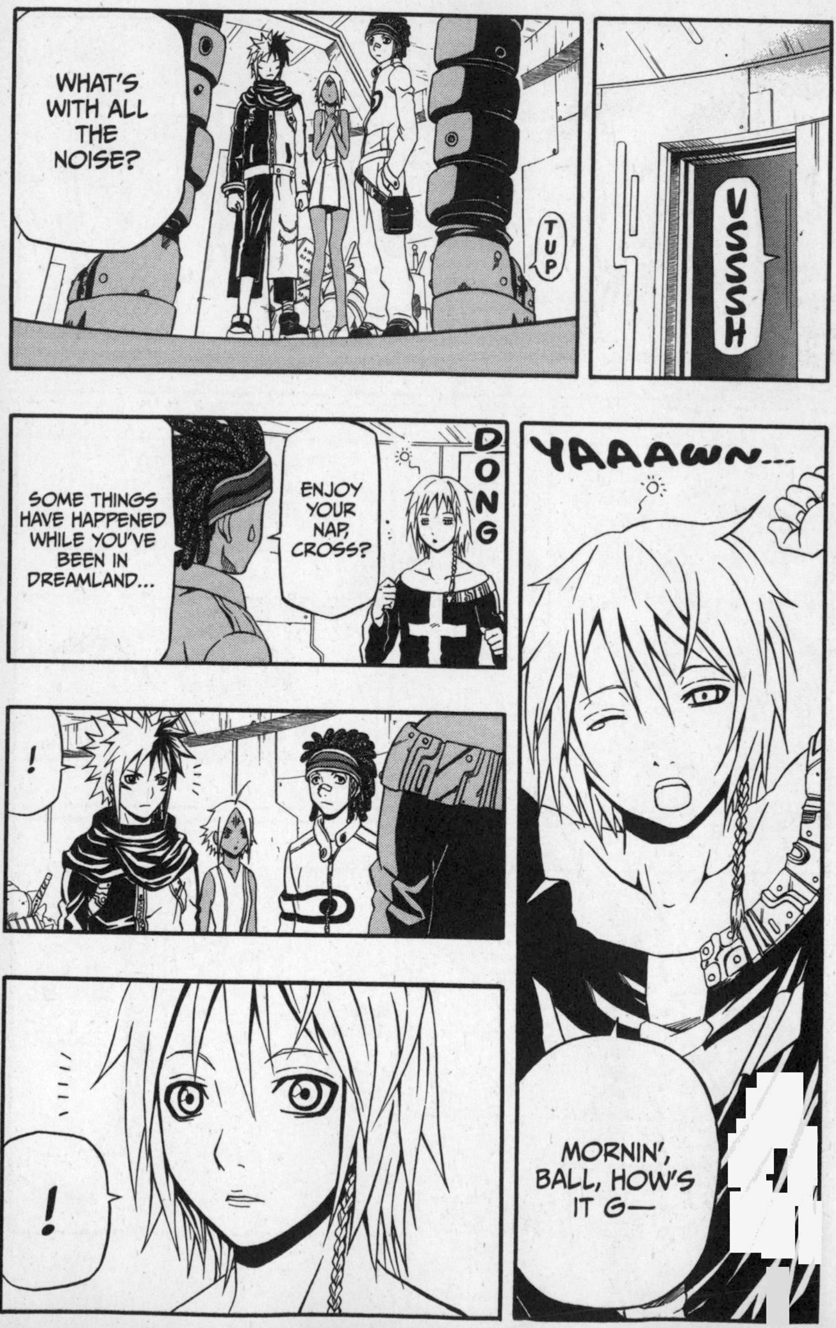
VSSSH
TUP
WHAT'S WITH ALL THE NOISE?
YAAAWN...
MORNIN', BALL, HOW'S IT G—
DONG
ENJOY YOUR NAP, CROSS?
SOME THINGS HAVE HAPPENED WHILE YOU'VE BEEN IN DREAMLAND...
!
!

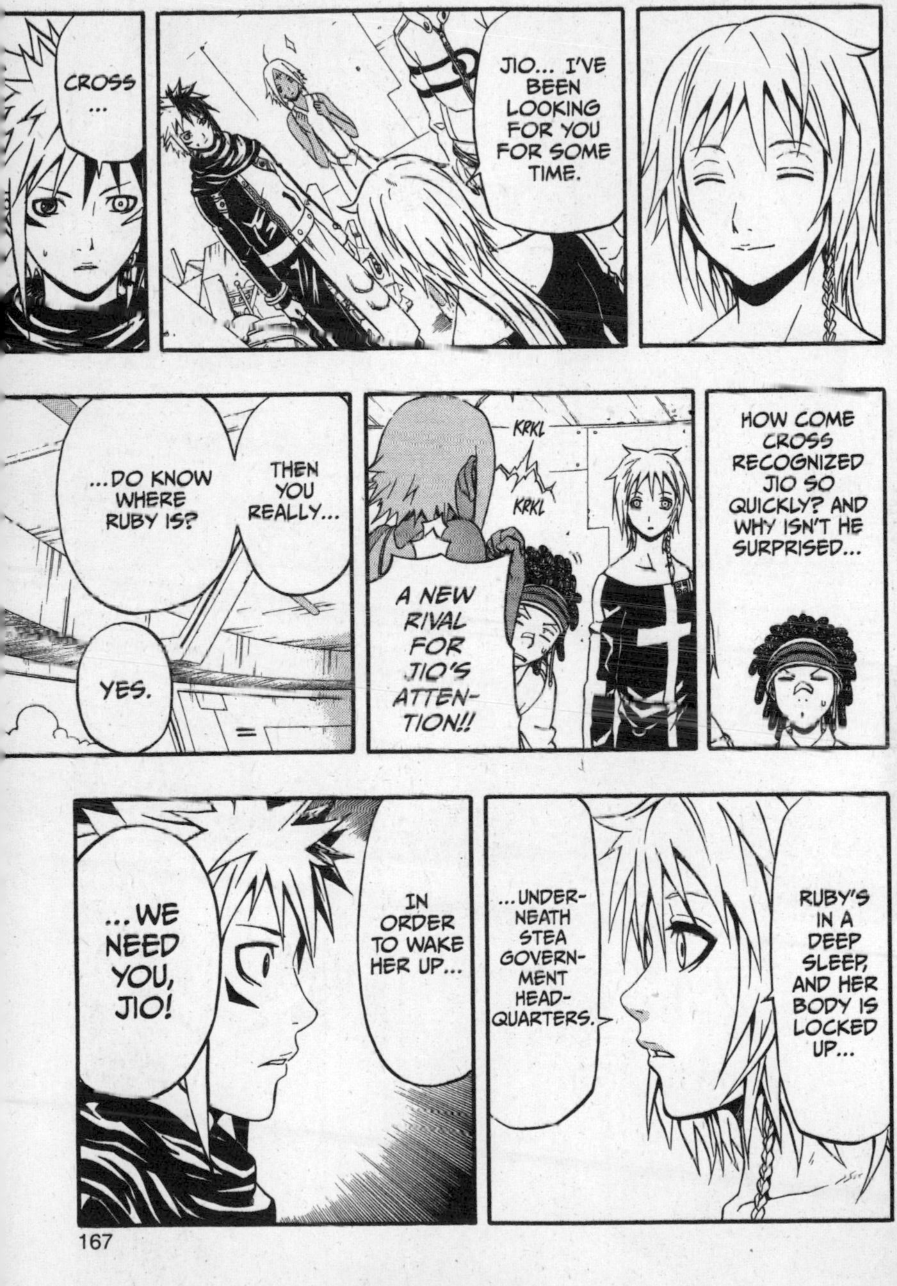
JIO... I'VE BEEN LOOKING FOR YOU FOR SOME TIME.
CROSS ...
HOW COME CROSS RECOGNIZED JIO SO QUICKLY? AND WHY ISN'T HE SURPRISED...
KRKL
KRKL
A NEW RIVAL FOR JIO'S ATTENTION!!
THEN YOU REALLY...
...DO KNOW WHERE RUBY IS?
YES.
RUBY'S IN A DEEP SLEEP, AND HER BODY IS LOCKED UP...
...UNDERNEATH STEA GOVERNMENT HEADQUARTERS.
IN ORDER TO WAKE HER UP...
...WE NEED YOU, JIO!

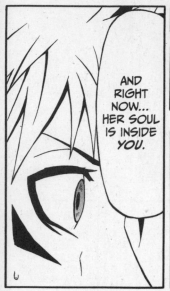

I PROMISE ...
...I'LL FIND HIM!!
FWAAAH
ABS-ORB!!!
RUBY CHOSE TO LET SATAN ABSORB HER SOUL... TO SAVE YOU, JIO.
AND RIGHT NOW... HER SOUL IS INSIDE YOU.
DON'T FORGET THAT YOU'RE NOT ALONE.
I'LL ALWAYS BE HERE, INSIDE YOUR HEART...
...PRO-TECTING YOU... ALWAYS.
SWUH
RUBY!!!

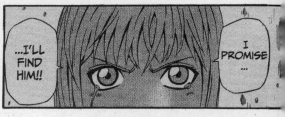

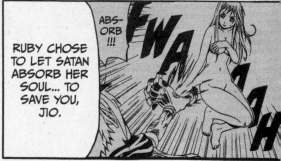

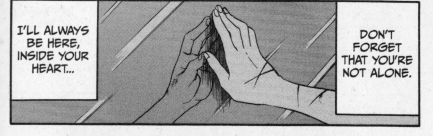

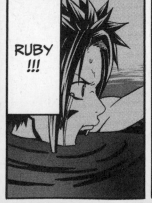

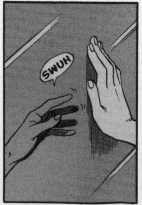

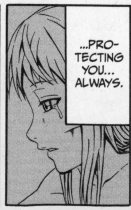

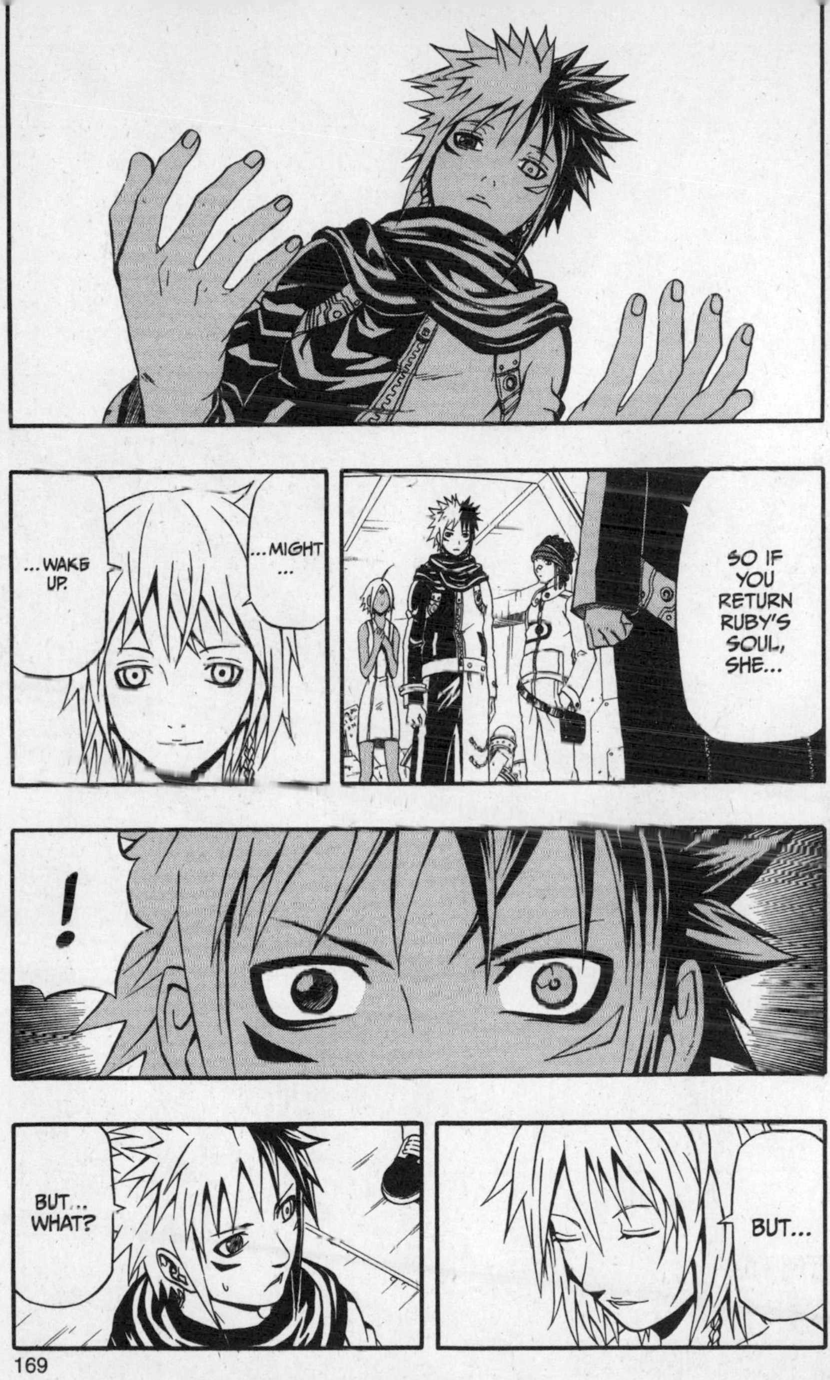
SO IF YOU RETURN RUBY'S SOUL, SHE...
...MIGHT ...
...WAKE UP.
!
BUT...
BUT... WHAT?

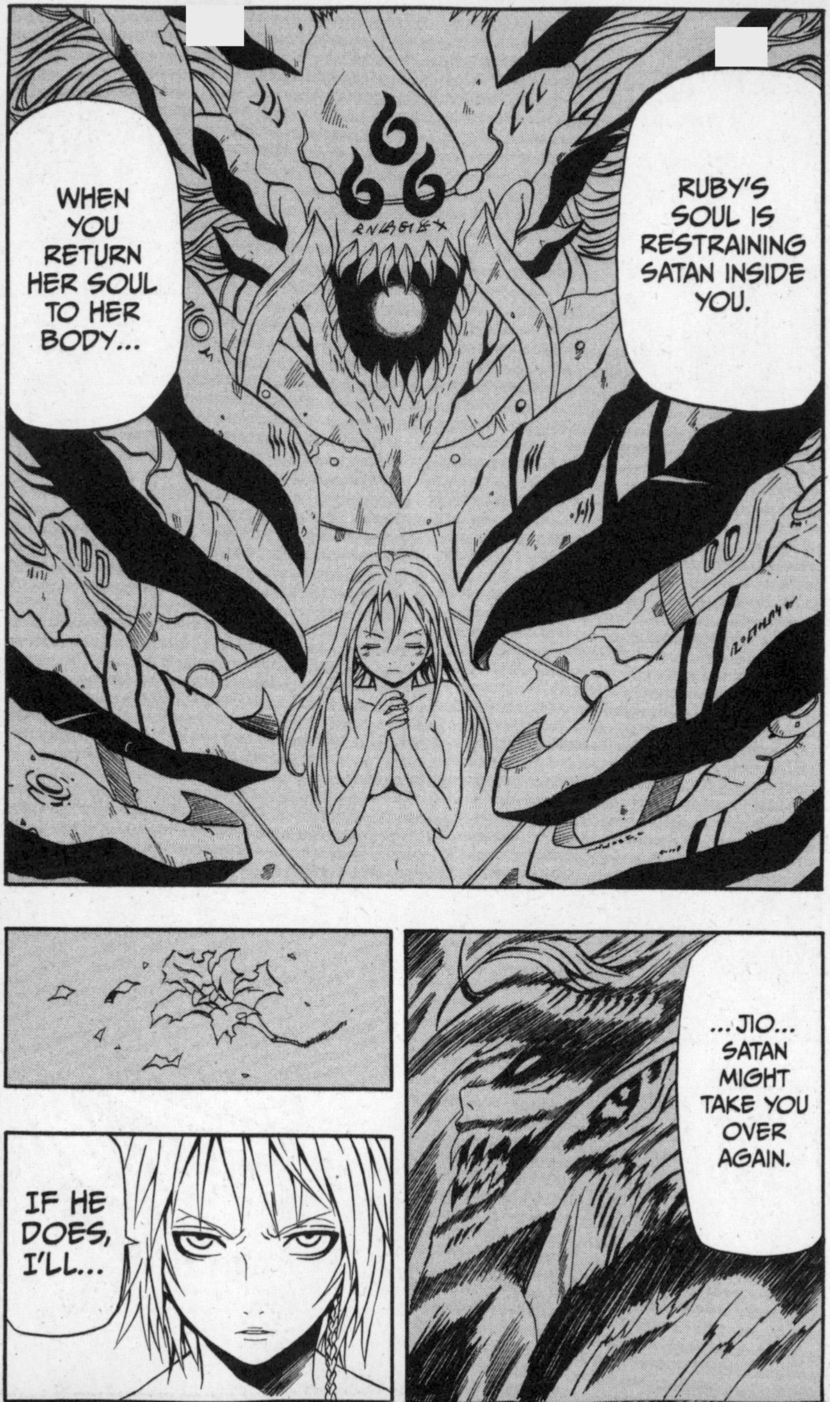
RUBY'S SOUL IS RESTRAINING SATAN INSIDE YOU.
WHEN YOU RETURN HER SOUL TO HER BODY...
...JIO... SATAN MIGHT TAKE YOU OVER AGAIN.
IF HE DOES, I'LL...

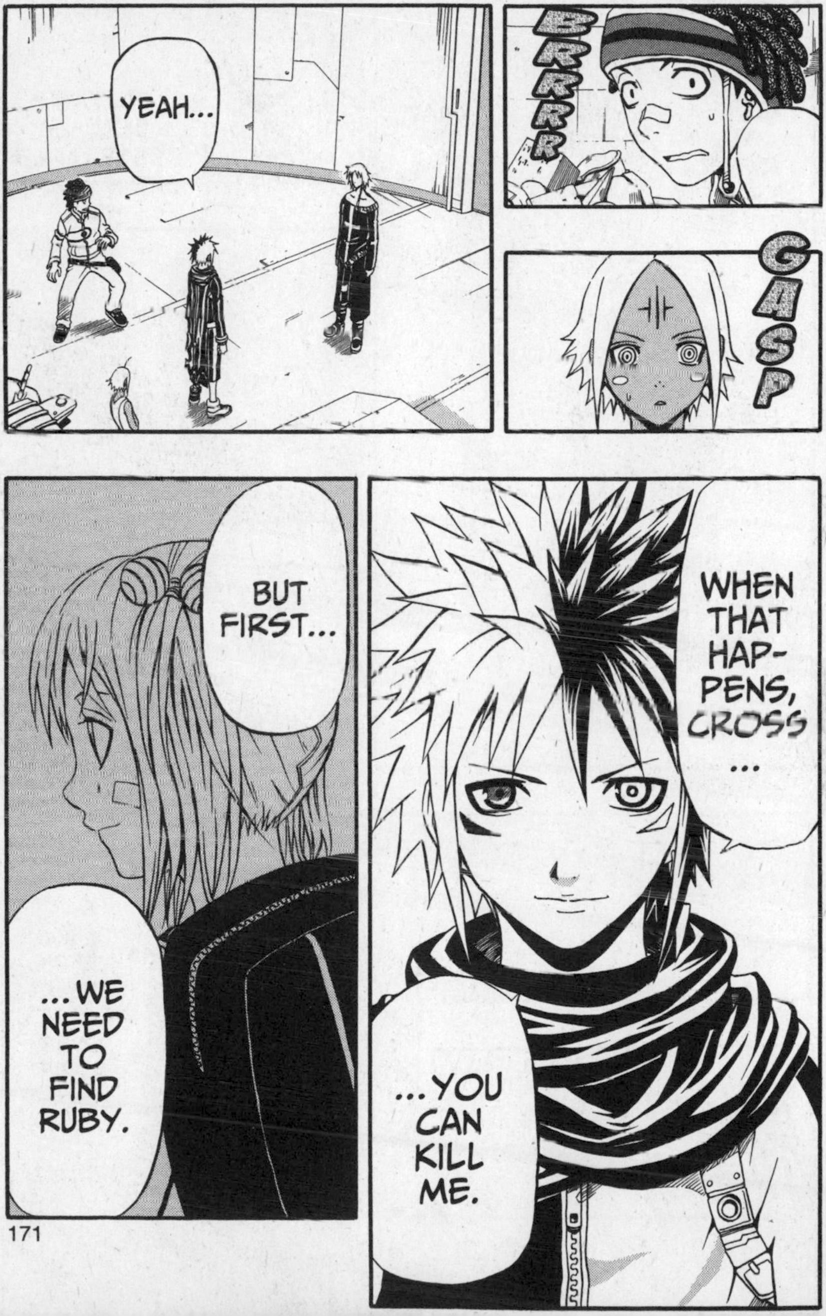
BRRRR
GASP
YEAH...
WHEN THAT HAP-PENS, CROSS ...
...YOU CAN KILL ME.
BUT FIRST...
...WE NEED TO FIND RUBY.

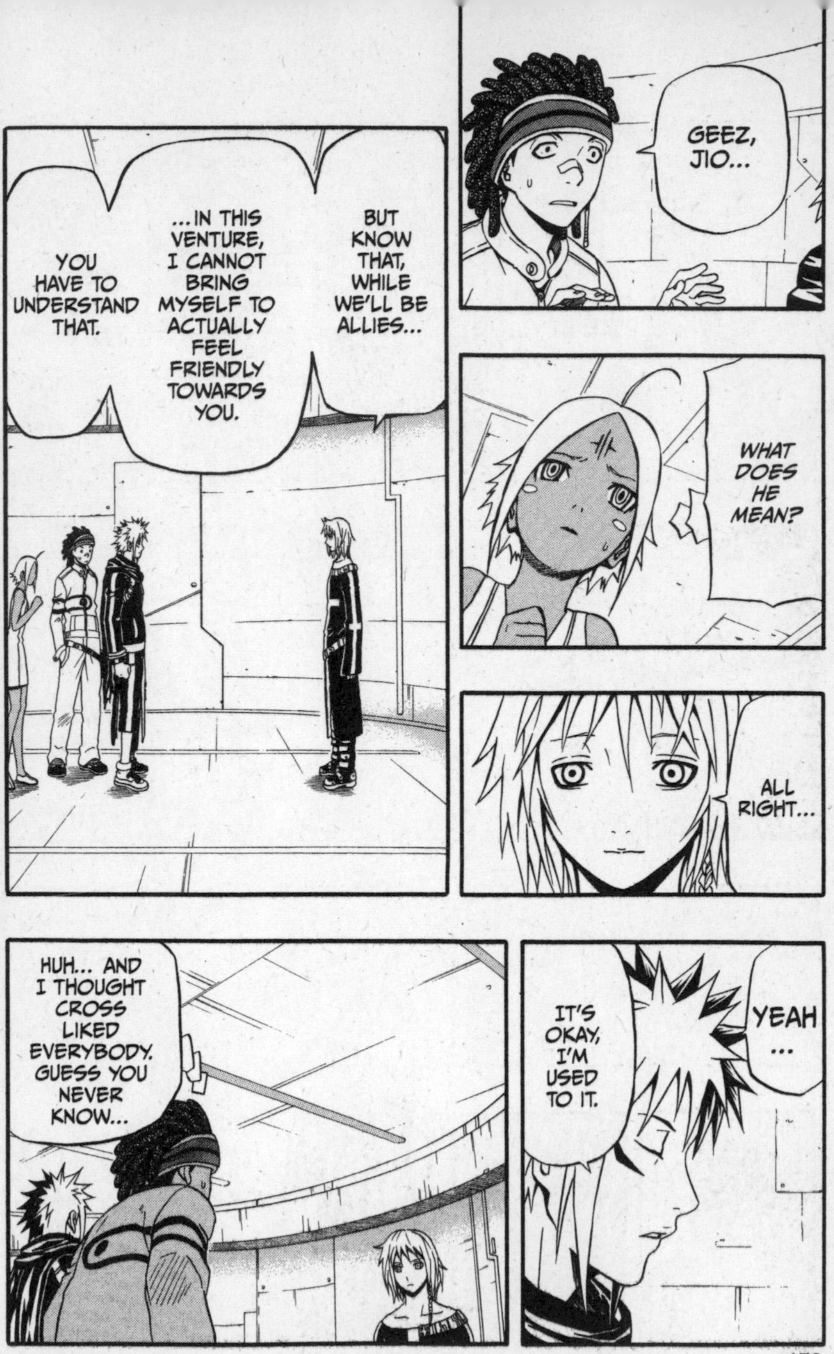
GEEZ, JIO...
WHAT DOES HE MEAN?
ALL RIGHT...
BUT KNOW THAT, WHILE WE'LL BE ALLIES...
...IN THIS VENTURE, I CANNOT BRING MYSELF TO ACTUALLY FEEL FRIENDLY TOWARDS YOU.
YOU HAVE TO UNDERSTAND THAT.
YEAH ...
IT'S OKAY, I'M USED TO IT.
HUH... AND I THOUGHT CROSS LIKED EVERYBODY. GUESS YOU NEVER KNOW...

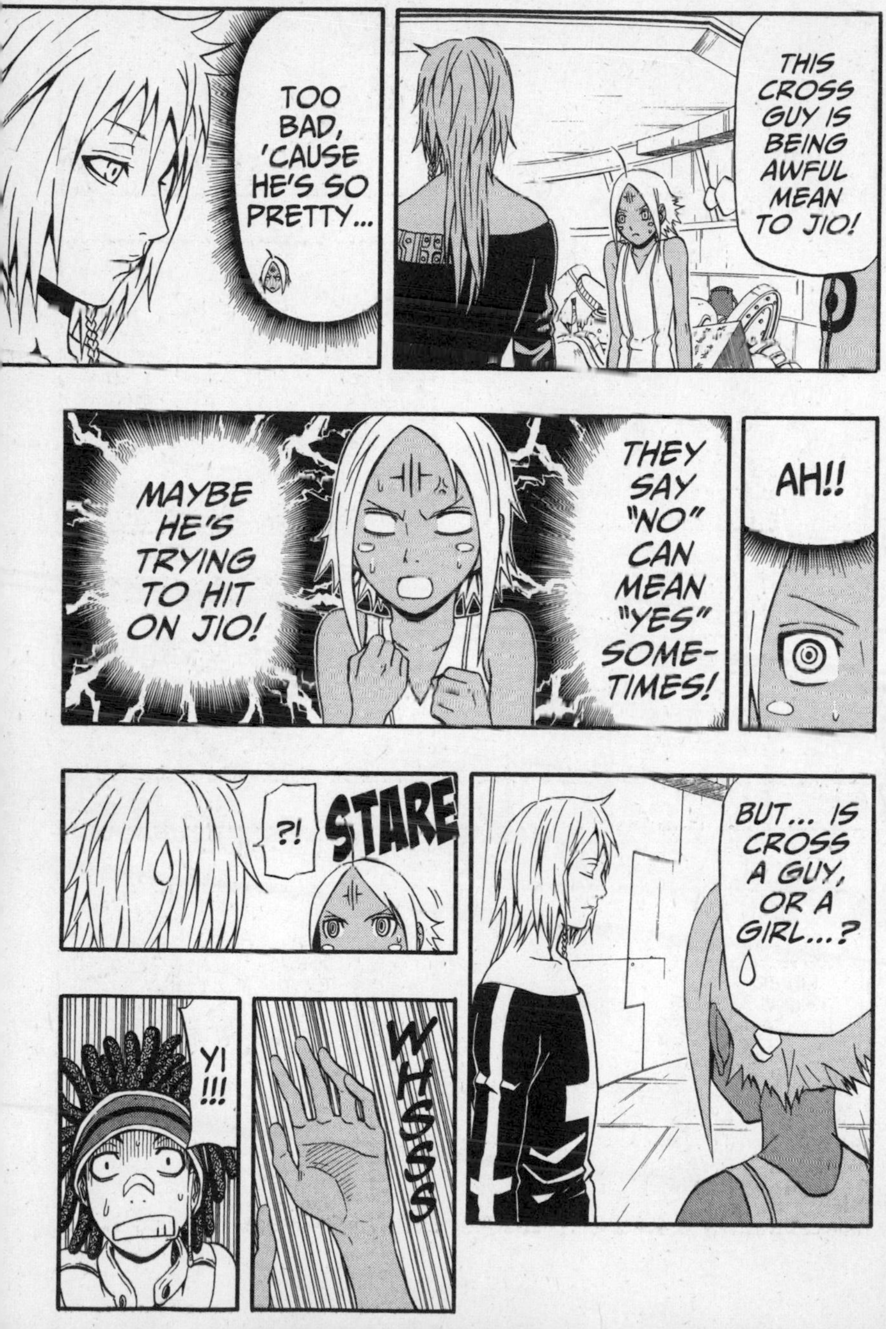
THIS CROSS GUY IS BEING AWFUL MEAN TO JIO!
TOO BAD, 'CAUSE HE'S SO PRETTY...
AH!!
THEY SAY "NO" CAN MEAN "YES" SOMETIMES!
MAYBE HE'S TRYING TO HIT ON JIO!
BUT... IS CROSS A GUY, OR A GIRL...?
STARE
?!
WHSSS
YI !!!

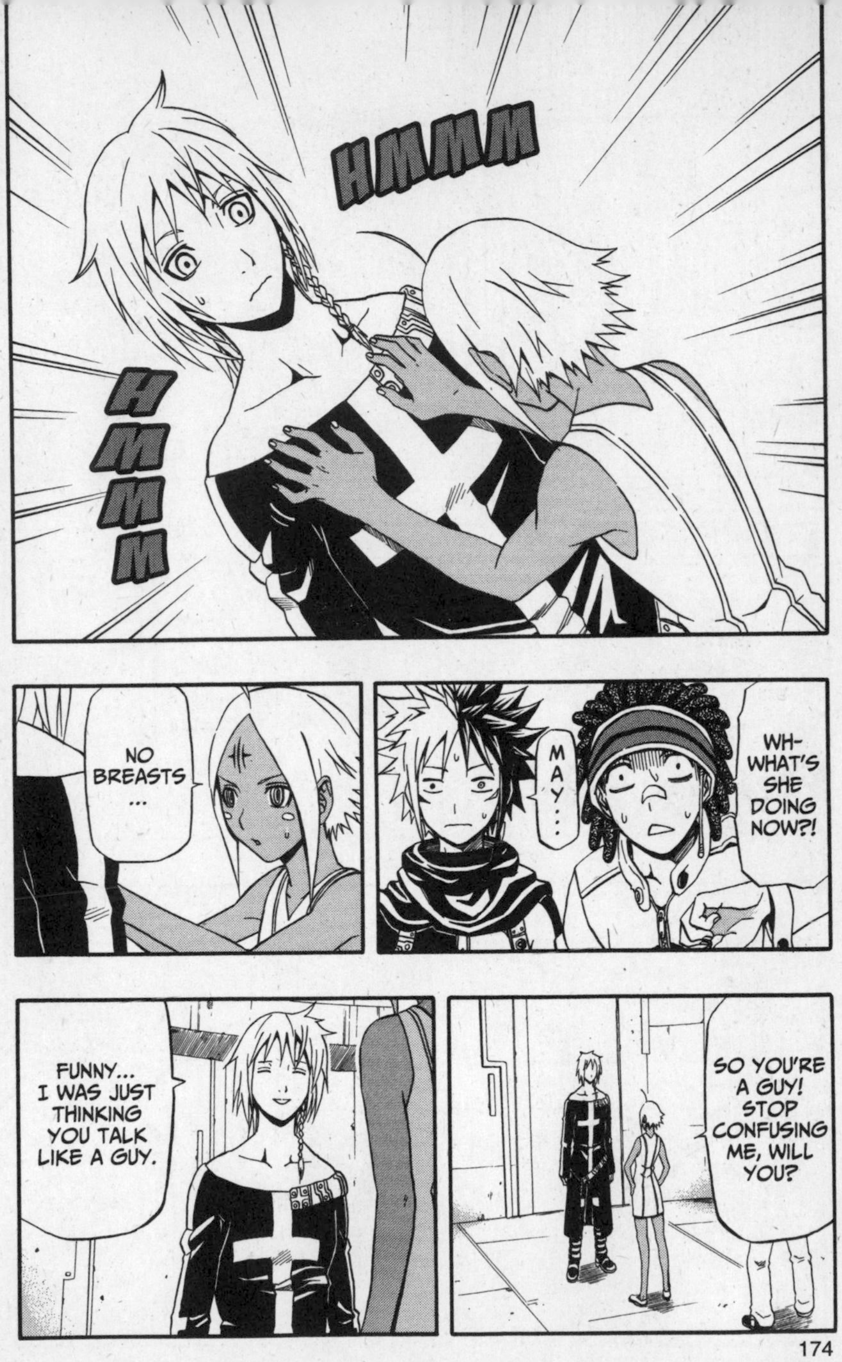
HMMM
HMMM
WH- WHAT'S SHE DOING NOW?!
MAY...
NO BREASTS ...
SO YOU'RE A GUY! STOP CONFUSING ME, WILL YOU?
FUNNY... I WAS JUST THINKING YOU TALK LIKE A GUY.

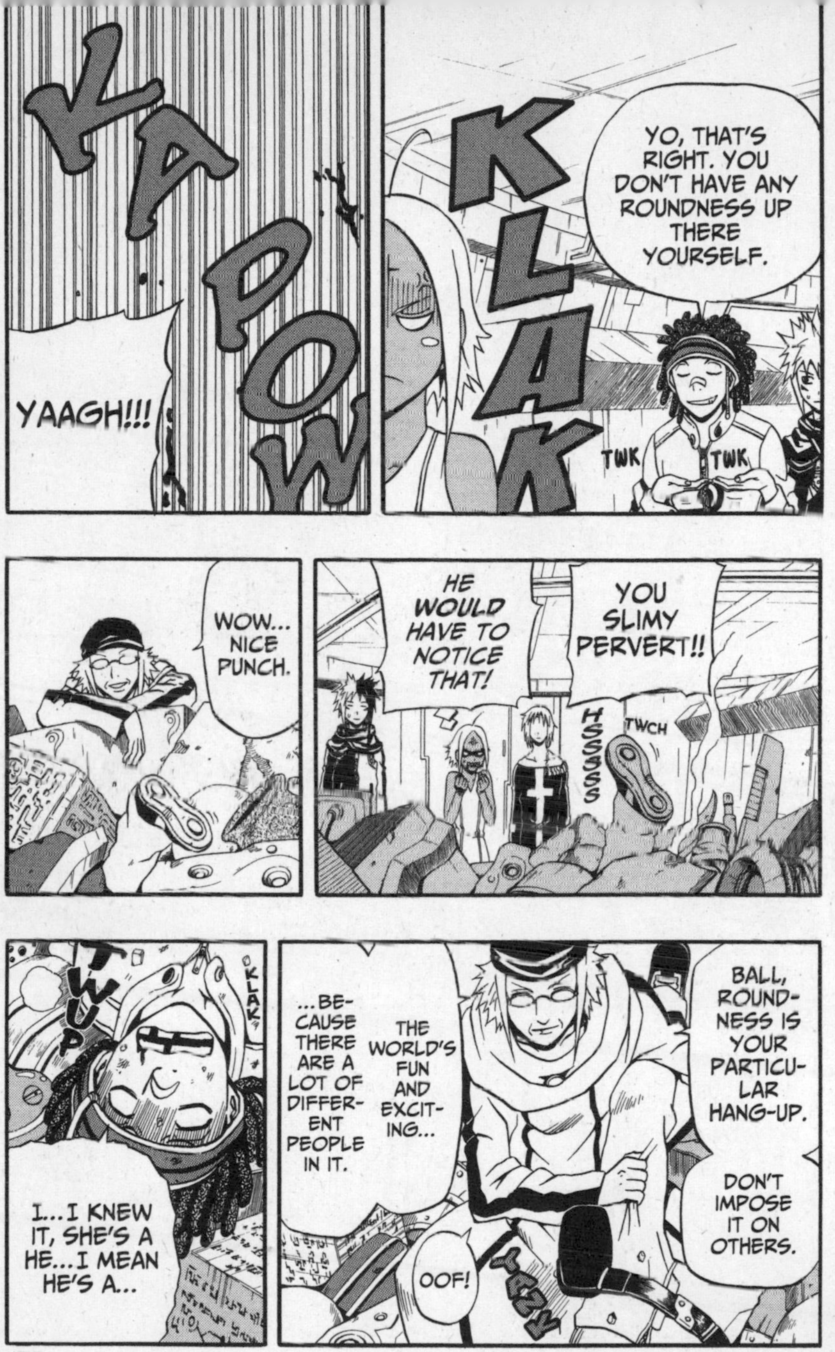
YO, THAT'S RIGHT. YOU DON'T HAVE ANY ROUNDNESS UP THERE YOURSELF.
KLAK
TWK TWK
KAPOW
YAAGH!!!
YOU SLIMY PERVERT!!
HE WOULD HAVE TO NOTICE THAT!
HSSSSS
TWCH
WOW... NICE PUNCH.
BALL, ROUNDNESS IS YOUR PARTICULAR HANG-UP.
DON'T IMPOSE IT ON OTHERS.
THE WORLD'S FUN AND EXCITING...
...BECAUSE THERE ARE A LOT OF DIFFERENT PEOPLE IN IT.
OOF!
TWUP
KLAK
I...I KNEW IT, SHE'S A HE...I MEAN HE'S A...

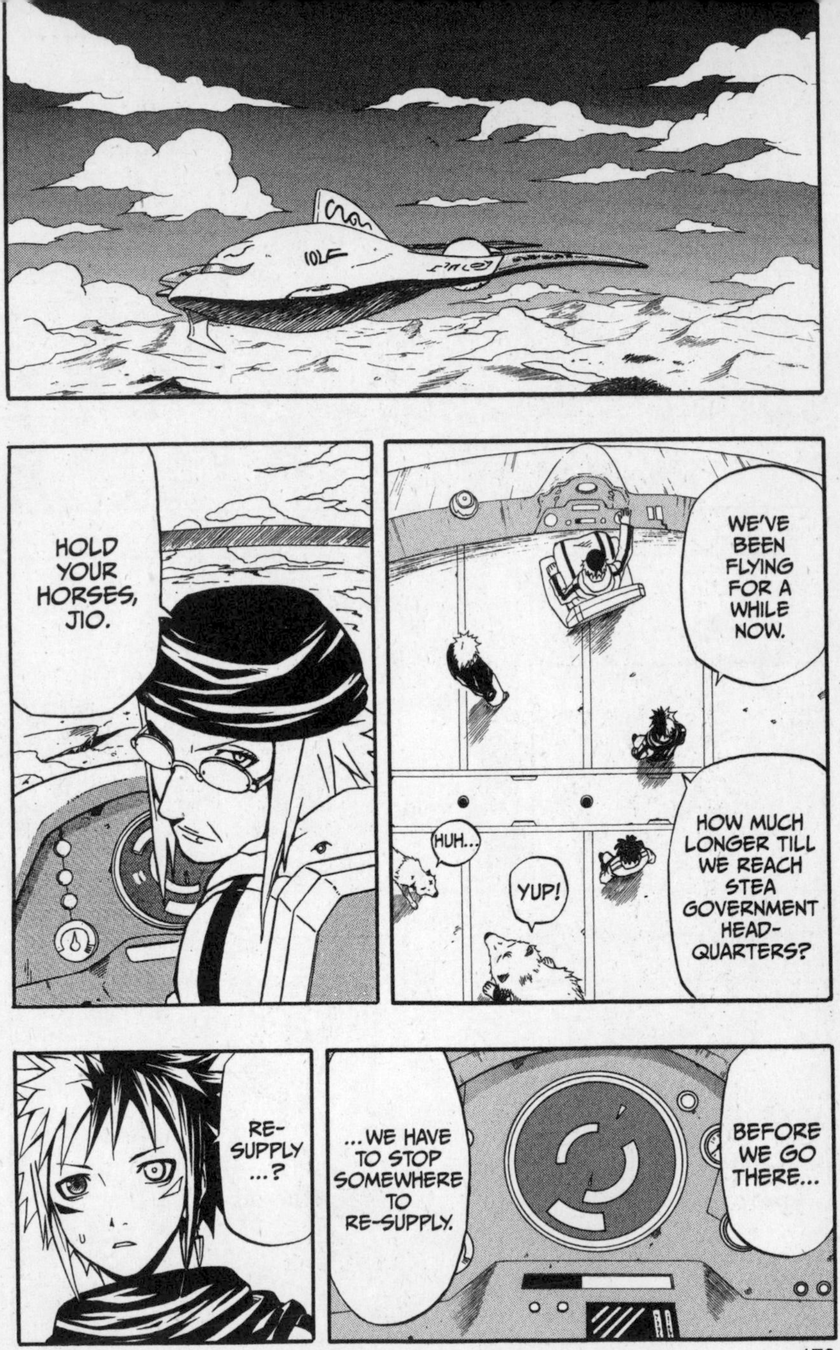
WE'VE BEEN FLYING FOR A WHILE NOW.
HOW MUCH LONGER TILL WE REACH STEA GOVERNMENT HEAD-QUARTERS?
HUH...
YUP!
HOLD YOUR HORSES, JIO.
BEFORE WE GO THERE...
...WE HAVE TO STOP SOMEWHERE TO RE-SUPPLY.
RE-SUPPLY...?

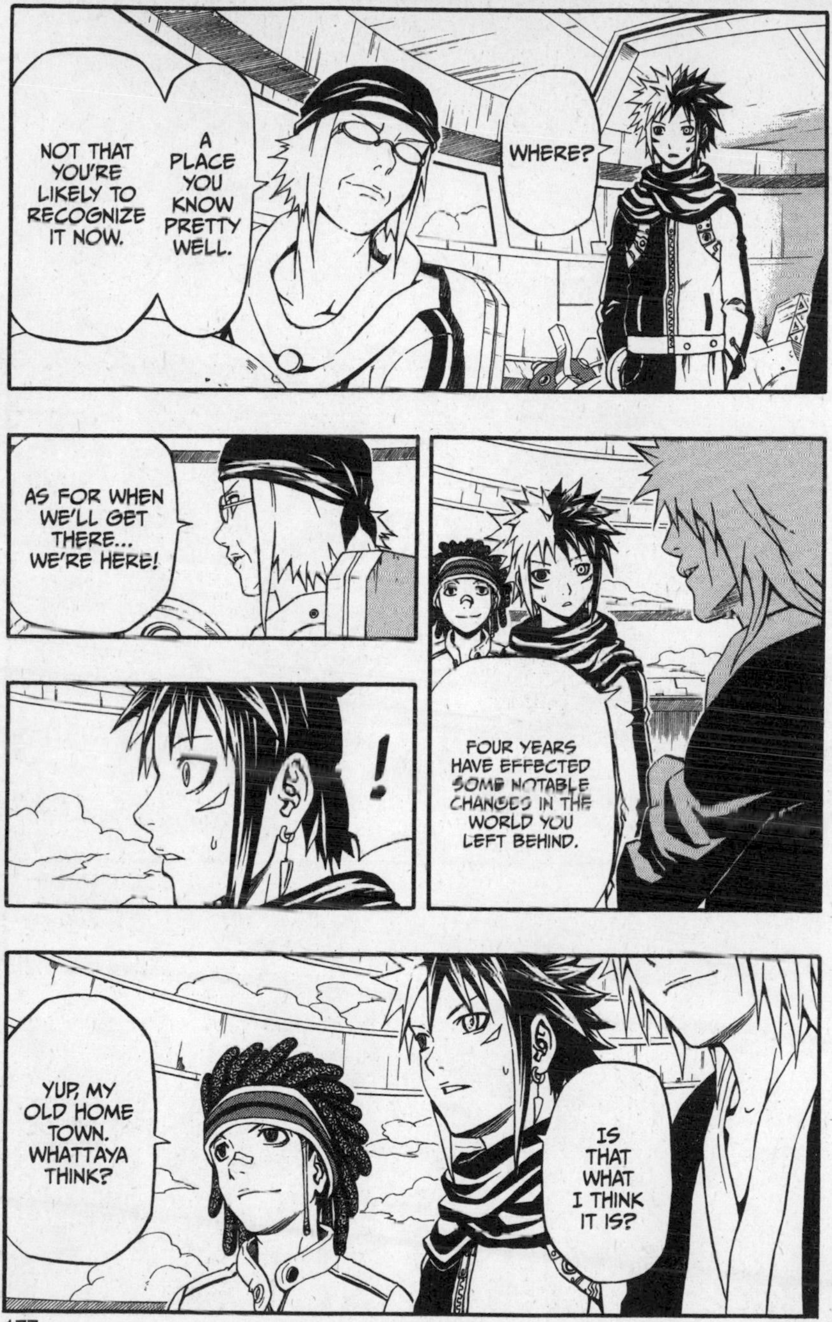
WHERE?
A PLACE YOU KNOW PRETTY WELL.
NOT THAT YOU'RE LIKELY TO RECOGNIZE IT NOW.
FOUR YEARS HAVE EFFECTED SOME NOTABLE CHANGES IN THE WORLD YOU LEFT BEHIND.
AS FOR WHEN WE'LL GET THERE... WE'RE HERE!
!
IS THAT WHAT I THINK IT IS?
YUP, MY OLD HOME TOWN. WHATTAYA THINK?

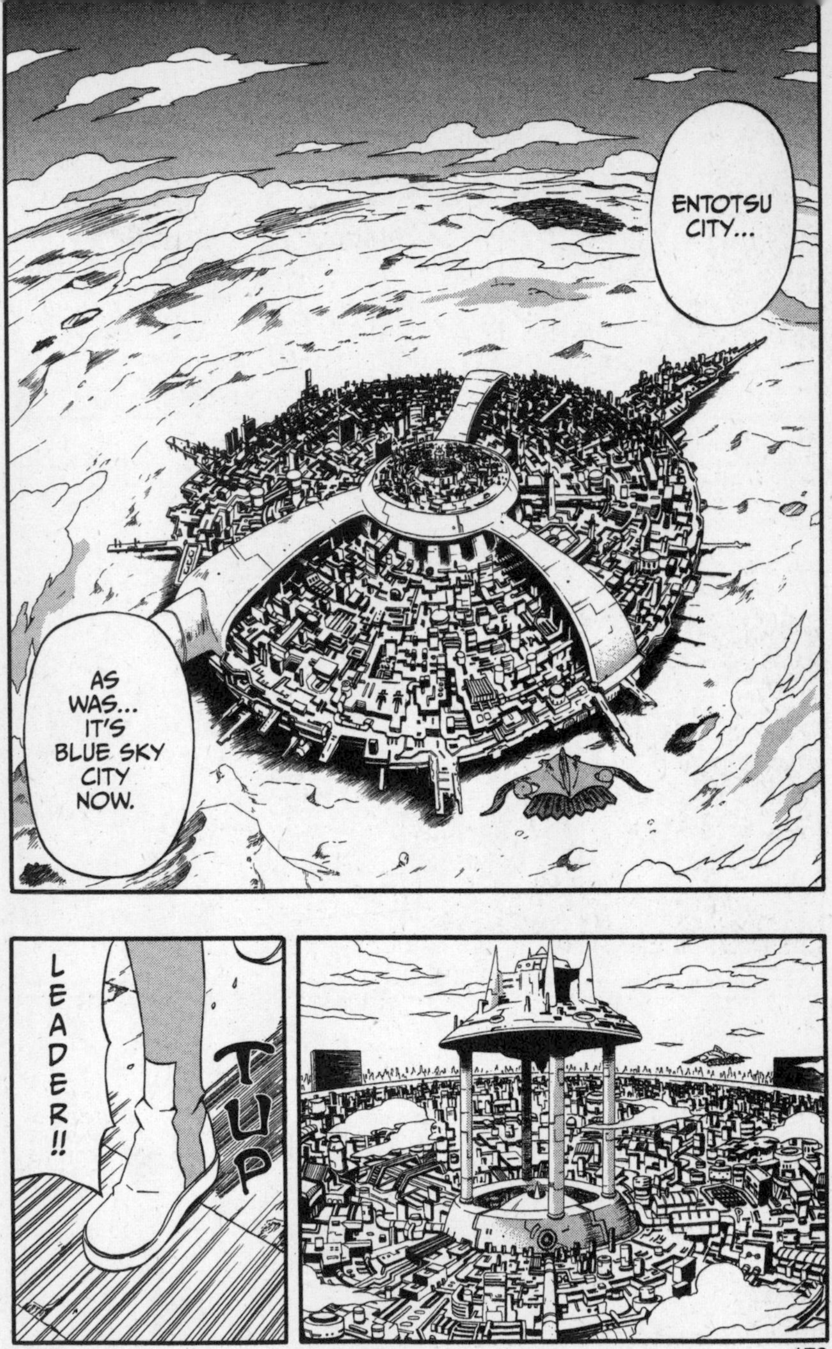
ENTOTSU CITY...
AS WAS... IT'S BLUE SKY CITY NOW.
LEADER!!
TUP

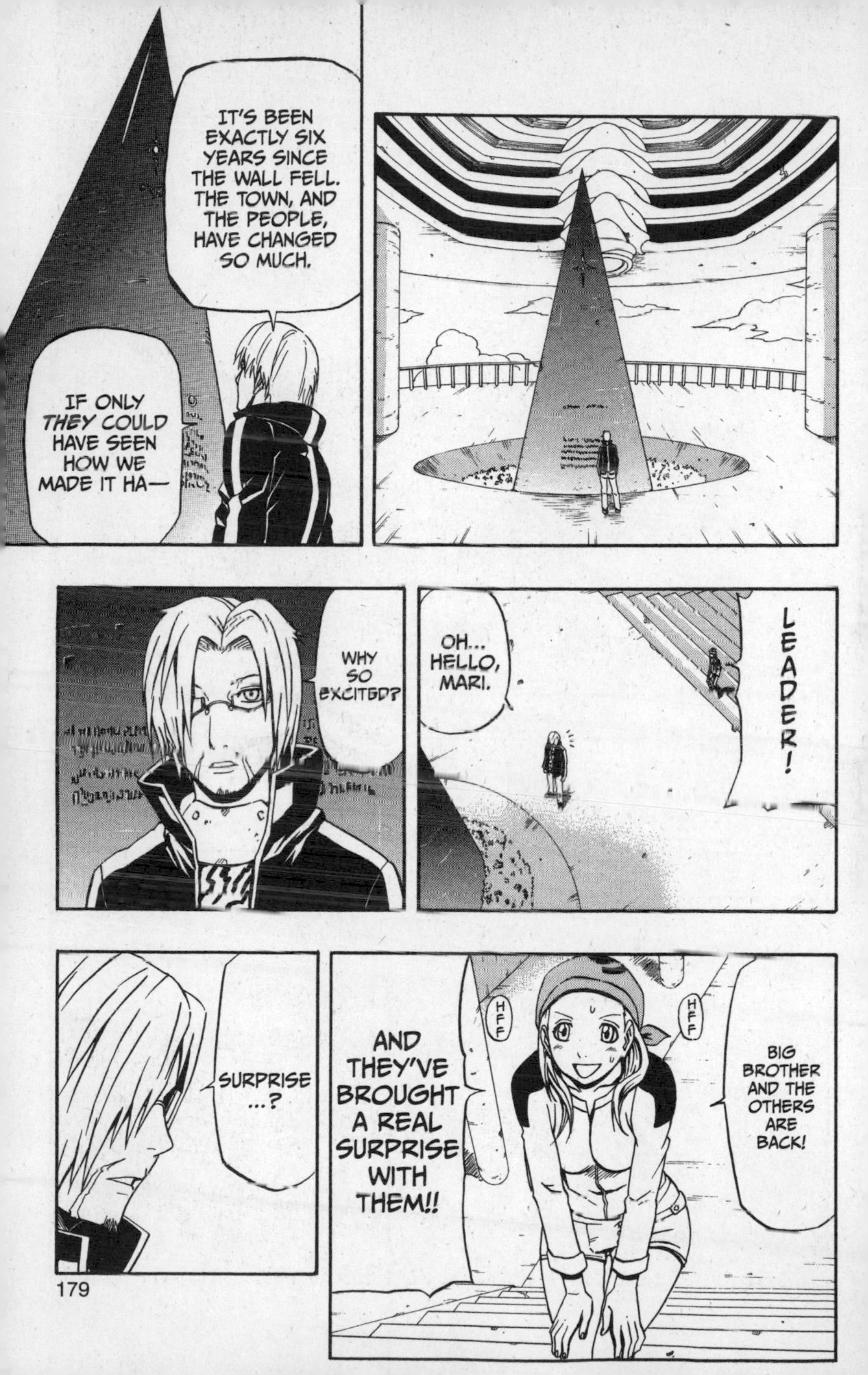
IT'S BEEN EXACTLY SIX YEARS SINCE THE WALL FELL. THE TOWN, AND THE PEOPLE, HAVE CHANGED SO MUCH.
IF ONLY THEY COULD HAVE SEEN HOW WE MADE IT HA—
LEADER!
OH... HELLO, MARI.
WHY SO EXCITED?
BIG BROTHER AND THE OTHERS ARE BACK!
HFF
HFF
AND THEY'VE BROUGHT A REAL SURPRISE WITH THEM!!
SURPRISE ...?

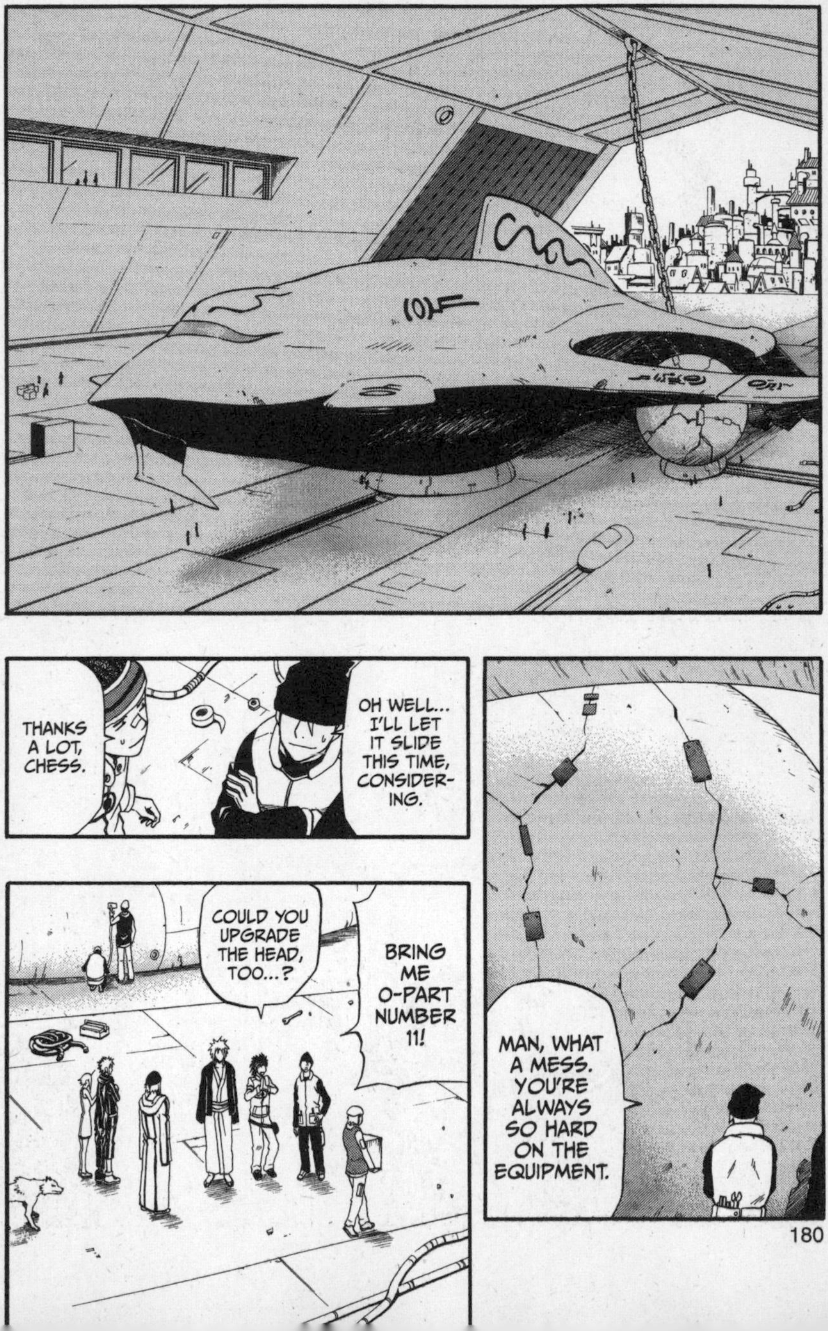
MAN, WHAT A MESS. YOU'RE ALWAYS SO HARD ON THE EQUIPMENT.
OH WELL... I'LL LET IT SLIDE THIS TIME, CONSIDER-ING.
THANKS A LOT, CHESS.
BRING ME O-PART NUMBER 11!
COULD YOU UPGRADE THE HEAD, TOO...?

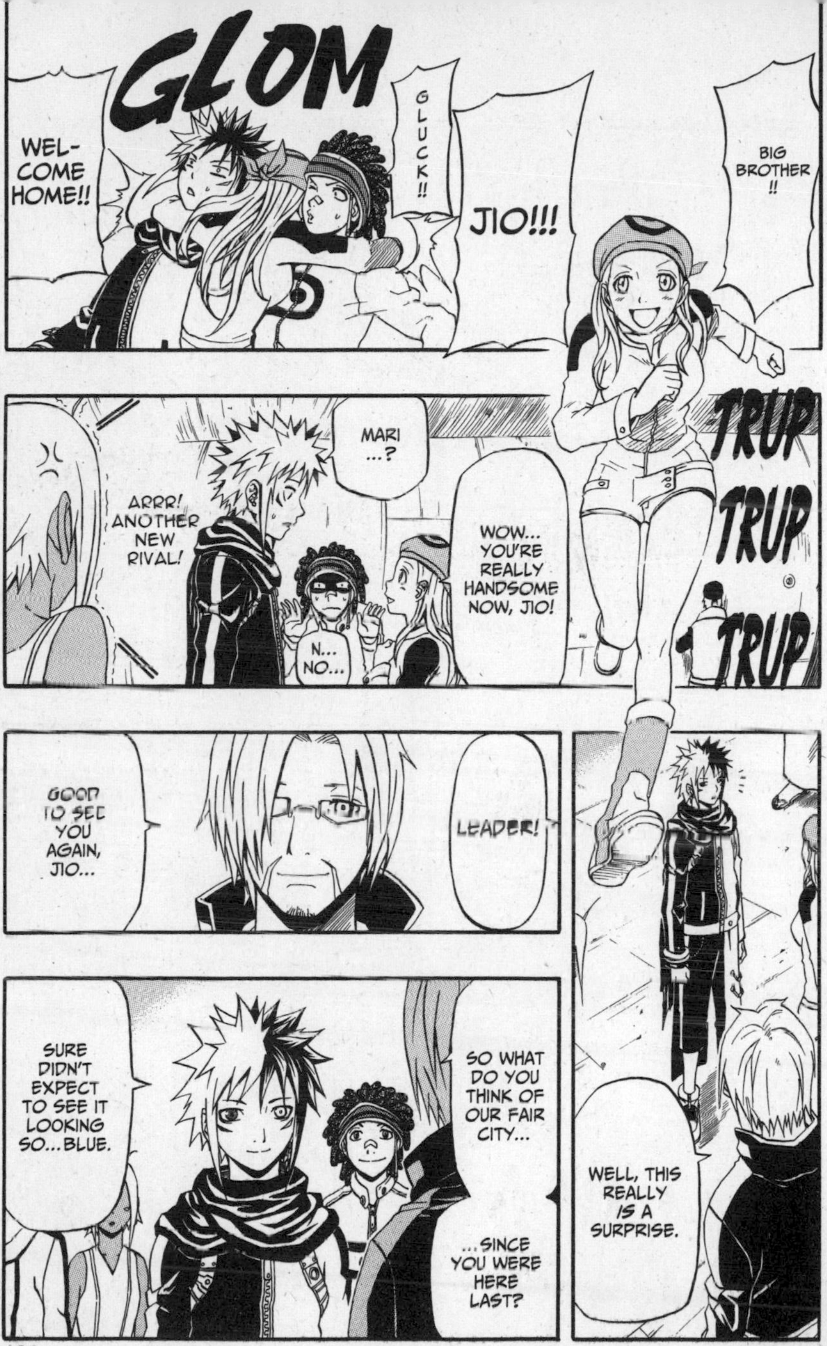
BIG BROTHER!!
JIO!!!
GLUCK!!
GLOM
WEL-COME HOME!!
TRUP TRUP TRUP
WOW... YOU'RE REALLY HANDSOME NOW, JIO!
MARI ...?
N... NO...
ARRR! ANOTHER NEW RIVAL!
WELL, THIS REALLY IS A SURPRISE.
LEADER!
GOOD TO SEE YOU AGAIN, JIO...
SO WHAT DO YOU THINK OF OUR FAIR CITY...
...SINCE YOU WERE HERE LAST?
SURE DIDN'T EXPECT TO SEE IT LOOKING SO...BLUE.

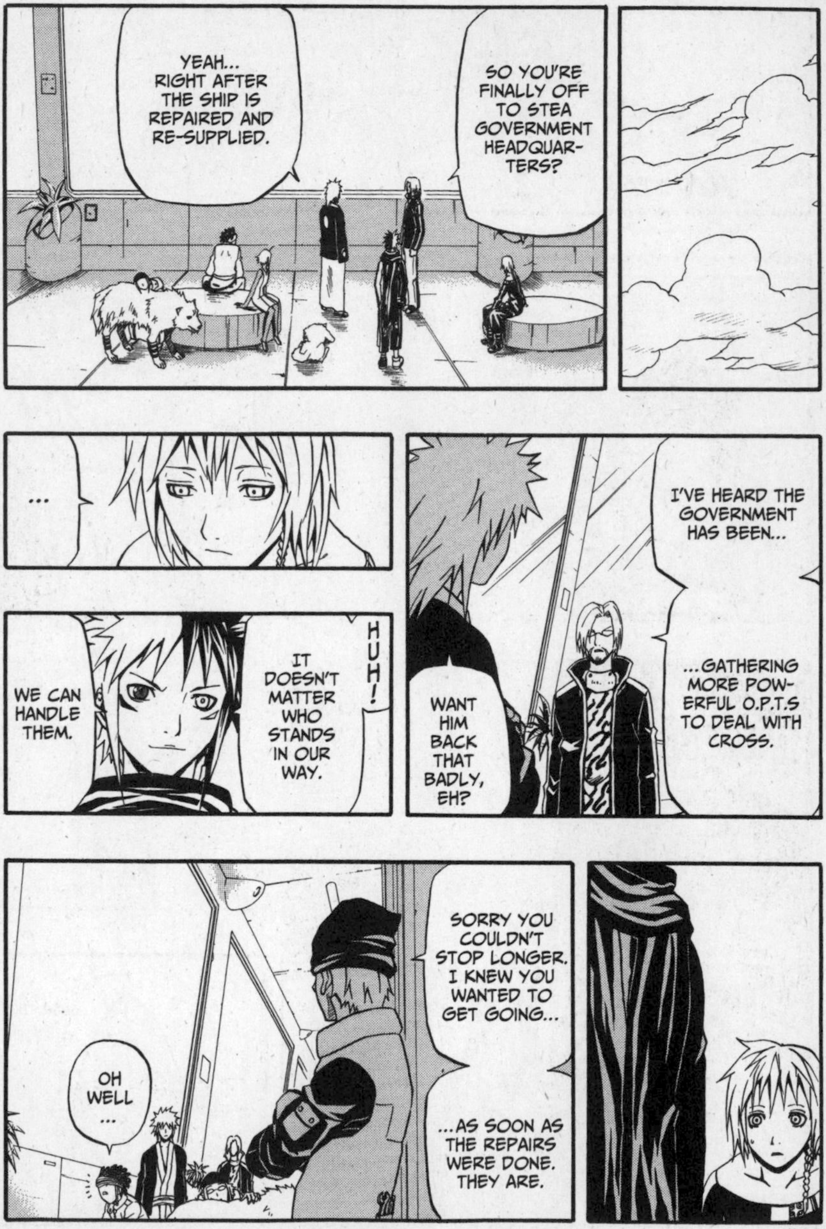
SO YOU'RE FINALLY OFF TO STEA GOVERNMENT HEADQUAR-TERS?
YEAH... RIGHT AFTER THE SHIP IS REPAIRED AND RE-SUPPLIED.
I'VE HEARD THE GOVERNMENT HAS BEEN...
...GATHERING MORE POW-ERFUL O.P.T.S TO DEAL WITH CROSS.
WANT HIM BACK THAT BADLY, EH?
...
HUH!
IT DOESN'T MATTER WHO STANDS IN OUR WAY.
WE CAN HANDLE THEM.
SORRY YOU COULDN'T STOP LONGER. I KNEW YOU WANTED TO GET GOING...
...AS SOON AS THE REPAIRS WERE DONE. THEY ARE.
OH WELL ...

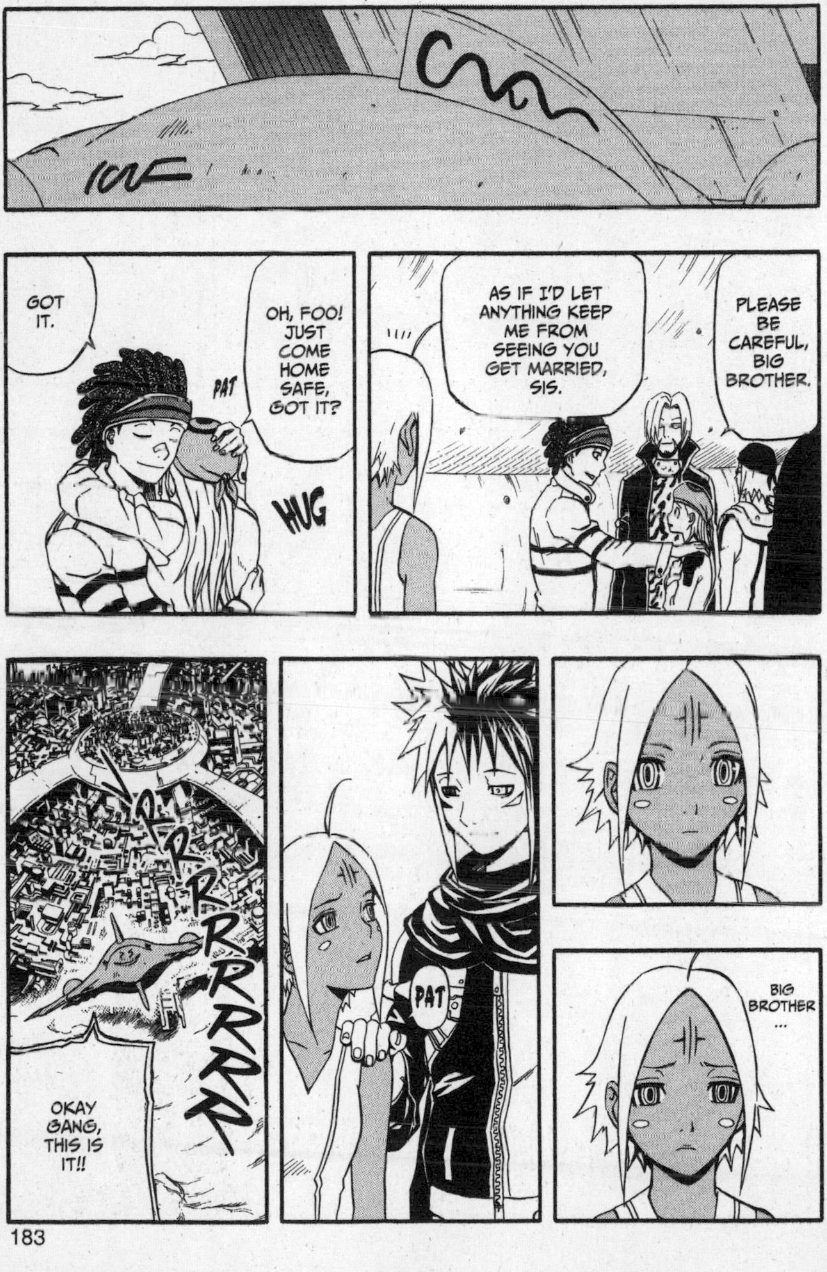
PLEASE BE CAREFUL, BIG BROTHER.
AS IF I'D LET ANYTHING KEEP ME FROM SEEING YOU GET MARRIED, SIS.
OH, FOO! JUST COME HOME SAFE, GOT IT?
PAT
HUG
GOT IT.
BIG BROTHER ...
PAT
RRRRRRR
OKAY GANG, THIS IS IT!!

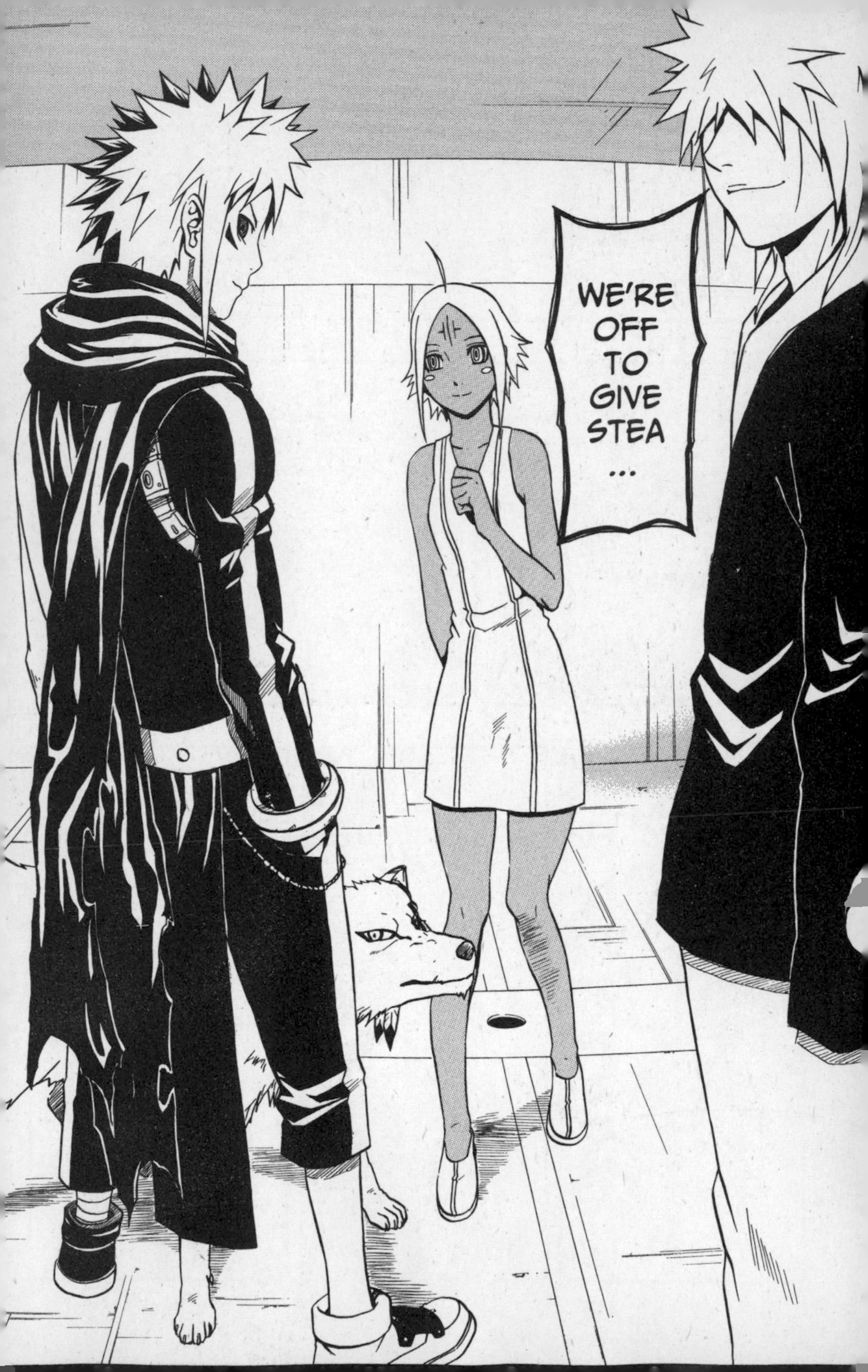
WE'RE OFF TO GIVE STEA ...

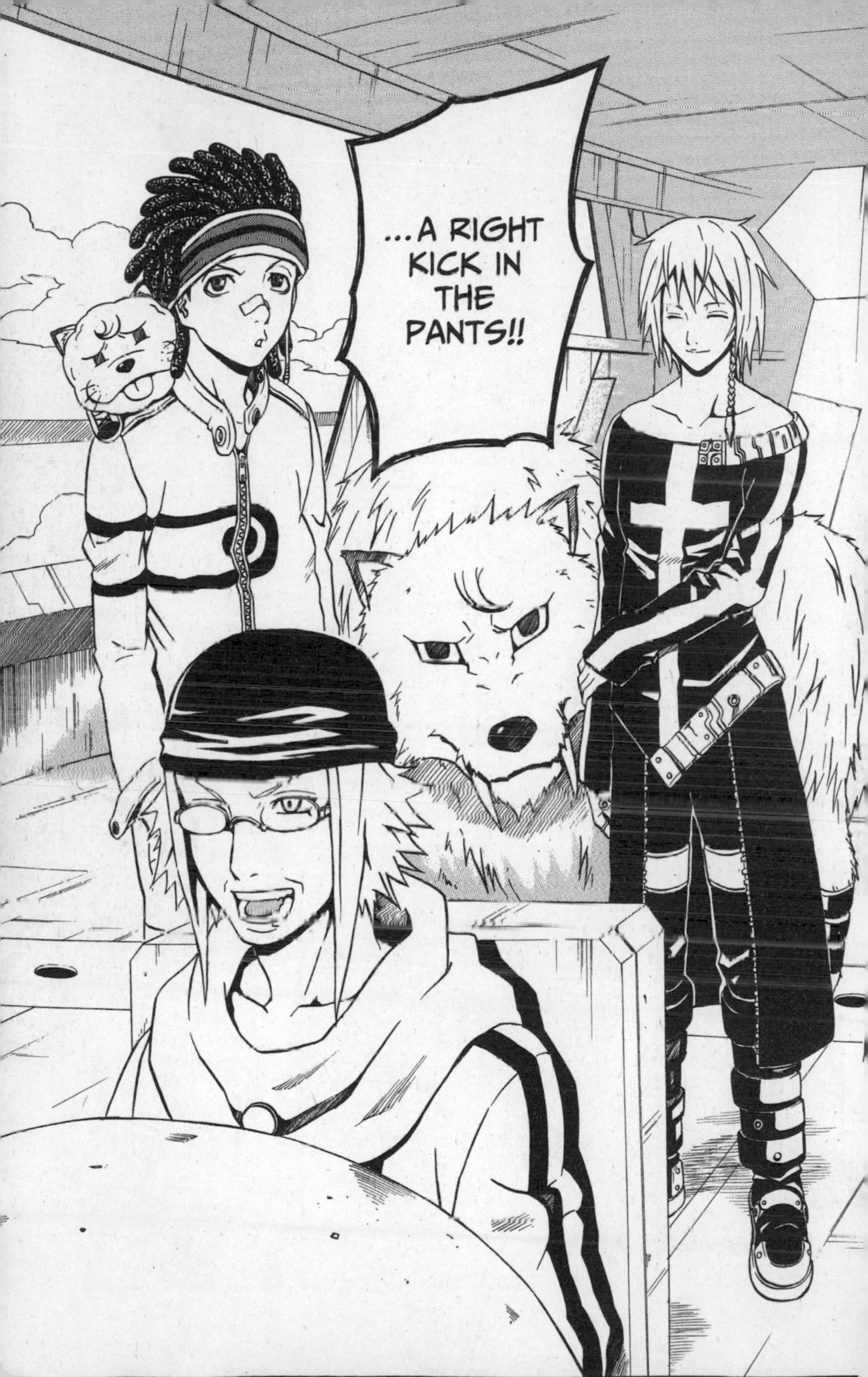
...A RIGHT KICK IN THE PANTS!!

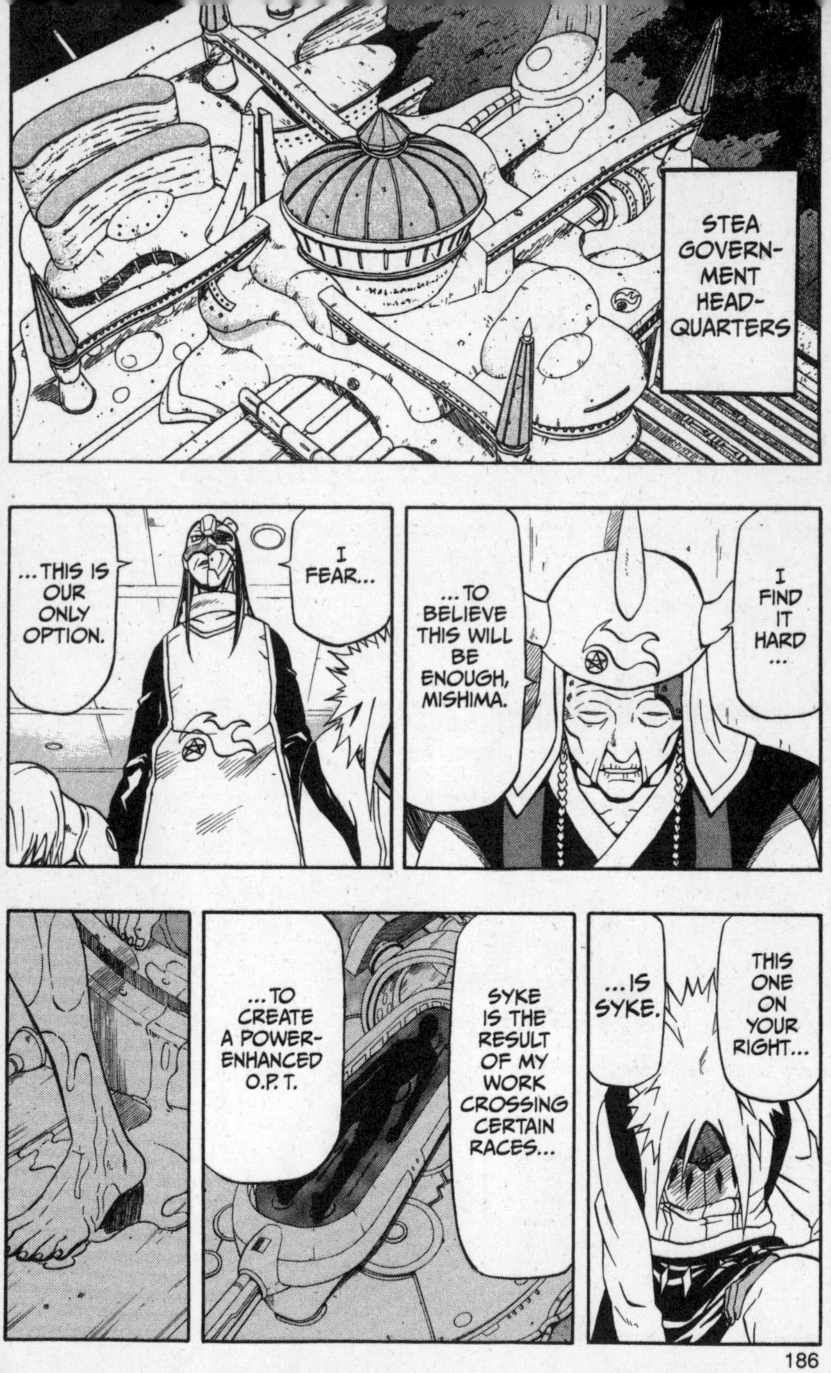
STEA GOVERNMENT HEADQUARTERS
I FIND IT HARD...
...TO BELIEVE THIS WILL BE ENOUGH, MISHIMA.
I FEAR...
...THIS IS OUR ONLY OPTION.
THIS ONE ON YOUR RIGHT...
...IS SYKE.
SYKE IS THE RESULT OF MY WORK CROSSING CERTAIN RACES...
...TO CREATE A POWER-ENHANCED O.P.T.

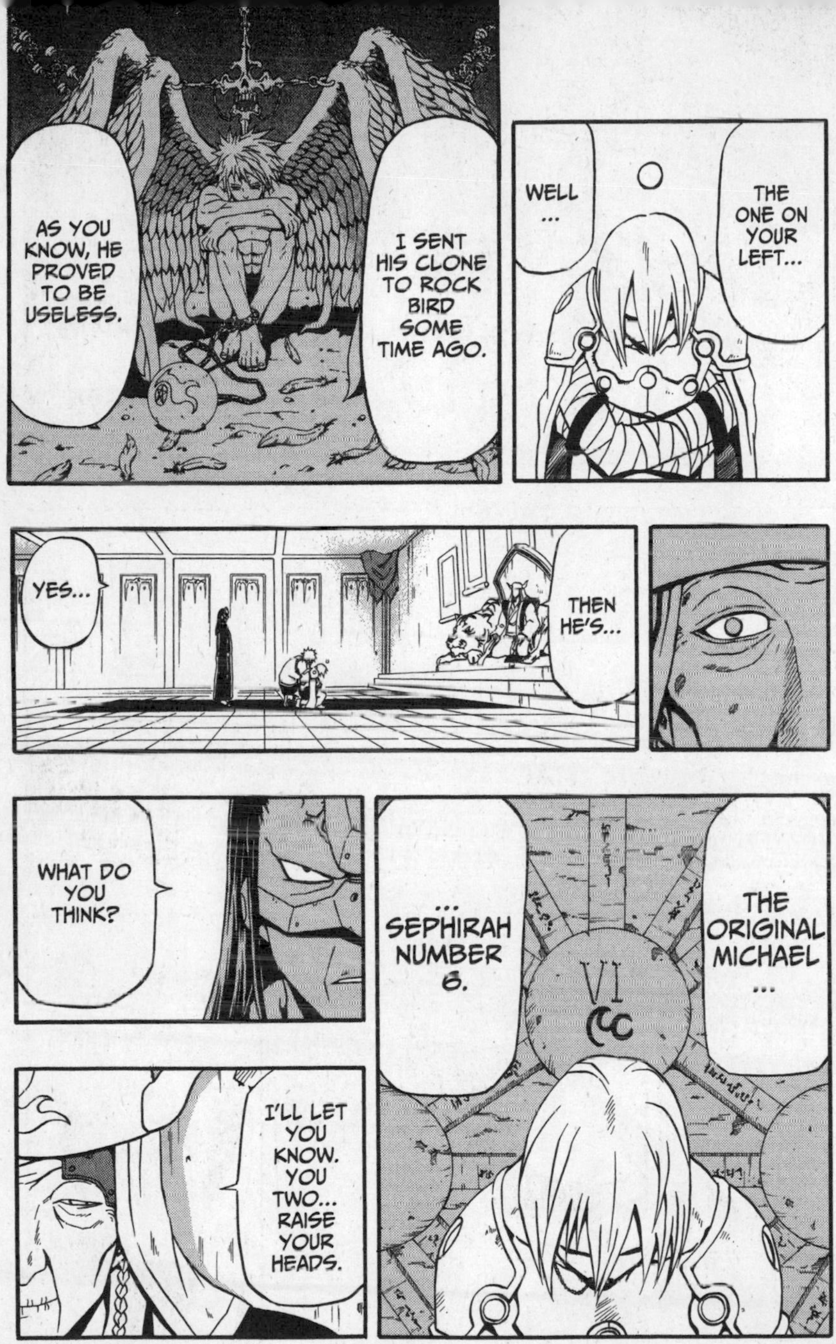
THE ONE ON YOUR LEFT...
WELL ...
I SENT HIS CLONE TO ROCK BIRD SOME TIME AGO.
AS YOU KNOW, HE PROVED TO BE USELESS.
THEN HE'S...
YES...
THE ORIGINAL MICHAEL ...
... SEPHIRAH NUMBER 6.
VI
WHAT DO YOU THINK?
I'LL LET YOU KNOW. YOU TWO... RAISE YOUR HEADS.

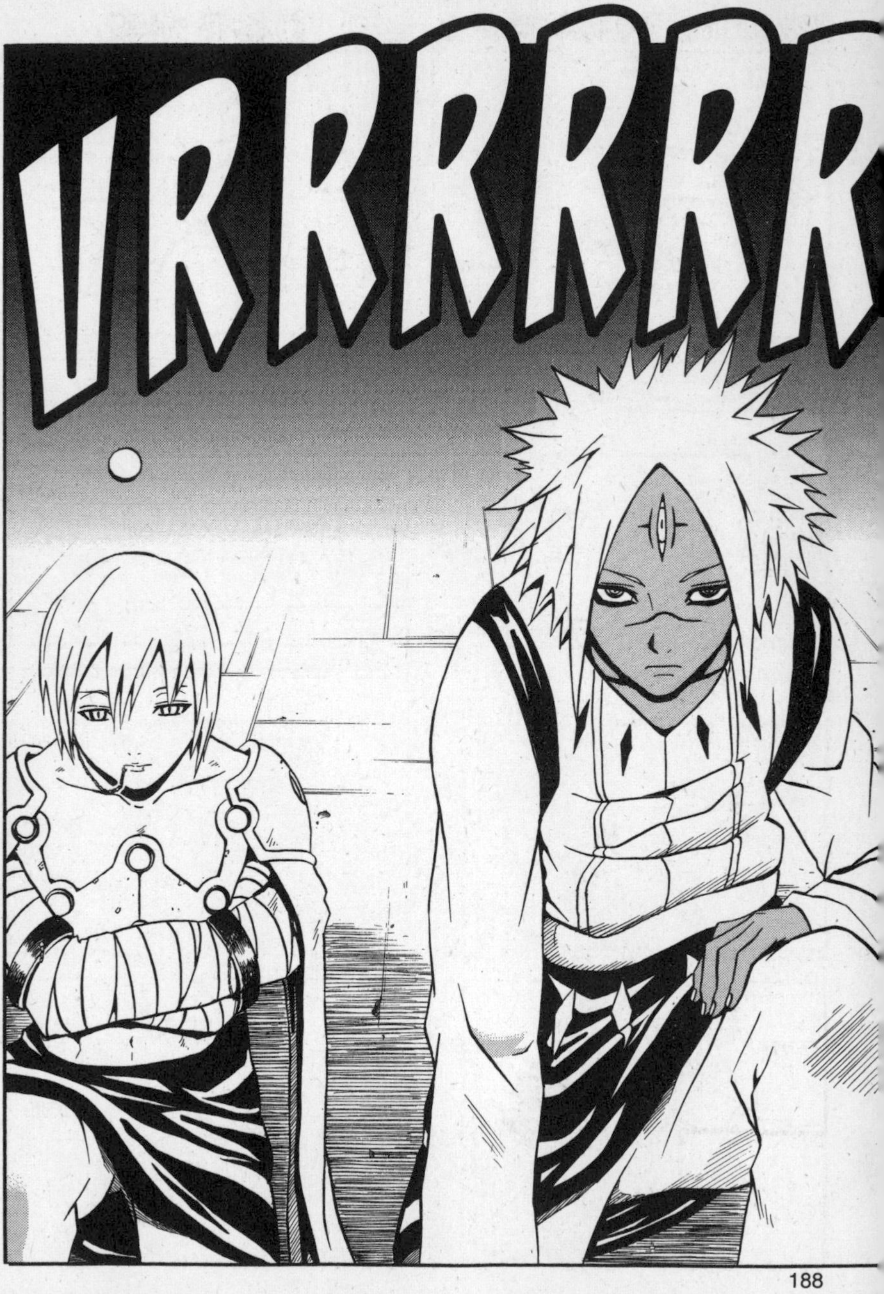
VRRRRR

SEISHI AND THE BIRDCAGE

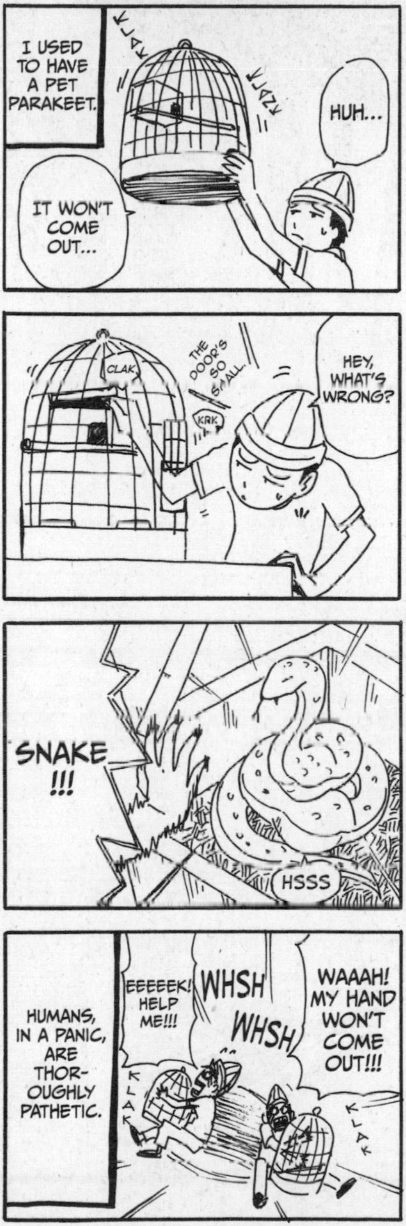
HUH...
KLAK
KLAK
I USED TO HAVE A PET PARAKEET.
IT WON'T COME OUT...
HEY, WHAT'S WRONG?
THE DOOR'S SO SMALL.
CLAK
KRK
SNAKE !!!
HSSS
WAAAH! MY HAND WON'T COME OUT!!!
WHSH
WHSH
EEEEEK! HELP ME!!!
HUMANS, IN A PANIC, ARE THOR-OUGHLY PATHETIC.
KLAK
KLAK

SEISHI AND THE SEASONAL WARDROBE CHANGE

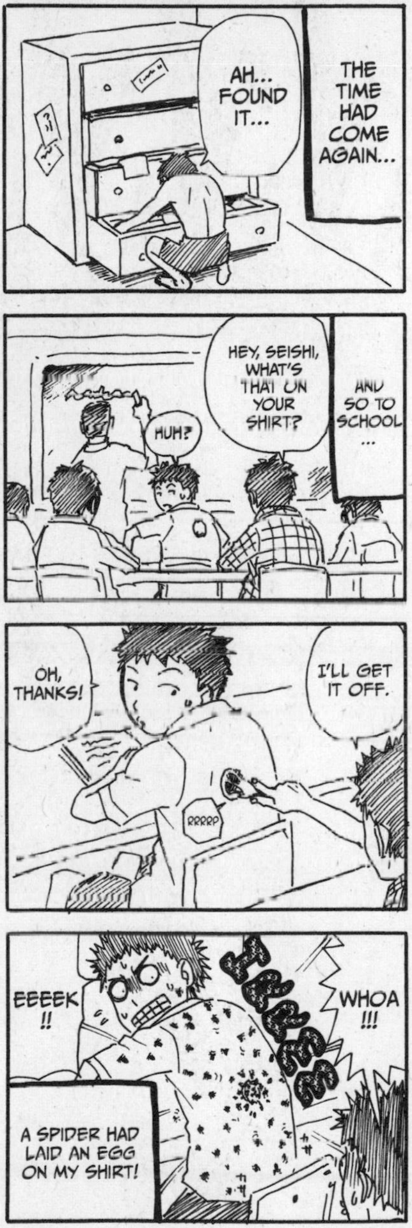
THE TIME HAD COME AGAIN...
AH... FOUND IT...
AND SO TO SCHOOL...
HEY, SEISHI, WHAT'S THAT ON YOUR SHIRT?
HUH?
I'LL GET IT OFF.
OH, THANKS!
RRRRP
WHOA !!!
EEEEK !!
A SPIDER HAD LAID AN EGG ON MY SHIRT!

O-Parts CATALOGUE⑭

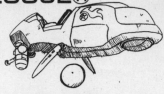

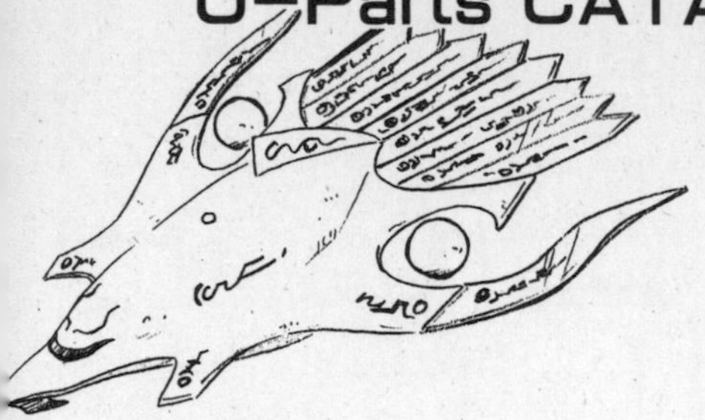

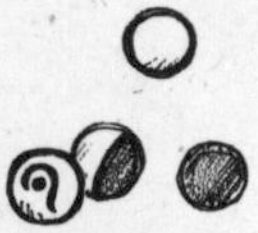

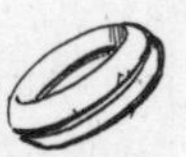

O-PART:BEEPHEN
O-PART RANK: C
EFFECT: FLIGHT
EACH BEEPHEN MOUNTS A WEAPON TO THE RIDER'S LIKING. THEY USUALLY ATTACK IN HUGE SWARMS, LIKE BEES.

O-PART: NEW BIG ORPHAN
O-PART RANK: B
EFFECT: FLIGHT
A LARGE VEHICLE THAT CAN FLY IN ALL DIRECTIONS.

-PART: TRICKY
-PART RANK: B
FFECT: MAGNETISM
MALLER THAN BALL'S LD O-PART, BUT TRONGER AND RICKIER.

O-PART: NEW ZERO-SHIKI R
O-PART RANK: B
EFFECT: CREATES ITS BLADES IN RELATION TO ITS OPPONENT'S LEVEL OF HATRED. HOW WOULD IT WORK ON JIO?

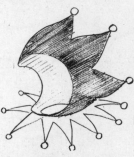

O-PART: JOKER HOOD
O-PART RANK: C
EFFECT: FLATTENS YOU LIKE A PLAYING CARD. ORIGINALLY USED FOR SPYING PURPOSES BY THE ZENOM SYNDICATE.

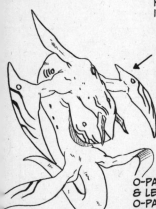

O-PART: GARAIA
O-PART RANK: B
EFFECT:① FLIGHT AND ② RUST BEAT, WHICH TURNS ANYTHING IT BITES TO RUST.
A VERY POWERFUL O-PART, BUT BALL HAD BECOME SO STRONG THAT IT WAS EASILY DEFEATED.

O-PART: RIGHT-HAND & LEFT-HAND
O-PART RANK: B
EFFECT: SUPER-TIGHT GRIP. IT CAN SQUEEZE THE BLOOD OUT OF A PERSON.

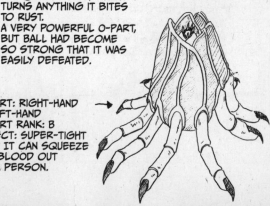

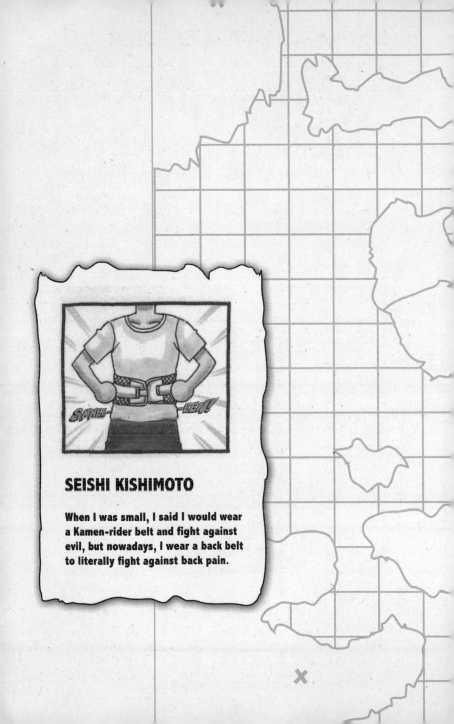

SEISHI KISHIMOTO

When I was small, I said I would wear a Kamen-rider belt and fight against evil, but nowadays, I wear a back belt to literally fight against back pain.

O-Parts HUNTER 14

VIZ Media Edition
STORY AND ART BY SEISHI KISHIMOTO

English Adaptation/David R. Valois
Translation/Tetsuichiro Miyaki
Touch-up Art & Lettering/HudsonYards
Design/Andrea Rice
Editor/Gary Leach

VP, Production/Alvin Lu
VP, Sales & Product Marketing/Gonzalo Ferreyra
VP, Creative/Linda Espinosa
Publisher/Hyoe Narita

Printed in the U.S.A.

Published by VIZ Media, LLC
P.O. Box 77010
San Francisco, CA 94107

10 9 8 7 6 5 4 3 2
First printing, February 2009
Second printing, July 2009

www.viz.com